The Showgirl and the Writer

Also by Marnie Mueller

Green Fires Assault on Eden:
A Novel of the Ecuadorian Rainforest

The Climate of the Country:
A Novel

My Mother's Island:
A Novel

The Showgirl and the Writer

A Friendship Forged in the Aftermath
of the Japanese American Incarceration

Marnie Mueller

A PEACE CORPS WRITERS BOOK

2023

THE SHOWGIRL AND THE WRITER:
A FRIENDSHIP FORGED IN THE AFTERMATH
OF THE JAPANESE AMERICAN INCARCERATION

A Peace Corps Writers Book — an imprint of
Peace Corps Worldwide

Edit and design by Marian Haley Beil
Cover design by Helene Silverman

Cover Art: "Classmates" from Roger Shimomura's
Minidoka on My Mind series,
exhibited at the Missoula Art Museum 2007.
Courtesy of Roger Shimomura

Shimomura was incarcerated in Minidoka Camp as a three-year-old.

For more information, contact peacecorpsworldwide@gmail.com.
Peace Corps Writers and the Peace Corps Writers colophon
are trademarks of PeaceCorpsWorldwide.org.

ISBN-13: 978-1-950444-58-8
Library of Congress Control Number: 2023912589

First Peace Corps Writers Edition, July 2023

Dedication

To the resilience, honor, perseverance,
and courage of the Nisei

Contents

Foreword

WHEN WE WERE YOUNG, AUNTIE MARY LOOMED LARGER THAN LIFE.
WE always sat cross-legged at her feet, enthralled to watch as each
spidery false lash magically transformed her eye-
lids.

Our dad's older sister and sole sibling was
Mary Watanabe. To us, "Mary Mon Toy" was
just her catchy showbiz moniker, not realizing it
hid her Japaneseness so deftly that her obituary
shocked her hometown community when it revealed that she was not Chinese.

Lori
Watanabe
Saginaw

We now see the grit and resilience that Mary
(Mon Toy Watanabe) needed in order to gain a professional foothold
in an America embedded with prejudice against Asians, and with
particular hostility toward Japanese Americans after the war's end.

In her heyday, roles for an "oriental" actress, dancer or singer
were rare, humiliating, or nonexistent. To pay the rent, her repertoire included songs like "*Hava Nagila*," the anthem of the Catskills'
Jewish nightclub circuit. She rehearsed the two of us to parrot it
back in unison. Standing at attention, we belted out our phonetic
Hebrew, eager for her praise.

Any crumb from her exotic life was titillating. Good seats at Liza
Minelli's first off-Broadway show. A magical moment hidden in the
wings, glimpsing her graceful burlesque on stage before our mother
whisked us away. Did she care what we thought? Likely not. Our

lives were tiny and irrelevant compared to the rigor and demands of her career and its hard won rewards.

Soon after Mary's death, Marnie found us, introducing herself as a friend and executor of our aunt's will. We were Mary's next of kin so she was obligated to tell us that there was nothing left to us.

"Will you contest it?" she asked. "No," we answered. We felt little connection to Mary.

Wendy
Watanabe

What we did feel was the incongruous timing of Marnie's phone call on December 7th. A date that smolders on the calendar because it marks the irreversible and painful turning point in the lives of two generations of our family members on both sides. To learn of Mary's passing on Pearl Harbor Day was an eerily ironic curtain call. That day's trauma and all that ensued reverberates even with us who only know it indirectly.

What followed was an intimate memorial held inside Mary's West 88th Street apartment building, a New York City street address we knew by heart because she had lived there forever. And while digging through boxes of her belongings packed by Marnie, we heard the first of many eye-opening anecdotes about our mysterious aunt.

Since then, Marnie has interwoven the threads of Mary's life and her own into this book. Left with only scarce details about the Watanabe side of our family, particularly during and after their incarceration, Marnie's accounting restores a link in our lineage otherwise lost to us and to Mary's grand nephews, Zachary and Benjamin.

The story of the relationship Marnie forged with our aunt, serves to document a Japanese American woman's dream-seeking and survival. Although we feel its significance as our family story, it adds an important chapter to comprehending the totality of the impact on those imprisoned in America's concentration camps.

Mary was like others in persecuted groups who are given the paradoxical choice to "pass" by masking their true identities, and who then bear an internal weight and cost for that decision for the remainder of their lives.

Our aunt's story now stands in the light. Rest in peace and truth, Mary Mon Toy Watanabe.

Mary Mon Toy's nieces,
Lori Watanabe Saginaw and Wendy Watanabe

Preface

MARY MON TOY, A JAPANESE AMERICAN PERFORMER, AND I ENCOUN-
tered each other by chance. Soon after, she sought me out. Both our
lives changed as we began to meet, and our friendship developed. I
ask myself now, years later, why I was drawn to Mary and she to me?

There is no easy answer. There were many layers of our relationship, in which we presented true and false identities, and intermit-
tently were both caring and resentful. Our ambivalence makes sense
if you think of this as a love story of sorts spanning generations, art,
politics, race, and ethnicity — driven by the bond of the incarceration of Japanese Americans during World War II. What follows is a
tale of a fifteen-year friendship between two women — one Asian,
one Caucasian of Jewish descent, one an actress and showgirl, one a
fiction writer — who kept secrets as much from each other as we did
from ourselves and the world.

How It Began

The place where I was born no longer exists. All that's left are a few deteriorating barracks on a dry, windswept lake bed of black volcanic sand. A plaque on the side of the road identifies it as the site of the Tule Lake Japanese American Segregation Camp. Here, in this high desert in Northern California on a hot summer day in 1942, my life began.

Fifty-two years later, on a snowy New York City evening in 1994, I attended a focus group for the Japanese American National Museum. Group members were invited to answer questions and offer programming ideas for the museum. I'd been included because I'd written an essay for a national magazine about being born in Tule Lake. We sat at a large boardroom table in a prestigious law office high above Park Avenue. I was the only Caucasian in the room, and I stood out among the well-dressed Japanese American professionals.

As we waited to begin, an elderly Asian woman in a black wool cape, with a red AIDS ribbon pinned to her collar, walked in leaning on a cane. She seemed more out of place than I did, especially after she took off her cape to reveal a sequined black sweater and purple sweat pants. Her hair was a mass of unruly black curls which I later learned was one of her many wigs. When she raised her head, and smiled brightly at the group, I saw that she was perfectly made up, with the smooth, ivory skin of a young woman. She told us her name was Mary Mon Toy and that she was an actress. "I was in the Minidoka camp, but I got out early because Mrs. Roosevelt came to give us IQ tests and asked if we were being treated well. She heard that I was a singer and she procured me a scholarship to Juilliard School."

Introducing ourselves around the table, it became clear that Mary Mon Toy and I were the only two there who had direct experience in the camps. I explained to the group that my father — a declared conscientious objector on philosophical grounds, who hadn't yet been called up for service, was a labor economist, active in establishing the early consumer and farmer co-operatives in the United States. He was assigned the job of organizing the prisoner-operated co-operative store system in the Tule Lake Camp. My mother signed on to teach in the schools. I wanted to make sure they understood that my parents had chosen to work in the Tule Lake Camp in order to try to make an intolerable situation less onerous for those incarcerated there.

Mary observed me with close interest throughout the rest of the meeting and stopped me at the door as we left.

"I live on West Eighty-eighth Street," she told me. "What about you?"

"On West Seventy-seventh Street."

"Good. We're neighbors. We can take the bus together."

I would rather have taken a taxi at that hour — I'd had a long day — but, I agreed to the bus ride because I was curious.

We went out into a thick snowfall that muffled the thumping of Mary's painted bamboo cane. Even with the cane's help, she had difficulty walking. When the bus arrived and wheezed lower, she had trouble climbing the stairs. Once aboard, we settled into seats designated for the disabled and the elderly.

She did all the talking as the bus lumbered up Madison Avenue. She told me a long story of how she'd tripped on carpeting at the Sheraton Hotel on Seventh Avenue and broken her hip. The good news, she said, was that her lawyer had sued and won her a substantial settlement.

As the bus turned west across Central Park, she began on her theatrical career. "I was a tits-and-ass showgirl and I made it to Broadway. They loved me. I was tall for an oriental girl and I had it up here."

She grabbed her breasts through the heavy black cape and gave them a shake. "The face is still good, but the bod's given out. The casting directors still call me up, 'Mary Mon Toy, we need an oriental girl for the show,' but I can't go to auditions with this hip. I'll come back though." With that she spread her arms wide, still holding her cane, and began to sing "Curtain up. Light the lights. You got nothing to hit but the heights."

Her voice wasn't loud, but it carried all the way to the back of the bus. Everyone was staring at us. "Projection," she would tell me later. "They made us sing to the top of the house. The young ones can't do that anymore. They have those mikes stuck to their heads."

THESE DAYS, ON THE WALL ABOVE MY DESK, THERE IS A ROW OF black-and-white photographs of Mary. In one she's adjusting the bra of her Latin Quarter costume while a laughing Christine Jorgensen, the first publicly acknowledged transgender, looks on.

Mary Mon Toy and Christine Jorgenson at the Latin Quarter
Written on the sign,
"To Mary, WOW!!! Christine Jorgenson Latin Quarter New York 1954"

This photo is from 1954 showing Mary being fitted by the British award-winning costume designer, Oliver Messel, for her role of Mamselle Honolulu on Broadway in *House of Flowers*.

Costume fitting for Broadway's *House of Flowers* with
Mary Mon Toy and Oliver Messel

In another photo, Mary stands on a regional theater stage, her expression intently focused, a total professional, as she plays Helen Chao in *Flower Drum Song*.

Mary Mon Toy as Helen Chao in a regional production of *Flower Drum Song*

My favorite is a shot of her posing languorously on an Art Deco spiral staircase. It's the 1950s and, according to her, she had just broken race barriers to become the first Asian runway model for Christian Dior in Paris. There is no indication in her delicate youthful face that she has suffered indignities or racial insults, no hint of lingering anger about her incarceration in Minidoka camp, nor of the secrets she kept.

Mary on the staircase
in Nouvelle Eve Club, Paris, France

My introduction to the weight of memory she endured occurred on an evening early in our friendship as we waited in a theater lobby. It was December 7, the anniversary of the bombing of Pearl Harbor in Hawai'i, the event that set in motion the incarceration of people of Japanese descent in the United States, and the country entering World War II.

Thinking it was a solemn date we shared, I said to her, "Mary, do you know what day this is?" She turned on me with fury in her eyes. "Yes, I know, and I'd rather not be reminded."

I was confused by her reaction, since she had attended the focus group for the Japanese American Museum, and had spoken openly there about her time in camp. Why was she closing down on me?

The reasons given for the wholesale sweep of Japanese American communities on the western perimeters of America during WWII were explained variously. The Department of War said it was necessary after Pearl Harbor, in order to protect the country from acts of espionage by traitors still loyal to Japan. Others in the Roosevelt administration put forth the more benign-sounding notion that it was to protect them from attack by Caucasian citizens.

Later, when there was no evidence of disloyalty among the Japanese American population, historians followed the economic causes, and contended that Caucasian Nativist farmers' organizations, such as the Sons of the Golden West, wanted the Japanese farmers off the land. With their cultivation skills and industrious labor, the Japanese immigrants had made previously unproductive acres bloom, and now the white farmers wanted the land back.

Farmers are a powerful lobby during a time of war when a nation and its fighting forces have to be fed, and they took advantage of the wartime fear and used it to pressure Roosevelt. Historians have also postulated that Roosevelt deferred to the military's judgment because he was up for re-election and the military position had great public support.

BUT NO ACADEMIC ANALYSIS AMELIORATES THE SUFFERING; ONLY through the gradual peeling of the hundreds of thousands of individual stories coming out of the camps can we hope to heal ourselves and our nation from the consequences of our denial of this grievous history.

The telling is complicated by generational differences and political pressures.

The *Issei* were the Japanese immigrants who were still denied the possibility of United States citizenship when they were remanded to the camps. Their children, the *Nisei*, like Mary, were American born citizens. The *Kibei* were *Nisei* who had been sent back to Japan by their families to be schooled and acculturated in Japanese ways. Their status had no bearing on their incarceration; they were all uprooted based on race and ethnicity. But their different statehood standings tore at their hearts and self-esteem in conflicting ways that would influence the positions they took in camp as well as having an enormous impact on their recovery after their release.

The repercussions of the Incarceration are far reaching. Just as African Americans migrated from the Deep South to the north, a trip as harrowing in its own way as the earlier middle passage from Africa, so too Japanese Americans, after years behind barbed wire, had to travel from the camps back into America where they were reviled, and remake lives for themselves by putting this traumatic piece of their personal and historical pasts behind them. They were like the refugees coming out of Europe, only they were refugees in their own land.

Everyone was affected, even those of us who were white.

THE SHOWGIRL AND THE WRITER

PART I

My Story

The author is on her father's knee on the front row right,
and her mother is standing behind in a light shirt dress
They are at the Tule Lake High Security Camp with a group of Japanese
Americans.

1

The First Caucasian Baby

It has always been difficult for me to explain my history as a resident of a Japanese American Concentration Camp. How could anyone — Caucasian or Japanese American — ever understand what it meant to be a white person born in a concentration camp in America, and how the experience within my family, situated in the context of the subjugation of another race, connected politics and history inextricably with my sense of self?

My birth was announced in a staff newsletter: "The first Caucasian baby was born today in Tule Lake, Margaret Grace Elberson, seven-pound daughter, to Donald Elberson and Ruth Siegel Elberson." The description would follow me through the years, publicly and explicitly defining who I was by my race, something that would rarely occur in any other place in America when a white child is born. What it has said to me is that I'm non-Japanese and non-Asian, just as most people of color in our country are declared non-white; in my mind I am the perpetual outsider who doesn't belong in mainstream America because of the odd circumstances of my birth, while simultaneously feeling no right to my place in reclaiming the history and politics of the Japanese American Incarceration because I am Caucasian.

It came to the foreground when I began to write in the 1980s. Did I have permission to tell my own life's story, my heritage and personal history garnered from having been born in the Tule

Lake camp? Did I have the consent to address the sorrows of those who were forcibly ripped from their previous lives? Could I tell a personal cultural story I have carried within me my entire life?

W HEN I WAS EIGHT YEARS OLD, A CHANCE ENCOUNTER IN A HOTEL elevator alerted me to the problem. I was riding down to the lobby to meet my parents, when two middle-aged Asian couples got on. The men were wearing black suits, white shirts, and silk ties, and the women, cocktail dresses and furs. Subtle perfume filled the air of the cab. I peeked admiringly at them as they talked among themselves.

Suddenly I realized one of the men had said "Tule Lake Camp," and "the day we arrived there." They were talking about the place where I was born The place I'd never heard mentioned, except by my parents. I waited for a lull in the conversation, then volunteered in an excited voice, "I was born in Tule Lake Camp in California." As they turned slowly to look at me, their expressions turned to stone.

When we reached the lobby, they walked out without a word to me. I was mortified. What had I done wrong? It was only years later that I wondered, in their eyes, given the extreme politics of Tule Lake, had they only seen me as a child of their jailers.

A FTER TULE LAKE, MY FAMILY OF THREE MOVED EAST ACROSS THE country, following my father's work organizing farmers into co-operatives, and each time I entered a new school district, I was invariably asked where I came from. I answered that I'd been born in a Japanese American prison camp in California. After a couple of teachers looked at me in disbelief and told me that they didn't think I had my story right — that there was no such thing as concentration camps in the United States — I settled on saying, simply, that I was born in northern California. I didn't name a town, because after 1946 there was no existing town to call my birthplace. The story of the camps was never taught in any of my schools, including the university I attended. Since my country had expunged Tule Lake from our history lessons, I decided it was best to be quiet about that part of my past.

From as far back as I can remember I have kept secrets about my identity. When we settled in places that were openly anti-Semitic, I hid that part of my birthright, never telling my friends that my mother was Jewish, concealing this piece of myself behind my father's non-Jewish surname. If asked what denomination I was, I gauged what denomination the questioner was before answering. If she was Methodist, I said I was Episcopalian; if she was Presbyterian, I said I was Lutheran. I lived in fear of being found out. If I felt I was about to be caught in my religious subterfuge an electric current like spasm shot through my body.

Nor did I want other children to know that my father was a socialist, an organizer with the left-wing Co-operative Movement, a pacifist who hadn't fought in the war. By the time I reached high school I had created an all-American persona for myself, camouflaged by bleached blond hair and bobby socks.

I carried on the subterfuge through my university years.

I've often wondered if my country's failure to atone for the crime I was born into contributed to my creating my alternate persona.

MY PARENTS WERE IN FULL AGREEMENT THAT THEY HAD TO TRY THEIR hands at changing the world.

They had spent their honeymoon and the first year of their marriage in 1938 working in a Farm Security Camp for displaced Dust Bowl farmers, featured at the end of John Steinbeck's *Grapes of Wrath*.

Seated in their stifling dirt-floored pup tent, my mother penned proper thank-you notes for wedding gifts of silverware and linen stored away back in Palo Alto that June, when my father decided to leave the ivy tower of Stanford University where he was working on his Ph.D. in economics, and plunged into the real world of political organizing.

It was during that year that my mother witnessed the farm women's grief when their babies were stillborn or died within days because of insufficient prenatal nutrition, and the trauma of their months of dislocation.

My parents reported to Tule Lake camp in May of 1942. My mother was twenty-six, my father had just turned thirty. They were assigned to a staff barracks unit containing a kitchen with, as yet, no stove, a tiny living room sparsely appointed with Army issued Sears and Roebuck furniture, a bedroom with no closet, and a primitive bathroom.

My mother set about to making their space habitable, cleaning and putting out the few personal objects they'd brought along — some pieces of Fiesta ware, a couple of tablecloths, and a Mexican rug they'd purchased on a trip to Tijuana.

She soon discovered that she had to sweep and dust at least three times daily to keep the place free of the black grit stirred up off the dried lake bed by the omnipresent wind. It sifted in through the cracks in the walls and windows, coating every surface and eating into fabrics. After a few days, she put the rug back into a trunk and settled for the linoleum that covered the floors.

My mother boiled the mineral-hardened water. Her pots and pans were coated white with crystallization; her linens turned gray, her dark curly hair became stiff with dust. Her olive complexion became rough and reddened in the dry, high altitude climate. But she never let adversity and sacrifice dampen her determination.

One day while she was cleaning, my mother heard hammering and sawing coming from across a vast firebreak from the prisoner side of the camp. Lines of tar paper-covered barracks were still being thrown up even as the evacuees arrived.

The barracks were 100' long, open buildings that were being divided into units of various sizes, with 20' x 25' units being most numerous, followed by 16½' x 20', 20' x 20'. They were assigned to

Tule Lake High Security Segregation Camp near Castle Rock,
in northern California. *photo*: Densho National Archives

families based on their size. The buildings were organized around a
square that was called a "block." Within each was a mess hall, communal lavatories, shower rooms, and laundry rooms.

AT THAT TIME SHE WAS SIX MONTHS PREGNANT WITH ME — HER
first and only child, but what she found more immediately demanding were her preparations for teaching the incoming children at Tule
Lake. It was important to set them down to work as quickly as possible to lessen their distress, and to bring them up to date with state
education requirements as they had missed months of schooling already since their dislocation.

The high school was housed in a barracks that had been parti-
tioned into three classrooms. As my mother told it,

> There were no desks or chairs, not even a clock in the room.
> I corralled some of the construction workers to make picnic
> tables and benches. But there were no school books to teach

from, and no notebooks for the children to write in. There wasn't a blackboard or a piece of chalk to be found, and no mechanism for putting in a purchase order. I stole sheets of newsprint from the newspaper office and tacked them to the wall and wrote the lessons on them with crayons.

My FATHER DESCRIBED THOSE FIRST WEEKS IN TULE LAKE CAMP AS chaotic and brutal. Some days there were over five hundred arrivals. He helped people down from the trains — university students, teenagers, fragile old men and women, young couples with babies and small children.

His next task was to line up the arrivals so they could be finger-printed and have their pictures taken, all the while balancing finding milk for crying toddlers and private spots for nursing mothers.

In the midst of the turmoil, he tried to identify Nisei-generation leaders who spoke Japanese to act as translators for the elderly Issei and comfort those who were frightened and infirm.

"People were pretty damn shaken coming off the trains and seeing the twenty-foot-high fences with barbed wire on top, and the armed soldiers in the watchtowers," my father said.

But nothing mitigated the moment when he escorted the families to their new living quarters, "walking with them across the barren firebreaks. I had to take them into those dingy excuses for rooms, with walls that didn't reach the ceilings, steel bed frames, rolled empty mattress ticking they had to stuff themselves from piles of straw, and a potbellied stove. These were people who'd left everything behind, even fine houses. I learned not to enter with the family, but to stand outside. It was too terrible to witness the pain in people's faces, especially the Issei women, too shameful for them to be seen in that degrading situation."

My MOTHER GAVE BIRTH TO ME IN THE LATE AFTERNOON OF AUGUST 6, 1942 in a tarpaper-covered building that served as the camp hospital. On a mimeographed list of births, the baby born before me was number "22, Donald Takeshi Hashimoto, Male," and the baby after me, "Sumiko Tanaka, Female, number 24"; I was number 23.

Still troubled by the infant deaths she had seen earlier at the Farm Security Camp, my mother decided not to look into my eyes for a week so she wouldn't fall in love with me before she was sure I would live. As was her wont, she stuck to her resolve, but she did ask the doctor "Is the baby intact?" When he told her I was perfect, with all my fingers and toes, she asked what she really needed to know, "Do her ears stick out?" She was relieved to hear that they were snug to my head, as she was afraid I would be burdened with what she considered a Jewish trait — protruding ears — a stigma that would have been inherited from her and would make her daughter a target in a dangerous world.

When she eventually did gaze at me, she was disappointed. "All the Japanese babies in the nursery with their round faces and thick black hair and smooth skin were beautiful, while you were scrawny and red-faced and bald." I had no Jewish traits that would identify me with her, but she had still given birth to an imperfect child.

THE ENORMOUS DAILY OPERATION OF THE CAMP SITE'S 1,100 ACRES, which eventually housed 18,000 prisoners, was carried out to some degree by white staff, but even more so by prisoners who were paid $19 a month for their efforts, the top wage scale in the camp. We're talking about professionals such as the Issei and Nisei doctors and nurses in the hospital who attended to my birth, and teachers, as compared to the $16 and $12 a month salary for mess hall staff, and farm workers who sowed and later harvested produce for the population on the extensive camp outlying fields, and sanitation workers in charge of keeping the primitive plumbing operational.

MY FATHER BEGAN THE WORK OF ESTABLISHING THE CONSUMER CO-OP system. The co-op philosophy was based on participatory democracy, profit-sharing among the membership, and nondiscrimination principles. The irony was that he was organizing behind barbed wire with prisoners who were incarcerated for the crime of their race and ethnicity, and whose frozen bank accounts were, for a while, inaccessible to them.

He believed fervently in the principles of the Co-operative Movement; he was convinced that it was the answer to the little guy winning against the corporate state. That year he dedicated himself to tirelessly persuading people of the efficacy of learning skills that would lead to possibilities for gaining political and economic power once they were back out in the world.

He was most proud of how he'd engaged with the three groups in the co-op: the Nisei, Kibei, and Issei. Many of the Issei spoke only Japanese, adding communication and generational complexity to the decision making.

Gradually the owner-operated board of directors had coalesced, but not without wrangling; the participant internees, especially the Kibei and Issei were, with good reason, suspicious of the War Relocation Authority's motives in wanting to develop co-ops within the camps.

After endless hours and months of sometimes contentious meetings, the effort resulted in a member-operated grocery store, a dry goods store, shoe repair shop, furniture store, barber shop, and even a taxi service, all of which were capitalized with five-dollar membership fees per person.

MY FATHER'S EFFORTS HAD REPERCUSSIONS WITHIN OUR OWN SMALL family unit as he was out most nights at meetings or trudging night and day from barracks to barracks, addressing people's concerns. He was consumed with making the project work, rarely making it home for dinner with his wife and new baby.

In a contemporaneous document dated a week after my birth, a Nisei man wrote that my father had lost his cool in a meeting, distressed that people were dragging their feet at a critical point in setting up the co-op.

"Elberson is shaking with emotion. He's been trying to get the floor. Finally, he stands to say, 'You give Fumi [my father's female Nisei assistant] and me the power to make decisions and then you crab. Fumi and I have been working our butts off on this. I've been doing it to the detriment of my family life. Do this for me. Do it for Fumi.'"

In another document a Nisei man told of a conversation in our barracks while enjoying a Christmas dinner of my mother's roast beef and cherry pie. They were talking about how hard my father had been working on the co-op, when at one point, the man wrote, "Mrs. Elberson smiled sweetly and said, 'Yes, baby plays with rattle, while Daddy plays with co-op.'" The writer found nothing untoward about her comment, but reading the document fifty years later I recognized only too well her barely suppressed rage beneath the sarcasm, the biting undertone that informed my childhood and their marriage.

Her anger had already erupted over a seemingly small incident. A month after my birth they took me to a photographer's studio just over the state line in the town of Klamath Falls, Oregon. The sepia-toned pictures were a symbol for my mother — like the wedding thank-you notes she'd written in the tent — of holding onto some semblance of a normal life, of maintaining a ritual propriety despite difficult circumstances. She wanted to send the formal photo back home to her parents, proof that she made the right decision in marrying my Gentile father.

My father was to pick up the pictures on one of his regular trips to Klamath Falls, where he went to buy provisions for various detainees, special items they couldn't get in camp or through catalogs. Twice he returned home laden with supplies for others, but empty-handed for her, having forgotten to stop by the studio.

When he finally did bring the photos back, my mother carefully lifted the gray cardboard overlay. She stared in disbelief at me lying on the blanket with a ragged, ripped hem that she remembered from that day. The photographer hadn't bothered to crop the picture to hide the edge. "You didn't even look at your daughter's picture," she let loose in a merciless fury. "You care more about your work than about us. Everybody else's needs come before ours." She never forgot her grievance about that incident, and would repeat the story innumerable times over the years.

Perhaps my mother's rage could have been triggered by postpartum vulnerability, or by an ambivalence about motherhood. She was a brilliant woman with an IQ in the high genius range, who had her own professional ambitions. She had excelled at both UC Berkeley and the University of Washington.

From the moment my parents met, their love was predicated on respect for each other's talents and intelligence; their first glimpse of each other established the guideposts.

My father was a graduate student at the University of Washington, working on his Master's degree, and as a teaching fellow he had proctored a final exam that my mother was taking.

Of that day my mother said, "he stared at me throughout the exam, interfering with my concentration, and then had the temerity to give me a B grade on it, my only B in my entire four years and I confronted him on it."

An early feminist, she had insisted that the words "to obey" be stricken from her wedding vows, and here she was, left alone in a grim barracks in a prison wasteland with an infant while her husband was out doing the work he loved. Or maybe it was her growing distress concerning the news she was receiving from her mother about the plight of Jews in Europe, while her own husband had chosen not to fight in the war.

My parents had married in a civil ceremony in 1938, at a time when it was a radical act for a Jew and Gentile to come together in what was considered a mixed marriage. They both gave up their respective religions so they would have no conflict, a seemingly logical solution, but they hadn't anticipated the Holocaust.

I'm sure it was more of a sacrifice for her than for him. Religion *per se* wasn't what she lost, rather she relinquished the millennium of Jewish tradition passed down through customs like the familial Seders she had participated in at her beloved grandmother Annie's home in Seattle.

It was many years later, after my mother had died, that I discovered that that same Annie Kahane Kahan and her first cousin, my great-grandfather Louis Kahan, had escaped the pogroms in Russia in 1885 and come to America to homestead in North Dakota in a Jewish community where they celebrated the High Holy Days in the town hall of Devils Lake. A valiant, iconoclastic Jewish story to be proud of, but instead was hidden away and never became one of those tales proudly related to one's child.

My formidable maternal grandmother, Sarah Seigel, liked that my father was working on his Ph.D. when she met him, a degree that she herself had worked toward. She had trained as a chemist.

Family lore has it that she went on to do post-doctoral studies in Frieberg, Germany, before World War I. All I could find in my research was that she taught chemistry at the University of Washington in 1906, and later at Broadway High School in Seattle, where her teaching was so highly regarded that she was looked to as a conduit for providing talented premed students to universities across U.S.

Though my grandmother was charmed by my father — he was able to work his magic on even her — she was an active and ardent Zionist, and by 1942 she must have known what was happening to Jews under the racial laws of the Third Reich . . . and she must have had feelings about his choosing not to fight.

When my mother returned to work teaching at Tule Lake, an Issei woman and her husband were hired to care for me. At first it felt to my mother like exploitation to employ this woman "at practically slave wages," but in the end, she said, the woman was as grateful for the work and the income, as she herself was to be relieved of childcare, and again able to go back into the classroom.

I've been told that I loved this elderly couple — especially the woman — whose names I've never learned, but in all my poems about the Incarceration and in my fiction — including my second novel, set in Tule Lake — and in my dreams I call them Mr. and Mrs. Takaetsue, a name I made up before I began my research on the camps.

My first words were spoken to them, and they were in Japanese. Mrs. Takaetsue doted on me, spoiling me, at least in my mother's eyes.

When my parents had to be away from the camp for a week, she and her husband moved into our barracks, and my mother asked our neighbor in the adjoining apartment to keep a watch on us. In what became an iconic story in our household, the neighbor reported that each morning around nine, the husband stepped outside with a broom. He swept a path to an area a few feet from our front door. He went back inside, to emerge minutes later with my folded playpen, which he opened out and placed at the end of the path. He returned to the barracks and came out again with the broom and swept a trail around the playpen, after which he got a pan of water and sprinkled the paths, wetting down the fine black lava dust. Only then did his wife appear in the doorway holding me, the princess, dressed in a fresh bonnet and playsuit, and waited for him to give the signal. When given, she ceremoniously carried me high in her arms over to the playpen, gave me a kiss, and settled me gently down for the morning. Several times before lunch, the husband would return to re-sprinkle the paths.

My caretakers were classified as immigrant aliens. To understand the political implications of their status for them and other Issei in the next phase of life in camp, we have to go back to 1922

Author in her playpen in Tule Lake Japanese American
High Security Segregation Camp in northern California

when Takao Ozawa, a Japanese immigrant who had lived in the United States for twenty years filed for citizenship under the Naturalization Act of 1906. The act allowed only "free white persons" and "persons of African nativity" to naturalize, making it clear that Asians weren't welcome. Ozawa contended that he was eligible by dint of the shade of his skin.

His case, Ozawa v. United States, made it to the United States Supreme Court where he, acting as his own attorney, contended before the nine sitting justices that beneath his clothing his skin was as white as theirs. Legend has it that he rolled up his sleeves in court to prove his point. The nine justices ruled unanimously against him saying that his skin may be white, but he was not of the Caucasian race, reaffirming the ban on Japanese immigrants from becoming citizens, and leading to the Oriental Exclusion Act of 1924, passed by Congress, effectively ending all Japanese immigration to the United States for twenty-eight years.

THE SITUATION IN TULE LAKE AND THE OTHER NINE CAMPS worsened after January of 1943 when the government initiated a camp-wide mandatory requirement that all evacuees over the age of seventeen had to sign loyalty oaths. Washington had decided that Japanese Americans incarcerated in camps could volunteer for the army and serve in a racially segregated unit, but before they could do so they had to prove their loyalty to the United States by answering correctly 28 questions on "The Loyalty Questionnaire."

THERE WERE TWO QUESTIONS THAT CAUSED CONSIDERABLE CONSTERnation and upheaval among the internees. They came to be known as Question # 27, which asked —

"Are you willing to serve in the armed forces of the United States on combat duty, wherever ordered?

Question #28, was —

"Will you swear unqualified allegiance to the United States of America and faithfully defend the United States from any and all attack by foreign or domestic forces, and forswear any form of allegiance to the Japanese Emperor or any other foreign government, or organization?"

Even though the ostensible goal was to recruit able-bodied men to fight, everyone over seventeen years of age, men and women, the elderly, citizens and alien residents, were impelled to register and take the oaths. The questions tore apart families and shredded the fabric of the community because if the Issei, who like the Takaetsues, had not been allowed to become citizens of the United States, forswore allegiance to Japan and the emperor, they became people without a country, and because the emperor was literally their god, they would be without a divine being to protect them.

Or more starkly put, our government would, like the Nazi's did to Jews, eradicate their right to citizenship in any country, thus wiping out their national identity, leaving them stateless, and erasing their connection to their culture and religion.

As political philosopher Hannah Arendt said, "the state's ability to sentence someone to death was minor compared to its right to denaturalization because it put the person beyond the pale of law."

Their children, the Nisei, feared if they swore their allegiance to America, they could be separated from their parents. As a result, many native-born Nisei answered as their parents did, and checked off "no" to the two questions pertaining to their loyalty to the United States. Other Nisei chose to check off "no" thinking that they didn't have to declare loyalty to a nation that had imprisoned them, nor did they have to fight for the country while their parents remained behind barbed wire.

As it turned out, a significant percentage of Tule Lake inmates refused to register.

Those who signed "no" from the other nine concentration camps were dubbed "No-No's," and were rounded up and sent to Tule Lake, turning it into a high security camp.

My father said the word from Washington D. C was that it was to be the "black camp," — a prison within a prison, — replete with stockades and steel solitary confinement cages for the most rebellious.

The two populations — "loyals" and "disloyals"— lived side by side in the barracks, as a resistance movement against inscription into the armed forces built and became increasingly militant.

19

In the ensuing months the factions attacked one another, causing both psychological and physical harm.

At the height of the conflict there was an attempted takeover of the administration area of the camp by more militant residents, described later in outside newspapers as "a riot in the camps by radicals," though my mother said "the evacuees had a right to demonstrate, that's all it was, just a demonstration."

My father later defended the actions of the demonstrators saying they were simply expressing their unhappiness with the increasingly repressive dictates from the administration, and rumors that food meant for the prison population was being stolen from the warehouses by Caucasian staff.

BUT FOR ME, ONE-AND-HALF-YEARS-OLD BY THEN, WALKING, TALKING in simple sentences, and certainly absorbing the stark desert prison world we lived in, the night of the insurrection had a grave impact, with implications well into my adulthood.

Earlier that evening my parents had driven to Klamath Falls to see a movie. When they returned, the camp was under martial law and Army tanks had moved inside the fence.

My mother and father were stopped at the front gate by the military police who had no information on where I was. My father was told to report immediately to the administration area leaving my mother to go alone on a frantic search for me.

I wasn't in our barracks where they'd left me. The arrangement had been made that the neighbors would listen through the thin walls and in case I cried they would go in to see about me. The lights were out in the neighbors' barracks rooms and the door was padlocked.

My mother ran through the cold November night past military tanks that were moving deeper into the camp, as the search lights mounted high on fences swept the area. She asked whomever she passed where the staff had been sent. None of the soldiers knew. She was frantic by the time a jeep pulled up beside her.

It was Harold Jacoby, a close friend and compatriot among the liberals on the staff, whose job it was to head the civilian police force. "We took everyone to the community center," he shouted and told her to jump into his jeep. She held on to the roof as he raced across the rutted, snow covered expanse. He dropped her at the door of the quonset hut. "She's in there, Ruth, I'm sure," he said.

My mother entered the noisy, hot room. Still decorated for a Halloween party from the previous week, the streamers of black and orange crepe paper loops sagged off the ceiling in the damp body heat of scores of staff people.

She spotted me across the room sitting stock still in my flannel nightie, my spine rigid, staring blankly into space. Even when she approached calling my name, her arms reaching for me.

I didn't respond, I didn't look at her.

"I picked you up. Your little body was stiff with fear. I held you for the longest time before you finally relaxed against me and began to cry. Your wail was heartbreaking, unearthly."

The turmoil continued for months and culminated in a knifing murder of the Nisei co-op general manager. No one was ever brought up on charges.

MY FATHER WAS DEEPLY SHAKEN BY THE KILLING, FOR THE LOSS OF life, but also for the undermining of all the hard work they'd put into building the co-op. The long-standing racist attitudes held by certain conservative staff members were turning virulent.

In a contemporaneous document it was said that staffers were calling the internees "yellow monkeys" to their faces; ". . . references were made to the evacuees as 'those goddamned yellow sons-of-bitch-es,' '. . . those goddamned yellow bastards,' and 'those slant-eyed . . ..'"

This vile naming brought my father to an ethical crossroads. Years later his face was etched with angry incredulity, his voice trembling, when he said to me —

"I was adamantly against any use of violence, but after a time I became furious at their [certain of the staff's] racism. They expected Japanese Americans to be grateful for whatever morsel they got in camp and said they were spoiled and bel-ly-aching when they stood up for themselves. I realized there were circumstances where I could take up arms, if my family was being threatened, or if people who couldn't defend themselves were being treated intolerably unfairly. A part of me had the capacity to be violent if the injustice was too great. I couldn't in good conscience say I was a pure pacifist."

At the time, he angrily wrote, "Some people expect the sort of gratitude a serf would feel when the feudal lord bestowed some good on him."

He traveled down to San Francisco to change his status and sign up to fight. When the officials heard he worked up in the Tule Lake Camp, they asked him, "what's your position on the internment of the Japs?" He answered that it was an egregious injustice. "They called me a 'Jap Lover' and closed the books on me," my father told me. They refused to take him into the Army, and re-categorized him as "unfit to fight."

My father didn't want to fight. He remained a pacifist his entire life. But certain of his motives for that trip to San Francisco will always be unclear, and somewhat disturbing to me. Over the years, whenever he spoke of this incident, he never connected having opted to change his draft status to the suffering of Jews in Germany, nor what it must have meant to my mother that he wasn't fighting for her people.

On a visit home after I'd been delving deeper into their experiences in Tule Lake, in the presence of my mother, for the first time I shored up my courage to ask my father how he had felt about being a conscientious objector, given that Jews were being slaughtered in Europe. I could sense the silent tension coming off my mother as I waited for his response. Finally, he said, "We didn't know the grue-some details back then."

I didn't dare press further. I felt I was stepping into dangerous territory, for them, for me. Our family's mixed identity — my mother being Jewish — marked my father's work at other junctures as well.

A little later we were talking of the time after Tule Lake when we lived in a farm community in southeastern Ohio and how diffi-cult that had been for my mother. It was at the end of the war, and the farmers my father was organizing into rural electrification co-op-eratives through the Farm Bureau were mostly German American, many of whom blamed the Jews for the war. My mother said quietly, "I don't think it was helpful to Don to have me as his wife."

My father responded, "That's the problem with being a commu-nity organizer. You often have to subsume your own opinions and your closely held beliefs in order to get the job done."

As I heard their restrained statements, I was glad I'd gone no further, because they brought back an incident in Vermont when my father was working with a Protestant minister in order to reach the community.

I was with him one Sunday morning when he parked me in a Sunday school class so he could make his presence known at the service. I see that room in the church basement with the technicolor images of Christ. I feel my pleasure at being there. But then I see and hear my mother's rage-fueled reaction when she somehow found out he had betrayed their pact. It was one thing for him to sit in the church for his work, quite another to send me to Sunday school.

I also remember how, after her fury, she took to her bed, falling into a profound sleep only to wake in a stuporous state, a pattern re-peated throughout her life. The sleeping, or as I learned to call it, her depression, and her disappearances into fugue states, were equally as frightening as her anger. It was dangerous territory for me to enter, even as an adult.

Amidst the Dark Forces of America

TURBULENCE WOULD BE A CONSTANT VISITOR DURING MY GROWING up and young-adult years. Periods of stability were rare. The strong winds of those years were created by the political climate, marital strife, and emotional struggles, my own and my mother's.

In late 1943 my father began to travel back and forth from the Tule Lake camp to the Washington D.C. War Relocation Authority headquarters, and from there a long stint in Manzanar camp, and then accompanied a group of Nisei leaders on the train to Chicago for a major Co-op meeting. In May 1944, he traveled to Arkansas to see to the disbanding of the co-op in the Jerome War Relocation Center. This was the first real disruption and uprooting of our family.

While he was in Arkansas, my mother, with me in tow, drove to Palo Alto, where they had lived earlier, in our old, second-hand car to claim our few possessions from storage. We stayed there while my mother organized our journey across the country where we were to meet up later with my father in Chicago.

My mother has said that during this period I was missing my father terribly, and that I would attach myself to every man in sight. "You'd cling to them, which I suppose they found charming, but it was disconcerting, and then one day a package came from your father with a cloth doll inside, and you clutched it to your chest and wouldn't let it go. After that you stopped grabbing onto male strangers."

WE BEGAN OUR JOURNEY DRIVING THROUGH THE MOUNTAINS ON small, precariously twisting roads. As my mother told it, one day as we began our continental push on flatland straightaways across grassland plains she was overcome by sadness and loneliness. She pulled the car to the side of the road and sat, her hands gripping the steering wheel, staring ahead for a long while into the flat distance. Then turning to me, she said, "You're my best friend, my best companion. Today is mommy's birthday," and she taught me to sing "Happy Birthday, Mommy."

For two solid days, I stood on the passenger seat, and sang my two-year-old version of the song to her, with the hot air off the plains blowing through the car as we made our way, from morning until the sun was setting behind us, belting out the words.

At the end of the second day, her laughter bringing on tears, she yelled over my singing, "For God's sakes, sweetheart, stop, my birthday is over." By then I must already have learned a powerful lesson; there was a way to make my mother happy, avoiding both her anger and her psychic disappearances. There were to be countless episodes with her during my childhood and adulthood — including as my mother was dying — that I attended to her emotional life.

SHE AND I ARRIVED IN CHICAGO, AND SHE QUICKLY FOUND A JOB and temporary home for the two of us in a welfare summer camp on the outskirts of the city to tide us over while we waited for my father. She was assigned to sleep in the bunk room with the teenaged girls, and I was left each night in a metal crib with high sides in a cavernous dormitory where families with small children were housed. I would wake before dawn every morning, screaming, shaking the metal spokes like prison bars until my mother was sent for, and, as she told it, "I had to row you around the lake until you calmed down. You see I had it hard, too."

I long wondered what had engendered my anguish: Was it being separated from my father, or did it have to do with being torn from the loving comfort of my caretakers at Tule Lake or was it simply leaving familiar surroundings? The question I now ask myself: Was I terrified each night that my mother had left me as well? Perhaps there's a clue in a recurring nightmare I've had throughout my life. I am standing outside a prison. I reach in though a high chain-link fence to a beautiful dark-haired woman in a long scarlet dress. I cry out, begging to be let in because only there will I find comfort and relief, only there will I belong. But the question remains, is the woman in red my mother or a stand-in for my father, or my Issei caretaker?

As the story goes, Mrs. Takaetsue confronted my mother when we were leaving, saying she was afraid my mother couldn't take care of me properly. Had she witnessed my mother's anger at me or at my father? It was highly unusual for an Issei woman to confront a Caucasian, but then the camp was a setup for unusual disruptions of ordinary mores.

Professionally, my mother was tremendously competent, ambitious, and inventive in her teaching. She was brave as well. In the mid-1950s she would set about successfully integrating the school system in the high school where she served as head of her department, by hiring Black teachers, against great resistance.

She was the breadwinner in our family; the person who would pack us up over and over again, and move us bodily to our next home; and the person who made all my clothes, took care of my physical well-being, and cooked the meals even as she held down full-time positions.

Her ability to take matters into her own hands and drive us across the country during wartime lived as a metaphor for me for her outer strength and independence.

But in fact, she was emotionally fragile, prone to tears if she felt slighted by my father or me, and when she and I were alone, susceptible to sudden eruptions of anger at me, nasty snipping, and even physical cruelty when she felt most vulnerable. She confessed to me in later life that there was a period, "when I had to hit you every day."

I don't remember the spankings. I suspect it was when I was five-years-old and had been prescribed new corrective lenses for my lazy eye, but the optometrist had made a seriously wrong calculation in the prescription. I constantly overturned my glass of milk when reaching for it because I couldn't properly judge depth.

We'd recently moved to a ramshackle farm, in Shelburne, Vermont on the outskirts of Burlington. I'm guessing it was then, because I remember that I was filled with trepidation as I went down each morning for breakfast wondering who I would meet: the furious mother, or the mother staring into space lost in her own world who, when she looked up, didn't meet my eyes, or the too-happy mother, the latter chilling in her over-excitable enthusiasm.

WE WERE AGAIN JUST THE TWO OF US BECAUSE MY FATHER HAD A new job, and he was out and about, driving up and down the state organizing farmers. I began to fear that my mother was putting poison into my orange juice. I believed I could escape her poison and save my life by holding my breath and silently — bringing to bear a new skill — count to ten as I gulped down the juice.

To stave off her anger I also employed my ability to entertain, singing or happily telling stories, though that too could bring on her irritation as she sternly instructed me to "calm down." If her rage or mania was too enormous for me to handle, I simply stayed out of her way by going outside "to play," secretly crossing the road to our new neighbor's house for succor.

When she finally found a high school teaching position in the factory city of Winooski, Vermont, her anger and her excitability lifted. She placed me in an elementary school a few blocks from the high school. Since I was five years old and there was no kindergarten, the first-grade teacher said I could play quietly in the back of her class.

My mother and I would take the long bus ride from Shelburne, through Burlington, and across the river to Winooski and back again at the end of the day. She became a normally happy person that year. She had a friend at school who would sometimes drive us home. From the back seat of the car, I once heard my mother say, "I don't know what I would have done if I hadn't gotten this job. I'd kill myself if I had to stay home with a child for any longer."

AS A COMMUNITY ORGANIZER MY FATHER EARNED MINIMAL SALARIES, and according to my mother he often "plowed his earnings and some of mine into his projects." When we eventually moved into Burlington, we changed apartments five times over eight years, whenever the rents rose above $35 a month.

Decades later, I chipped a portion of paint off the second-hand wooden kitchen table and matching chairs we'd carried from place to place, and counted eight layers of color; my mother had applied a fresh hue most times we moved, but evidently not all because by my thirteenth birthday we had lived in fourteen different homes.

I STOLE AS A CHILD.

My attic-room closet in our last apartment in downtown Burlington had a carton filled with my stash, everything and anything: comic books I was forbidden to read that I adroitly slipped under my tee shirt when the store owner wasn't looking, maple sugar candy which I wasn't allowed to eat, cans of ripe olives which I craved, small toys, lipstick for dress-up, ornaments for my hair, all sundry of five-and ten-cent-store items that I really didn't want, but couldn't stop myself from snatching, and bottles of Evening in Paris perfume which I thought epitomized glamour.

One year when I didn't want a Christian friend to know I wasn't going to church on Easter, I stole money from my mother's pocketbook, as I often did until I had accrued enough to go with my friend and her mother to Abernathy's, Burlington's most elegant department store at the top of Church Street to buy an Easter bonnet. I snuck the hat into the house and hid it in the carton. On Easter morning, alone by the windows of my bedroom that overlooked two main churches in downtown Burlington, I watched the parishioners in their finery parade up the paths and through the doors into the sanctuary as I ate an entire box of maple sugar candy bears, which I'd shoplifted the day before, prolonging the comfort as each bear slowly melted on my tongue. I didn't dare put on my beautiful bonnet with its wide brim and long blue grosgrain ribbon for fear my mother would walk in.

They say that many children don't know they're poor. That wasn't entirely true for me. We did live in another time than now, when there's such a proliferation of stuff to make a poor child feel deprived, but I knew I had less than other children. I lied to friends about the toys I hadn't received on Christmas. I once drew blood from a girl's arm whom I bit in a fury of jealousy because she had dolls — one of which she had just snatched back from me — and a play kitchen and all sorts of other trappings in her fancy bedroom, whereas I didn't have a room for my nonexistent toys. That year in Burlington I slept on a cot tight up against my parents' bed. I don't want to make more of this than it was, because in many of the neighborhoods where we settled, the children were much poorer, lived in more cramped conditions, and in dark dank places.

WHEN I WAS TWELVE, SUSAN, MY BEST FRIEND, WENT OUT IN A snowstorm without a coat or shoes in the middle of the night, and ran three blocks to our apartment because a man visiting her mother had climbed into bed with Susan and tried to rape her. She stayed with us that night. I held her shaking body under the covers of my own bed. Her nightgown was as stiff and frigid as sheets dried on a clothesline in winter. She stuck her finger up me, to show me what had happened and the erotic sensation both thrilled and repelled me.

Susan's mother was a waitress and had to make money on the side because she was the sole support; Susan had no father that I ever saw.

Mrs. Talbot did what she had to do to make a life for Susan, buying her lovely frilly dresses, patent leather Mary Janes, and ruffled socks, and purchasing Toni "natural wave" to perm her hair. She brought men into their home where they paid for sex with her. I loved Mrs. Talbot more than I pretended to love my own mother. I had always looked forward to her day-off afternoons when she would sit with us in her pink silk robe with a glass of whiskey, the ice tinkling as she sipped, while we pranced about dressed up in her satin negligees and mules with the ostrich feathers fluttering in the breeze-we made, acting parts of glamorous actresses we'd seen on the screen, until she put down her drink and said, "come over here girls, let me paint your nails." She would scrub my nails clean with remover before I left for home, saying "I know your mother doesn't like such fancy stuff," and I'd go to bed those nights inhaling the left-over banana-scented fumes, and dream of snuggling close to her on the sofa.

Susan lived with us for months after the incident. Police escorted us to and from school because Mrs. Talbot went wild with agony when she wasn't allowed to see Susan.

One night she smashed the window glass in the door to the staircase leading to our second-floor apartment, demanding her daughter's return. "You prigg'n fuckers, give me back my daughter." After that my mother had the authorities commit Mrs. Talbot to the asylum for women in Waterbury, and we could freely walk to and from school, and ice skate on the frozen shores of Lake Champlain, and go each Saturday to five-hour movie matinees for twelve cents.

But Susan was anything but free. To get to the movie house we passed the cocktail lounge where her mother used to waitress, and Susan would fall silent with what I knew was sorrow. She cried most nights and I comforted her, holding her in the big bed we shared and describing the pictures made by the frost on our moon-lit window.

I hated my mother for what she'd done because I knew how much Mrs. Talbot loved Susan. Eventually Mrs. Talbot's family took my mother to court where the judge said if Mrs. Talbot went across the border to New York State, Susan could go with her. Mrs. Talbot came for Susan at school just after mud season, the afternoon of the hearing. I could see Mrs. Talbot in the hallway through the classroom door window while the teacher gathered Susan's belongings from her first row seat, and Susan strained her body forward into the aisle, waiting for permission to leave. My best friend, almost a sister, left in a rush without looking back at me and disappeared from my life.

Despite the difficulties, I think we never would have left Burlington if we didn't have to. My mother would say whenever we crossed the state line after a vacation, "You know immediately when you're in Vermont, even without a sign. It's the most beautiful state in the country." My parents had found a place where they could belong. It was resoundingly Republican but there was a small, intellectual progressive community and there were Jews associated with the University of Vermont. There was high culture — Martha Graham came to dance. If my mother and father wanted ballet or opera they could travel across the border to Montreal for a weekend.

BURLINGTON WAS WHERE I BEGAN TO STUDY MODERN DANCE AT THE Fleming Art Museum. Every Saturday I'd climb the museum's grand marble staircase to the second floor to my classroom, where for two hours I danced my fantasies of a flower unfurling, or a deer leaping, or a violently erupting volcano under the tutelage of my teacher, a devotee of Martha Graham and Pearl Primus. In that room, where I could express my most secret emotions in movement, I was safe. No one could know who I really was inside as I leaped higher than anyone else in class, my bare feet strong and flexible as springboards propelling me into the air and my muscular legs protecting my landing, where I could thrust my pelvis, sensing the sexuality of the action, while maintaining my innocence. When I later performed before audiences in my early teens, in recitals of my own choreography at the museum, winning a juried talent contest in Burlington, dancing before my entire summer camp, I moved people to cheers and tears.

One night I was carried on the shoulders of my fellow campers down the moonlit, pine-tree lined path from the performance center through the camp grounds in joyous celebration of my dancing. It was said by teachers and audience alike that I had a gift. But when we had to leave Vermont, I lost the confidence in my ability to dance and, never went back to it.

As the explanation went, the pressure to leave Burlington began in late 1954 when the Red Scare caught up to us, and my father was called a Communist on the front page of the *Burlington Free Press*. He lost his job, and though he looked far and wide during that fall and into 1955, he couldn't find another one in either Vermont or New Hampshire.

I could never find that article in the *Burlington Free Press*; the story I remembered my parents telling me could have been an apocryphal family tale distorted by time and my own faulty memory. Though chillingly, in 1955, my father abruptly disappeared from the pages of the Burlington Free Press, after being cited regularly in community news articles in 1953 and 1955.

Another regional newspaper told me more about the political climate and how my father could have been a target. The *Burlington Daily News*, now defunct, was published by William Loeb III, a virulent anti-communist whose tactic was to publish the names of "Communists" on the front-page editorials of his paper. People who had worked for the 1948 Henry Wallace campaign for President were especially targeted by Loeb. My father had proudly worked for Wallace's election.

Henry Wallace was the Bernie Sanders of his time. His platform stood for universal government health insurance, an end to the Cold War that was just beginning, full voting rights for Blacks, and an end to segregation. During his national run, he campaigned side-by-side with Blacks in the South, and refused to speak before segregated audiences or to eat in segregated restaurants or sleep in hotels that didn't provide lodging for Blacks. Wallace's ultimate crime, that led to his resounding loss, was that he was endorsed by the United States Communist Party, which he refused to disavow.

My father once told me that he had never been a member of the Communist Party, but had been attracted to them in the 1930s because, "they were the only ones speaking out about injustice and racial inequality."

Over the years he grew to dislike the party. Though he never mentioned Stalin, he did say, "they were too doctrinaire for me, too rigid for my liking, and were authoritarian." By the time we arrived in Vermont, he defined himself as a progressive populist of the sort that originated on the west coast, or a Eugene Debs Socialist, in the manner of Scandinavian farmers who settled in the Midwest. But political subtleties didn't matter to Joseph McCarthy and his followers, like William Loeb; my father, who wanted nothing more than to make America live up to its ideals, was caught in the poisonous HUAC (House Un-American Activities Committee) web.

During the 1960s, "the personal is the political," became the movement mantra; political awareness emerged out of recognition of one's own feelings of oppression. But in my family's case, and in the lives of thousands of others who lost their jobs and had to go into hiding, or for the hundreds of thousands of Japanese Americans who were incarcerated, a more accurate description would had been, "the political became the personal."

I HAVE VERY FEW MEMORIES OF THE YEAR 1954 INTO 1955 IN BURlington. What I do remember is: we moved "downstreet" as it was called in Burlington, to a railroad apartment in a dark, unappealing, four-family building.

That was when I began to steal, my friends couldn't visit me, and my parents stopped sleeping in a double bed. My mother was again angry all the time, and once when I didn't do my chore of vacuuming on a Saturday morning, she screamed at me, whipped the vacuum out of the closet, and struck me hard with it before dragging me by the collar down the long hallway to instruct me where I should start.

BUT THE QUESTION REMAINED — WHY DID WE HAVE TO LEAVE WHEN others who were as active as my parents stayed in Burlington?

Recently I located and spoke with a former childhood friend who now lives in Arizona. He was the son of a Quaker, a liberal activist, and a close friend of my parents.

I was forewarned that he'd become an ardent supporter of Trump, and that I should steer clear of the subject, which I did, even though I was curious what caused such an extreme conversion from his progressive upbringing. We talked for hours on the phone, reminiscing about the farm where his family lived, and which I loved to visit.

He gradually opened up about how he had been attacked in school and called a communist because of his mother's activities, but it wasn't until almost the end of our conversation that I began to understand where the experience of our parents, especially his mother's, diverged.

His mother, the "matriarch" — his word — was originally from mainline Philadelphia society. She could clip her coupons, he said bitterly, while she carried on with her political work. As I listened to his complaints, I understood why she could stay in Vermont even as my parents had to leave. She felt entitled to speak out. Her class and her high WASP background protected her and her family. Her husband was from a long line of Vermonters, which made her more acceptable than we were in the community. We were outsiders, having only lived there for seven years.

My mother was Jewish. The most renowned person forced to leave Vermont during the Red Scare was a brilliant cancer researcher at the University of Vermont who was Jewish. William Loeb had also gone way out of his way to disprove "rumors" that he himself was Jewish, even putting a statement to that effect on the notorious front page of his newspaper.

35

The fact that the McCarthy era reared up only five years after the end of the Holocaust, when the news of the camps was just seeping out of Europe, had to have been very frightening for my mother. Ethel and Julius Rosenberg were Jews and they were electrocuted in 1953 by the United States government. As a Jew my mother couldn't have felt safe speaking out. Nor were we embedded in the relative safety of the Jewish community or a synagogue in Burlington.

Additionally we weren't independently wealthy or even middle class. We could not afford to sustain ourselves, and save money for the future, on my mother's Vermont teaching salary of less than $1,500 a year.

My father lost his sense of self when he couldn't get a job; similar to the Japanese American male heads of household who lost their dignity in the camps. My father had stood up valiantly for them against the administration, but he never could stand up for himself, not to my mother, nor to a boss. He made room for others to speak and advocate for themselves; but he couldn't do the same for himself or for us as a consequence.

I HAD JUST TURNED THIRTEEN WHEN WE MOVED FROM BURLINGTON to Uniondale, New York, on Long Island, a mostly working-class community of people who had recently relocated from the outer boroughs of New York City in order to make a better life.

My parents chose it because my mother insisted on attaining a good paying teaching position, and the new Uniondale School system, in order to quickly staff the sprawling high school, was offering an unheard-of salary, for us, of $5,500 a year, with opportunity for advancement, which was important to her. Her pay proved necessary because my father couldn't find a position for over a year, even in New York City.

We arrived in mid-summer of 1955, before school began, with no resources, and settled into an apartment on the poor side of town, in a two-family house at the dead-end of a dreary and sparsely populated street of run-down houses and no sidewalks, abutting the chain link fence separating our street from the cemetery.

My father drove into the city each day to look for work, and my mother went to the high school, where she was to teach, in order to prepare her classroom. I had no friends other than the large family of seven next door. Their house was without a floor, only packed dirt underfoot, and was permeated with a stale stench of furniture scavenged from the local dump by the brutal man who was the father of the five children and husband to his beaten-down wife.

I regularly hung out in their kitchen that August, starting in the morning and on into the afternoon and sometimes then staying for dinners of Sicilian red sauce spaghetti. That was followed by giggle fests over dirty stories with the four daughters as we huddled together on moldy bunk beds in their tiny bedroom, just off their parents' sleeping area.

At some point, Chickie — the oldest girl, who looked different than the other dark-haired children with her pale skin and wild curly red hair — and I began to play strip poker with Rudy, her eighteen-year-old brother and his buddy Bobby, in Rudy's sunporch-bedroom that smelled of dried urine because he still wet himself most nights. It was degrading, though enticingly furtive.

It wasn't dangerous until one evening when my parents were out and I was alone in our apartment. I was in the bathroom combing my hair. Hearing a noise, I turned to find Rudy in the hallway just outside the open door with a rifle trained on me. I froze. He laughed, emitting a demented, high-pitched sound, and then lowered the gun and left saying nothing. Don't ask me what I felt, beyond shock. And despite any fear I may have harbored, I continued to play strip poker in his bedroom. I had no other place to go for company. I never told my parents about the gun.

THAT WINTER I OPENLY WEPT IN THE SCHOOL CAFETERIA IN FRONT of my new classmates when over the loudspeaker, they played, "I'm

Dreaming of a White Christmas." Shortly after that I stopped going to my modern dance classes my mother had signed me up for.

My father began to drink, at first only a Martini each night and gradually he upped it to three and it turned out he'd been downing cocktails at lunch in Manhattan where he worked as a volunteer for the United Housing Foundation, an urban development group dedicated to building below market priced, middle income co-operative housing.

They finally hired him a year on in to be their Education Director, teaching co-op principles to the new member-owners.

After he got the job, he would regularly arrive home late from the city. It was like he was working overtime to save his new life. My mother would spend the long evening hours waiting for him, sitting straight-backed on the sofa, watching shows on our very first television, and playing hand-after-hand of solitaire, snapping the cards into place with what I can only describe as wrath.

Our poverty was no longer a lack of money and material goods, but one of a more consequential nature for me, caused by my parents having cut loose from their backgrounds, their families on the west coast, their religions. By the time we arrived in Uniondale, it became clear that we had no church, no synagogue, no tribe, no permanent family home, no postage stamp as William Faulkner called it — that place where roots go deep. I had no cousins on our side of the continent, no community of Jewish people to counteract the anti-Semitism and racism I heard in abundance in school, no place to go for cultural, political, and even class identity where I could feel free to be who I was.

What I did have were my parent's political beliefs, which were too dangerous to speak of, their good works, their intelligence, their commitment to making a better world, that in the everyday reality of my life, left me pretty much to my own devices to find my way during my teenage years.

It took my parents some time to recover from being cast out of the Eden of Burlington. My father continued drinking; my mother continued being angry. We'd come up against the "darker forces of America," as James Baldwin called them. America had turned into a treacherous place for us and we were unprepared.

I BECAME A CHAMELEON: TAILORING WHO I WAS TO WHAT I SENSED would make them like me.

I became whatever persona was necessary. I was so good at it that I became a magnet for people, always popular, always loved. I could walk into any new social group or culture other than my own and instinctively know what was expected of me. I listened well and deeply. I was like a highly tuned antennae for cultural, racial, and class differences. I believed my lie about myself and became cemented to it, much to my parents' grave chagrin.

I hung with a rough crowd of kids who'd brought their gang affiliations from Brooklyn to Uniondale. I went along in my boyfriends' hopped-up cars, drag-racing in the streets and on the highways, drinking and smoking and doing poorly in school. I snuck out of house in the middle of night to be with boyfriends. I enjoyed the disguise of being a rebel, loved the recklessness.

Much to my highly educated parents' dismay, I was so successful at failing in high school, that only one university would even consider my application, and eventually accepted me with caveats. My parents took out a $2000 loan from their credit union for my tuition; I worked during the school year as a waitress in the dining room of my dormitory as in-kind payment for my room and board. In summers I slung food behind the counter in luncheonettes.

After a semester of struggle with my studies and confusion about my class identity vis-a-vis the other students, I caught on to the mid-western mores of Ohio and became a popular co-ed; I was runner up to Homecoming Queen in my freshman year, and later was crowned May Queen.

I still had a rebel streak, now politically focused on the civil rights movement. I graduated with honors, and held so many leadership positions that I was one of five women in my class tapped by the national Mortar Board Honor Society for "exemplary scholarship, leadership, and service." But all the while I carefully guarded my secret, never letting anyone know I was Jewish.

Upon graduation in 1963, I joined the Peace Corps and decided from then on I wouldn't hide my Jewish heritage. My relief at coming out was enormous, but I would find later, that the damage of hiding lived within me and continued to take its toll.

3

Write It, Warts and All

THE CLEAREST INDICATION OF THE PSYCHOLOGICAL TROUBLE I was in from those years of concealing who I was, came to the fore in 1978, when in my mid-thirties, living in New York, I was in a high-pressure, all-consuming job as the program director of Pacifica affiliate WBAI-FM, a left leaning, listener-sponsored radio station. Work had become my salvation; I excelled at it and it provided the most genuine aspect of identity for me, but now I was unraveling. I had completely burned out from the political intensity and ego-filled dramas of the place.

I resigned from my job and within two weeks I had bought myself a Smith Corona typewriter, and for no reason that I could discern at the time, I started to write fiction. Before this, I had never formulated anything more than letters and grant proposals. I had never had aspirations as a child of becoming a writer. I'd been schooled to be an activist.

I didn't foresee any conflict between creating a fictional world and the historical political context of my stories. My life up to then would offer me a windfall of unusual content; from birth my worldview was inextricably connected with the events of the incarceration of Japanese Americans during WWII. My parents' ongoing commitment to racial and economic equality had allowed me to live within many disparate communities in America. Despite resenting their single-minded focus on fighting for their beliefs at the expense of family, when it came time to decide my own life course, I had chosen activism, following their lead by joining the Peace Corps, and spending two years doing community organizing in an urban *barrio* in Guayaquil, Ecuador.

When I'd returned home, I worked as a community organizer in New York's *El Barrio* and in the South Bronx. I'd also served in the John Lindsay mayoral administration from 1968 to 1970 where one of my responsibilities was working with under-served communities to bring arts programs into their streets, and for a while I ran a business producing rock and folk concerts for non-profit groups, as well as an outdoor festival for twenty thousand people to promote Off-Off Broadway theaters. All rich material.

But I soon found that it was harder than I thought to figure out how to harness the complex mix of historical and political experiences into a compelling narrative of fictional truths. One day I was stunned to realize that the creative source had to be my inner life, and to get there I needed to tunnel into the emotional vortex of my family, and at its heart, myself. Not an easy task for someone indoctrinated with the principle of holding the needs and hardships of others above my own.

As I applied myself each day, an account began to emerge of a white man's experiences in a Japanese American prison camp in Northern California. There were scenes of an army takeover of the camp, and of a traumatized Caucasian child who is separated from her parents during the disturbance. The words poured out with such force that the keycaps of the keys of my new Smith Corona flew off, and I had to rush to the typewriter repair shop around the corner, where the owner, Mr. Adelman, a survivor of four concentration camps, including Auschwitz, with whom I'd shared my history, dropped everything to reaffix them and send me back to work.

As I continued, I felt a deep resonance with the material, but one day I came to an abrupt halt. When I tried to advance the narrative beyond the child's distress, I met a complete block. What was going on? Wasn't this my story? Why couldn't I write it?

42

LOOKING FOR ANSWERS, I WENT TO VISIT MY PARENTS WHO HAD retired to Puerto Rico, and were living, as was their way, in a poor and working class *urbanisación* half an hour to the west of San Juan. All their neighbors were Puerto Rican except for one Haitian family that lived across the street. My father, who had quickly become bored with sitting on the beach, had organized a political group called the *Comite de Trabajadores y Consumadores*, made up of young university-educated radical activists committed to bettering the lives of the people on their island. My mother had returned to teaching in a local high school.

We settled in the small yard of their modest bungalow, serenaded by a background chorus of cocks crowing off schedule, faint salsa music from across the street, and the melodic late afternoon calls of *coquis*, the endemic frogs of the island. My mother, in a prim floral sundress, sat stiffly in a plastic chair. I was at the picnic table taking notes on my typewriter. My father, darkly handsome, his hair still black with only threads of white, wore his favorite shirt, a colorfully embroidered *guayabera*. He lay in the hammock strung from the wrought iron bars of their *marcesina* — carport — to the chain-link fence that separated their yard from their neighbors on three sides. Hands behind his head, he swung to and fro, pushing off the ground with one trailing foot, answering my questions.

HE BEGAN WITH THE STORY I'D HEARD OVER THE YEARS OF HOW he had come to Tule Lake to organize the camp's co-op system. He spoke as usual with nostalgia about Noboru Honda, a close Nisei associate in the co-op who still sent us Christmas cards each year, and Koso Takemoto, a young Kibei he'd had high regard for as an organizer.

Then he unexpectedly said to me, "I hope if you write this book, you'll tell it warts and all." With that he shifted focus and began to explain that President Franklin D. Roosevelt, a master of politics, in a pragmatic move, had signed the executive order that sent people to the camps.

But then, to ameliorate the devastating action, Roosevelt, the so-cialist, had decided he didn't want American corporations like Sears Roebuck and Penney's providing goods and services to the inmates, and he reached out to the progressive Co-operative League of Amer-ica to remedy the situation. "That's where I came in," my father said. "The league assigned me to Tule Lake." He paused.

When he spoke again, he surprised me by talking about his as-signment after leaving Tule Lake, an episode he'd rarely mentioned. His speech was measured, but underneath it resonated with pain. He reminded me that while my mother and I had driven to Chicago he had gone to the camp in Jerome, Arkansas.

"It was late in the game, and my task was to start to dismantle the co-op in preparation for closing the camp, without letting people know exactly what was going on because many Issei were afraid to go back into America. They were traumatized by the loyalty oath debacle, and were resisting leaving. I wasn't supposed to tell them what was in store for them. "'Just do your job, government officials told me.'"

He stopped and for a while was silent and seemed to be far away, remembering. When he resumed, his tone had hardened. In a tense voice he explained that after the loyalty oaths, men who had an-swered "yes" to the two questions, started signing up for the military to prove their allegiance to America, thinking white America would see them differently. "They were doing it out of personal loyalty to the country, but also to bring honor on all those who had been and were still incarcerated for the crime of being Japanese American, es-pecially their own parents who remained behind barbed wire. By the time I got to Arkansas the 442nd 'Go for Broke' segregated Army unit was in training just across the state border in Shelby, Mississippi. Bringing suffering and humiliation to the Japanese American sol-diers in what should have been their fine moment, they found that Jim Crow applied to them as well. In those southern towns, proudly dressed in uniform, they had to step off the sidewalk to let white

44

people pass. The 442nd ended up being the bravest unit in the war. They died in droves in Italy proving their loyalty to America." The hammock ceased swinging.

"One day in May, some of the soldiers were on leave before shipping out, and had come into camp to be with those who were still prisoners. Maybe to shore up people's belief in themselves. That afternoon the camp population, staff, and honored guests assembled on the parade grounds in the devilishly hot sun," my father said.

"I'll never forget standing there. The place was packed with the soldiers in uniform, families, old folks, and Nikkei Boy Scout troops, in proud formation. The flag was raised. Everyone began to pledge allegiance. I looked up. I saw Old Glory flapping in the wind and in the distance, the watch towers with soldiers standing guard, and the glint of barbed wire coiled along the high chain link fence that enclosed the entire prison camp. It all went together for me. Here were these people paying obeisance to the flag of the country that had put them there." His voice faltered. He lurched half out of the hammock, as though to escape, his feet just catching his fall. He covered his face. "Oh, my God," he said and began to weep.

I had never seen my father cry before. It frightened me. I didn't want to know what sorrow lived in him from those days. If there was an emotional center to our family of three, it was he. In all he was a joyful, charismatic person, his laughter contagious and distinctive. When my parents went to movies in whatever town we lived in, people often came up to my mother the next day to say, "You must have enjoyed the movie last night. We heard Don laughing to beat the band."

I adored my father, but when I'd decided to come down to Puerto Rico to question him a suspicion had crept in that he might have contributed to the problems of the incarceration. What if he had refused to work in the camps to start with? If he'd not committed himself to making life in the camp more palatable for people, maybe they would have resisted earlier and he could have joined in fighting the incarceration.

The Seventies was a time on the left when one had to be either militant or considered an accommodator or worse, a collaborator, nothing in between was permissible. Now I was torn between wanting him to be politically pure, and worried that I may have hurt him by pushing him too far in my questioning. I sat in agony, staring at his bowed head, his face buried in his hands, his shoulders shaking, wondering what else beyond sympathy contributed to his long-submerged sadness. Was he crying because these brave men had made a sacrifice for the honor of their families and for the country that had imprisoned them, while he, even with a Jewish wife, had not fought in that same war? Was he ashamed in front of my mother, who sat in silence as he told his story? Or had he felt guilt for not being honest with the families about the camp closing and that they would have to go back out into America without their sons to help them? Could it be that he felt he had let me down with this new version of what it meant to be involved in the camps? I wondered if he struggled, as I had in my organizing work, with feeling it was just too hard to stay the course and do the right thing.

I'll never know for sure.

When he cried I realized I couldn't continue with my novel. If I did, I felt I would have to become a spy in the house of Elberson, undermining whatever good he had done. I put aside the book after that day and though I spoke perfunctorily with him from time to time about the camps, I would not pick it up again until long after my father had died. As frightened as I'd been by his weeping, what was worse was my sense that at the core of his being, there was some terrible weakness that I didn't want to expose, let alone explore.

I began to understand that when I walked away from the political drama entailed in my work at WBAI, and began to write, I had been incredibly naïve about the price I would have to pay to transform politics and identity in the United States, into fiction.

In Puerto Rico I should have understood the pain, contradictions, and moral paradoxes that plague an organizer's life. And by extension I shouldn't have been taken by surprise that the melding of the personal and the political in writing would be easy. In fact my whole being by then was exemplified by such conflicts, or one might say, I was living a novel long before I ever dreamed of creating one.

Wedding photo of Fritz Mueller and Marnie Elberson Mueller
New York City — Chelsea district of Manhattan

In 1969 I married Fritz Mueller, a German national, and though I loved him — in fact it was a passionate love — we were oddly both compatible and incompatible. He had lived through World War II as a child, and had left Germany for the United States in 1964 after earning his Ph.D. in chemistry, with a job and a permanent green card in hand, as part of the country's scientific brain-drain.

Neither of us were a good fit for our own societies. There was an unspoken love-across-history and the horrors of war to our bond. I'm not sure how much we really understood what we were getting into or why we were instantly attracted to one another. We were attached in a place beyond the rational. It was not a sensible or a deeply-considered match.

For our honeymoon, I proposed that we travel to the Ande an region of South American, covering Peru and Bolivia, but first stopping in Guayaquil, Ecuador to visit my old *barrio,* and then up and over the Andes, into the Amazonian region for a week, to then travel down the Rio Napo.

It was on the Napo, that I, without realizing, began gathering dramatic and tragic incidents for what would be my first novel, the intimate, psychological story of a newlywed German man and his Jewish American bride, set against the napalming atrocities of the first incursions of the oil companies into the Amazon.

During that trip, long before the encounter with my father, I had experienced traumatic flashes in my dreams from episodes in my urban barrio, of a dead baby, of riots, of stones being hurled at me, of being trapped in a dark space while rocks ricocheted overhead off a corrugated metal roof, merging with the old recurring images of prisons and prison camps, and a woman in scarlet calling to me from behind a chain link fence, triggering my desire to return to her arms for safety and comfort.

Paradoxically, it was the story of the Rio Napo journey that in 1980 I innocently turned to when I couldn't go forward with the novel about Tule Lake. I soon found that I was diving into another whirlpool of intense emotion and personal ambivalence about my place in the world. In addition to intimate, unresolved family issues, I was confronted with troubling memories from my Peace Corps tenure.

Cerro Santa Ana, where I had lived and worked, was a tough, dangerous barrio of dirt-floored, ramshackle cane shacks with no plumbing, their interiors half-covered by dilapidated corrugated iron roofs, sprawled up a hill or *cerro* on the northern most reach of the city. It was situated on high, dry land with the brown, flotsam-filled river Guayas sweeping by to the left, its current carrying in laden banana boats from the south. The city was built on a filled-in swamp spreading out below.

Cerro Santa Ana was romantic to the untutored eye, but brutal in its living conditions, settled by a tough population of original squatters and drug dealers, and the profoundly impoverished, with only a small infusion of those aspiring to the middle class — taxi drivers and university-bound young people and shop owners.

I was there to help them better their lives through self-determination promulgated in the activities surrounding the new community center built by the previous Peace Corps volunteers at the base of the hill. Assigned as a community organizer, I gradually convinced people that I was not there to give handouts, but rather to work with them to achieve their desires and goals. Through our day-to-day successes and failures, in our year and a half journey toward progress, I'd become deeply, emotionally connected to my neighbors. I had grown to trust them, as they seemed to finally trust me. I was my father's daughter.

Everything went well until toward the end of my service, a new Peace Corps representative for the district replaced my previous supervisor who had supported me and the community in our endeavors. In his first month the new man called the volunteers into his office and excitedly proposed bringing gifts of luxurious items from an American church into the barrio. In the meeting I argued vigorously against doing so, saying it would contradict everything I'd promised people I wouldn't do, and furthermore, offering objects they could never afford or even dream of would cause a riot in the neighborhood. He refused to listen and a few days later a long flatbed truck pulled up to the bottom of the hill laden with four-foot-tall dolls — larger than six-year-old children with malnutrition in our community — bolts of rich brocade fabric, world class soccer balls, regulation baseball bats, and more luxury items.

The word flew up the *cerro* and within minutes people were streaming down the cement staircase and into the community center's yard; in no time people were bloodied from fighting with each other over the treasures, ripping arms, legs, and heads from the dolls in their desperation for the toys . . . the lucky ones carrying off whole bolts of fabric.

The community leaders and I tried to move the goods into the storage room, but the now furious mob — the same people I'd won over in the past year — turned on me, hurling rocks, cement blocks, dirt and whatever rubble they could get their hands on. The center's local president and treasurer rushed me inside, and we bolted the door from within.

We stayed for hours in the dark, sweltering building while rocks thundered down on the corrugated metal roof.

Silence finally returned. People had given up and climbed back up the hill to their homes, and we decided it was safe to leave. Stepping outside I saw remnants of dolls, torn fabric, and shards of plastic and glass littering the yard, glittering in the blast of noonday equatorial sun.

When I turned to padlock the door, hearing the warning shouts of the other two who had walked out before me, I came face to face with thick human excrement smeared across the wood. In that moment the world lost all color, my vision physically transmuting to gray and white. Remembering, as I write this, I wonder if the draining of color could have brought back the tar-paper-covered barracks and the black lava sand mixed with snow of that November night in Tule Lake.

It took me years to be able, without spasms of trembling, to tell of the dangerous stupidity and arrogance of the Peace Corps Rep and the retaliatory fury aimed at me by the people of the *barrio*, whose trust I had betrayed. A year and a half of hard, hopeful purpose had

50

been ruined in an hour and the community leaders were vilified in the process.

This was so similar to what must have happened to my father's aspirations, and the efforts of the co-op leadership in dealing with the violence during the signing of the loyalty oaths, culminating in the later death of the co-op manager. And not unlike my father's mandated-by-Washington-betrayal of the Japanese Americans in the Jerome, Arkansas camp, who did not know of the precipitous plans to send them back out into an unwelcoming America.

I WOULD WORK FOR YEARS THROUGH THE 1980S ON THE RIO NAPO novel, which would eventually be published as *Green Fires: An Assault on Eden*, but not without a decade's long battle to come to terms with what had happened. As the barely fictionalized bride in the novel, married to a German, I was trying to understand what it meant to be me, decoding the emotional parallels between being born white in Tule Lake prison with the choices I made to work within poor communities. Equally as crucial, was the question of why had I chosen to marry a man whose family had spent the war on the side of the enemy, who could have potentially been complicit in my family's annihilation. And what did it mean that I found more emotional comfort with this man than I had in my own family, and who taught me how to love, at least as much as I was capable of in the early days of our marriage?

During those years of self-discovery and working on *Green Fires*, I permitted myself once again to think about the novel set in the Tule Lake camp, and to attempt to do some research. I went to the New York Public Library in the mid-1980s, where I found *Years of Infamy: The Untold Story of America's Concentration Camps*, the early, seminal treatise by Michi Weglyn. I opened Weglyn's book to photos of Tule Lake, of black sand, chain link fences and watch towers, and in full view of others in the reading room I began to weep inconsolably. I didn't know why I cried, but I sensed it as relief at finding confirmation that the camp where I was born did exist outside my family stories. It was documented in a book. More important, the pictures looked like the backgrounds in my baby snapshots, like the photo of me in my playpen, set out on the wasteland of the dried lake bed by the Issei couple who had so lovingly watched over me.

Over the next years I continued on to The *Kikuchi Diary* (1973), by Charles Kikuchi to Reverend Daisuke Kitagawa's *Issei and Nisei: The Internment Years* (1967), and many other books written by people with firsthand knowledge of the camps.

ONE DAY IN 1991 I WAS READING THOMAS JAMES'S *EXILE WITHIN: The Schooling of Japanese Americans 1942-1945* (1987), a book about the camp-wide educational system, when I came upon my father's name in a footnote. As if by a miracle I found the reference on his birthday. He would have been seventy-nine.

I had begun to worry that he was slipping away from me: I was having trouble remembering the timbre of his voice, the sound of his laughter, the look of his hands, and the smell of him. When I phoned Thomas James, he said, "Yes, Don Elberson showed up extensively in my research." He directed me to the National Archives in Washington and the University of California's Bancroft Library at Berkeley.

A MONTH LATER I RODE THE TRAIN TO WASHINGTON, DC, NERVOUS about what I might discover. What man was I to encounter? My father had related his view of his place in the camp, but what would the documents reveal?

I had called ahead to the National Archives, given them my father's name, and been told they would have the material ready for me on my arrival. As I sat waiting at the long wooden table under the high, vaulted ceiling of the old Research Room, surrounded by the soothing sound of turning pages and the soft scratch of assigned pencils on paper, I imagined that the librarians had found nothing: my father might have been paramount to me, but to the greater world he probably wasn't worth the space of a file.

Then a man came toward me pushing a three-tiered book cart filled with boxes. "You're waiting for the material on Don Elberson in Tule Lake camp?" he asked matter-of-factly.

There were eighteen boxes on the cart and they were jammed with my father's letters, memos, meeting minutes, and everyday notes asking about mundane topics like health insurance and petty cash refunds. There before me was my father's signature on letter after letter dated 1942, 1943, and 1944. I read documents written in my father's distinctive syntax, requesting leave clearance for Japanese Americans — and in those passionate narratives, he spoke of racism, of the specific discrimination against Japanese Americans in this country, of the need to undo the harm of incarceration.

In one letter dated February 10, 1943, he was trying to obtain leave clearance for an *Issei* man who had worked closely with him in the co-op. He wanted to secure him a job with the Consumers Cooperative Association in Kansas City, but there was resistance on the other end because of fear of racist reprisals from the local white community. My father wrote:

> It's rather inconceivable to me that employment of one Japanese in an organization the size of the Consumers Cooperative Association could be sufficient to split your organization on a racial question.
>
> The co-operative movement professes that it puts into practice racial tolerance where other groups merely talk about it. We, who attempt to sell the co-operative movement to the Japanese as an instrument to be used for their general welfare, have made much of this point, and I feel that it is quite obvious that the co-operative movement, as a whole, does not practice these things because it thinks that its existence is more important than the platforms it announces.

53

When tears again blurred my vision, I admonished myself, "Stop crying, you'll have time for that later." It was like having my father back again. The voice in the letter was my father's own — straightforward, pragmatic, idealistic and not adverse to biting irony to make a point.

The Bancroft Library provided an equally rich trove. In *The Kikuchi Diary*, Charles Kikuchi had written about his time in the Tanforan Assembly Detention Center in the Tanforan racetrack in San Bruno, California, based on daily journals he had kept for the Japanese Evacuation and Relocation Study, a project initiated in 1942 by Berkeley sociologist Dorothy Swaine Thomas.

I had gone to the Bancroft with the hope of finding similar journals written in Tule Lake. And they were there — daily journals written by two *Nisei* intellectuals, S. Frank Miyamoto and James M. Sakoda, who was *Kibei*, for the same study. Both of these young men would go on to esteemed careers in academia: Sakoda was a pioneering figure in computer programming while directing the Social Science Computer Laboratory at Brown University, and serving on the National Institutes of Health Computer Advisory Committee; Miyamoto returned after the incarceration to the University of Washington, where he finished his doctoral degree, which was then based on his Tule Lake research. He remained as a full professor and later assumed chairmanship of the sociology department from 1966 to 1971. He became associate dean of the College of Arts and Sciences in 1975 and acting dean of the college in 1978.

Two twelve-inch-high stacks of the original typed pages were set before me on the long Bancroft library table. I had no idea where to start so I plunged in at random. Within two pages I came upon Frank Miyamoto writing "I think there's only one man in the administration that we can trust, and that's Elberson."

I moved through the immense documents which gave intimate day-to-day accounts of the life and politics within the camp. They proved to be gossipy, erudite, angry and sanguine and read like the great novels of the nineteenth century. I heard my father's voice in the carefully observed dialogue from meetings of the co-op, as he negotiated among the factions of *Issei*, *Nisei*, and *Kibei*.

Just as my father had told me, there on the pages were Koso Takemoto, Noboru Honda, and Fumi Sakamoto. James Sakoda describes Fumi as a "gritty young gal who sure knows how to dress." He writes that she was blunt, impatient, and sometimes aggressive in going after what she wanted. In one vivid image she is said to have a cigarette toughly hanging from her mouth. These details fit my father; he liked his women smart and assertive. My mother matched that model, and I'd been groomed to be outspoken. I learned from Frank Miyamoto that my father preferred to work behind the scenes and that he didn't discriminate "because of race," which "made it possible for him to deal with Japanese without taking a superior attitude that so many other Caucasian staff members tended to do."

On my last research session at Bancroft Library, looking up from the journals at the end of the day, and out the windows to the sun-warmed Campanile, I thought about how my mother and father had come of age and become politically radicalized during the 1930s and 1940s on the western coast of our continent, and I wondered how that had informed their choice to work in Tule Lake.

Sakoda had also written that my father had sensitivity to racial issues, explaining that, "Don has no experience with racial minority groups, but he has worked with minority groups such as trade unions, Okies, and co-ops. He believes that this understanding of present social structure makes it easy for him to understand problems here . . .. As Don put it: 'You work hard with people and you don't notice race.'"

My father would have loved to know that the role of the co-op enterprise was fully documented and archived in the Bancroft library. He would have loved to read the historical acknowledgment and proof of how intrepid the camp inmates were in making something good out of such an intolerable situation. It might have eased the guilt, and sorrow he felt on that day he told me of the *Nisei* soldiers and Boy Scouts pledging allegiance to "Old Glory," while behind the flag the barbed wire glinted in the sun.

Sakoda's statement, coupled with Miyamoto's comment that my father liked to work behind the scenes brought back another memory of how when I was a child of eight and he was organizing independent farmers into co-ops in Vermont. He and my mother would take me along to meetings in farmhouses and put me to sleep upstairs.

One night I sneaked out of bed, over to the heating vent to peer down into the parlor where the farm men and women sat in a discussion circle with the distinctive mélange of odors of their labor — milk, sweat, manure, and hay, barely disguised by the scent of soap — wafting up to me.

I watched my father, white shirtsleeves rolled, and tie loosened, sit forward with his elbows on his knees, listening, rarely saying much at all, a question here or there to this or that person, but mostly just letting the farmers talk. I asked him the next day, "How come you don't say more?" and he laughed, kidding me that I was spying on him, but then he said, "You have to allow people their needs and encourage them to raise their voices, let them find what they think, especially when you disagree with what they say." Even in his listening silence I saw his ability to draw people out and recognized how they trusted him.

Now I'd learned that on the cusp of his turning thirty, which was how old he was in the Tule Lake Camp, he was already applying those principles.

I WAS CLOSER TO BEING ABLE TO WRITE MY TULE LAKE NOVEL AFTER the days spent in the archives, but another mission lay before me. If I was going to set the story in the camp, I needed to revisit it as an adult. Once again, as in our trip to South America, Fritz joined me for this pilgrimage to my birthplace, fifty years after the fact.

We flew to Seattle, stopping there to walk the campus of the University of Washington while my mother's description played in my imagination of how "Don grew so thin I was alarmed." She asked him, and he confessed that he was skipping lunch and eating meager dinners to save what little money he had so he could take her to tea dances and the movies.

I recalled as well, her telling me how he was desired and sought after by the Gentile girls, but he had chosen her, and how it pleased her to have the sorority girls watch enviously as he picked her up from the Independents' House, the only available place for her as a Jewish girl to room on campus.

We then rented a car and began the drive through Washington State into Oregon. We were to spend the night in Klamath Falls. When we arrived we found that all the motels and hotels were booked for a lumbering conference. The only place left was an RV camp where we set up our little orange pup tent between two towering recreational trailers. To add to the surrealistic yet apt setting, the camp was protected by a chain link fence with barbed wire on top and we were given the locks' number combinations to the communal bath house and toilets when we checked in.

THE NEXT MORNING — A SUNNY AUGUST 6TH — WE MADE OUR way across the border into California. We drove through farmland and the wetlands of the Klamath Basin, finally arriving in the small town of Tule Lake.

It was only then that I realized I hadn't properly done my research; I didn't know where the camp was located. We hadn't passed anything that corresponded to the black-and-white photos I'd pored over.

We found an open 7-11 store. Inside some men were buying their take-out breakfasts. When I said that we were looking for the site of the Tule Lake Internment Camp, one of the men turned to the others and said, "Wasn't that the place they put the Japs?"

They directed us to a location a few miles out of town.

We almost passed by; it was practically indistinguishable from the other flatlands we'd been traveling through.

Fritz was the first to spot the plaque identifying it as the Tule Lake Japanese American Segregation Camp.

I felt nothing as we wandered about, even when I finally recognized the distinguishing craggy profiles of the prisoner re-named Castle Rock and Abalone Mountains in the surrounds that had figured in my baby photographs. There were a few buildings in disrepair, but the vast expanse of land was covered with high, golden grass, and the sky above was an intense blue.

There were no watch towers, no black tarpapered barracks. This was the Technicolor version of a more peaceful time rather than the black and white of war.

There was nothing of the past for me here. I'd been a fool to come. Fritz walked off a bit to watch birds, taking advantage of the fact that the Klamath Basin had become famous as a major flyway. Left alone I kept trying to bring some emotion to the fore.

Just as I was about to give up and join fritz where he stood by a canal, a hot wind arose, so strong I had to turn my back against it. When it died down, I wiped my face and then my neck. Both were coated with grit, the very black lava sand my mother had swept three times a day from our barracks.

In that instant I could imagine her, a slender, big-of-belly, raven-haired Jewish beauty pushing me out into the world in the baking hot tarpaper-covered hospital on a blazingly sunny August afternoon like this one, with my father nervously sitting in the room where fathers waited in those times, for the news of my arrival.

As I imagined my parents, two young people of conscience, who had chosen to sacrifice their own comfort to bring me into the world in a place where they could at the same time help others through the trials and tragedies of incarceration, I decided I would try my best to write their story, and my own, set against and within one of the greatest crimes perpetuated by our government. And I would tell it, as my father had challenged me to do, with "warts and all." My wise father was there ahead of me in his understanding of the difficult task I'd set out to accomplish. I was finally ready.

Little did I know that I would end up writing the story twice. The first time in the novel with them as the protagonists, and the second time in this book about Mary and me.

PART II

Mary and Me

Mary Mon Toy (l) and Marnie Mueller (r) in the lobby of Studio 54
for the production of Cabaret 1998.

4

What She Told Me

Soon after we met that snowy night in New York City in 1994 at the Japanese American National Museum focus group, Mary Mon Toy began to call me and ask me on a regular basis to join her at the theater or accompany her to benefits and special screenings of movies.

Three out of four times I had to say no because by March I was often on my way to another city on an endless tour to promote my first book, *Green Fires*. I also made-up false excuses because I was conflicted about becoming her friend. I was drawn to her because of our mutual connection to the camps, but I have a strong tendency — some of my friends would say a compulsion—to be pulled in by another person's neediness, especially when I'm feeling vulnerable.

I was coming off an emotionally draining October through December in Puerto Rico tending to my mother as she died. Despite our difficulties over the years, I decided that she had given me life and it was my place to help her into death. I left my anger outside the bright pink door of the little bungalow on Calle Maruja, and entered into caring for her with openness, respect, and intense longing for what could have been. By the end I felt in a state of grace and wanted to savor that unusual peaceful place and feeling of resolution as long as possible.

Mary's persistence eventually won out and I was gradually drawn along by her seeming loneliness as much as by her appealing offerings. She'd extend a tantalizing invitation to be her escort at an Actors Fund benefit starring tap dancer Savion Glover in *Bring in 'da Noise, Bring in 'da Funk* or to see Frank Langella in Noel Coward's *Present Laughter* and I'd acquiesce, thinking, "Just this once more, what can it hurt?"

I assumed all the tickets came through the Actors Fund and the Screen Actors Guild, as she was a member of both; when I questioned her, I discovered that she was also standing in line for hours to get free passes to previews of movies that would be shown to the general public at first-run theaters. She'd get on the bus, go down to the local multiplex or the offices of *New York Magazine* or whatever other venue was offering the tickets and wait with the crowd until they were distributed. Then she'd travel back home and phone me. She was like a bee after pollen and would have gone out every night if she'd had a companion.

"Let's start to celebrate our birthdays together," Mary phoned me at the end of May that first year. "Mine is next week. I read an article in *New York Magazine* about a restaurant in a Japanese hotel. It caters to Japanese businessmen and diplomats who expect the best. The review said it's very refined. Everything is presented in *bento* boxes. It's my treat."

I felt her wish for a special personal connection entering me, breaking through my protective boundaries and upping the ante of our friendship. I'm particularly susceptible to people's birthday hopes. The story of my singing Happy Birthday to my mother was the touchstone for my helping others at the expense of my own needs.

"No, the dinner is my treat, Mary. It'll be my present to you."

"We'll see. Remember," she prompted, "it's very refined. We have to dress up."

When she said she wanted to go to the restaurant on her actual birthday — June 3 — I realized it was just eight days before my mother's birthday. If my mother were alive, she'd be celebrating her seventy-eighth year.

That night I witnessed a new side to Mary. She could be as proper and refined as the meal we were served, as restrained in her gestures as the subdued environment of blonde wood tables adorned with a single orchid sprig, tatami mats on the floor, and the subtle silk-textured walls of our private room. As each course arrived in lacquered containers, with women in kimonos offering whispered service, Mary spoke softly to them in what seemed to be fluent Japanese. She had dressed in a floral-patterned silk blouse and black skirt; the wig she'd chosen for the occasion was short and smartly coifed. Her makeup was perfectly applied, as if by a professional. When I said as much, she laughed, "It should be perfect, it took me all afternoon."

It was during the tempura course that I said, "My mother's birthday is eight days from now. She was born on June 11, 1916."

"I was born in 1916, too! I'm seventy-eight today."

I was astounded by the coincidence but also because I'd thought she was a decade younger.

"I was born in Hawaii. My father was Chinese. He was a doctor working in Father Damien's leper colony in Molokai. My mother was Japanese, so I'm half Japanese, but they still sent me to camp."

"I didn't think people from Hawaii were interned."

"You're right. You know more about camp than most people. We didn't live in Hawaii then. My father died of a terrible disease when I was two. My mother remarried a Japanese man. He was a chiropractor, the first oriental chiropractor in Washington state. We moved to Seattle."

"That's incredible," I said. "My mother grew up in Seattle."

I was beginning to feel as though by some fluke of nature Mary had been sent to me as a replacement for my mother. "My mother went to Broadway High."

"I did too."

"That's even more incredible. My mother could have been in your class."

"What was her name?"

"Ruth Siegel."

"I don't recall that name. Did she go out for sports?"

"She wasn't at all athletic, in fact, the opposite. She was mostly just a good student."

"I was a good student *and* an athlete. My mother always said that studies came first, but once they were done I could take singing lessons and play sports. I was on the field hockey team."

"Maybe you knew my grandmother, Dr. Seigel. She taught chemistry at Broadway High."

Mary considered the question as she plucked a tempura shrimp from the black *bento* box.

"I think I do remember her," she said, although she looked uncertain. "I was very good at sports, you know. You're sure your mother wasn't on any team?"

"I'm certain." I chose a piece of sweet potato, dipping it in sauce, devouring it hungrily, and changing the subject from my mother, I said, "I'm sorry about your father's early death. It must have been very difficult.

"It was okay. I don't remember him. You handle your chopsticks like an Oriental."

"Thank you." I lifted my sake cup. "Happy birthday, Mary. May you live to be one hundred."

"I plan to," she raised her cup. "And I plan to write my own obituary so I'm certain it's correct. People can get facts mixed up. I have big breasts and long legs, because my father was Chinese. Japanese women are flat-chested and short-legged."

"If I'm still alive, I'll help you write it. Maybe we can work that line in."

She laughed. She had a robust, throaty laugh. "*Kampai.* That's what we say before we drink."

"*Kampai.*"

"Perfect. You pronounce it like an Oriental. To your mother."

"To my mother," I said.

"Are you sure she didn't play sports? I would have known her if she played field hockey."

At home I went straight for the drawer where I keep my tiny collection of historical family memorabilia: some Brownie camera shots from Tule Lake and the Farm Security Camp; half a dozen formal portraits of my grandparents and mother and father; the baby picture my parents had fought about. Not much more. I scrambled through until I uncovered the graduation photo of my mother's class of 1933. There were four rows of students, two rows of girls and two of boys. The girls were resplendent in their white organdy floor-length dresses. I inspected the faces. Not an Asian among them. I was both disappointed and relieved, and a little suspicious of Mary. Perhaps she was simply trying to ingratiate herself with me suggesting the possibility of being my mother's classmate. But the coincidence of their birth dates and the mere possibility that their lives had crossed, aroused a new sort of desire to be pulled into another's life. What if Mary could open up a whole chest of knowledge about my family that I knew nothing about? Just being in her presence had triggered a potent, unfamiliar necessity in me I couldn't quite put my finger on. What I did know was that I wanted more.

5

Blue Eyes, Brando, Sammy Davis Jr., and a Husband

On a July dog-day Mary and I sat on a bench on the Broadway malls — the medians that separate the uptown from the downtown traffic at 100th Street. We were waiting for a movie to start in a nearby theater so we could escape the low, dirty-gray skies and sweltering humid air for a few hours. She was wearing her eccentric garb, dressed in fluttery rayon, mid-thigh shorts to show off her "gams," which were at seventy-eight years of wear and tear, no longer the beautiful specimens that the producers used to lust after. "Show me your legs," Mary said they'd command, "lift that skirt higher, higher. Okay, you got the job, Mon Toy." She wore clogs with dainty ruffled white anklets, her favorite rhinestone-studded tee shirt, and on her head a wide-brimmed black straw hat. Her cane lay across her lap.

We'd known each other for over a year. Though we'd been attending movies and shows with some regularity, I was still a reluctant participant. I never knew when she'd arrive in a get-up like today's, or would break into song in public, or tell smutty, edging on racist jokes and stories at full volume in the back of a cab driven by a person of color.

One of her favorite tales took place in Vegas when she was performing there.

"Sammy Davis Jr. invited me to a party in his room. The elevator operator who took me up to his floor, a Black man, said to me, 'Ah don't think you want to do that, honey. You look like a nice girl.' He waited for me while I rang the bell. Sammy opened the door, stark naked, a drink in his hand. 'Come on in.' I said no thanks and turned right around and got into the elevator. That elevator man got the last laugh, 'Don't say ah didn't try to warn you, honey'"

IT TOOK EFFORT TO HAVE A REAL CONVERSATION WITH HER, AS SHE mostly repeated these same anecdotes, over and over. I'd sat through many iterations, gradually growing bored, wanting badly to go deeper or move beyond the set pieces to more substantive talks.

It's not easy for anyone to be an artist; I wanted to know about her struggles, thinking it was a topic we could share in. I'd given up on asking her Broadway High School questions because they proffered no insights and little information. I did wish she would speak of her incarceration and its aftermath, but I held back on pushing her after our tense moment on Pearl Harbor Day. The early episode on the elevator when I announced my birthplace to the Japanese American couple had also left an indelible impression of how premature questions or statements could be misinterpreted, coming from a Caucasian.

But Mary never tired of telling entertainment stories. Another one began, "When I was in Las Vegas, Ol' Blue Eyes asked me out after the show. We drove up to the hills in his convertible and parked. Then just like that he fell asleep and didn't wake up until the sun rose. He was upset and made me promise not to tell anyone, afraid it would ruin his reputation with the girls. When we got back to the club all the kids were buzzing. 'Ooh, Mary Mon Toy and Sinatra, they're an item.' But I never told."

Then there was the occasion when Marlon Brando had wanted her cast opposite him in *Sayonara* and she didn't get the part because she was too tall: "I was five feet six inches, tall for an oriental girl, and you know he was short." He took her out to dinner at a fine restaurant. "But we couldn't have a private meal because people kept coming up to him for autographs, so he had a table set up for the two of us in the kitchen. That's where we stayed talking with all the waiters rushing by." Later, she had an affair with Brando. "You know he liked his oriental girls. Lots of guys did, but mostly because they were curious. They'd heard we had horizontal slits down there. Brando knew better."

Or the story about when she performed with Mel Brooks in the Poconos, he'd always introduce her as his sister and everyone would laugh.

She was most proud of the fact that she'd made it to Broadway. "How many oriental girls accomplished what I did?" was her frequent refrain. "I did it my way, and all on my own."

And though she went on to get television and movie roles, the story she most loved to tell was how Lou Walters, Barbara Walters' father, discovered her performing in a club in Paris, and how he brought her to the States to play the Latin Quarter. Once in New York, Walters overheard her speaking in English to the stage manager and confronted her, "Whaddaya mean you speak English? I thought you were real Chinese. How come you didn't tell me?" "Cause you never asked," was Mary's sassy retort.

BUT THAT DAY ON THE BENCH, OUT OF NOWHERE, HER EXPRESSION thoughtful, she said, "Maybe being sent to the camp was better in the end."

"How so?" I said, alert but cautious, not wanting to close her down.

"If I hadn't been sent to camp I'd be married and have children and I wouldn't have gone on the stage. I was married when I went to camp. He was okay when we went in, but then after a while he drank and gambled his days away. When Mrs. Roosevelt visited the camp to see how we were doing, she met with us and said, 'I'm here on behalf of Franklin. We want to know if you are being mistreated or spoiled, but everybody must take an IQ test.'" Mary, her nose in the air, perfectly recreated Eleanor Roosevelt's high-pitched, breathy locution. "We all got IQ tests and she asked around about me and they told her I was a singer. She procured me a scholarship to Juilliard. My brother was given a scholarship to Syracuse University. He was a star tennis player at the University of Washington before everything happened, so we both got out of camp. He left first."

"And your husband?" As many times as I'd heard this story, this was the first mention of a husband.

"I never saw him again."

"Never? You left him there?"

"What time is the movie?"

"We have ten minutes more."

"Curtain call!" She flung out her arms, hitting my thigh with her cane. "Curtain call, Ms. Mon Toy!" And she stood. "Time to go. We don't want to be late."

As we made our way across Broadway to the movie house, her arm in mine for balance, I saw her on a train traveling to New York City alone, having left her husband behind — a young, identifiably Asian woman in a sea of soldiers.

Before my father died, he told me he hated to be on the trains during the war because they were often used as troop transports and he felt that everyone was silently questioning why he wasn't also in uniform. In Mary's case she looked like the enemy.

In 1944 my father accompanied a group of Nisei men on a trip to a co-op conference in Salt Lake City. They sat in a private sleeping compartment so as not to be conspicuous. A Negro porter came in to take their order for dinner. After he'd served them, one of the Nisei men tried to tip him, but the porter refused to take the money, saying, "Plenty bad's being done to my people, but nothing compared to what's being done to yours, incarcerating and all."

Had Mary left her seat the entire trip? Had she been allowed in the dining car or did a Negro porter have to bring her a sandwich? I tried to imagine what she'd been thinking and feeling as she looked out the window to the majesty of mountains and endless plains and amber waves of grain. Any soldiers on the train were probably suspicious and resentful of her being in their company.

I had come across a distressing story in my curiosity about other Nisei performers. Kimiye Tsunemitsu, at nineteen, had just left a camp, and was traveling alone on a train to New York City, her first time away from her parents and siblings who had remained in camp, when a soldier angrily refused to sit beside her, yelling that she was the enemy. She had been frozen with lonely terror until a friendly civilian man came to her aid and took the seat beside her.

For Mary's journey to freedom, I wished her kind passengers as the locomotive carved its way through the mountains and chugged across the vast plains toward the Big Apple where she was to attend the most famous and elite music school in America. Even so, her joy had to have been tempered by anxiety about what was in store for her on the outside.

And who was this husband? When had she married him? How did she really feel about leaving him behind? I wouldn't get a clear answer to those questions for fifteen more years, though along the way I would hear descriptive variations on the theme of her husband. No divorce papers had yet been submitted at the time when she would have been on that train moving east. The young woman, in brimmed hat, gloves, and a spring suit, in a May 1944 snapshot, who stood primly under a flowering cherry tree in a park near Juilliard School, was still married.

6

Together on Ellis Island — Spring 1998

A WRITTEN INVITATION ARRIVED FROM MARY, ASKING IF I WOULD accompany her to the gala opening of an exhibit on Ellis Island about
the camps, where there was to be a life-sized replica of a barracks.
Reading her note, I was as tremulous as an adopted child about to
meet her birth mother. Even though I had visited the Tule Lake
camp with Fritz, this offered the possibility of "going home" in the
company of others who had lived the experience, who knew what
neither my friends nor Fritz knew about the place and conditions
where I was born. It was to be a reunion, albeit a reunion of strangers
who were connected by a dark thread of American history.

LEADING UP TO THE EVENT, AN UNSEEMLY DIALOGUE OCCURRED
between leaders of the Japanese American community and those of
Jewish American organizations. The Japanese American Museum,
the designer of the exhibit, had used the words "concentration camp"
to describe the camps, which was immediately met with objections
from some members of the Jewish community: Only survivors of the
Holocaust could use that term. It would diminish the horror of the
Nazi extermination as the American version were not killing camps.
The Japanese American leadership agreed that they were not death
camps, but argued that people had been concentrated and incarcerated on the basis of their race and ethnicity.

Senator Daniel Inouye, who was on the board of the museum,
and who fought in the all-Nisei segregated unit during the war, ar-

gued "Suffering has many faces. Jewish suffering has the most terrible face. But suffering is suffering."

In the meeting I attended, I was shocked at the insensitivity of this group of Jewish Americans. I was torn in my loyalty to the two sides. Both were right in their individual ways, but I felt that Jews should be more understanding about the evil power of such discrimination and of the criminalization of ethnicity. As I sat there listening to the argument, I was reminded of something that happened when Fritz and I had visited the Tule Lake camp. Driving through the town of Tule Lake I had noticed housing developments that looked very much like the prison barracks at the camp, one hundred feet long with five doors spaced about twenty feet apart, but instead of black tarpaper they were covered with green aluminum siding.

When I pointed this out, Fritz said, "That's not possible, it would be like moving the barracks from Dachau into my town." Dachau is forty kilometers from Fritz's home city of Augsburg. We pass it whenever we drive to Munich.

A day later we visited a small museum in the local fairgrounds. It contained a collection of artifacts from the camp, and I asked the woman in charge about the houses in town. "Yes, indeed," she said. "After the war they were auctioned off to returning servicemen and moved into town. The strangest thing was they had no insulation; there were gaping spaces in the walls even with the tarpaper covering. How could people have lived in them given our weather up here? It can go over a hundred degrees in the summer and thirty below in the winter."

In the end, the Ellis Island exhibit opened under the title "America's Concentration Camps," but the heated argument has continued to this day about which is the correct terminology to use when referring to the ten camps.

On the day of the gala event I had my hair done and dressed formally in a new black crepe dress. The town car I'd hired for the drive to Battery Park — where we were to get the ferry to Ellis Island — picked me up first; Mary was waiting for me outside her apartment building as she always was when we went anywhere together. "In the theater you have to be on time," she had repeatedly told me, her subtle indictment of my tendency to be late. She was elegant that evening, in black silk pants and a gray-blue Chinese brocade jacket, her face made up, and sporting her finest wig, a tumble of bouffant curls. The sun was just setting and in the soft rose-tinted light she could have been twenty-five.

"You look beautiful," I said.

"Thanks, you look pretty good yourself. I like your new haircut."

"I'm really happy to be going with you," I said, warmed by her compliment.

She smiled regally. "I'm glad you're coming with me too."

We rode on the bow of the ferry across the night-black waters of the bay to Ellis Island, facing into the unseasonably mild air and gentle breeze. In the distance the building that in years gone by had provided an often-troubling entrance to America was lit up like Gatsby's mansion. As we drew closer, Mary put her hand over mine on the railing and left it there. She had never touched me before except to lean on my arm for support.

Inside the majestic main Immigration Hall, we thrilled to the sight of banquet tables aglow with candlelight, and the grand room filled with formally dressed attendees. Various illustrious Japanese Americans were present; I scanned the room for George Takei of *Star Trek* fame, who I knew had been incarcerated in Tule Lake as a child, but didn't see him in the crowd. I'd hoped to meet him here. Nonetheless, it was enough for me to be a part of the gathering.

We didn't mingle with the rest of the guests — Mary seemed reluctant to do so — but she was vivacious and entertaining as we drank our cocktails; she chatted away, clearly energized by the festive atmosphere. "That's Senator Inouye." She pointed into the crowd to the famous, distinguished man in a dark blue suit. "He lost his arm fighting in the war. He comes from Hawaii like I do."

When we moved out of the glittering party and filed into the subdued lighting of the exhibit, a silence fell around her, as it did for everyone there. We came to a stop before the replica of the tar-paper-covered barracks, with the fourth wall cut away to expose the twenty-by-twenty-foot family unit. The floor was covered with floral-patterned linoleum that would have been provided by the evacuees themselves, bought perhaps through the camp co-op. Two sleeping areas were closed off for privacy with hand-stitched drapes, and a third bed was partially out of sight behind a standing bookcase. In the center of the room was the coal stove. A table with open school books and four chairs stood nearby. The one window had blue-and-white-checked curtains. Upended orange crates served as storage for personal items — a hairbrush, a mirror, shaving supplies — the ordinary objects that told you people had made the best out of life in such an unfortunate space.

We remained at the barracks as other guests came and went. I was brimming with thoughts of my parents and choked with emotions at the sight of the room. I glanced at Mary. Though she strained forward to get a closer look, she appeared untouched as she coolly surveyed every detail, until, in a gruff voice, she said, "That's where they put us. It looks exactly the same," and abruptly turned her back on the exhibit.

We walked away, and in a matter of moments she returned to her prior ebullience, her tone tuneful, light, and lilting. It was a startling transformation. "Did I ever tell you about when Eleanor Roosevelt came to camp to see if we were being treated properly or if they were spoiling us? She found out that I sang and she procured me a scholarship to Juilliard."

This time I heard Mary's story for its poignancy, for how it relieved the pressure of that traumatic time, like a safety valve letting off steam, and preserved her dignity in the process. I yearned to put my arms around her, but remembered my father remaining outside a barrack room as the Issei women struggled with their shame, and I knew I couldn't embrace her. I had to stand apart and allow her privacy for her emotions.

AFTER THAT EXCURSION I WAS MORE AMENABLE TO ACCEPTING Mary's invitations, less conflicted, more caring of her and less resistant to any warm feelings I had for her. I'd had a glimpse of her pain and now had a better understanding of why she kept her stories so encapsulated.

Even so, her life after camp remained a mystery to me. Though she stated over and over how lucky she'd been in her career, I still didn't quite believe in her accomplishments. We went to the theater together more often, and at special Actors Fund benefit performances of hit Broadway shows we paraded down the central aisle to our front row seats as she, on my arm, accepted greetings from fellow performers. But she never once introduced me to any of them, and in the five years I'd known her, until then, not one friend of hers had materialized to confirm the stories she told.

LATER THAT SPRING, MARY INVITED ME TO SEE CABARET. "THERE'S A new young actor, Alan Cumming, in the lead. We can't miss him." She said a friend had house seats for us and we were to meet her at the theater.

We waited in the lobby of the Roundabout Theater's Studio 54 venue. The tide of excited attendees became a crowd and then thinned as people entered the theater. It was almost curtain time. I was about to give up, worrying that Mary's friend had abandoned her, if indeed she really existed, when a tiny, delicately featured beauty appeared in an ankle-length mink coat, rushing toward us with tickets held high.

"There you are, Mary dear. I've been waiting outside for you. I said to myself, she's always early, maybe she's in the lobby. And here you are." Her voice, with its hint of foreign accent, was more trilled song than spoken word. She hugged Mary, kissing her on both cheeks before turning to me. "I'm Mary's friend Cely Onrubia. I'm so happy to finally meet you. Mary speaks of you all the time. She tells me what good friends you are. It's so nice for her to have you."

A group of people who had come in with her were standing off to the side waiting. "I can't stay. I'm so sorry. I'd made these other plans before Mary called. But you two have a wonderful time." And with that she left, her equally glamorous companions in tow, as I stood marveling that such a being would be somehow connected to Mary.

"Your friend is gorgeous. Have you known her long?"

"Since I was on Broadway in *The World of Suzie Wong* and she was in *Flower Drum Song* across the street. She understudied for the part of Mei Li, and later took over the role. Gene Kelly asked me to be in *Flower Drum*, but I already was in Suzie Wong. I played Minnie Ho, the girl who enjoyed her work so much that she forgot to ask for money." She laughed uproariously.

"I ad libbed that line, and Joshua Logan kept it in. *The New York Times* said I had a gift for comedy."

As we settled in at our cabaret table, front center, Mary said, "Cely's daughter, Cynthia Onrubia, is a famous dancer and choreographer. She's the associate choreographer in this show. That's how we got the house seats. And she was Connie in the original *Chorus Line* and Victoria in *Cats,* and taught Richard Gere his steps for *Chicago,* the movie. She and Cely are Philippine. It's quite an accomplishment."

And with that, a dose of reality — in the personages of Cely and her daughter, added to Josh Logan and Gene Kelly whose ballet in "Dancing in the Rain," was my all-time favorite sequence in American film — illuminated the stories Mary told. It was a lesson that would be repeated over my years with Mary, and after her death, a lesson that I too often failed to heed: don't underestimate the prior life of elderly people. Listen closely to what they say, because even if they are embellishing their tales or lying about their adventures, there can also be rich lives to unearth. In Mary's case it would be a complicated mix.

Reacting to 9/11

SEPTEMBER 11, 2001 — I LEFT HOME AT EIGHT IN THE MORNING FOR jury duty in Lower Manhattan. As the subway headed downtown, we were stopped several times mid-station. The public-address system came on to inform us that we were being slowed because something had happened at the World Trade Center.

When we reached Fourteenth Street, people boarding our car told us that a plane had just crashed into one of the towers, and when the train pulled into Chambers Street the conductor announced that we all had to vacate and walk calmly out of the station onto the street. The train couldn't travel any further south.

We climbed the stairs to the street into blinding sunshine and pandemonium. We craned our heads to look where others pointed and saw, what until then was unimaginable, five short blocks from us the World Trade towers were on fire.

At first sight what we saw was uncannily beautiful; the shooting flames penetrated the massive silver structures which stood against brilliant luminous blue sky as millions of shimmering fragments of glass fell, scattering like translucent flakes in a Christmas snow globe. I was riveted to the spot until people began to scream, "They're jumping!" and I had to turn away. Crowds began to rush toward us, running from the burning buildings. I thought, *the towers could fall on us or we'll be crushed by the stampede of people.*

I half-walked, half-ran east, wending my way through the crowds, trying to cover the seven blocks toward Federal Plaza, and worrying that I was late for jury duty and hoping I wouldn't be penalized. But halfway I stopped for coffee and a donut at a coffee cart, thinking, I'll need to eat in the jury room. What the mind does in times of crisis! When I reached the courthouse made famous by TV shows and movies, with its expansive flight of steps, I jogged up and stood in line in the lobby with other distraught people until those in charge said there was no way they could process us and sent us back outside.

Standing beneath the portico, not knowing what to do or where to go, a roar greeted us from the west and as one we reflexively crouched and covered our heads, anticipating another plane. Someone shouted, "The tower is down."

A man huddled beside me said, "That's impossible, it's hidden behind the other tower." But when we stood all we could see was a thick cloud rising from the ground from where it had disappeared. Streams of people, some weeping, others grim-faced were entering the plaza. Women limped along barefoot, carrying their high heels; young men and women clutched briefcases, their faces gray with dust, their hair matted and wet. "The sprinklers went off in the stairwells," they told us as we joined the exodus north, first walking in the street following the shouted instructions of the anxious police — one of whom was so agitated that he spun in circles, saying "What should I do, oh, my God, what should I do?"

Then the police changed their minds and ordered us onto the sidewalk, when in a panic they realized that emergency vehicles couldn't get in if we clogged the arteries. We trudged slowly uptown in silence. No cell phones operated. Office workers from the buildings we passed had set up tables and handed us plastic cups of water. Radios blared the news that the Pentagon had been attacked. We stopped to take a drink, trying to make sense of the reports. After maybe five more minutes of walking, just before we reached Canal Street, another roar, and we looked back to see the second tower go down.

Fritz wasn't able to return home from work. His lab at Ciba Geigy Chemicals was located in Westchester County. He spent the night at the home of his assistant technician where they had a giant TV screen, and by the time he found his way into Manhattan the next day he was more traumatized than I. He had become dizzy and nauseated watching the endlessly repeated images of the planes slamming into the building, slicing through steel and glass until the towers collapsed into monstrously booming clouds of dust.

For a week after the event, when we woke, we lingered in bed talking, reluctant to go on with our regular lives.

For Fritz, the aftermath of the World Trade Center buildings collapsing brought back the nighttime bombing by the British of Augsburg. "It was in February of 1944 when the Americans bombed the factories during the day, and Brits terrorized the populous at night.

"At the warning sirens we raced on our bicycles to the bunker across town where we would listen to the reports of the bombers' approach. On the worst night of the raids we didn't have time to leave the house and had to go down to our own bunker in the basement of our house. Our neighbors also came," he said in a voice devoid of emotion. Held in his mother's arms he had felt the impact of hits on nearby targets, and had watched the sand spill in rivulets down the walls. "I saw flashes of light, but I don't know if I really saw them or if the impact caused me to think so." He'd been eight years old.

In the morning, when the all-clear signals had sounded, "Mutti rushed me, Lore, and Beate to get dressed while she packed extra underwear and a few things into suitcases. They were evacuating us to the countryside. We walked the four kilometers to the train station. The city was destroyed. I couldn't recognize where we were. The snow was black and what was left of buildings was just smoldering debris, flying pieces of soot, and empty burning window frames against a sulfurous sky."

Fritz's sister Beate, who was living in Munich, wept for days after 9/11; many Germans of their generation reacted similarly. Those that had lived through the war and the civilian bombings had rarely if ever spoken of wartime and if they did, they, like Fritz, often made light of their experiences, saying that it was fun to collect the shrapnel left on the piles of rubble in the city, or how on the farms when they were evacuated, they could walk barefoot to a one room schoolhouse, milk cows, and play in the hay with the local children.

As they came of age in the 1950s and 1960s and learned of the slaughter of hundreds of thousands of Jewish children, these *Kriegskinder* or war children, felt their memories were too inconsequential, indulgent, and shameful to speak of. The destruction of an iconic American building, which many of them had visited, and its visual aftermath somehow broke through the taboo against acknowledging their own suffering in a war in which their nation and their parents were seen as the villains of the world, or evil incarnate.

THAT FRITZ WAS A KRIEGSKINDER WAS ONE OF THE REASONS I'D BEEN attracted to him. He had experienced firsthand what most of our friends hadn't known, namely war. There was no equivalency between what he and I been through during that world war — being bombed as a child, living for years in the aftermath of the rubble that had once been his beautiful city, as well as enduring the guilt of his nation for something he didn't bring about, was far worse. I felt sympathy for what he couldn't completely acknowledge, and for the hope of his generation during the Occupation for a peaceful, united Europe. It was why he had lived in the United States for forty years before applying for American citizenship, holding out until he was assured of dual citizenship with Germany and as such, in the EU.

When friends began to place American flag decals on their cars, and hang flags out the windows of their apartments, Fritz and I couldn't do the same. He has an aversion to any display of nationalism and patriotism, knowing where it can lead. He challenged,

"What flag should I fly?" I felt like an outlier not putting out the flag, being seen as a person with no sense of loyalty to my nation, but my entire being resisted a hollow demonstration of allegiance. Waving the stars and stripes was for me a simplistic and unacceptable stance in response to the horror of the act, the rising xenophobic furor across the country, and the *ad hominem* attacks on people who dared to wonder if maybe some of our own global political positions could have led to the attack. When friends questioned my refusal, saying what's wrong with a little patriotism under the circumstances, I answered, "You just have to remember where I was born."

I don't recall where mary was on 9/11, but I do know that in the following days she went on as though nothing had happened in Lower Manhattan, and even as the wind turned and the foul plume of smoke billowed over our neighborhood, and her sinuses began to bleed profusely, she wouldn't acknowledge that there was any connection between the bleeding and the poisonous air.

We were beginning to hear that Muslims were being rounded up and whisked away under such heavy cover that families couldn't find if they'd been incarcerated or even if they were alive. I trod carefully with Mary afraid that she might relate this to what transpired within forty-eight hours of the bombing of Pearl Harbor, when the FBI began arresting Japanese immigrants they identified as community leaders: priests, language teachers, newspaper publishers, and presidents of organizations. The agents showed up in the night, forcibly removing the heads of household. Some families went for months before finding where their loved ones were imprisoned, as racist taunts and physical attacks increased exponentially on Japanese business establishments and individuals, and signs went up in cities and towns broadcasting in huge letters, NO JAPS WANTED HERE. Rumors ran rampant through the Japanese community that everyone was going to be sent to Japan — even those who were American born citizens who had never been to Japan, didn't speak

Japanese, were fully assimilated patriotic Americans who had bought war bonds, and wanted nothing to do with the country we were at war with. When I gently said to Mary that I'd heard that Japanese Americans in California were in the street demonstrating against the rumor and threat that the government was planning to build camps to incarcerate Muslim Americans, she said nothing. I tried again, "I think it's very brave that they're on the street like this, protecting other people from what happened to you," but she wouldn't meet my eye.

I now realize that I underestimated the full impact on Mary of the events of September 11, as I hadn't taken into account the bombing of Hiroshima. By August of 1945, Mary was living in Manhattan and her parents had left camp only two weeks before. Mary's cousins and aunts and uncles were in Japan. No matter how all-American Mary may have felt, I was certain she wouldn't have joined the tens of thousands of people who rejoiced in Times Square on V-J Day. More than one hundred thousand Japanese had been killed, and hundreds of thousands maimed in the first atomic bombing of Hiroshima. Three days later the second atom bomb was dropped on Nagasaki.

If she hadn't adverted her eyes from me during the days that followed the World Trade Center attack, I imagine I would have seen rage in her eyes, reading in them her silent voice that said the tragedy of September 11 paled in comparison with the civilian bombings of Hiroshima and Nagasaki by her nation of birth.

It may have been the same reason that, despite all the times we celebrated our birthdays together, she always got the date of my birthday wrong. Otherwise the most exacting of people about dates and times of arrival, she would think it was August 3 or 4 or August 8, when it is actually August 6, Hiroshima Day.

8

Getting Deeper in Debt

IN THE FALL OF 2000, I HAD ALLOWED MARY TO MAKE ME THE co-executor of her estate along with her lawyer. I say "allowed" because she basically steamrolled me into going to the lawyer's office to change the execu-  tor from her brother Frank to me. I didn't ask why she was altering his role, while still designating him as her sole heir.

I don't know why I wasn't curious about any of this. At the time I had no idea what it meant to be the executor of an estate. I simply sat in the claustrophobic conference room of the lawyer's cluttered offices and signed my name at the bottom of the codicil to the will.

Mary Mon Toy with brother Frank Chusei Watanabe circa 1922

Years later I asked Mary why she had made me the executor.

She said it was because she had given her brother a copy of my novel set in Tule Lake camp, which I had published with some trepidation the year before. I was worried because it dealt with a troubling episode in the camps, when factions within the community had turned on each other over volunteering to fight in the war versus resisting induction into the United States Army. Mary told me that after Frank had read it he said, "She understands us, you can trust her."

FRANK DIED THAT DECEMBER. MARY BURNED INCENSE BEFORE A Buddha statuette in her apartment and wasn't interested in going out. She didn't speak about her grief, but I could see in her expression and in her level of distraction that she carried her loss heavily. She never told me much about Frank except to say that he was a tennis pro who taught Princess Grace in Monaco, and had "a little something going" with her daughter Caroline, which I viewed with skepticism.

Mary had lent him a considerable amount of money to buy a house for himself and his current wife, a Caucasian French-Canadian woman.

I worried that Mary was impoverishing herself with the loan and asked her on a number of occasions if he was repaying her, saying, "You'll need that money for yourself." She was evasive, answering only that he'd paid her back "a little bit." After he died, she didn't respond to my questions and I pulled back; this was her family business, not mine.

2001 WAS A DIFFICULT YEAR FOR MARY ON ANOTHER ACCOUNT. In the spring she had a recurrence of breast cancer. I hadn't known she'd had a previous bout, but she said it had been over ten years before, and she only had a lumpectomy. This time Mary had another lumpectomy, but she had to have radiation.

"Could you go with me?" she asked apologetically. It was unlike her to ask for emotional help, or reveal any neediness, which told me she was frightened.

When my mother was diagnosed with a cancer that had metastasized at a vigorous rate, she refused any treatment. We sat together in the doctor's office in San Juan while he explained the options. She held firm. "I've lived a good life," she said. "I don't want to spend my last days blasted with radiation and chemo." Then as though contradicting herself she began to shiver in spams until I embraced her and held on tightly to quell her terror. But once we left the doctor's office she remained resolute in her decision, and stoic to the end.

Now I HELD MARY'S HAND AND WRAPPED MY ARM ABOUT HER shoulders to try to keep her warm in the over-air-conditioned radiation unit as she told me her mother had died of breast cancer. "She was young and beautiful. I still miss her."

Mary was not unlike my mother in her own stoicism. After the first treatment she informed me that going forward she could get to the appointments by herself and wouldn't need my help. Months later she revealed that in lieu of my offer to take her by taxi, or at least pay for a car service, she had traveled back and forth alone on the bus each day for six weeks.

It was difficult enough for her to mount the bus stairs in the best of health. She was eighty-five and debilitated from the radiation, but she forged ahead, continuing to get us front row seats at the Actors Fund benefits, still standing on line for free passes to screenings, still searching out the best Japanese restaurants for our dinners. Nothing I said dissuaded her from her constant, almost desperate activity.

Her fortitude and determination pulled me ever more deeply into her orbit. I felt her need to prove she could do it on her own as if it were my own battle for survival. Here but for the grace of some god went I. I'm married and have a large family of friends, but I have no children to look out for me in my old age. Caring for

Mary clarified this reality. I sometimes wondered if I was setting up a bargain with a higher power so as not to be abandoned in my own decrepitude.

It's not clear to me when exactly Mary began to go downhill. There could have been a long continuum beginning from before I met her, but in early 2004 our interactions noticeably changed.

We rarely ventured out to the theater or movies, and when we did it was usually with door-to-door car service.

Occasionally we walked, though at a slower-than-snail's pace, to her favorite nearby neighborhood restaurant, which served what she called "country Japanese food, just like my mother used to make." It took us fifteen minutes to cover the tree-lined block between Columbus and Amsterdam Avenues as she hobbled along, clinging to my arm and balancing on her cane.

The restaurant, furnished with crude, hand-crafted wooden tables and one booth, was frequented by silently studying young people, and older Upper West Siders who looked to have acquired their alternative-lifestyle food tastes in the 1960s.

The young waitress was Japanese, and Mary always placed our orders in Japanese. The woman was respectful of Mary, making certain that the restaurant's booth was held for us if we called ahead.

The food was simple and delicious . . . salmon with various choices of sauce, brown rice, and Mary's favorite chunks of steamed and lightly sauced squash. Despite the warm *sake* it seemed more like health food than Japanese cuisine, but Mary swore it was exactly what her mother had cooked.

"When I had parties, she made sushi, but at home this is the food we always ate. I gave the best parties. All the theater kids came. They loved my mother and her food."

"In the same place you live now?"

"Of course, I've lived there for forty-five years."

I liked to imagine her apartment at that time, sophisticated, where martinis were served from the 1950s-style bar in her entryway as her mother prepared Japanese delicacies in the kitchenette. Somehow it didn't seem probable that sushi was being eaten in the 1950s, even in a theater crowd. But I savored the thought.

ONE EVENING WHILE WAITING FOR OUR ORDER, OUT OF THE BLUE Mary said, "My mother never saw me perform. It's my one regret. I wish she had."

I asked her why that was, thinking maybe she'd died too early. I waited for Mary's answer. She was looking down. By now I knew the signs of her refusal to speak of certain things.

We drank our *sake*, toasting with our ritual "*kampai*." She complimented me on my pronunciation and my ability to use chopsticks, as she did every time, and once again she instructed me on how to remove and tie the protective paper on chopsticks into a light knot.

"You rub the chopsticks together to make sure there are no splinters. Like this." She briskly illustrated the operation. "Then you place them on the paper, so the tips don't touch the table."

I carefully followed her directives, pleased to be rewarded with a "Very good. Just like an Oriental," but I longed to know why her beloved mother had never seen her on stage? How could that be? She had cooked for Mary's theater friends. Had she never been curious to see her daughter and her friends perform?

We ate in silence, Mary concentrating on her food and relishing each bite. Her expression evinced total peace, as though she'd been thrown back into a more perfect time.

By then we rarely had a real conversation. She occasionally asked me how I was doing, how my writing was going, and I asked similar questions of her about her daily life and she reported that she'd seen this or that person — whom I didn't know — or that she'd gone to Thanksgiving in New Jersey, which I doubted. The only friend of Mary's I'd met over the past nine years was Cely.

It was during this period that Mary's stays in the hospital began. I'd get a call as her health proxy telling me, "Ms. Mary Mon Toy has fallen," and I'd rush to the hospital to find her lying in the Emergency Room, dazed, waiting patiently to be taken care of.

Often when I introduced myself to the attending doctor or to one of the nurses, the first question to me was, "Does she need a translator?" It was my early insight into what being Asian in America must have meant to her on a daily basis — always the foreigner, always "the other." It was a small slight, made by well-meaning people, but a slight nonetheless, and I felt angry enough in her behalf to answer, "she speaks better English than all of us," or simply, "no, she was born here."

In the spring a new phase set in for me, with duties that expanded exponentially as Mary required more assistance with her everyday living. She never expressed her requests as needs, but as demands, or so I heard them. I was sent on grocery expeditions with punctilious instructions: "Get the chicken from the takeout place on Broadway and Eighty-sixth Street, the daikon from West Side Market, the fish from Citarella's, and the broccoli from Fairway." When I suggested that she order home delivery from the stores — this was New York City after all — she answered, "They never send the best. They think they can get away with giving me inferior food if I'm not there."

Week after week and month upon month of pushing the laden shopping cart from store to store up and down Broadway, two blocks east along 86th Street, two more blocks north, began to wear on me. By mid-summer I was miserable. Sweaty and scruffy, trudging the streets. I had better things to do with my time. Why was I allowing this to happen to me, acting a martyr to her demands? What did I owe her? What was I getting in return was the real question and one I couldn't answer. I didn't yet understand the need in me that I was trying to fulfill, the endless need to do the right thing in order to atone for some unnamed sin. The only clue to this was a recurring dream I began to have of being pursued by people with guns who wanted to kill me, punishment for some untoward act on my part. The pervasive aura in the dream was of guilt, though I had no idea of my crime.

THEN THE SPECIAL ERRANDS BEGAN: HER WATCH TO BE FIXED AT THE jeweler's, her tax receipts packaged and sent by messenger to her accountant, gifts purchased for relatives in Japan to be taken to the post office, and all with adamant insistence on receipts for anything I purchased, even when I paid, which was usually the case because judging by her increasing parsimony, I was certain she was indigent. She used low-watt bulbs and when I moved from one room to the next in her apartment, she'd call to me, "You didn't turn off the light after yourself." When she went out alone, barely able to walk, she would trudge five blocks north pushing her shopping cart, to buy beer at Gristedes.

"Mary, for heaven's sake, why don't you go to the supermarket around the corner?" I asked.

"Because the six-packs are a dollar cheaper at Gristedes."

It took all my will not to give into her, and offer myself up to shop at Gristedes for her. "*Don't do it,*" Marnie, I said to myself, "*don't you dare do it.*"

OUTWARDLY I MAINTAINED MY SHOW OF GENEROSITY TOWARD HER, inside I was an angry, indentured servant. My resentment intensified when it seemed she was trying to keep her hold on me by giving me presents, and there was nothing I wanted — old coats, tiny candies wrapped in yellowing cellophane plucked from accumulating shopping bags, boxes of chocolate-covered macadamias that a Linda Lee regularly sent from Hawaii, care packages from Japan of miso soup mix and other products whose contents I could never use because the preparation instructions on the plastic packets were in Japanese.

My solution was to take the gifts, express great gratitude, then drop them in various garbage baskets as I walked home, making sure I was far enough from her place that she wouldn't spy them if she took a walk. I knew this was crazy, but my frustration was turning into an angry paranoia. I wanted out or at least to be free of the almost daily requests. Fritz's attitude didn't help; he thought I was a saint for taking care of her: "You're such a good person to be doing this."

Pity for her growing weakness, and shame about my resentment, rose up when she began to fall at home with more regularity and was rendered helpless until a kindly neighbor or the mailman found her, and called me or EMS directly, who took her, as required by law, in an ambulance to the hospital.

Each calamity was followed by a new story of why she had landed on the floor. In one version she had turned her apartment over to a film crew who had pleaded: "'Please be in our movie, Ms. Mon Toy,'" she archly described. "They begged me, but I said no, absolutely not, I wouldn't be in their film, and I went to a party to get out of there. I came home after midnight to a mess and tripped over equipment they'd left, and I woke up on the floor."

The hospital staff was skeptical, "Is this possible?" or "Is Ms. Mon Toy suffering from dementia?"

"She usually remembers all current events down to the last details," I said.

"Who is the president, Ms. Mon Toy?" they tested her.

"George Bush," she answered, wrinkling her nose in disgust.

"And the mayor of New York?

"Bloomberg, of course, for what he's worth."

They agreed that for an almost-ninety-year-old woman, she had "remarkable intellectual acuity."

And *"powers of invention,"* I thought to myself, but didn't say.

CELY ONRUBIA, WHO KINDLY AND REGULARLY CHECKED ON MARY, pushed me to do something about Mary's living circumstances.

"Mary can't take care of herself anymore. If she won't have a home aide, she should go to the Actors Fund Home in New Jersey. It's beautiful there."

The possibility of finding a safe place for her to live where she would be fed and looked after, sounded like a welcome step toward my release.

In the past she had rejected any mention of a senior residence, but her next fall was especially debilitating. She'd been on the floor for twelve hours before anyone found her, and was in the hospital for two weeks.

The doctor prescribed a week-long stay in a rehab center, which was conveniently only four blocks from her apartment.

When she was released, I cautiously broached the subject of finding a place for her to live.

"We can go to visit the Actor's Fund residence with no commitment. We'll just look at it. It's completely up to you, but I'd like it if you could keep an open mind. I want you to be safe"

She went silent on me.

"There are a lot of actors there," I said.

"Naturally."

"You can share stories with them and I'm sure they put on performances."

"We'll see."

Her expression was its most opaque, which should have told me that this was a no-go from the start, that only her sense of etiquette kept her from outright refusing to see the facility.

The town car I hired picked us up at her apartment and we glided north on the Henry Hudson Parkway toward the George Washington Bridge.

She had dressed respectably in black trousers and an oversized black sweater. She'd forgone her ruffled socks for conservative black anklets with her clogs. She'd spent hours on her makeup and wore a plain, though stylish, black wig. She was startlingly rejuvenated by her time in rehab.

We moved along quiet tree-lined residential streets, until the car turned into a drive and swept under a portico to the front door of a modern mansion set back from a coiffed, green lawn. No one was out and about. We entered the main lobby, painted a pale blue, and there were met by the director, a plain looking young woman who appeared straight out of social work school.

"We're so happy to have you here, Ms. Mon Toy. Your reputation has preceded you. A lot of your old friends are here."

As if on cue, people descended on us from various directions, all women save one slender, attractive white-haired man who looked to be an Irish charmer.

"Mary Mon Toy! Are you going to stay?"

"Mary, it's been so long since we've seen you."

I was thrilled. She was a star here, a queen. How could she resist?

Mary was graciously imperious as she air-kissed two women. Then the man pulled her aside and began a *sub-rosa tête-à-tête*. Mary looked interested in what he was saying, nodding as he spoke and rolling her eyes coquettishly as she flashed him a flirtatious smile.

We followed the young woman — no match for Mary, I began to fear — into the empty main living room where there was a grand piano. The room was airy and bright with sunshine, and again decorated in various shades of cool blue.

"Most people rest after lunch," the woman was saying. "If you'll stay a bit, we usually gather at the piano or in the library for drinks before dinner."

"We can't stay," Mary said.

The woman maintained her composure though looked a bit taken aback by her brusqueness. I refrained from apologizing for Mary, fighting an impulse to ingratiate ourselves. What was the matter with her? This was a terrific place.

"Let me show you a sample room, Ms. Mon Toy. I'm sure you'd like to see one."

"Fine."

She thumped along on her cane more loudly than usual, and showed no scintilla of interest in the sunlit bedrooms.

On our way out, we encountered the white-haired man smoking a cigarette under the portico, leaning against a column.

"Remember what I told you, Mary, about this place," he said, ominously, like Joseph Cotton in a Grade B *noir*.

We drove through the lush green streets of New Jersey in silence. I held off speaking until we were on the bridge crossing over to Manhattan.

"So what did that man say to you?"

Her chin tipped high and haughty, her profile to me, she spelled it out. "Don't come near this place. It's lonely. It's not New York. There isn't even a bar to hang out in. And nobody comes to visit. And you have to share a bathroom."

"That's not true, Mary. The two rooms we saw had private bathrooms."

"No, you have to share a bathroom. I won't share a bathroom with anybody."

That was it. Done.

She gave me a look that said, you want to put me into a prison, but I refuse. Frustrated by her recalcitrance, I still understood. She would never ever again let anyone condemn her to an institutional living environment.

Back home, Fritz was out for the evening. He'd left me a note, "hope you had success."

I just wanted to go to bed.

I thought, *I can't do this any longer.* My sad-sack reflection in the bathroom mirror as I brushed my teeth told me how stressed I was. My hair looked ratty even though I'd washed it that morning for the visit. I made inventory of my situation. My friendships were taking second place to my attention to Mary's needs. I was known as someone others could rely on for a sympathetic ear for their troubles, but I had no time or patience for them.

I HAD PUBLISHED A THIRD BOOK, A NOVEL ABOUT MY MOTHER'S death in Puerto Rico, which had been easy and cathartic to write — as I described it, an ecstasy of sorrow — but now my work was suffering as I struggled with a novel that was too complex for my tired mind.

This was a big book centering on the Pinochet coup in Chile, fueled by unresolved emotion from what had happened to me in Guayaquil.

I was spineless in regard to Mary. My tendency to help others was out of control. I was as much at fault as she was; she would go on making demands of my time as long as I provided it. Short of going cold turkey, I could see no way out.

9

Glimmers of Love

In June of 2006 I received a call from a woman who introduced herself as Diane Carrion, the tenant living across the hall from Mary. "She gave me your number in case of an emergency," she said, "and she talks about you all the time." A man in the building, Michael Estwanik, was giving Mary a surprise party for her ninetieth birthday, and because Mary was announcing to everyone that I would be the executor of her estate when she died, he wanted to make certain that I knew of his plans; he didn't want to step on any toes.

"We love Mary," Michael Estwanik said when I reached him. "She's such a grand person."

It's very nice of you to be doing this."

"It's the least I can do for her. And nothing compared to what I've heard about you and all the help you've given her. She says you're her best friend, that you do everything for her."

"Not really," I said, hearing my voice grown small, feeling like a fraud as I'd pulled back on my attention, and hadn't seen her for weeks.

"Oh, don't be so modest, my dear. Own your goodness."

I called Cely to invite her.

"I'm not going. She shouldn't be taking charity from strangers. She has enough money to make her own party, and invite her closest friends." She was still harboring anger at Mary for her rejection of the Actors Fund Home.

"She'd really like to have you there. You'll be her only friend. It's all people from the building."

"No. I refuse to encourage her. She shouldn't take from people, including from you. She has to have pride in herself. And she has enough money. I know that. I'll send my gift."

I was learning that once Cely made a decision, she couldn't be swayed, a strength and weakness she and Mary shared. No wonder they were friends.

THE DAY OF THE PARTY ARRIVED, A BALMY SUMMER SUNDAY. THE plan was for me to go directly up to Michael's and not let Mary see me. For a cover story, Michael had invited her in for a private lunch with a few people from the building.

When I got there, Michael was bustling around his extraordinary one-bedroom apartment, slightly larger than Mary's, resplendent with his treasures — crystal and China in glass-faced cabinets, paintings covering the walls, Tiffany lamps, and a grand piano at the far end of the sunken living room. In the bathroom his shower curtain had specially designed outer plastic pockets to hold theatre playbills, and the walls were a display of other Broadway memorabilia. It was personal and cozy, as was Michael . . . middle-aged, attractive, just slipping over into pudgy, dressed in a garish Hawaiian shirt, "especially for our Hawaiian Mary," he explained when I commented on the obvious theme of the party.

We stood by a table in the dining area, a groaning board of all variety of food: smoked salmon flown in from his favorite source in Washington state, cookies and cakes, whitefish salad, tropical fruit platters, and macaroni salads. The Hawaiian motif played out on the paper tablecloth, plates, and napkins with images of cute hula dancers under palm trees and a stack of psychedelic-colored plastic leis to be worn by all the guests. Michael dropped two florescent pink and orange leis over my head and then relieved me of my bundle of two dozen peonies that I'd splurged on to make up for my recent negligence of Mary, and because she somehow reminded me of a peony. Michael led me into the kitchenette so I could get them into water.

More food was being plated in the crowded, narrow space as wine and glassware were ferried over my head from the pantry closet to the dinette where a bar was set up. Dozens of people began to arrive with more food under saran wrap and tin foil.

A young, full-figured woman with ruddy brown skin and shiny straight black hair squeezed her way into the kitchen.

"I'm Diane, I'm so glad to meet you. And this is Stan," she said, pulling a man in behind her. "Stan lives upstairs, Mary loves him."

"Not as much as I love her," Stan said. He was nice looking, in his early fifties, edging on hip, dressed in a brown Indian shirt over jeans. "I'm here to document the great event," he said, holding up his camera as he backed out into the main room.

Diane, with loving amusement, regaled me with tales of Mary while I arranged the peonies in a glass vase.

"The way she dresses! She goes out to the mailbox in a long tee shirt and underpants with those frilly socks and clogs. It's okay around all of us, we're used to her, but when my folks visit, oh my God! We're a conservative Chicano family. Mary comes to the door and I think I'm going to die. My mother is so shocked. I try to explain to her that Mary was in show business and she doesn't have the same idea of modesty that we do."

The next people to press into the kitchen to introduce themselves were Mary's New Jersey friends, Mary Louise and Bill Britten, the couple who had supposedly invited her for Thanksgiving. She'd recently told me that Mary Louise used to be lead singer with the Cab Calloway orchestra during the 1930s. Mary Louise was slender and high-cheek-boned, a light complexioned African American. "I'm the person who sends her the dirty jokes," she laughed.

Bill was the original Bozo the Clown, but the older, sedate, white man introducing himself seemed anything but a clown.

"Mary has said such nice things about you. We're so happy to finally meet you."

As I was making space for the fragrant peonies in the center of the food table, Fritz arrived. The gathering had built to over fifty adults and ten or so small children. Incredulous as I was, he asked, "What is this? Who are they? I thought no one else cared about her but you."

Mary Louise, by my side, whispered knowingly, "She's Maureen Moore," nodding toward a delicate, exceptionally pretty strawberry blonde who beamed at the group of admiring men and women who met her at the door. "She's an understudy to all the greats, Bernadette Peters and Patty LuPone, to name a few. When she steps in, she gets reviewed in the *Times*. She's currently Christine Ebersole's understudy in *Grey Gardens*."

MICHAEL RUSHED OVER TO ME. "MARY'S NOT HERE. I TOLD HER to come at one and it's almost two. I just don't understand, she's so reliable about dates. Keep a watch on things for me." He grabbed the birthday tee shirt he'd had silk-screened for her and hurried out to find his guest of honor.

Half an hour later the front door opened to a troubled Michael standing behind a bewildered Mary, who wore the tee shirt that read, "Mary at 90." She hadn't put on a wig and her cropped white hair was sticking out every which way. Her face was shiny and swollen with sleep. We all shouted "happy birthday," but she didn't take it in. I went to her and gave her a kiss and combed my fingers through her hair so she wouldn't look so disheveled. I'd never seen her without a wig.

"What are you doing here?" she asked, confused.

"It's your birthday, Mary. We've come to celebrate with you."

"How nice of everyone. What have I done to deserve this?" She gave me a vague smile.

Michael whispered to me, "She didn't remember that she was to come upstairs."

It was then I realized she was truly deteriorating mentally.

As the afternoon went on, I became unusually tender toward her. She appeared fragile and frightened by all the attention, so I led her to a chair — which she was grateful for — and asked her what she wanted to eat, listing the possibilities. When she replied, "Just some salmon," I worried. This was a person who loved to eat and always did so with gusto. She barely nibbled at the food on the plate I made up for her.

A few of the partygoers began to sing show tunes, accompanied by a friend Michael had hired to play the piano. His name was also Michael, and his repertoire of musical theater was so extensive he could play any song requested, in any key each person asked for.

"Mary, sing something from the shows you were in," Maureen Moore said.

"Oh, I'm not in voice," she demurred.

Mary Louise settled on the arm of Mary's chair. "How about 'I Enjoy Being a Girl' from *Flower Drum Song?*' Do you know it, Michael?"

"Of course," he said and began to play.

"You remember it, Mary. But too bad Cely isn't here. It was her big role," Mary Louise said.

Mary perked up and started to repeat the old story. "Cely was across the street playing the lead in *Flower Drum Song* when I was in *The World of Suzie Wong.*"

Mary Louise began to sing, "'I enjoy being a girl...' C'mon, Mary, help me out."

"I don't know if I remember."

"Of course, you do. You toured with the show."

A picture of concentration, Mary slowly picked up the thread of the song, and soon she had the tune and the lyrics, her voice growing stronger. She was transformed, her head high, her diction perfect, and her face alive with purpose. She wasn't an old lady anymore on a Broadway bench, but a professional performer, a trooper, belting a song that was lodged deep in her memory. They sang together, on key throughout, the pair of them gathering steam, the blending of their voices lasting to the final note.

We applauded energetically and before our adulation faded, Mary Louise began to sing, "Some enchanted evening, you will meet a stranger."

Mary singing with Mary Louise Britten at Mary's 90th birthday.
The song "Some Enchanted Evening"
from *South Pacific* by Rogers & Hammerstein.

Mary listened, focusing on the tempo and the key, her head nodding, her finger tapping out the beats, until she gauged the moment to join in on the line, "And somehow you know, you know even then . . . ," her soprano soaring above Mary Louise's alto. She sang with all the longing of a young woman who has never before found true love, her voice filled with desire for what could be.

When they'd finished and we were complimenting them, Mary looked into the distance as though at the scene in the song, the crowded room, the man whose eyes she'd met. "I love that song," she said quietly, to herself.

Their last song that day was "Bali Ha'i," with its mournful melody, and words of yearning. By now the two Marys were in perfect voice and harmony, any roughness smoothed away. "Some people live on a lonely island . . .."

A contemplative Mary after singing "Some Enchanted Evening"

I COULD BARELY CONTAIN MY EMOTION AND THE TEARS THAT THREATened. I felt so proud of her. This was who she was, this was what she loved, what she had lived.

Many years later, after her death, I would read an interview in which she'd confided to the young man asking the questions, "I can't perform anymore because of my hip. I really miss it." I had to put my hand to my chest to contain my sadness, because at her birthday party I had fleetingly witnessed who she had been, what time passing had caused her to lose. By then I knew the full extent of her past, how she had trod the boards night after night on Broadway, on tour, in nightclubs, brave acts in themselves. It took courage and toughness and talent to survive that life, and she had all three. But that birthday afternoon in Michael's place surrounded by old friends, I only had a hint of who she'd been.

Mary and Mary Louise could have gone on singing for hours as far as I was concerned, but Mary was fading.

She turned to me, saying nothing.

"Should we get you home, Mary?"

"Oh, wouldn't that be nice," she said, calling up a faint, flirtatious smile.

I WAS EMOTIONALLY TRANSPORTED THAT AFTERNOON, BUT SOON AFTER I distanced myself from her again. Maybe I was just too tired of going shopping and increasingly often footing the bill for what I bought her, or maybe I had reached the limit of my altruism, or my intrinsic selfishness had kicked in — I still don't fully understand why at that particular moment I stopped helping her, but I do know that, though wracked by self-blame, I abandoned her for weeks, turning my back on her needs. I even considered writing her lawyers, saying that I wanted to be released from being the executor of her estate. My suspicion that she'd manipulated me made it a little easier for me to stay away.

In defense of my behavior, let me say that shortly after the party Fritz's ninety-three-year-old mother, Margret, in Germany, began to fail and was rendered bedridden. Fritz's three sisters split the supervision and spelled each other visiting Margret. Fritz was the only son and the only member of the family who had left Europe for America. He felt he had to take some of the burden off of his sisters. I went with him for support.

I HAD MY OWN COMPLICATED RELATIONSHIP WITH MARGRET. I'd arrived on the scene only two decades from the end of World War II; suspicious of any German her age, I spent the first five years of our acquaintance wondering what she had done during the war. Added to that, she lived in an elegantly appointed townhouse, and was always perfectly dressed in matching cashmere sweater sets, pearls, and suit ensembles of the softest wool. She had a personal tailor who arrived with fabric, emblematically, a cashmere mix, to cut her suits. I had no understanding of such a life, nor did she have of mine. I felt that my lack of class, in her mind, threatened her social position. There were certain friends she went out of her way not to introduce me to. I lost all my sense of self, becoming almost mute around her. Fritz didn't understand what was happening to me. "Why can't you be yourself around her? I want her to see what a beautiful woman I've chosen to be with." I both wanted to fit into her life and resisted giving into that desire, which upended my chameleon resources for becoming the other, for adapting. It was too steep a climb.

Over decades of my visits to Germany as I grasped the complexities and moral ambiguities of Germans living under the Nazis and what it took to survive the war under the Third Reich, I softened in my feelings toward her. She too came around. "I understand now," she said to an art-collector confidant, I'd impressed with my knowledge of art, "she's an artist." When a friend asked me if I thought she was anti-Semitic, I said I didn't think so, at least not more than the average European of her generation. But she'd undoubtedly made her compromises during the war.

Prior to our visit to Germany that June, the agency that provided some nursing care had called the family in to say that Margret, who had always used her money to control her children, and those who worked for her, had been handing out tips to the home aides in great quantities each day, which was not allowed.

When Fritz's sisters investigated, they found Euros stuffed under her pillow, and scattered through out her bedclothes. Although she was almost blind and couldn't read the denominations, she had been intimidating her housekeeper to cash checks, which she could still sign in order to replenish the cash.

We all decided that the money outlay had to be monitored. Panicked at the fact that she was losing control, Margret screamed, berating her children and me, and on one occasion hurled her heavy telephone striking Fritz's head. Fritz and I left Germany exhausted.

Unable to tolerate caring for one more elderly woman, I left Mary by the wayside, rarely phoning her, and only seeing her when pressed.

10

One Asian Woman to Another

A MESSAGE FROM CELY CAME INTO MY OFFICE PHONE IN THE MIDDLE of an afternoon in late July.

"Mary called me. She sounds terrible. I've never heard her sound so bad."

When I phoned back, Cely breathlessly reported, "The postman found her. You know how proud she is. She doesn't like to ask for help but she fell and couldn't get off the floor. Her door was un-locked and he had brought in her the mail because her box was too full. She can't go on like this. She could die."

I'd procrastinated about contacting her during the current heat wave even with all the radio stations warning listeners about the dan-ger to the elderly. I'd convinced myself that her neighbors would look in on her. I was now engulfed with remorse.

"I'll go up to see to her, Cely."

"You're so good to her. She's so lucky to have you," she said, making me feel worse.

When I arrived, Mary was sitting on a bench, barely upright, in the dark entryway of her shadow-shrouded apartment. The stench of urine was overwhelming.

I stood by the front door, arms crossed as I tried to hold back the anger and resentment that had returned on my taxi ride to her apartment.

"How did you know to come?" she whispered.

"Cely phoned. She's worried about you."

"Oh, isn't she a lovely person. You know, she always puts on full makeup to go to the mailbox. She says you never can tell when you'll meet a casting agent."

"Not now, Mary. Why didn't you push your alarm button?"

I switched on the overhead light, all forty watts of it.

"You aren't even wearing your pendant. Why?"

"I took a bath. I didn't want to get it wet."

"But that's exactly when you should have put it on, for your safety.

She looked up at me with sorrowful eyes, her cheeks hollow, her neck gone scrawny.

"When did you last eat or drink?"

She shrugged.

"Why haven't you eaten?"

"I fell on the floor and couldn't get up."

"How long were you there?"

She shrugged again. "I peed in my pants." She began to cry.

My resistance gave way. I put my hand to her silken cheek. "You have to go to the hospital."

"Nooooo, I don't want to go to the hospital."

"You don't have a say in this, Mary. Where's your pendant?"

"I don't know."

I found it on the table by her bed amid stacks of unopened mail, wadded Kleenex, bits of food, and pills, the detritus of illness and old age.

"Okay, I'm pushing the button for the ambulance."

"Please, no," she whimpered.

"I have to. You're starving and dehydrated. I can't let you die."

I poured her a glass of water while we waited for the ambulance. She dutifully drank it.

It'll be good for you to be taken care of," I said, combing her hair.

The intercom sounded and I buzzed-in the EMS people. A tall, heavy-set African American man, whom I recognized from other

Mary emergencies, was the first one through the doorway, filling it with his bulk.

"Hey, Ms. Mon Toy, you getting yourself into trouble again? Don't you worry, we'll have you fixed up, sweetheart, and back on stage again."

Mary gave him a flirtatious look and then, her eyelids growing heavy, she fell asleep against his arm as he began his procedures.

Mary remained in the hospital for a month recuperating from her fall. Those thirty-six hours on the floor of her apartment had taken their toll. She had come so close to death that it took weeks before she was sufficiently hydrated and had regained the weight she'd lost. I'd stopped by every day to check on her and to make certain the staff knew she had someone looking after her.

At the end of the month I met with a social worker as she was preparing to check Mary out of the hospital. She was a nervous, distracted woman, with straw-like orange hair. Her head was down as she shuffled and reshuffled papers on her cluttered desk.

"It says here that she lives alone. She's ninety-years-old. She sure doesn't look it."

"She's a beauty. She was an actress on Broadway," I said, with a surge of pride.

"As she's told all of us. She's had quite a life, but she can't seem to take care of herself anymore. What arrangements have you made? You're her health proxy, right?"

"Yes, but . . .."

The woman's head went up. "What's the but in this?"

"I thought maybe she could go to a rehab center at the Katery Residence to get her strength back. The hospital has seen to that before. She likes it there."

She riffled through the papers again and found the record. "So I see. What are you trying to say to me?"

"That maybe if she goes back to the Katery rehab center in her condition and is comfortable there she'll agree to stay on another floor of their facility for good. I'd like to give it a try."

"You're tired, aren't you?"

"I am."

"You've bitten off a lot taking care of a person you're not even related to. It's hard enough for a family member. It's a real *mitzvah*. She's lucky to have you."

"I don't know how people can do it alone. What happens to them?"

"They die unseemly deaths."

I WENT TO MARY'S ROOM AFTER THE MEETING. SHE'D OUTLASTED her roommate, and now had the bed by the window, looking onto the Hudson River, though previously she hadn't shown any interest in the view.

When I entered, her eyes were closed. She was still wan from her near-death experience, but she was beautiful, her skin smooth, her face more filled out, her striking cheekbones as prominent as ever. Her full lips, with their little valentine peaks, were a rich mauve as though she'd applied the newest shade of lipstick, her cropped white hair stuck up around her head like a punk rock star.

She opened her eyes, blinking in the bright daylight. It took her a moment to get her bearings, but when she did, Mary smiled at me with a radiance I hadn't seen in some time.

"I love you," she said, reaching for my hand.

"I love you too," I said, filled to the point of rapture with affection for this woman who was my burden. "How are you feeling?"

"I'm still tired."

"I believe it. We're trying to get you into rehab again, so you can regain your strength."

"What a good idea. You have such good ideas. I'm so lucky. What have I done to be so lucky to have you?"

I knew this adoring response would be short-lived once she got wind of what I was planning.

The social worker was successful in getting Mary assigned to a private room at Katery. I called Diane to tell her of the move. She volunteered to put up a sign suggesting that people visit Mary.

The social worker expedited Mary's transport to the residence while I went to pick up her mail and some clothes. I arrived to find Stan and Diane in the lobby, waiting for me.

"I can keep collecting her mail, or whatever you need," Diane said.

"We love Mary," Stan said, offering to come into the apartment to help.

I said I was fine with it, worried what I would find there, what it would reveal of Mary's state.

Entering, I was shocked anew and saddened to see how household duties had gotten away from her. I'd been so focused on rescuing her three weeks earlier, I hadn't taken in the full extent of disorder and disrepair. The smell had ripened to an intolerable mélange of dried urine, dust, decaying food products, old paper, and dirt.

The top of the cocktail bar was overflowing with unopened mail and half-standing, half-toppled birthday, Christmas, and Easter cards. I balanced the shopping bag of mail Diane had collected on the one bar stool that wasn't already precariously piled with paper and shopping bags.

On the wall behind the bar dozens of smudged-glass black-and-white celebrity photos had shifted every-which-way, and were only faintly discernable in the dimness.

Desperate to bring life into the place, I marched from room to room, switching on lights, rebellious in my profligacy with her electricity, irritation and loyalty shifting like mercury as I felt her shadowing me, demanding, "Shut off the hall light behind you."

The Formica table in the tiny dinette off the kitchen was stacked three feet high with boxes of the chocolate candies from Hawaii, other meticulously wrapped — unopened — packages from Japan, and carton upon carton of vitamins and youth-enhancing elixirs from a company in Canada. The narrow counters of her kitchenette were washed clean — she'd maintained this island of order — and the sink was free of dirty dishes. Stuffed under the window between a rolling cart and the stove were dozens of neatly folded plastic bags, which I used to dump moldering vegetables from the refrigerator. I stripped her bed in the living room and bagged the stained sheets and a blanket to be thrown out.

After I'd packed some clothing and toiletries into a weekend bag, I stood in the foyer. By now twilight had set in and the panes of the two windows were frosted mauve, bathing the living room in a melancholy lilac. I couldn't cope with doing more. I'd come back another day.

SHE LOOKED TINY AND WEAKENED IN THE BED, HER FACE DRAWN, her eyes vaguely meeting mine.

The quilted bedspread, pulled up under her chin, was a muddy floral affair of gray-greens, ocher, and mauve. With the thought that this might be her home for the rest of her life, I recognized what a dreary place it was — no adornments on the walls except for a painting of Christ and a wooden cross, everything lit by dim fluorescent bulbs. Why couldn't they at least warm the room with pink-toned lights? I opened her locker to unfamiliar clothing.

I tracked down an aide in the hallway who said the clothes were from discarded wardrobes of former residents. "She came with nothing. It's better she wears these. Her own things will get stolen."

I PULLED THE CHAIR CLOSE TO MARY'S BEDSIDE AND TOOK HER HAND in mine.

"You okay?"

"Yes," she whispered.

"You're tired, aren't you?"

She eked out a nod.

"We've got to get you rested."

"Yes," and she closed her eyes.

I stayed with her until she was sleeping soundly.

Descending in the elevator, waves of urine stench greeted me at each stop on the nursing home floors. With the odor lingering in my nostrils, I walked along the dark, shadowy, tree-lined street.

AUTUMN HAD ARRIVED SINCE THAT SUFFOCATING DAY WHEN I'D found Mary in her apartment. It was almost Labor Day and an early crisp breeze came off the Hudson. Dried leaves littered the sidewalks. Mary's care had been in limbo for over a month.

My wish had been fulfilled, to have her assigned to this rehab center where she'd been before. But now that the possibility of her remaining there loomed, what had seemed like a reasonable solution — placement in a safe, humane residence — presented an intolerable future for her: fragile and alone in the drabbest of settings, housed with people who soiled their beds, and attended to by overworked aides.

Nothing would be gained by a move. I wouldn't be able to do it. I couldn't betray her trust by assigning her to this custodial institution for old people — one prison was enough for a lifetime, especially when condemned for no fault of one's own — so I'd have to find another solution.

The weeks passed with gradual improvement in Mary. I observed her in occupational therapy sessions and exercise classes where she worked hard to keep up. I sat with her at lunch or dinner in a functional but cramped dining room where an oversized television blared during the meals.

Mary, never complaining, was either intentionally or unconsciously oblivious to her surroundings. She no longer languished in bed, and though still weak, she didn't need a wheelchair to go to dinner or classes.

THE SOCIAL WORKER, STACEY, CALLED ME IN FOR A MEETING. SHE was a beautiful young woman, stylishly dressed, with curly dark hair framing her lovely face. She bore a resemblance to photos of my mother taken when she'd just met my father, her expression eager, intelligent, with a hint of irony. I liked her immediately.

"She's a piece of work," Stacey laughed. "She's charmed the staff. What's with the tits-and-ass business?"

"That's what she was. She performed at the Latin Quarter."

"Wow." She took a moment to read her notes. "She's ninety and still living alone. Does she have help?"

I told her my concerns about Mary — that I didn't think she could be maintained in her apartment. I related the story of our visit to the Actors' Fund Home. Stacey agreed that the Actors Fund was a beautiful locale, but she could understand Mary's reluctance to move across the river. "She's right, nobody would visit her after the first month." When I said I'd considered having Mary remain at Katery, she said she had another idea: that there was a wonderful facility just around the corner on Eighty-sixth Street. "It's costlier, but fabulous. Do you know the state of Ms. Mon Toy's finances?" I agreed to check on them and she said she'd set up an appointment for me at the Vista Residence.

PATRICK BRADY, MARY'S FINANCIAL PLANNER AT A BANK TWO BLOCKS from her apartment, adored her and got a kick out of her eccentric ways, how she would pop in without an appointment to pass the time of day. "I love to see her and hear her theater stories, even though I've heard them a hundred times before," he chuckled. Patrick was a jovial young man, but I noted that he was cautiously appraising me during our initial light banter, which I found reassuring. It signaled that he could be trusted and counted on to protect Mary's financial concerns. He gave me a general picture of her money situation, but without actual figures until I had power of attorney: "You might want to begin thinking about that, especially if you're finding her a place. And honestly, I think it would be a good idea because, sad to say, she's definitely losing her grip a little."

When I explained my connection to Mary, our mutual history in the camps and how we'd met, it was clear from the bewildered expression on his young face that he didn't know about the camps.

"She never let on. You never know, do you, what burdens people carry around with them?"

And with that he told me that Mary had well over three quarters of a million dollars in investments. "Actually, it's closer to one million."

"What?" I was dumbfounded. "How did she accrue all that?"

He shrugged. "It's been a good market. We've invested her conservatively but well, and she's receiving a good solid return. She gets her Social Security and two actors' pensions, some residuals from movies and television programs she was in, and she doesn't come close to spending through all that. You may have noticed she's pretty frugal." He chuckled again, at his understatement. "I'll analyze the figures further, but I can tell you now, she could stay at just about any home for the elderly and she wouldn't run out of money even if she lived to be one hundred and ten."

FLYING HIGH, WEST EIGHTY-SIXTH STREET NEVER LOOKED SO hospitable. I could put Mary in a fancy residence close enough to my home to visit her regularly, but others would be responsible for her. She would be safe and doted on. It was a perfect solution.

Thank you, Mary, I thought, praising her for her frugality and her perspicacity in planning for her old age. Money had never been important to me, as a child of socially conscious people who were dedicated to their work, not their salaries. Now I saw its value — money sets you free. It would buy my liberation from this burden.

There were hurdles to overcome, but who cared? The future would be mine. The first obstacle was going to be the one I feared most: I would have to convince Mary to give up her apartment.

Before i tackled that, i visited the vista residence.

It was everything I'd hoped for and more. Anita, a perky blonde woman in her forties, in charge of admissions, gave me a tour from top to bottom, beginning with the penthouse dining area and large terrace. "For special events and family affairs," she said in her southern accent. "We have a room set aside in the main dining room for private parties, but many people like the elegance of this, and the view." And what a view it was, a 360-degree sweep of the Hudson River up to the George Washington Bridge, across to New Jersey, down to Lower Manhattan, over to the east side of Manhattan and beyond that to Queens and the Triborough Bridge.

She showed me two available studios, one for $3,500 dollars a month, with housekeeping, three meals a day in the beautifully appointed dining room, and innumerable activities — visits to museums and concert halls — included. It was a nice enough room, but the windows looked out onto an airshaft. The second space was on the twentieth floor with a wide vista to the east. *Morning sun*, I thought, *air*. It cost $4,000, still a bargain by New York standards. I remembered Patrick's words — Mary could afford it. "I'll take it," I said.

When I told Cely that Mary could afford the luxurious Manhattan residence, she said, "Don't you go see her tonight. I'm going to have a talk with her, one Asian woman to another."

The next morning Cely called. "I told Mary she couldn't continue to do this to herself and to you. She listened, but she didn't say anything. I may have lost my friend, but it had to be done."

That evening I sat by Mary's bed. She was solemn, pensive, not looking at me as I began.

"I know you spoke with Cely. I realize this is terribly difficult for you, but I found you a beautiful place to stay just around the corner. It's like a five-star hotel with a fine dining room, a penthouse garden for entertaining, a beauty parlor, movies every night, and a terrific apartment that someone will clean once a week. And you can afford it, I've talked to Patrick. He says you can live to be one hundred and ten and still afford it. You are almost a millionaire."

"I am? A millionaire? How is that?" she said, coming alive.

"You're a smart businesswoman. You saved your money, now you should be enjoying it. Spending your money on yourself is how you'll remain independent. In your apartment you have to rely on the goodwill and charity of others. This is the next stage in your life. Be as smart about this as you were about your career. What do you say?"

I waited, trying to keep calm.

"Okay. I'll do it."

"Really?" I paused, unable to believe it had been so easy. "Cely will be relieved. She's afraid you won't ever speak to her again."

"Oh, Cely. She is such a stitch. Tell her, of course I'll speak to her."

By moving day, I was not only Mary's estate executor and her health care proxy, but I had signed on to hold her power of attorney, responsible for all her legal and financial interactions.

In hindsight I see myself rushing headlong into a deep hole of accountability, fueled by my eagerness to find a solution to an insoluble problem — the care of an elderly person in modern-day America. But back then I was filled with joy and hope that I was doing the right thing and belief that my burden would be lifted.

11

The Convergence of Past and Present

CLEARING OUT A PERSON'S APARTMENT BEFORE SHE'S DEAD, CREATES its own set of problems. For one, how much do you involve her in the decision making? Mary's cognitive processes were slipping. She was a serious, long-time hoarder, possibly stemming from the trauma of leaving behind all her worldly belongings when she was sent to camp, and I was making her move again. If I enlisted her help, we would never finish. I was cautioned not to close up Mary's home until after she'd adjusted to the new place, but I felt I had no other option. She couldn't go back to living alone, so she'd have to stay at Vista or some other residence.

It soon became obvious I had made the right choice in not involving her. The situation was far worse than I had thought. A hall closet was stuffed with scores of neatly stacked boxes filled with unwearable shoes and leather boots, as well as dozens and dozens of worn-out handbags, and two high stacks of broken suitcases and carryalls. Another hall closet contained outmoded coats, not one that I'd ever seen her wear, hats of all styles — some dating back to the forties. The walk-in closet in the bedroom — jammed with more unusable clothing — required a week to clear out.

Her generous neighbors insisted on pitching in: Diane, Michael, Stan, and Claire, a book editor, who lived next door to Mary. For weeks, each evening after work we sifted and sorted. Michael was a master at deciding what to keep, what to throw out, and what to donate to Housing Works, a thrift store whose proceeds went toward housing for indigent people with AIDS. Mary regularly gave substantial amounts of money for housing for actors with AIDs via the Actors Fund so I thought she'd approve. Claire had an eye for what was valuable, particularly when it came to distinguishing the difference between fine jewelry and paste, and other items of value, like the Lalique perfume bottle in the glass-fronted vitrine in Mary's living room. Diane was willing to deliver clothing to the dry cleaner nearby, once we agreed on what would be good enough for Mary's life in the upscale residence. She did countless loads of laundry in the building's basement of underwear, socks, and tee shirts. Mary loved her tee shirts so we didn't want to deprive her of them, "But tell her she has to wear slacks with them when she goes down for meals," Stan said with impish glee.

A glamorous life unfolded before us in satin evening wraps and petite Dior coats and dresses and sweeping gowns of silk and taffeta. As we unzipped the dust-laden cloudy plastic wardrobe bags we women exclaimed with delight and Michael cooed. Stan made sardonic quips about her seducing men when skimpy, sexy lingerie in pink satin and black silk confirmed the stories Mary had told of a multitude of lovers, as did the ribbon-tied packets of adoring letters from various men — a three-time Prime Minister of Thailand, a Tony and Oscar awarded actor, a Tony winning stage manager, an official member of the Philippine Mission to the United Nations, and by cryptic, suggestive notes from the likes of acclaimed director Peter Brook and the film actor Robert Ryan. We allowed ourselves only a minute or two to glance through before packing them away. Albums of photographs told a tale of Mary's emergence from a shy young woman with long legs, sylphlike torso, and ivory skin to a seductive, self-assured showgirl, savvy about marketing her assets.

We pulled grimy boxes from beneath the beds. They were five feet long and three feet wide, made of a strong synthetic cardboard-like material, held together with wide fabric straps. They contained twenty years' worth of receipts for her taxes, but we decided that they must originally have been her costume boxes when she toured. MARY MON TOY was prominently stenciled in large letters on the top of each. They conjured visions of one-night stops in towns across America when she'd gone on tour with Broadway shows. I once asked Mary what touring was like. She became totally serious and in a professional voice said, "We kids worked hard. Nobody ever works as hard as kids on the road." No sassy stories, nor sexy embellishments.

A large wooden chest confounded us. There was no key and no lock. Then one day, feeling around under the cover's rim, I accidentally pushed a button and magically the top sprung open a crack, letting out a whiff of cedar scent. Inside were packages wrapped in parchment paper inscribed with calligraphic Japanese characters, the paper tied together with jute cords. We unwrapped one to find an exquisite kimono; the silk was a swirl of color — peach, yellow, coral, accented with purple. Others we peeked at were equally beautiful: red carnations on a cream background with a touch of royal blue; a grass green foreground accented by lemon flowers — and there were twenty more kimonos in the chest. We carefully stacked them, still in wrappers, on Mary's now-cleared dining table. Mary would later tell me the kimonos belonged to her mother, who didn't trust the American dry cleaners and would ship them back to Japan for cleaning. The next prizes were formal *obis*, *getas*, fans, and lacquered paper parasols.

At the bottom of the chest was an extravagant white fox stole. I couldn't resist: I slipped it around my shoulders, the soft fur caressing my cheek, and paraded the room, experiencing the intoxicating power of glamour and reminding me of the afternoons my childhood friend Susan and I had dressed up in her mother's satin negligees. As I sashayed like a beauty queen, I recalled the last chapter of our friendship. It was 1966 and I had recently returned from the Peace Corps. I lived in a tiny apartment in the East Village. My parents had given me a black and white television which I turned on one night to catch the end of the Miss America contest, just at the moment when they announced that Miss New York State had won the Miss Congeniality award. There on the small screen receiving the honor was Susan, her face not as rounded as it had been, but as she beamed with pleasure, the dimple I knew so well dug into her left cheek and her eyes squinted almost shut, like upside down smiles. The announcer said she was loved by all the other girls and everyone else she'd come into contact with during the competition. Like Mary, my beloved friend had survived on her beauty and her gift for reaching out and charming others. Both attributes had saved her as a child. They never mentioned her name, but I knew she was my Susan, which years later was confirmed when I researched her for a short story about our friendship.

"Fabulous," Michael said, as I took off the stole. "You have to ask Mary to leave it to you."

When I eventually asked Mary what she wanted done with it, she said, "Save it. I'm going to wear it on my 100th birthday."

Catching grime on shelves were eight glass-encased, handmade Japanese dolls. The most extraordinary was a pair of dolls — one male, one female — an emperor and his young wife, seated on thrones. When I included Mary in the decision about what dolls to take to her room at the Vista, she said she only wanted the elegant geisha girl her mother had made.

One evening after everyone had left, I was working my way through the last box in the hallway closet when I came upon yet another grungy plastic carryall. All the purses and weekend bags we'd found had been filled with objects that turned out to be junk, but I opened this one nonetheless and pried out an army-brown canvas duffel bag, stiff with age and soiled from heavy use. I unfolded it, exposing a white cotton cloth stitched on by hand and printed with the name, Yoshizo Watanabe. Suspecting what it was, I brought it to Mary the next night. She said, "My stepfather put our things in it when we went to camp. I don't want it. Send it to the Japanese

American Museum." I carried the bag away that evening, holding it close like a baby as I walked down Broadway, powerfully moved by its history, and wondering about the last name, Watanabe.

THE DAY WAS APPROACHING WHEN MARY WOULD LEAVE KATERY AND take on her new life. I purchased outright the model furniture that Vista had used to decorate the room for showing it to prospective residents — anything to make my task easier.

We'd rid the old apartment of nonessential items, but now there was nowhere to put the possessions that should be saved: the cedar chest of kimonos, thirty wigs in large hat boxes, seven dolls encased in glass, a file cabinet of song sheets and scripts, old playbills, other personal theatre artifacts, voluminous scrapbooks filled with press clippings, old steamer trunks, art work, love letters, family photographs, the albums of theater photos, and on it went. I rented a storage unit, and hired movers to take the memorabilia over there and transported the remaining items to the Vista.

While Michael hung the new entry wall with theatrical photos — Alvin Ailey, Pearl Bailey, France Nuyen, Telly Savalas, a very young William Shatner, to name only a few illustrious performers, as well as Mary herself — I made up Mary's bed with brand new sheets and quilt. Together we found places for a painting of a Paris street scene with a café beneath a large awning, two large oil portraits of Mary, a four-foot tall, hand-colored photo of her in an Asian-influenced costume complete with dramatic Thai-headdress, and formal framed studio photos of her family. Her mother's doll stood on the bureau, her brother's headshot was on a shelf by the window alongside a lovely photographic portrait of her mother in a kimono, under a cherry tree. Michael and I *kvelled* like loving parents. "Isn't this great," he kept saying. "She's going to be so happy here. This is so much better than that dark, dank old place."

After Michael left, I rested for a few minutes in a wingback chair, taking in the peaceful apartment. The setting sun reflected off the buildings' windows to the east, filling the space with a rosy glow. Mary's presence had emerged stronger as we'd honed her possessions to the essentials, like editors excising redundant prose to reveal the story. Her theatre connections took on life. I saw for the first time that she had a strong identification with things Japanese, at least as they related to her family. *We've done well by her*, I thought. All the same I was glad she hadn't witnessed the dismantling of her home of forty-plus years.

On a cold october day, mary checked out of katery. They lent us a wheelchair. I piled her lap with shopping bags filled with items she had accumulated during her stay, and we set out with the wind rushing off the Hudson River, smacking us in the face. The wheelchair was unruly, an antiquated relic with stiff wheels and no steering.

"Hang on, Mary, we'll get there," I yelled into the wind.

She was clutching the bags close to her chest and holding tightly to the armrest with her free hand when I lost control of the chair and it swerved and crashed into the pole of a construction overhang. After the first shock, we started to laugh, she wheezing with pleasure and I with the absurdity of the situation.

On one knee in front of her, I took her hands in mine.

"Bear with me. I'll do better."

She nodded, now sober, as wind-and-laughter-induced tears leaked from the corners of her eyes. With a gesture that I would come to know well over the next few years, she lifted her arm and with the back of her hand, she wiped the tears gracefully from one eye and then the other, all the while studying my face with a fierce intensity.

I rose and kissed her on the forehead before we continued our short journey to her new home.

Mary was astonished when we entered the elegant lobby and she was greeted by the receptionist, "You must be Ms. Mon Toy. We're so happy to meet you."

"Is this where I'm staying?" she asked, her voice filled with wonder.

"It is," I said, with relief. "Wait until you see your room."

We rode the elevator in silence to the twentieth floor. I wheeled her along the wall-to-wall carpet, around the corner, down the short hallway to room 2007, and opened the door. The room was filled with light. I'd bought a large bouquet of oversized yellow chrysanthemums for the round dining table. Mary took in the kitchenette, the flowers, her theater pictures on the wall, her mother's doll, the photo portrait of her brother, the bed made up in white and lavender, the wingback chair, the television, and the paintings.

"Where am I? We must be in Paris."

12

Good Fortune Smiles on Us

The next day I met with the registered nurse who coordinated the aides for the residence's in-house home provider, to work out payment and procedures.

Abigay Jackson was a hefty Jamaican woman, dressed neatly in a patterned blouse of muted mauve and blue and a black tailored skirt. She exuded intelligence and competence, and barely smiled.

There was a preponderance of Jamaican women working at the residence, I would learn, and formidable seemed to be a distinguishing cultural trait. From that first meeting I tried to endear myself to Abigay through compliments and adopting a slightly obsequious manner, to no avail. She had a job to do and a middle-aged white woman was just one more family member to contend with . . . or I might be a paid guardian reaping thousands of dollars a month off the elderly.

Mary began to thoroughly enjoy herself at the residence, joining in many of the activities. She was rarely in her room. Loving the weekly sing-alongs in the penthouse, she made it known to the visiting cocktail lounge pianist that she'd been a performer, and he encouraged her to lead the songs she knew. She went every day to the concerts in the large community room off the lobby. It was where I looked for her if I dropped by in the afternoon. I would stand in the doorway and observe her sitting in the front row of chairs, completely rapt, as a group of young classical musicians from Juilliard played, or a pianist gave a concert of show tunes, or a flamenco dancer strutted, clicking her heels on the marble floor. Most evenings Mary went to the movies in the back room. Once the movie started, she forgot the discomfort of the hard classroom chairs usually used for bingo games and watched with total absorption the old and the new, the funny and the tragic, movies she'd seen many times before or ones that had only come out the year before. She was in heaven, which made me happier than I can describe. She brightened in those first months, became more talkative, more alive to the world than she had been for the past year. Seeing her blossom made me understand the thrill of watching your child thrive. For the moment, all was well.

ABIGAY PHONED ME.

"We have two little problems," she said.

I never like it when people preface "problems" with "little."

"Tell me," I said.

"Ms. Mon Toy needs more clothing. She doesn't have really appropriate attire."

My face burned. As I'd feared, Mary wasn't dressed properly for this fancy residence.

"You think I need to buy her some more outfits."

"That would be a good idea. Ms. Mon Toy has been wandering the halls in the middle of the night in tee shirt and panties. She's gone down into the kitchen at midnight to ask when dinner is served."

"That's not good. She must be confused."

"It seems so."

"Are you kicking her out?" Panic surged.

"No, no, of course not. We love Ms. Mon Toy. But she needs more care. I'm afraid it's time for her to transition to a private aide."

That afternoon I went to the local Talbots, and purchased half a dozen outfits for Mary.

"All this is for me?" Mary exclaimed as I unfurled one item after another from the white tissue paper and laid them out on her bed. "Oooh, so beautiful." Dressed in each new outfit, she examined her reflection, turning from side to side. She carried the clothes beautifully, and she was enchanted with this new iteration, her delight brought healthier color to her face. It was as though I'd made a Christmas morning for Mary. I reveled in her happiness. Perhaps she didn't need an aide.

ABIGAY REFERRED TO A STACK OF CLIPPED PAPERS AS WE MET IN HER tidy office.

"What I recommend for Ms. Mon Toy is to begin with a twelve-hour shift for one of our in-house private aides. We can start the aide at 10:00 a.m. I understand Ms. Mon Toy has a late breakfast in her room?"

"Yes, she still keeps theater hours."

"The aide will be with her until 10:00 p.m. when she prepares her for bed after the movie. This way she'll have supervision into the evening."

"Does this mean the aide will be in the apartment with Mary all the time?"

"Yes, except when they go downstairs for activities."

Mary now would have her own private guard, no longer free to come and go on her own. This would be worse for her than sharing a bathroom.

"Mary won't tolerate that. She's always lived on her own." I didn't have confidence that bringing up her incarceration would help. There were certainly Holocaust survivors living here who had adapted to the rules. It was the Upper West Side after all.

"There's no other option."

"She'll fire the aide."

"Ms. Mon Toy will have to accept that the aide is there. I'm sure she'll adjust."

"So, how much would this cost?" I sensed the only way to negotiate was to keep my cool.

"You'll be billed $16 an hour, for seven days a week. That's $192 a day and $1,344 a week or $6,048 a month."

"How much is that per year?" What had I gotten us into?

"Just a minute." She did the tabulations on her calculator, then raised it to show me.

I read $72,576. Added to that was the $28,000 we paid for Mary's room and board, or $100,000 a year.

"Does Medicare cover any of this?" I asked, dry-mouthed with anxiety.

"No."

"Maybe we could begin with an eight-hour shift and see how it goes?"

That wouldn't deal with the evenings, and that's where we're having the problem. You're free to hire your own people from the outside."

"Then you wouldn't get coverage when an aide doesn't show. I'd have to do it all myself."

"That's right."

"I don't have the time for that, I'm doing this voluntarily, but I'm responsible for Ms. Mon Toy's money. I don't want her to run out."

Abigay's eyes narrowed as she took in what I'd just said. It was the first time I'd told her I wasn't getting paid for the job. I saw a glimmer of sympathy. "Let's make an exception and try out an eight-hour shift. I'll add a visit during the night from the general aides, to check that Ms. Mon Toy is in her room. I won't charge you extra for that."

I was awash with gratitude, excitedly agreeing to the new numbers that were slightly less shocking than the original amount.

Needing reassurance that I hadn't sold us down the river, I stopped in to see Patrick.

"Whoa, it's really costly. I had no idea these places are so expensive.'

"Me neither," I said.

He opened up Mary's accounts on his computer screen, and ran the data, explaining again how much she was earning on her stocks.

"She could spend twice as much and still come out ahead. This is going to be okay."

Even with his optimistic view, I left his office thinking that this wasn't anywhere near as much fun as buying her new clothing.

MARY'S AIDE BEGAN IMMEDIATELY.

I worried all weekend that I'd get a call on Monday morning from the front office informing me that it wasn't working out and Mary wanted her gone, but no call came.

On Friday I arrived at the Vista filled with trepidation. I rang Mary's bell. Moments later the door opened and standing before me was a gorgeous, statuesque young Black woman. She smiled broadly when I introduced myself and told me her name was Rose Baptiste. She had a distinctive French accent with a Caribbean lilt.

"She's been waiting all afternoon for you."

"Is she doing all right?"

"She's doing good. You'll see."

I followed her down the picture-lined hallway into the main room.

"Look who's here, Mary, come to see you." She practically sang the sentences.

Mary sat erect in the wingback chair, dressed in her new navy-blue ensemble with crisp white trim. Her hair had been cut into a boyish, gamine style. Her face was subtly made up with foundation, blush, eye shadow, and lipstick; she appeared twenty years younger.

"Mary, you look spectacular."

Mary smiled, taking in the compliment.

"Did you put on your own makeup? It looks great."

"She did it," she said, pointing to her new aide.

"I do her makeup every day," Rose said.

"Did you cut her hair?"

"I took her downstairs to the beauty parlor."

"Look at my nails," Mary held up her hands. Her nails were filed and painted pale pink.

They do the manicure at the same time as her hair," Rose said.

Over the next month as I got to know rose, I felt we'd been assigned Vista's best aide.

Perhaps it was because the staff liked Mary; whenever anyone discovered that I was connected to her, they'd exclaim, "Oh, I love Ms. Mon Toy, she's so nice." Mary was polite to everyone, she never complained. "I always say thank you," she often told me. "People appreciate that." Another explanation could have been that because many of the staff had been in and out of Mary's room, they had seen the corridor of theater photos, with the personally autographed pictures of renowned African American, Asian American, and Latino performers. Mary was in many of the ensemble publicity shots. Even if they weren't familiar with these iconic American theater artists, they had to recognize that they were celebrities and that they were people of color.

We'd hosted a couple of dinner parties in the private dining room, attended by Mary's friends Mary Louise, Dr. Glory Van Scott, Dianne from her old building, and Cely Onrubia, among others, most of whom were either nonwhite or of a distinct ethnicity. This couldn't have gone unnoticed by the staff, who with the exception of the top administration and the head of the dining room, were all Black or Southeast Asian, serving the 99.9 per cent white resident population. Nothing was ever said, but I was sure it made a difference in how Mary was treated. I felt it must have filtered up to Abigay and affected her decision to assign Rose to Mary.

Mary instantly took a liking to rose, a single mother of a six-year-old son, Haitian and regal in her bearing, with an infectious sense of humor and a great well of kindness and love for the elderly.

Mary had quickly sized her up; not only was Rose beautiful with softly rounded, dark brown features and ever-changing hair styles that included fabulous wigs, she was classy; she spoke French and had an elegant manner. She was tall, close to six feet and thin. Mary especially disliked people who were heavy.

When she, Rose, and I were in the elevator going down for dinner, Mary often would proclaim in a loud voice, "I don't know why some people let themselves get so fat."

The overweight Caribbean aides, in the crowded space, acted as though they hadn't heard. I cringed and Rose looked straight ahead, but I could see her working to suppress her pleasure at Mary's insulting behavior. Though the majority of workers were from the Caribbean, Rose was the only Haitian, placing her at a disadvantage in the staff social milieu, thus her delight in having Mary as a devilish and irreverent mouthpiece.

Rose Baptiste and Mary

I began to look forward to our Friday afternoons, to the coziness of gossiping with Rose and watching Oprah, Ellen, and Judge Judy with Mary and her.

It had become ever more difficult to have a conversation with Mary, but I grew interested in the way her old stories were increasingly conflated. She rolled the Catskills story of Mel Brooks into the dinner with Marlon Brando, and the night on the ridge with Ol' Blue Eyes became a night with Brando on the ridge, and from there to the Catskills again, only the performer was Alan Alda.

I was sitting with her on the bed when she said, "I dreamed about Alan Alda last night. It was so beautiful. He said he loved me. I woke up crying. We had a thing, you know, when we were in the Catskills. He would open the show saying, 'And now I want to introduce you to my sister.' And I'd walk out and everyone would laugh. But you'd better believe I was no sister to him. When I woke up this morning I was crying."

Her reminiscences were becoming prose poems.

13

Resident of the Month

WINTER 2006 — MARY MAINTAINED THE CONVICTION THAT HER old apartment was still intact. Even though I had kept her abreast of the dismantling, had occasionally asked her advice about who should get what, had let her know that I'd donated certain items, had told her I'd put her memorabilia in storage, and had informed her when the job was completed, she could not comprehend that the apartment and its contents were no longer hers. There was one item in particular that she focused on: her typewriter. It was a manual, over fifty years old, a bona fide antique.

"I need my typewriter," she demanded. "It's in my apartment, in the bedroom, on the shelf over the desk."

She was correct; that was exactly where I'd found it.

"I'm sorry, Mary, but I gave it away."

"You what! That's not possible. It's in my bedroom on that shelf over the desk."

"I know where it was, but I gave it to Stan."

"To Stan? Why to Stan?"

"Because he likes old machines."

"I need it. I'm going to write my obituary for the *Times*."

"Your obituary, isn't that a little premature? It'd be very difficult on that typewriter. It doesn't have a ribbon anymore."

"Then you have to get one. I need to write my obituary for the *Times*."

"I can put it on my computer. You can dictate it to me ahead of time."

"I have to do it myself. No one else can get it right. Go to my apartment and go into the bedroom and over the desk is a shelf and it's on the shelf."

With that I gave up. I called Stan. "Mary wants her typewriter back, to write her obituary."

"Oh, my dear Mary. Is she ill?"

"She just wants to be prepared."

I retrieved the typewriter, brought it to Mary, who had me stash it under her table, never to be touched or requested again.

Mary continued to be insistent that no one else should write about her. When a local paper was doing a piece on the Vista and wanted to profile some of the residents, Mary was suggested as a possibility, but she stonily refused.

"You have such a good story to tell, Mary."

She shook her head, giving me a puckered prune face of disapproval.

"You don't want people to know about your life and your career?"

"No."

And that was that.

THE RECREATION DIRECTOR CALLED ME TO SAY THAT MARY WAS TO be named "Resident of the Month," with an article in the residents' newsletter. I jumped at the opportunity to write about her. He was relieved to have one less obligation. I thought if I wrote the article her story would be told accurately. Even if she was willing to be interviewed, confusion and conflation would make the stories incomprehensible to any outside person. I had to protect her from looking foolish.

I confess that throughout I sought to bask in a little reflected glory. I loved that she was in the theater. During the 1970s, in the two years before I'd been the Program Director at WBAI, I'd produced live rock and folk concerts for the radio station, and later, when I left the station, I'd run my own business producing city-wide festivals, including a two week out-of-door's promotion of Off-Off Broadway theaters, and concerts in venues like Manhattan's Town Hall. I was always behind the scenes, but I fed on the magic and precariousness of live performances. I admired anyone with the courage to trod-the-boards night after night, whereas I had long ago given up becoming a dancer. Mary had faced the risks and stepped out into the lights. I wanted her fellow residents to know this about her.

My plan was to get details about Mary's early life directly from her, without her realizing what I was up to. I began with the story of her being born in Hawaii to a Japanese mother and a Chinese father who was a physician working in Father Damien's leper colony.

The Friday I chose to interview Mary was, fortuitously, one of her better days. As we sat together on her bed, I massaged her achy shoulders and asked about her life as a child.

"What island was the leper colony on?"

"Molokai."

"Did you live near the water?"

"Oh, yes, it was beautiful. Our house was on the beach."

"Did you often go swimming?"

"My mother and I did. Most days." Her voice came from a far-off place.

"And your father?"

"He was at work. In the colony. And then he died."

"From what?"

"Some illness he got. I was a little girl."

"I'm sorry, Mary."

"Thanks."

"Then what happened?"

"My mother remarried. To a Japanese man. And we moved to Seattle."

"Was Frank with you?"

"He wasn't born yet."

"He was your stepfather's son then? Your half-brother."

She stared at me. She seemed confused.

Answering, she said, "My father was the first Japanese chiropractor in Washington. He got his degree in Idaho."

"*How strange,*" I thought, "*Idaho was where Minidoka camp was located.*"

"You mean your stepfather."

She looked perplexed, pausing before saying, "Yes, my stepfather. My mother remarried and we moved to Seattle."

"In those days, in Japanese culture there was no problem about her remarrying?"

She thought a moment, puzzling over this last question.

"She came from a wealthy family, that made it okay. Her family owned a lot of land in Japan and they bred silkworms."

"Have you ever seen that land and met the family?"

"Yes." She was slightly breathless now. "I went with my mother and met everyone."

"Before the war or after?"

"I'm tired. I'd like to lie down."

She flopped over on her side, her legs hanging off the bed, her head missing the pillow.

I lifted her head to the pillow and arranged her legs in a more comfortable position, covering them with the spread. Within moments she was asleep.

Rose had been listening to us from her place on the wingback chair.

"Is that Hawai'i that she's talking about?"

"Yes. Where she was born."

"She always talks about Hawai'i, how beautiful it is, how nice it was when she was a little girl. How her father died. Mary loves her Hawai'i."

Mary Mon Toy
Resident of the Month

Mary Mon Toy's life story is a truly American tale in which, to paraphrase Frank Sinatra, "she did it her way." Ms. Mon Toy was born in Hawaii on June 3, 1912 to a Japanese mother and a Chinese father. Her mother came from a wealthy land-owning family, and her father was a medical doctor who dedicated his life to working in Father Damien's Leprosy Hospital in Hawaii. He died when Mary was two years old; her mother remarried and the family moved to Seattle, Washington.

The family lived there until March of 1942 when they were uprooted to the Minidoka Japanese-American Internment Camp in Idaho. Fortunately for Mary, Eleanor Roosevelt made an early visit to the camp; hearing of Mary's theatrical abilities, she arranged for a scholarship to The Juilliard School.

She became the first Asian runway model in Paris, France. She danced as a showgirl in Parisian nightclubs, where she was singled out by Lou Walters (Barbara's father) to join his *Revue a la Folies Bergere* in Las Vegas, and from there on to the Latin Quarter in New York City. She was "discovered" in the Latin Quarter by Harold Arlen, Peter Brook, Truman Capote, and Balanchine for the Broadway musical, *House of Flowers*, for which she received excellent reviews.

A triple threat, Mary was next cast by Josh Logan in the original Broadway show, *The World of Suzy Wong*, again to outstanding notices. She later joined the National Tour of *Suzy Wong*, which became the first legitimate Broad-way show to play Las Vegas. Additionally, Mary toured with *South Pacific* and *The King and I*.

She has appeared in many television commercials. Her television theatrical credits include, *Teahouse of the August Moon* as well as episodes of *Kojak, I Spy, Nurse, Drs. Hospital,* and for many years she was a regular on the soap opera, *Ryan's Hope.* Her movie credits include *Year of the Horse, Airplane II,* and Bob Fosse's classic, *All That Jazz.*

Recently Mary related to a friend how she loved opening nights, and how, as cast members, they would peek through the curtains to see the audience arrive, and then the thrill of the curtain rising on the performance, and afterward the celebration at Sardi's as they awaited the reviews. She ended her reminiscence by saying, "I've had a great life. I've had it all."

"MARY'S MAD," ROSE GREETED ME AT THE DOOR WHEN I ARRIVED on Friday. She was laughing. "She's mad because they got her birth date wrong."

I took the already dog-eared newsletter from Mary, who sat steaming on the edge of the bed, and saw that sure enough I had written that she was born in 1912. That made her four years older, ninety-six as opposed to ninety-two.

"Make them change it," Mary said sternly.

"I can't, Mary. It's too late. Anyway, it was my mistake."

She looked at me with a mixture of fury and disbelief. "Make them change it."

"Mary, I can't. Anyway, people will think you look even younger for your age. Already no one believes how old you are. Now they'll be more astonished."

Mary let loose with her wonderful laugh, hearty, and spontaneous, especially when the joke was on her. "The bod's given out, but the face is still good."

She took the newsletter back from me and began to read intently, her head bowed low.

"Mary loves that article," Rose said. "She carries it everywhere in her walker basket. She sleeps with it."

"So, Mary, is the rest of the article okay? Did I get it right?" I asked after a few minutes.

She nodded. "It's well written. But they got my birthday wrong. Make sure they change it."

14

Wishing We Could Do this Every Night

SPRING 2007 — MARY'S IMPULSE CONTROL WAS LOOSENING. ONE day she asked Rose, in a belligerent tone, if she knew what S.O.B. meant. Rose didn't. "It means son of a bitch. She's an S.O.B," Mary said, pointing to Kathy, who was in charge of the dining room. She'd also been telling loud, smutty jokes in the packed residence elevator.

WHEN A CARD ARRIVED INVITING MARY TO A ONE-NIGHT CABARET performance by Mary Louise, my first reaction was that Mary couldn't go — not in her current condition. I put the invitation aside.

Then Michael called.

"I assume you got the invite to Mary Louise's cabaret night. We should all go together, you, Mary, Rose, and me, and Mary's old friends from Eighty-eighth Street. So, are you up for it?

"I don't think she could last through an entire performance."

"Sure she can."

"She's not in the best shape."

"It'll be good for her."

"But how do I get her there?"

"We'll get her a limo. She can travel in style."

Of course . . . a car service. I was avoiding the obvious solution because I didn't want the others to see how much she'd deteriorated. "I can't do it on my own. Rose will be off duty by then."

"I'll come by and help you. She needs to get out more. It'll be stimulation for her."

When I asked, Rose was eager to go. She'd never been to a movie, much less cabaret or the theater. I told Michael we'd meet him at the theater. Mary, beside herself with excitement about the event, hadn't been this animated in months. I bought her a new outfit for the occasion, black silk pants and a black sequined top.

Mary Louise had reserved a place for Mary in the front of the house. Rose and I were seated at a table behind her. Gradually the house filled with friends and acquaintances of Mary Louise and Bill, several people from Mary's old building, including Claire, and Dianne. Maureen Moore was there and of course Michael, at his most debonair.

"You look divine, Mary." He kissed her on both cheeks.

"Thank you, you look pretty darn good yourself."

Bill Britten gave Mary a hug and a kiss and shook hands with the rest of us.

The musicians, a jazz quartet of piano, bass, drums, and sax, settled into place on the small stage. The waiters took our orders for drinks and sandwiches. Then Mary Louise entered stage left, ravishing in a narrow black skirt, a pale pink pleated over-blouse, and strappy spike heels. Her hair was perfectly done, her makeup subtly theatrical, her skin tone firm and smooth, and her liquid black eyes gleaming. In that moment, even a young Lena Horne wouldn't have been competition for her. With no introduction she cued the musicians and began to sing.

Mary was in thrall to the musicians and Mary Louise. She sat in rapt concentration, closely following each song and musical interlude. She entered the music, devouring every note and chord, her eyes half-closed and her mouth pursed in pleasure as if kissing the air.

When Mary Louise completed her set, everyone applauded but Mary. She was still caught up in the tunes playing in her head. Mary Louise thanked several people and introduced the musicians, and just when it seemed she was finished, she said, "But most of all I want to thank my friend Mary Mon Toy for coming to hear me sing.

She is a great performer and it gives me such pleasure to have her here."

Mary graciously accepted the applause, her head held high, at a queenly tilt.

"Did you hear that?" Rose said in the lobby during the break. "Did you hear what she said about our Mary? In front of everybody!"

I brought Mary home by myself. I'd waved Michael off when he'd offered to help because the East Indian driver had promised to assist getting her in and out of the car. He was as gentle and patient with her as if she were his own grandmother.

"Take your time, madam, we are in no hurry, just let me lift you and now, madam, bring your leg inside. Oops, we go, one more leg and we're all done."

At the residence our luck continued: two men in their forties, strapping and attractive, came to our aid and walked Mary into the building, each taking an arm, as she slid her eyes coquettishly from one to the other, purring and exclaiming, "You are so gallant. Thank you. Would you like to come up for a drink?"

"Maybe another night, we'll take a rain check," the more handsome man said.

When we got her inside, resting on a chair in the lobby, I told them she was an actress.

"Could've guessed that on my own," the blond said, waving goodnight.

In the elevator, Mary said. "I think that blond one kinda liked me. I've still got something, you know. Men see it right away."

"That may be so, but I'm pretty sure they were gay."

"Nooo, I could tell there was a spark."

"You could be right. Gay men have been known to fall in love with women."

"There was something there. I've got that *je ne sais quoi* they pick up on. Did I tell you the story of when Marlon Brando took me out to dinner after I didn't get the role in *Sayonara*? He wanted me for the part. He had a thing for me."

We'd reached Mary's floor. She cut off the story, needing all her concentration to navigate her way carefully around the corner to her door.

Rose had left the standing lamp on, and its soft light imbued the apartment with a sense of home. I helped Mary to the wingback chair; she wasn't ready for bed.

"It's cozy here," I said.

"Yes. You did this for me. You found me this place. I could never have done it without you."

"Thank you, Mary. I appreciate that."

"Did you hear what Mary Louise said about me?"

"I certainly did."

"Mary Louise was just a kid when I met her in *House of Flowers*. I'd already been around awhile. Pearl Bailey took one look at me and she had it in for me. She said, 'This here's a colored show, what you doing in it?' I said, 'I'm adding my own atmosphere and color, madam.' The others never could have answered her like that. But I had experience, I'd been to Europe and most of the kids in the show, they had no idea how to be. I showed them the ropes. They looked up to me."

"They must have."

She contemplated that for a few moments and then said, "I wish we could do this every night."

"It would be fun, but shouldn't we get you ready for bed now?"

"I could stay up all night."

"I know, but let's get you ready for bed and then we can talk some more."

"Okay," she answered in a tiny voice.

Finally, out of her silks and sequins and into her bed, I bent over her and nuzzled her cheek, breathing in the pungent scent of Joy by Dior.

"Ooh, that feels good," she said. "I like that."

WALKING HOME DOWN BROADWAY IN THE BALMY NIGHT AIR, I wished I were a better person, the sort who could fulfill all of Mary's needs, regularly taking her to shows, movies, and cabaret. Michael had been right. She hadn't been this cogent in years. It would be good for her to get out more often, but we'd come smack up against the wall of old age: you no longer have the energy or physical stability to go out on your own, many of your friends have died or fallen away, and those who are left simply don't have the desire or the time to shepherd you around. Mostly, though, they just don't want to. As your days become increasingly circumscribed and dull, so goes your once-vibrant mind, making you a less sought-after date. In the end, nothing can make up for the rhythm and excitement of the life you once conceived and built; it never will exist again.

In Mary's ever-optimistic thoughts she remained young and beautiful, sexually alluring to men, and a mentor to the kids in the show. She was like a young man I'd read about who had suffered a severe brain injury and had lived to talk about it. He described how during the period of his rehabilitation, his mind continued to tell him he could run a marathon, it just couldn't communicate that information to his legs. But in Mary's case, that last synapse was missing. She didn't even know she'd lost the ability to communicate the reality of her situation. Her brain was so compromised that she didn't know she'd become someone else, someone who was not young Mary. Perhaps it was better to live with the illusion of youthful vigor, or so I tried to convince myself. But it tore at my soul that I couldn't do more to bring true joy into the reality of her old age.

What also troubled me was that when Mary Louise had spoken so admiringly of Mary as a performer, I'd been surprised. I had to admit that I still had my doubts about Mary's career and even questions about whether or not she was talented. Sure, I showed her off to people, telling everyone about her career, especially that she'd broken through racially, but in fact I didn't really know the latter to be the case. I had a fleeting suspicion that evening that I was proud of her simply because she was a Japanese American woman who had come out of the camps and had made her way on her own, and I was using her example to prove some point. Did she have to be exceptional to confirm her worth? Did I think if she was so talented it would reflect well on my taking care of her as evidence that I wasn't doing it out of pity for her as a Japanese American who had been incarcerated? Or was it that her talent would prove to others that it had been wrong to incarcerate her on racial grounds? If I could elevate her, she could be the example that demonstrated the injustice. But only if she *was* exceptional. One couldn't be just an ordinary, smart, or talented citizen. One had to be the best! Maybe that was why I was embarrassed by and became uncomfortable with her smutty jokes and iconoclastic behavior — it kept her from being perfect. I didn't like to think of myself that way; I pushed it from my thoughts and was free of the discomfort by the time I'd reached home.

15

The Color of Citizenship

FALL, 2008 — THE PRESIDENTIAL ELECTION WAS IN FULL SWING.
I WAS rooting for Hillary against Barack Obama during the primaries
and to my surprise Rose and many of the home aides were as well.
I suspected it was simply what they told the white people they took
care of, but Rose convinced me that it was indeed the case.

"I trust Hillary to get me health care. I don't trust him on that,"
she said. "I think women do better. Hillary's stronger."

As for Mary, she chose Hillary.

Mary had always voted, but I had failed to change her registration
when she'd moved to the residence, so I set about to reregister her.

Rose had only recently obtained her American citizenship, a very
exciting achievement for her, and she hadn't yet registered to vote.
Only after the primary did her voter registration card arrive. But she
was thrilled when Obama won.

"I've never voted," she said. "It wasn't worth it in Haiti. We all
knew before the election who would win. It was corrupt and dangerous to vote."

"Now you can vote for Obama," I said.

"Yes," she smiled. "I'll vote for a Black man for president. I still
love Hillary, but I like voting for a Black man. Who are you voting
for, Mary?"

"Hillary," she said firmly.

"You can't vote for Hillary," I said. "She's not running anymore.
Obama beat her."

"He did?" Her eyes widened in disbelief.

"She lost the primary."

"I don't care, I'm voting for Hillary."

"Mary doesn't want to vote for a Black man," Rose teased.

"Is that true, Mary? Are you prejudiced against him because he's Black?" I asked.

She shrugged and returned to watching the television.

"He's from Hawaii. Did you know that?"

"He is?" She turned back to us.

"He grew up in Hawaii. Will you vote for him now?"

"Okay," she said.

I HAD COME TO TERMS WITH MY DISAPPOINTMENT OVER THE months between Hillary's loss and Obama becoming the candidate. I still felt she was the most qualified, but he was a Democrat and, by all accounts, he was a brilliant man. I had been a fan of his after reading his first book, *Dreams from My Father*. As the daughter of a community organizer, a community activist myself, and as a person who'd also lived across cultures and was still working to put my own disparate cultural, racial, and class identity together to understand who I was and where I belonged in America, I found communality with the voice of quandary that cried out in his writing. What I didn't like was the deification of him by white Americans, an adoration that seemed driven by the fact that he was the perfect Black. A "good, clean, articulate Black" as Joe Biden had said. I'd done my own research on Obama and found some questionable actions of his as a legislator in Illinois. He was no saint. He was a pol to some degree. Whenever I raised those points with friends, I was shot down with accusations that I only wanted Hillary because she was a woman. Some of the anger toward me by even my closest friends was also tinged with subtle insinuations that I was being racist. To my mind, it was they who were being racist by not being willing to discuss any flaws he might have, as though there had to be a wall of purity around him, and to make him human was to harm him. It hit me particularly hard because my parents' Black friends and colleagues were middle class intellectuals and highly educated professionals, like Obama, and in two cases couples in mixed marriages of Black and White, like Obama's parents. It's who I grew up knowing and from whom I first learned about racism in America. Obama would have fit right in at the political discussions we had in our home when they were present. Obama was too familiar for me to hold him in higher regard, simply based on race. But now he was the candidate and the right to vote was my passion, my religion. Every time I enter the voting booth, I weep from the privilege of giving voice. There was no way I was going to let African American voters, or anyone for that matter, be disenfranchised as they had been in by the Republican hierarchy in Ohio in the 2004 election for president. So, on the Friday before Election Day, having cast my absentee ballot, I left for Cincinnati, Ohio to work under the auspices of the Black Lawyers Association as an Election Protection volunteer.

A little before dawn on Election Day I was on the way to their headquarters in Cincinnati when my cell phone rang. It was Rose.

"I voted," she cried.

"Already?"

"I got here at four. There was already a line. By the time I went inside the line was down the street and around the corner."

"That many people that early?"

"We're all Black people in my neighborhood, Marnie. We want to be sure we get to vote."

Eighteen hours later when I finally returned to the house where I was staying, I settled down with friends in their study, in front of the television. Just after eleven the network anchor announced that Ohio had gone for Obama and we knew he'd won. Shortly before midnight my cell phone rang.

"He won, Obama won," Rose screamed. "A Black man is going to be president of America."

Cell phone pressed to my ear I left the television room and the house and went out to the driveway, into the clear night. I looked up to the star-filled sky.

Rose was crying and laughing. "Obama won and I voted for him. I can't believe it."

"Beginner's luck, Rose." My eyes brimmed with tears. "Don't expect to pick a winner every time. We aren't usually that lucky."

Before we hung up, I said, "Be sure to tell Mary tomorrow, even if she doesn't understand."

I stayed outside in the cool air and silence for a long time. It was a night to remember for many reasons, not the least of which was that we three had voted for a winner.

16

Crices

January, 2009 — mary's expression had become dull, increasingly mask-like, and she lost interest in the activities offered at Vista. She fell with some regularity, and I'd get phone messages in the middle of the night to inform me that she'd been sent to the hospital, where she would stay for a week.

Abigay had left, and a new person, Delyse, called me in to say it was time to have round-the-clock coverage with private aides, to the tune of sixteen thousand dollars a month on top of the five thousand a month for room and board. The impact of the 2008 financial crash was diminishing Mary's portfolio. I worried as the money seeped out of her account.

At no point had Mary asked me how much the stay at Vista and Rose's salary were costing her. She had to have known that the residence and its services were expensive. Where money was concerned, she was one of the savviest people I've ever met, and I wondered if her silence was because I had told her she was close to being a millionaire, and from the perspective of her generation, being a millionaire was the pinnacle of wealth and represented having a sum she could never run through. Or it could have been that she wanted to close her eyes to how much it was costing. She liked the luxury, the meals, and the care she was receiving from Rose. Or had she lost too much of her cognitive function to notice.

In the beginning I had told her that she alone had earned the money and it was now there for her to spend on herself. I reminded her that most women of her generation had husbands who'd taken care of them, but she'd done it all on her own and she should reap the rewards for herself. "You have no children," I'd said, "no one to whom you have to leave money." It was at this point that she usually brought up her brother's children, two nieces with whom she'd had a falling-out after Frank's death. She asserted angrily that they hadn't been sensitive to her loss at the time; they hadn't even called her to express their condolences. "I wrote into the will that they should only get one dollar each. That way they can't inherit anything." I knew this wasn't the case, as I'd recently seen her will; it only stated that the sole recipient of her estate was now to be her first cousin in Japan, but I didn't contradict her.

Mary entered a new phase whereby every five minutes she proclaimed her need to "go wee-wee." Rose would remind her that she'd just gone. Mary would accept the information — and five minutes later she would repeat the need. She would sit on the toilet, doing nothing, get off with Rose's help, and flush the toilet. After a while the ritual morphed into a new variation. She would make the same demand, but when Rose accompanied her to the bathroom, Mary wouldn't even sit. She'd simply flush the toilet, turn around, and leave. I worried that the administration would trace the excessive water usage to us, and add a surcharge to our bill. On some days Mary could repeat the ritual ten times within an hour until, exhausted, she collapsed in a heap on the bed and took a nap.

With no warning, the screen actors guild, usually meticulous in their accounting, made a simple clerical error that threw hundreds of their members off Medicare. I needed Mary's password to enter the government system, so I could help clear up the problem, as she was too mentally deteriorated to speak with the Medicare representative herself. A sympathetic clerk hinted that the password that was listed on the application was Mary's mother's maiden name, but she couldn't tell me what that was. I knew that Mary's correspondence from Medicare, Social Security, and SAG all had her name as Mary Mon Toy Okada, so I asked if Okada was her mother's name. The clerk said she was sorry, but that was not the password. My only recourse was to get the name from Mary.

Mary was sitting on the edge of her bed watching television when I arrived. Rose turned off the television, and I knelt down before Mary. "You must help me. I need your mother's maiden name. I can't pay your medical bills without it."

Mary stared into my eyes, furrowing her brow as she concentrated. I could see her trying with all her might to bring up the information. She looked ready to cry. I was torturing her.

"Just relax," I said, "think of your beloved mother. Think how beautiful she was. What was her maiden name, her name before she married?"

More time went by. I glanced over at Rose who strained forward in the wingback chair, as though she could will Mary to come up with the name. Rose knew how crucial this was, how difficult it would be to enter the bureaucracy without the password. It felt like ten minutes had passed. What was I going to do if Mary couldn't come up with the name? I was about to give up when Mary's gaze darted left then right, as though she was seeing something, and her face relaxed.

"Yusa," she said, her voice strong.

"That was your mother's name?"

She nodded, though she looked unusually sad. It had taken an emotional toll to remember her mother.

I called the Medicare office. "Yusa," I said when the woman asked me for her password. "Fine," she said, "now let's see what we can do to straighten out this mess."

It took a sixty-hour week to get her reinstated, even with the extra help of a young Japanese American man at the Guild headquarters who went out of his way when he heard that Mary had been in a camp.

I began to feel like a martyr again. This is not to say that Mary's community wasn't there to help. Whenever I needed something specific from them, they came through. If I reminded her friends that her birthday was coming, they all sent cards. I often heard from Rose that a visitor had come for Mary, or a bouquet of two dozen roses would appear and I would read the note to find that Dr. Glory Van Scott had dropped them off. Stan brought his dog so Mary could cuddle him. Maureen brought her dog too, stopping in regularly to visit with Mary. If Mary would be wearing a new nightie, Rose would tell me that Cely had visited. Bradley Whitford, a star of the television series *West Wing*, who had lived in her building, came by with Michael, making quite a stir with the other residents.

Even with Rose taking on more and more of the administrative duties — ordering all the everyday necessities such as adult diapers, tissues, analgesics, and lotions; supervising the evening and weekend aides, leaving long, handwritten instruction sheets taped to the wall — in the end, the main responsibility was mine. Someone had to be in charge.

Added to my stress was the fact that my agent was sending out my new novel about Chile. She thought it was going to be my big, breakout book, but so far eight editors had turned it down. She now wanted me to do some extensive rewrites. Friends cautioned me about turning my life over to Mary at this critical juncture in my career, instead of concentrating full time on the book, and I countered defensively that I had to see her care through to the end. I had to finish what I'd begun. Despite my adamant resistance to stopping, I knew there was a truth in what they said; I was sacrificing too much of my own existence to Mary's well-being.

A lawyer friend advised me to get a court-appointed guardian for Mary. There was a short period when I considered that possibility — until I read up on what it entailed and I saw that not all her needs would be attended to under a guardianship, and it would impose a substantial drain on her financial resources.

More to the point, I would feel ashamed for abandoning her. I could not bear the thought of her sadness if I didn't show up again. Perhaps it was foolish and self-aggrandizing to assume that she would miss me, especially since lately she'd been angry at me.

I'd watched her transfer her love to Rose, and I told myself that her anger probably came from a sense that I was already abandoning her, by visiting less often, or so she thought, as she was having trouble remembering when I'd last been there and expressed her disappointment on not seeing me more. On my regular visits I had trouble coming up with items to talk about and I found myself speaking too loudly, almost shouting, as if she were deaf or spoke a foreign language. When I accompanied her to dinner, I constantly asked her what she planned to eat, how it tasted, if she was enjoying it. She wouldn't answer. She stubbornly continued to eat silently, which only spurred me to try harder.

I sensed that I was replicating earlier behavior with my mother, but I couldn't stop myself. The more I pressed, the more silence descended around Mary, so the more I pressured her. "Are you having salmon again today? Mmm, your soup looks delicious, is it good? What did you eat for lunch? Did you like the salad?" Not that I cared about her answers. I simply wanted to engage her, wanted her to recognize that I was there. It had been the same with my mother when I would call her in Puerto Rico, grilling her at top volume, "How are you, Mom, how are you doing? What did you have to eat tonight?" until my mother said, "You don't have to try so hard, dear. I'm fine."

Deflated, forced to silence, I knew full well why I went on like that. I didn't want my mother to guess how much I hated the calls, how afraid of them I was, how I resented having to make them. It was the same with Mary. I didn't want to go to the residence each Friday evening, didn't want to have to tend to her. I pushed and shouted so that neither of us would recognize my anger. But of course, she did. Even as her brain become more addled, her conflated memories less and less available, and her intellect and Pollyanna diversions no longer served as protection against long submerged sadness, she sensed my resentment and she responded in the only way she could — with damning silence.

17

The Census Taker

FEBRUARY, 2009 — ROSE PHONED ME IN MY OFFICE.

"Mary says she wants you to come up right away."

"Is she sick?"

"No."

"Can you tell me what it is?"

"She just wants you to come right now. There's somebody here asking her questions she doesn't want to answer."

ROSE HAD LEFT THE APARTMENT DOOR AJAR. THERE WAS NO SOUND from the room. Perhaps the crisis had passed.

But no, the silence was a chilly standoff between Mary and an elderly white-haired, woman who sat at the table, her laptop opened. Mary was glaring at her from the bed. Rose raised her hands to say, I have no idea what's going on.

The woman was visibly relieved when I introduced myself as Mary's legal representative. She then explained that she was a United States census taker, here to ask Mary questions from the long form.

"The office downstairs recommended her as a good person to talk with."

"You're not interviewing everyone?"

"No, we usually pick only a few people to answer the long form. They said she'd be interesting to interview, that she's had an interesting life."

No, I thought, *it's because she's a different race from everyone here. They have quotas to fill.*

"Ms. Mon Toy said she doesn't want to answer the questions, and I explained that we wouldn't be using her name. That it's completely confidential." She eyed Mary, to see if this had changed her attitude. It hadn't. Mary looked more dug in; her expression had settled into a stubborn frown.

I detected a slight foreign accent in the woman's speech, but couldn't place it.

Sitting beside Mary, I put my arm around her, and said "She's with the census bureau. She asks these questions so she can ascertain the needs of people, also what kind of people live in the area. This helps all of us, especially older people who need services in our neighborhood and the city."

"Get rid of her." Mary startled me with the loud rudeness of her demand.

"She's not even going to take your name."

"Get rid of her." Louder still.

Then I understood.

"I'm afraid Ms. Mon Toy refuses to answer the questions. You'll have to leave."

"But they'll only send someone else."

"Get rid of her." Mary was furious now.

My hand on her chin, I turned her face toward me. "Do you want me to tell her why you won't answer? Do you want me to tell her about the camps?"

She nodded. I kept my arm around her shoulder.

"Ms. Mon Toy won't answer because she was placed in a concentration camp here in the United States during World War II. She was put there because of her Japanese ancestry, even though she was an American citizen. As a result, she doesn't trust the government with any information about herself. I don't know if you know about the camps."

"I do," the woman said. "I'm from Germany. Hamburg. I left in 1939 for Britain, where I was put into a detention camp even though I wasn't an enemy; I was in there with my enemies. I know something of how she feels."

"Get rid of her."

"I'm sorry, but tell your supervisors that if they want to talk with anyone, they'll have to talk with me. Ms. Mon Toy is not to be bothered with this." I could feel the tension in Mary's body as I held her closer. "This is traumatic for her. I have to insist that you leave."

With that, the woman slowly began to pack her computer into her briefcase. "I don't know how they're going to deal with this," she said.

By then I'd found a business card in my purse.

"Give your supervisor my card, please. Under no circumstances should anyone call Ms. Mon Toy."

THE MINUTE ROSE CLOSED THE DOOR BEHIND THE CENSUS TAKER, Mary relaxed, her eyes brightened and her actress voice took over.

"I don't know if I've told you that when Mrs. Roosevelt came to the camp to see how we were doing, she said, 'Franklin asked me to come here to see if you've been treated properly.'"

The trauma still lived within her; she called upon her old story to cover the emotional blow of her war experience. But, moments earlier, her simmering rage had been palpable as she refused to give up any personal information to officialdom. Her anguish had been so great that she'd let go of her pride and her cultural strictures and had directly asked for help from me, the one person who had enough knowledge of this episode in her past and its meaning to know how crucial it was for her to protect herself, who knew the genesis of her resistance.

Today Mary had let the curtain open momentarily and now she was drawing it closed by calling up her old coping mechanism, the story of the scholarship.

By then Rose had come to sit on the bed with us. "I didn't know what Mary had gone through. The hair went up on my arms when you told the woman." She wept as she held Mary and kissed her.

Mary remained erect, her face not betraying any sadness. As she went on relating the story again and again, I sat there thinking, what an extraordinary convergence of political history had just transpired. Of the four women in the room one had been incarcerated in a concentration camp in America during World War II, another had been incarcerated in England during the same war, another had been born in an American Segregation camp, and the fourth, the woman rocking Mary, a Haitian refugee who had voted for the first time in her life a few months earlier in an historic election of the first black president of the United States.

"Mary has suffered as much as the people of your country," I said quietly.

"That's right. My beautiful Mary has suffered too," Rose said.

THE ELEVATOR RIDE DOWN FROM MARY'S APARTMENT WAS INTERMI- nable, with stops on every floor as residents got on to go to dinner. Mary had missed her early seating and we'd had to call the kitchen to ask for a tray. She couldn't dine with this group; they were the elite. They needed no assistance with eating, nor did aides help them to and from their meals. They were well dressed and walked upright; they greeted each other by name and exchanged pleasantries.

More people got on, and I was edged to one side until I was standing by the control panel. I reached over and pushed the "close" button. Someone behind me leaned forward and sniffed my hair. Startled, I pulled away and saw that it was the tall, attractive man who had hurled abuse at Mary a few months before, shouting, "Why don't you go back to China?"

She'd been so terribly hurt that she didn't want to participate in activities for weeks afterward, angrily repeating, "Everyone thinks all Orientals work in laundries. My father was a doctor."

Emotionally drained from the afternoon I let the man's inappropriate behavior go by without a comment. At the first floor I squeezed out, leaving the others to descend to the basement.

In the quiet of the lobby, staring at the closed elevator door, I thought, *everyone in this building is suffering from the losses of old age; they all fall victim to the humiliations. No one gets off scot-free, not even the cruel ones.*

Mary was a truly kind elderly woman, never succumbing to self-pity; she never lashed out with the intent to wound and in facing the vicissitudes of old age, she was brave. There was no resisting my responsibilities anymore. I was in this for the duration. I could never abandon her.

In July there was a new wrinkle.

Rose used Mary's naptime when I showed up for my Friday visit to say, "I have something to tell you." She looked down. "I'm pregnant, Marnie. I'm having another baby."

I had no idea how to respond. The father of her son could barely help out with the child since he'd had a major heart attack a few years before and was on disability. He was kind to his boy and shared childcare with Rose, but he had married another woman for immigration purposes. Rose had recently begun to date other men after years of hoping there might be a future with her child's father.

"It was an accident."

"How far along are you?"

"Three months."

"You don't have to have the baby, you know."

"But I want the baby. I knew you would be mad at me."

"I'm not mad at you. I'm only saying you have a choice."

She looked about to cry.

"Marnie, I'm going to be forty. If I want another child, and I do, it has to be now."

"Is the man going to help?"

"I don't want him to. I want to take care of my baby on my own. This is for me and my family. I'm the only one of all my sisters and cousins with a grandchild for my mother. I want to do it for them and for my mother. I knew you'd be mad. You're not happy for me."

Her words struck like a physical blow. "That's not true. If you're happy, then I'm happy for you. I want what's good for you. And your baby will have the most wonderful mother in the world."

She looked at me closely before smiling, "Thank you, Marnie. I want you to be happy for me."

We hugged, but I was left deeply uncomfortable about having entered into what was a private choice for her. I was ashamed before her as a childless woman. In her world I was the oddity, someone to be pitied. We were culturally so different, and that difference played out in both psychological and intellectual ways. I didn't have a child because I didn't think I would be a good mother, fearful that I might harm a child. I also was afraid that my child would hate me as I often hated my mother, wouldn't want to touch me as I had avoided my mother's hand. I feared I wouldn't be able to balance taking care of someone else with taking care of myself. I'd either be engulfed by another's needs, as I was with Mary, or turn my back on them, fighting the impulse to withhold love as also kept happening with Mary. I was sure Rose would never consider any of this in her own selfless, loving, decision making.

We carried on in our usual manner. After an initial panic at the thought of losing Rose when she gave birth, I stopped counting down the days until she would be on maternity leave. Mary perked up, pleased with the idea that Rose was pregnant. As Rose grew larger Mary said, "You're having twins. You're so big." And Rose countered, "One for you and one for me."

Following each exchange Mary laughed, but on a Friday in late September she became unusually serious and articulate. "I wish I'd had a child. I was pregnant once. It would have been a beautiful baby, part Caucasian and part oriental." This confused me because whenever I'd asked Mary about her husband, he was one of two possible men or both: a Japanese American who, according to her, had been fine when she married him, but had turned to drink and gambling when they were in camp; and a more romantic version, a Japanese national, a diplomat who had to leave the country after war was declared on Japan. Whenever she spoke of the latter, she became dreamy, describing how handsome he was, and how classy. "He taught me to ski and play golf," she'd say. When I asked what had happened to him after the war, she said, "He died in Okinawa."

Perhaps she'd actually had two husbands, one before Pearl Harbor and one after. But today there seemed to be a third, a Caucasian, or maybe a lover. Maybe even Brando. Why not? Before I could pursue this new scenario, she switched gears. "But if I'd had a baby I wouldn't have gone on Broadway. I wouldn't have had my career. It was a good life." With that she drifted off into the conflated stories of her life on the stage and her many lovers. After five minutes she stopped abruptly, curled up on the bed, and was immediately asleep. She never again brought up pregnancy.

18

Mary Fails to Thrive

LATE OCTOBER 2009 — I WALKED THE TWENTY BLOCKS TO ROOS-evelt Hospital to calm myself. Once I was on Mary's floor a nurse recognized me and directed me to her room. "Miss Mon Toy is in a double, but we're trying to see that the poor sweetheart has it to herself."

Rose was sitting beside Mary's bed holding her hand. What I noticed first was how large Rose was. She was in her seventh month, due in early December with three months of maternity leave to follow. How were we going to manage without her?

Mary's face was badly bruised and swollen. She looked sadder than I'd ever seen her as she stared up at me through blackened eyes. Her wrist was swollen to twice its normal size and angled unnaturally.

"Did she go for an x-ray?"

Rose shook her head. "They want her to rest."

"What do you think happened?" I pulled a chair close to Rose.

Rose shrugged, but I could tell she had her thoughts.

"You think somebody hit her?" I whispered. "The doctor thinks so." A Dr. Chinn had called me at eight in the morning to tell me that they'd brought Mary in before dawn, and it appeared that she had been struck. "He said he'd have to report it to the police."

Rose shrugged. "It's not for me to say."

"Do you know the night aide?"

"She's the one who doesn't like to be told how to do anything. She gave me trouble before."

"Maybe Mary kept asking to go to the bathroom and the aide got fed up and left her on the toilet and Mary tried to stand and fell against the tub and onto the floor."

Rose looked off toward the window. "Could be," she said.

"The doctor said if someone hit her it would be a left-handed person. Is the night aide left-handed?"

"How would I know?" Rose sniffed.

Back at vista talk was rampant through the home aides' grapevine that I should sue the home aide company. No night report had been written up, indicating there was something to hide. By now we were paying close to $200,000 a year for 24-hour coverage. I'd been stonewalled recently, in my attempt to up Rose's salary, by the company CEO, an uncompromising white woman whom I felt was exploiting the aides who had no paid vacation, no health care, many of whom had been fired when there was an attempt to unionize the staff.

After Mary's fall, the CEO knocked off a dollar an hour from our bill, which told me she was worried. I passed the money on to Rose, augmenting her salary. It came to $24.00 a day, a total of more than $700 a month, or $8,400 for the year if Mary lasted that long.

Mary never came back to her full self, or in medical terminology, she "failed to thrive." Whether it was the physical trauma she'd endured or the devastating possibility that a person who was supposed to be caring for her had harmed her, she became mute with depression, and had no interest in food. She could barely sit up in her chair, and then only with her head listing despondently to one side.

Fritz came to take a photo of her in case we needed it later, and the shock on his face upon seeing her said everything.

I was tormented with the knowledge that I hadn't been able to protect her. She, who had as a young woman been torn from her life and sent to a prison camp, had now been grievously injured in the home where I'd placed her for her safety. Perhaps I should have sued on her behalf — though how would it have changed the situation for her? She could never testify and even if she won, she wouldn't personally gain from the result — it was too late for that — nor would she comprehend the victory. I decided that fighting for her rights in this instance would have been worse for her than doing nothing.

ONE DAY MARY TOLD ROSE THAT SOMEONE HAD PUT A CAMERA IN the room. "Up there, by the ceiling." She pointed to a new smoke detector. "They're watching me."

I wondered if the aide — replaced by a new night person but still working in the residence — had threatened Mary, telling her she'd be watching her through the camera.

I asked Rose if she thought that was possible.

"Could be," Rose said. "I explained to Mary it's not a camera, but she won't believe me."

Maybe she had been thrown back to her time in camp when the guards in the watchtowers had monitored the population and searchlights had illuminated the nights, but any hypotheses wouldn't change Mary's current situation.

I had to live with my own remorse.

MARY STOPPED EATING AND THE RESIDENCE'S DOCTOR, SENT HER back to the hospital. Rose and I accompanied her in the ambulance. All the tension had left Mary's face once she was lying on the gurney.

"Mary's happy to be going back to the hospital. She's afraid to be in Vista," I said as we careened through the streets with both Rose and me holding on to her to keep her steady, though she was strapped in.

"I think so too," Rose nodded.

Mary was put on intravenous fluids for rehydration, but when her electrolyte balance was finally restored, she still had no interest in food. When she wasn't sleeping, which is what she did most of the time, she lay staring into space. She was unresponsive except for a big smile when Rose arrived. Yet the smile would fade in moments and she would again drift off to sleep.

AFTER A FEW DAYS, THE HOSPITAL SOCIAL WORKER ASKED TO SPEAK to me. We met at the nurse's station and stood by the counter in the midst of the usual hectic activity. She was the person I'd dealt with from the very beginning, the harried woman with the straw like hair. Today she looked at me with compassion as she said, "I'd like to introduce you to Miss Costello." It was only then that I understood that the young woman standing to my right was to be included in our conference.

"She's our hospice representative. We've talked and we think it's time that Miss Mon Toy enters hospice."

I began to sob. My tears took me completely by surprise. I covered my face in shame at losing control so publicly. Why was I crying? What about my resentment at having her as burden? But as I wept, I knew. I loved Mary and they'd just told me she was dying.

The staff determined that Mary could go home, but that she would remain in the hospital until we could finish making the arrangements for hospice care in her room at the Vista. I sat with her to explain the plans. She kept her eyes closed as I spoke.

"You'll be going home in a few days," I said. "You're strong enough now to leave the hospital. A nurse will come to your apartment to check on you once in a while. Rose will be there every day. You'll have a hospital bed like this one for your room. We can make arrangements to have your food brought to your room. So, no dining room. Would that be good?"

She gave a short nod, opened her eyes, and looked into mine.

"Good," I said. "I'm glad we can do what you want."

Rose accompanied mary back to Vista in an ambulette.

She called me at my office: "You have to come up. Mary is talking like a young woman. I don't know what has happened."

The new hospital bed had been placed in the middle of the room, and Mary was sitting up, chattering away, holding court for a dozen well-wishers from the staff.

"How lovely that everyone has come to visit me. I wish I had something to offer you, at least some tea or cookies. It's not right to have guests and not offer them anything." She laughed and flirted, interacting and speaking more than she had in the entire last year. I pulled Rose aside.

"Has she been like this since you got back?"

"She hasn't stopped talking. Maybe we were wrong. Maybe she just needed fluids."

Because the full-electric bed was plugged into the only available outlet in the room, I had brought an extension cord and a power strip to expand our outlet capacity. Mary caught sight of the cardboard packaging and asked to see it.

"What is it? What's it for?" she asked.

I explained.

"Did you get that at camp?" she asked.

"At camp?"

"At Minidoka," she said impatiently.

"No, why do you think I got it there?"

"Because they make things like that there," she said, and then turned back to her visitors. "What did I do to deserve this attention? It's so nice of you all to come."

It was eerie. Something had shocked Mary to an earlier time. A neurotransmitter must have reactivated an old blocked synapse in her brain. She was a young woman again, but where exactly did she think she was? Why did she think I was bringing an item from the camp? Since then I've learned that it's not uncommon for people to leap into health for a short period before lapsing back into terminal illness. It often occurs twenty-four hours or less before death. Mary didn't die, but she did shut down a few hours after this incident, returning to her mute, withdrawn state.

I held onto her matter-of-fact reference to Minidoka, and how she took for granted that I would know what she was talking about. She assumed that we shared the same history, and in an indirect way she told me that she trusted me because I'd taken care of her, and that the trust was a source of solace in her life as well as in mine.

19

"Come Away, Come Away"

MARY FADED OVER THE NEXT WEEKS AND AS SHE DID, TWO IMMINENT events worried me. First, Rose was about to give birth and would be focusing solely on her new baby for several months; and second, Fritz and I had long ago planned a trip to Chile for our fortieth wedding anniversary. We were scheduled to fly out on the eighth of November, and wouldn't return until the end of that month. I had been looking forward to the trip for months. I hadn't been back to Latin America in a long time, and hadn't returned to Chile since I'd visited there during my Peace Corps time.

BEFORE OUR DEPARTURE DATE, ROSE TOOK HER ONE-WEEK VACATION allotment in order to make arrangements for the birth. "We can try out the new person for when I have my baby," she said.

The new aide, Malati, was a nice and proper Indian woman, and very professional, though she didn't have Rose's humor and élan.

When I arrived on Friday, Mary and Malati were downstairs in the café. Mary didn't greet me, and she was slumped in her wheelchair, her affect completely flat.

I stroked her hands and arms to rouse her.

"Would you like me to call Rose so you can talk to her?" She didn't say no.

"I'll take that as a yes," I said, tapping in Rose's cell number.

"Hallo, Marnie," Rose voice came through with its familiar warm lilt.

"Mary wants to talk with you. She wants to hear your voice and know you're coming back."

I put the phone to Mary's ear. Mary nodded. Then she said "yes" and "yes" again, to the questions Rose must have been asking.

When she handed back the phone her face was more animated, but as I talked with Rose, Mary sank back into her stupor. She'd already forgotten that she'd spoken with her love.

Hanging up, I was happy for Rose, but was as bereft with missing her as Mary was.

I WAS INCREASINGLY AFRAID MARY COULD DIE BEFORE I RETURNED from Chile, and made arrangements with a funeral home. I prepaid for her cremation just in case I didn't return in time. I couldn't bear the thought of her body waiting in cold storage. I asked Maureen Moore to be my stand-in as power of attorney during my time away.

Further complicating things, two days before our departure, we had a call from Germany in the middle of the night . . . Fritz's mother, Margret, had died. After much back and forth with his sisters it was decided that we should go to Chile, and Margret's ashes would be interred in December.

I HAD PLANNED TO USE THE TRIP TO VERIFY SOME OF THE FACTS AND images in my novel, but the book, even in its revised version, had over the last month received one rejection after another, and finally at number twenty-five, my agent called to say she would no longer be submitting it to publishers.

Maybe I hadn't been able to put my full artistic effort into it while caring for Mary. Or maybe I just wasn't a good enough writer, but whatever the cause, I was devastated, and this trip was to be as much sad homage as vacation.

So off we went, Fritz in a state of half denial and half mourning and, I, in mourning for my failed book, but having made all the arrangements for Mary's possible death, oddly at peace.

Our car trip through the spectacular Atacama Desert along the Pacific coast, and the driest place on earth, was a strange mélange of beauty and heightened poignancy with an unspoken subtext; Mary and Margret were representatives of a dying generation who had known World War II as young adults, Margret, on the wrong side of history and Mary, caught in the interstices between the two sides.

We stopped to pay tribute at memorial sites to the dead and the *desapa-recidos* (persons who have disappeared, presumed killed by members of the armed services or the police). Fritz had logged onto Google Earth before we'd left, and tracked them.

He found one site thirty kilometers outside of the small mining city of Calama. It consisted of a semi-circle of thirty-nine twenty-foot-tall, vibrant crimson, cylindrical steel stanchions set against the azure sky. Each pole signified a lost person. It was built by the citizens of Calama to memorialize their dead after the mothers of the disappeared had found a mass grave of bones there. The mothers had literally scratched the desert earth by hand for years, never giving up, as they combed the sere land to find their loved ones and unearth the dreaded truth. Once the discovery was made, the bones were analyzed for DNA to confirm they were the bodies of their children, husbands, brothers and sisters and cousins.

How many other times had I paid my respects at the sites of war: in Argentina at the Plaza de Mayo watching *Las Madres* with their white head-scarves inscribed with the names of their "disappeared" as they circled the square in front of a government building demanding information on their children and grandchildren; in Berlin at the Wall in 1978 long before it came down; at Dachau in 1968 the first time I visited Germany with Fritz; years later at a small overgrown Jewish cemetery Fritz and I had come across on a spring day hike near his home; and at my birthplace on that hot August day, when the wind had blown, scattering and coating me with black volcanic dust. On each occasion I'd wondered, where are the perpetrators of these crimes? They always vanish once the wars are over and the atrocities stop, silently slipping back into the general population, appearing to be the most normal of people if you chanced to meet them on a bus, or train, or across a dinner table. Many survivors also disappeared into the crowd out of fear of future harm. The exception are people like the mothers who stand up to authority, refusing to let go until the crime is confirmed, and, if nothing else, are able, with reverence and ritual, to rebury the bones of their loved ones. And thus, the dead speak.

I RETURNED TO NEW YORK TO DISCOVER THAT MARY WAS IN THE hospice section of Beth Israel Hospital. Rose had given birth to a baby girl. She was euphoric about her daughter, Kayleen Baptiste, but heart-broken that she'd had to put Mary in hospice.

I found Mary in a softly lit room she shared with a Chinese woman whose college-age son sat quietly by her bed. I wondered if they'd intentionally put two Asians in the same room thinking they'd be more compatible, but I let it go.

Mary was struggling for breath. Her arms, belly, and face were enormously swollen. Alarmed I went to look for someone on the staff.

A nurse told me, "The doctor's been waiting for you." I was escorted into an office, where an attractive blonde woman sat behind a desk, glaring at me.

Without any introductory pleasantries, she asked, "Are you certain that you're in accord with hospice care?"

"Yes, I made the decision."

"Her doctor came last night."

"Her doctor?"

"Yes, from the residence. He ordered the nurse on duty to up her intravenous to ninety percent. We had her on ten percent to ease any pain she might feel from dehydration, but with ninety percent her lungs are filling and her body is swollen with fluid."

"That doctor has nothing to say in this matter." He was a man I'd had arguments with in the past about over-prescribing medication to Mary.

"Then you'll have to talk to him. You're the family."

"I'll tell him he can't come here."

"That would help."

"Please, reinstate your procedures. I'm completely in accord with what you're doing. She's dying. And I know it's the most merciful way."

The doctor softened. "Thank you. Some people just don't understand."

It took twenty-four hours Mary's her lungs to dry out and her swollen limbs to return to their natural shape. Until they did, she was racked with deep, wet coughs. She was drowning in the extra fluid. She gasped and panicked before each eruption. I would put my hand on her chest and tell her she didn't have to cough. "You can relax, Mary. You don't have to get it up." That calmed her and she'd close her eyes and breathe shallowly.

We WERE IN THE PRE-HOLIDAY SEASON. MY TIME WAS FILLED WITH catching up on work, buying presents to take to Europe, and visiting Mary. I taped a photo of her, one that showed off her beautiful legs, to the wall beside her bed, so everyone would know how lovely and sexy she had been.

She absolutely refused to eat. When Malati tried to give her even a teaspoon of water, Mary clamped her mouth shut and slapped the spoon away.

"She doesn't want to eat," I said. "I don't think we should try anymore."

This upset Malati greatly and I could see that she suspected I was killing Mary. When my mother was dying and had stopped eating, I had begged her doctor in San Juan to let me put her on intravenous sustenance at home, but he said to me in the most sympathetic voice

I have ever heard, "What we're looking for here is not to prolong life, but to allow her a merciful death. If you're brave enough, it's better to not intervene."

Even as I did as he said, I feared I was unconsciously acting out my anger at her by starving her.

I sat with Mary for hours each day. I didn't know if she knew I was there, or if she wanted me to stay.

One afternoon a volunteer arrived, a well-meaning woman who tried to hold Mary's hand, even as Mary kept pulling hers away. The woman wouldn't give up, until Mary smacked her arm. When the woman hurried out of the room, I took Mary's hand; she let me keep hold and let me massage her arm and then her shoulders, and I knew that she recognized my touch.

She also responded to Rose's phone calls, listening intently without saying a word. I told her again that Rose had a beautiful baby and that she would try to visit. When I told her that I had to go to Europe because Fritz's mother had died, she wordlessly seemed to take that in.

Through it all, it was clear to me that she was dying. I don't know if she had decided her life wasn't worth continuing, or if she knew Rose and I were preoccupied with our own lives and didn't have as much energy for her or if she knew that she would have to share Rose's love with the new daughter. Whatever the reason, to me it seemed that she'd made a decision that she was done with this world.

The night before I was to leave for Europe I stayed late at the hospital. Mary had been agitated all afternoon. "I hurt all over," she whispered, so I arranged for the nurse to give her a little morphine to ease her discomfort. But half an hour later she was thrashing back and forth, whipping her emaciated body from side to side even as I caressed her face and arms. She cried out, begging, "Help me, help me." I didn't know if she meant help her to live or help her to die. Nothing I tried would soothe her panic, neither kissing her arms, shoulders and cheeks, nor reassuring her with words of endearment.

I began to sing to her even though I can't carry a tune. "Some people live on a lonely island . . .." Mary's eyes opened wide, looking directly into mine, and then she closed them and her breathing slowed and deepened as I continued to sing, "*Lost in the middle of a foggy sea, Most people long for another island, One where they know they will like to be, Bali Ha'i may call you . . . In your heart, you'll hear it call you, Come away, come away, ...*"

I sang imagining Mary as a tiny child on the Molokai beach with her mother, and picturing Mary when she had toured with *South Pacific*. I sang her to sleep.

I kissed her, my lips lingered on her smooth cheek, her skin, cool.

"Goodbye, Mary. Sleep peacefully." All strain had melted from her face and she could have been a young woman. I wished I could tell her how beautiful she was tonight. I said a silent farewell, as close to prayer as I've ever come, before rising and leaving her room.

Next morning the phone woke me at 8:30. It was the nurse from Beth Israel.

"Ms. Mueller, I'm sorry to bother you this early, but they asked me to call to inform you that Ms. Mon Toy passed away at 8:05 a.m. They said to tell you that she went peacefully."

Even though it wasn't a surprise, hearing the words was a shock.

"The doctor will be coming through to sign the death certificate. And you can see to the collection of her body."

"I've already made the arrangements. I can't get down there. I'm leaving shortly for Europe. My mother-in-law died and we're going for the burial."

"My, you poor dear. I'll have someone call you in a bit."

"Are you in Mary's room? Can you put Malati on? I want her to stay. I don't want Mary to be alone." My voice caught.

"I'll speak to her for you. I'm not in the room, but I'll go in after I hang up. I have to say, though, she looks a little uncomfortable being with the body."

"Ask her to call me. She has my number."

"I'll do that, dear. And you take care. I'm sorry for your loss."

It's not my loss, I thought, as I hung up. *She's not my family. She was my burden.* But I could feel the pressure of impending tears. Who was I kidding? She was family. What we didn't have was blood in common, nor the gift of childhood memories, but we had a shared history and out of that we'd made an unspoken commitment to each other. I got back into bed, curling close to Fritz.

"Who was that?" he asked.

"Hospice. Mary died half an hour ago."

He wrapped his arms around me.

"She wanted to go before any of us left her," I said.

"That could be."

"Do you realize what day this is?"

"December 7. We're leaving today."

"It's Pearl Harbor Day. She died on her most hated day." It was eight hours earlier in Hawaii. Mary had died five minutes into the new day on her own special island. "You have to hand it to her. She went out with a perfect sense of dramatic unity."

20

Estate Revelations

I RETURNED FROM GERMANY AND BEGAN THE JOB OF EXECUTOR OF Mary's will. The lawyers said that my first task was to track down Mary's nieces to get their permission to have the will probated so that I could proceed to locate Mary's first cousin Junichi Kato in Japan who was the beneficiary of all her money. Her will instructed that her ashes be interred in Japan in the same gravesite as her mother and her brother Frank. The box holding the ashes was sitting on a bookshelf in my office. I wanted it on its way to her chosen resting place.

I riffled through the faded and tattered cards of Mary's rickety Rolodex until I found a phone number for Linda Lee in Hawaii, the only person I knew who had any connection to Mary's family. She'd been a friend of Mary's brother, and she was the one who, until a year before, had sent her an endless supply of chocolate-covered macadamia nuts.

I reached her on the first try.

"Oh, no," she said when I told her Mary had died. "I'm so sad to hear that. My dear Mary. But I've been bad. I haven't been in touch for a year. The last few times I called she didn't seem to know me. I still should have kept trying. But I think I can help you. I met the nieces at Frank's funeral. I have their addresses somewhere. I'll have to get back to you."

A few hours later she emailed their names with what she thought were their current addresses.

I dialed a number in Michigan. On the third ring a woman answered.

"I'm trying to locate Lori Watanabe Saginaw. It's in regard to her aunt, Mary Mon Toy."

"I'm Lori. Is something the matter with Auntie Mary?

Auntie? I was surprised to hear such an intimate term of endearment.

I said how sorry I was to tell her that Mary had died.

"Oh, dear. My sister and I were just in New York and we passed by her street. We wondered if Auntie Mary even lived there anymore."

They cared enough to wonder about her? What was this?

I explained that as her friend, I'd had Mary's power of attorney. "I'm now the executor of her will, and the administrator of her estate."

"That's a big job. I know because we had to do it for my father. You must have been a good friend. She was lucky to have you."

I next explained that she and her sister Wendy had been left out of the will. "Mary's sole beneficiary is her first cousin, Junichi, in Japan."

"I didn't expect anything. Wendy doesn't either." she said. "Auntie Mary cut off from us after my father died, I don't know why. But I wonder if there are any family photos? We don't have much pertaining to our history. It would be nice to have anything like that, if you could spare it."

Lori seemed warm and modest. Mary had to have misconstrued the nieces' actions after Frank's death. Perhaps in her deep mourning state, I thought she'd wanted more sympathy from them than they were able to give at the time. She could have had family in her last years, caring nieces who would have come to visit. Why would she deny herself such comfort and closeness?

"There are a few family photos of your grandparents and some other mementos. Of course, you can have them," I said with the lawyer's voice playing in my head, telling me I had to make an inventory of Mary's property and that everything belonged to Junichi. I would have to get his permission if I wanted to give away items that weren't in the will. *But who would know from family photos,* I thought, *certainly not the first cousin.*

"I'm overwhelmed," Lori was saying. "It's a bit of a shock to have you call and bring back memories of Auntie Mary. We're not a close family. This is a lot to digest."

When I reached Wendy in Seattle, she was also moved by the idea of receiving items of family history. I liked these two women, felt for them, could identify with their not having much of a family nor much in the way of objects to connect to their heritage. We exchanged emails.

FRITZ WENT WITH ME TO THE STORAGE UNIT TO HELP TAKE INVENtory of Mary's belongings for Junichi. We began with the contents of the cedar chest. I lifted out the individually wrapped kimonos, untied the hemp strings and peeled back the wrapping with the ink-brushed Japanese characters. One by one we hung the kimonos and obis on the passageway walls, with Fritz taking photos of the richly patterned silk in riotous colors of purple, orange, blue, green, yellow, and pink vibrant against the institutional-ocher-painted cinder blocks.

After Fritz left, I tried to repack each kimono and soon realized there had been a method to the folding that I couldn't begin to replicate. Mary must have known how to do it, perhaps she had been taught by her mother. This was the traditional Japanese mother who had been married to the Chinese doctor, widowed in Hawaii, and remarried to a chiropractor in Seattle. This was the mother who had never seen Mary perform. But why not? There was so much I didn't know about her. I'd been too consumed with taking care of her to ask the questions.

I dragged a footlocker out into the hallway and opened it to photo albums and scrapbooks. I sat on the concrete floor poring over them. Hundreds of photos of Mary in various poses and venues: Mary with other Asian beauties in elaborate Chinese costumes; Mary in pasties performing on stage with a white woman and a Black woman; Mary in front of a three-way mirror as a tailor fitted the bodice of an elegant costume; and Mary posing seductively in a silk Chinese dress with a high slit exposing her leg, and around her shoulders the white-fox stole she had wanted to wear on her hundredth birthday.

Mary in her white fox stole, San Francisco, 1958

In some of the photos Mary appeared sweet, young, and innocent, in others she had a sexy, come-hither expression, but in most she had the confident look of a woman who knew she was beautiful.

There was another group of publicity shots of people, both Asian and Caucasian. Linking the names and images to the crumbling pages of press clippings in the scrapbooks, I understood these were vaudevillians with whom she had performed. There were dog acts, dancers, comedians, high wire aerialists, singers, and strippers, both known and unknown.

There were clippings about the China Doll Club dating to 1946, where she was initially referred to as Mary Mon and later as Mary Mon Toy. No mention of the name "Okada" that had appeared on her official documents. Reading on I developed a theory that her name must have been Mary Mon Toyokada and that she had split off the Okada for purposes of theatrical catchiness. But where did the Toyokada come from; a husband? Which husband? Did she never take the name of her stepfather, Watanabe, as her brother Frank had? All the articles spoke of her as the "Chinese nightingale." Where was the young Japanese American woman who'd been incarcerated for her ethnicity and race? The Japanese half of her ethnicity had disappeared or been stripped away.

By five o'clock I was stiff and achy from sitting for hours on the cold concrete floor. I'd spent the day in another world, a seamier side of show business than I'd imagined for Mary. From this material it was apparent that it had taken her years to put her career together. She hadn't just fallen into the glamour of the Latin Quarter and the Broadway stage. I closed the scrapbooks carefully, cautious not to damage the flaking, yellowed pages any further, and returned them and the photo albums to the footlocker. My fingertips were silky with dust and smelled of old newsprint. Clamping the padlock on the metal door of the storage unit, I knew I had to learn more.

THE E-MAIL ADDRESS FOR THE SON OF MARY'S COUSIN JUNICHI ARrived from Linda Lee.

"The father doesn't speak English and doesn't use e-mail," she told me. "It's better to deal with his son."

Yet again I had to inform them of Mary's death, and of her desire to have her remains sent to them in Japan. The lawyer said I couldn't tell him the exact numbers until the will was probated, but I could give him a range.

"It will be less than $500,000." I wrote the son, "but your father will receive more than $300,000." He was flabbergasted, or as publicly flabbergasted as a reserved Japanese man ever gets.

"We had no idea she had so much money and that she'd leave it to my father. She visited us once. But this will take care of my parents in their old age."

If only Mary could have been privy to our exchange. I saw why she'd left it all to her cousin. It wasn't solely familial loyalty or honoring her Japanese heritage. Rather, the large figures told her mother's family that she'd been a success. Whatever shame there may have been about being in show business and, despite her bravado, whatever discomfort she had about being a showgirl, she knew that when they inherited her money she would forever be — in their eyes — the beneficent, wealthy cousin in America. She had gotten the last word and honored her mother's memory.

The family in Japan wasn't the least interested in the kimonos and wrote that I should distribute them among her friends and nieces as I saw fit. They didn't want the kimonos, I realized, no matter how beautiful; what did they need with one more kimono or obi? Even the photos, scrapbooks, and dolls were of no interest to them, nor were any of the other Japanese items. They didn't want to have to deduct the money for the shipment from the inheritance. I could do what I wished with Mary's belongings.

I WOKE ONE MORNING REALIZING THAT MARY HAD BEEN DEAD FOR over a month, and I hadn't put an obituary in the *New York Times*, nor had I planned any sort of memorial service. I called Michael.

"We should have it here," he said. "I'll call the pianist and we'll have the piano tuned. You notify the others and see who wants to perform. It'll be marvelous. We'll continue the Hawai'i theme for our little Honolulu gal."

We set the date for January 31.

Lori Saginaw wrote that she was planning to visit her son in Brooklyn at the beginning of February. I invited her to the memorial.

She wrote back a day later. "I'm thrilled. I can't believe this is happening!" She said that the entire family would attend: her mother May who was Mary's brother's first wife; Wendy; Lori's two sons and the oldest son's girlfriend.

I placed the obituary notice in the *New York Times* for January 30 and 31.

Mary's obituary photo:
At the China Doll Club

MON TOY, Mary, died on December 7, 2009 in her beloved New York City. A triple threat: Latin Quarter showgirl; original Broadway cast member in *The World of Suzy Wong* and *House of Flowers*; on television on *Kojak, Ryan's Hope, Teahouse of the August Moon, I Spy* and *Drs. Hospital*; in movies in *Airplane II* and Bob Fosse's *All That Jazz*. She was the first Asian runway model in Paris. Born in Hawaii, her family moved to Seattle in the 1920s only to be uprooted and sent to the Minidoka Japanese American Internment Camp after Pearl Harbor. She left the camp in 1944 on a scholarship to Juilliard procured by Eleanor Roosevelt. The rest of her life was spent in New York City where she was an active member of Screen Actors Guild, AFTRA and Actors' Equity, and generous supporter of The Actors Fund, animal rights and The Japanese American National Museum. A celebration of her life will take place on Sunday, January 31 at 1pm.

I MADE A PLAN FOR THE FAMILY TO COME TO MY OFFICE TO GO through the belongings I'd moved there when Rose and I had closed down Mary's apartment. They arrived together the day before the memorial, filling my small studio with their energy and chatter. They were attractive and stylish.

Lori wore chic orange-rimmed glasses and her dark hair was streaked with platinum. I was impressed when I discovered that she was married to Paul Saginaw, founder of Zingerman Delicatessen in Ann Arbor, and that she herself was the creative founder of Food Gatherers, an organization whose mission is to serve the hungry.

Her sister Wendy projected efficiency and competence, so it was no surprise to learn that she ran her own business as a development consultant to organizations promoting racial and social equity. Zach, Lori's older son, in his twenties, was an avant-garde jazz musician who worked in a cutting-edge Brooklyn restaurant with his French girlfriend. The younger son, Ben, who lived in Michigan with Lori and his father, was still in high school but already making experimental videos. I regretted even more that Mary hadn't stayed in contact with them.

May Watanabe, a diminutive woman in her eighties, looked to be sixty with a lovely delicate face and black hair cropped close to her head. While I found the others slightly intimidating, I felt a strange, unexplainable connection to May, a sense of comfort, as though she could be family. Physically she was tiny like my aunt Harriet, but where my aunt had an acerbic wit camouflaged by an overly polite demeanor, May was pure sweetness; she was the calm center of her family's noisy expressiveness.

It hadn't occurred to me that Mary's nieces might be suspicious of me, or might not like me, but when I confronted with them I felt out of place in their tight circle, like an interloper who must be tolerated. I was embarrassed by my secret conviction that they could almost be family and, feared they might intuit in me a need to belong and judge me for it. I wanted to blurt out that I'd only taken care of Mary out of a self-imposed sense of duty, to deny that I'd loved her. A deep shame came over me that, at the time, I didn't understand. All I knew was that while they were in my office, I felt pathetic and a little creepy.

We went through the objects, large and small — paintings, jewelry, mostly paste, though there was a ring with tiny diamond chips that had belonged to their grandmother, clothing, dishes, decorative items, and books. Since I'd been feeling invaded by Mary's possessions and eager to get her clutter out of my office — and saw it as a way to ameliorate my sudden insecurity — I offered almost all of it, including Yoshizo's duffle bag, which I gave to Zach. It seemed more fitting that his great-grandson should have the significant memento than the Japanese American National Museum. I hoped Mary wouldn't mind.

There were more items in storage and I suggested that we go there on Monday, after the memorial, to sort through them. They took most everything in the office, so great was their hunger for any particle of personal history. This I attributed first to their grandparents' and parents' dislocation during the evacuation, and second to May and Frank's divorce. They were lucky that Mary had kept what little was left.

When the flurry of acquisition subsided, I described what was going to happen the next day — a small gathering in the building where Mary had lived, where they had visited in the past. There would be neighbors and old performing friends, reminiscences and songs. I hoped they would offer some of their own.

"We'll be doing a Hawaiian theme since Mary was born there."

Lori, Wendy, and May gave me looks of, "What did you just say?"

"We always do a Hawaiian motif for Mary. Actually, I think Frank was only a half-brother to Mary. After Mary's Chinese father died your grandmother remarried, left Molokai and moved to Seattle, a few years before your father was born."

"What are you talking about?" Wendy said. "What Chinese father?"

"Mary's father in Hawaii was Chinese. He was a doctor in Father Damien's leper colony."

They laughed. "Mary was born in Seattle," Lori said. "She and my father had the same father. And he was Issei. I don't know where you got that."

"From Mary. Are you sure?"

"Totally," Wendy said. "Our father only moved to Hawai'i when he left our family. Mary had never been to Hawai'i before she visited him there."

"Is that right?" Incredulous, I turned to May.

"I don't know much about the family, but I do know that Mary was born in Seattle and that she and Frank had the same father."

IT WAS TOO LATE TO CHANGE THE OBITUARY. IT HAD ALREADY APPEARED in the paper that morning. I'd included my office number in the notice, hoping to attract more of Mary's friends, and judging by the number of messages on my machine, a lot of people had already seen it.

There were calls from sleazy men looking to come to a funeral where they might meet showgirls. I deleted those. There was one from a forlorn ex-showgirl who wanted to attend, but who wasn't from Mary's era. I erased it. There were messages from old friends of Mary's I'd been wanting to reach, but couldn't locate them. I took down their numbers.

The last caller was a man in boca raton who said he'd dated Mary. I called him back right away.

"When I saw the obit, I couldn't believe it, Mary Mon Toy! he said. "But what really got me was that she was older than I am. She was ninety-three!"

"How old are you?" I asked.

"Ninety-two. I thought she was just a kid when I met her. How come you didn't call her Mei Li in the obit? That's what we always called her 'cause she was Chinese, you know, like the character in *Flower Drum Song*. And it didn't mention her being married to Lorne Greene."

"Lorne Greene?"

"Yeah, from *Bonanza*, the TV show. You sound too young to know him."

"Is that what she told you?"

"Yeah, she was divorced from him."

"When did you date her?"

"When she was on Broadway. We'd walked into Sardi's together and they'd treat her like a queen. But I can't believe she was older than me. She was a real looker, if you know what I mean."

Mary and I had a private routine. She'd begin, "I have big tits because I'm part Chinese. Japanese girls are flat-chested, but Chinese girls have it up here."

She'd grab her breasts and jiggle them, and I would joke, "Then you must have one flat one and one that sticks out," and she would roar with laughter.

I had bought Mary's story hook, line, and sinker. I could hear people saying, all Caucasians think all Asians look alike.

The joke was on me.

Later when I told my friend Charles, who is Eurasian, that she looked so Chinese to me, he would say, "Be careful what you write . . . racial Asian characteristics are on a continuum. She could have been in any national grouping."

Hanging up the phone after talking with Charles, I immediately googled "Lorne Greene." No marriage to a "Mary Mon Toy." Jesus! What other stories had she made up?

I googled Mary, and up popped tweets and articles and blogs already referring to the obituary, all loving the photo and the life story of a Japanese American showgirl who'd been born in Hawai'i.

I had inadvertently filed false information with the *New York Times* — and it was being picked up across the Internet and there was nothing I could do to stop it.

21

Memorial

It Takes a Village — Mary's family of friends, row one (l to r): Cely
Onrubia, Michael the pianist; row two: Marnie Mueller, Dr. Glory Van
Scott, Michael Estwanik, Mary Louise, Maureen Moore.
(Missing are Diane Carrion and Stan Schnier)

THE NEXT DAY THE OBITUARY WAS TAPED BESIDE THE INTERCOM IN
the entry to 66 West 88th Street, and to the outside of Michael Estwanik's door. I didn't have the heart to take them down. Everyone
was so excited to have seen it in the paper.

"Love the photo you chose," Maureen Moore said. "Mary would
adore everybody seeing her 'gams.'"

The room was abuzz with the high-intensity chatter of the most loyal mourners: Mary Louise and Bill Britten, Dr. Glory Van Scott, Maureen, Cely, Diane, and of course Michael, who was bustling around and tossing psychedelic leis — extras from the ninetieth birthday party — over our heads. The scents of fine perfumes and the aroma of good scotch and wine wafted through the room.

Cely was a nervous bird; she had a terrible lung infection and was afraid she couldn't do justice to "Bali Ha'i," but as soon as she began to work with Michael, the pianist, to find the key, she became a focused professional. Fritz poured drinks at the bar. Stan was shooting pictures as other friends and neighbors entered.

Rose arrived with her mother and son and the new baby. Kensley, her son, was in a dove gray suit, white shirt and pink tie, looking all the little man at seven-years -old. The baby was asleep in Rose's arms. Rose introduced me to her mother, who spoke only a Haitian French. I asked Rose to tell her how fabulous I thought Rose was. "I can't," Rose said. "She'll think I'm too proud. Anyway, today is for Mary."

Finally, the family appeared. I'd been so anxious and upset about the obituary, and the exposure of my gullibility at believing Mary's story, that I was sure Mary's family would boycott the memorial. But

The Watanabe Family, (l to r), Lori Watanabe Saginaw, Zachary Shigeto Saginaw, May Ohmura Watanabe, Benjamin Kenjiro Saginaw, Wendy Watanabe

they were all smiles as Mary's friends gathered around to welcome them, offer their condolences, and to say how sad they were that Mary hadn't kept contact with her family.

Michael called out, "Okay, everybody, grab your drinks and take your seats."

We refilled our Hawaiian-themed paper plates with the hula dancers being covered again with Michael's special salmon flown in from the Pacific Northwest. When everyone was comfortable and had quieted down, Michael told the assembled that this was going to be very casual, "as our friend Mary would have wanted it. We're here to honor her memory and celebrate her life. Marnie will begin, and after that, just come up front when the moment moves you. Remember, Mary is listening!"

I began by telling how our bond was the American concentration camps. When I said she had been incarcerated in the Minidoka camp I could see from the surprised looks on many of her friends' faces that they knew nothing of this.

I kept to myself the new information about her birthplace, which wasn't difficult because I still didn't quite believe it. She'd told the story of Molokai so often and so well that it didn't seem possible that she'd entirely made it up. Mary had once said, "in those days, Chinese and Japanese didn't get along. Objections came from both sides of the family and so, they weren't disowned, but they weren't favorably considered." Maybe even the nieces didn't really know the truth; maybe Frank had protected them from the history of a mixed marriage and a remarriage. Maybe Frank was ashamed that his mother had remarried.

As I described Mary's career, pointing out how unusual it was for an Asian woman of her generation to make it to Broadway, I felt pride in her refusal to let racism deter her, for not looking back after she got out of camp. I ended by telling how on our last evening in hospice I had sung to her and how astonished she'd seemed. "I didn't know if she was moved by hearing 'Bali Ha'i,' or horrified that I couldn't carry a tune." I didn't say that I'd sung it hoping she would find comfort being transported imaginatively to an island like her Hawai'i.

What followed were songs — a soulful blues rendition from Mary Louise, an exquisite "Bali Ha'i" from Cely, "I Enjoy Being a Girl" belted out by Maureen — and stories of Mary's exploits and lovers, memories of theater past, of her generosity and kindness to other performers, her outrageous outfits and stylish beauty.

Diane told the group, "Mary gave me a peek into her world and yours, into a place I knew nothing about. What a rich life. It was a privilege to know her and all of you."

Glory Van Scott, splendid in a raw-silk head wrap of gold, forest green and burnt sienna, told how she and Mary used to have peanut-butter-tasting parties with different jams and teas from around the world. "Mary loved her peanut butter. I'd say 'I only have an hour,' and four hours later we were still talking about the theater and all the people we knew. It was an education in the theater for me to talk with her."

Lori Saginaw rose. "I'm Lori, the oldest daughter of Mary's brother Frank, who left our family in 1969 to move to Hawai'i. Somehow, we were disconnected from Mary. I remember as a child watching her applying her false eyelashes and thinking it was the most amazing way to be a woman. We have more of a connection to her than she knew. We're all fighters like she was, for people being accepted for who they are no matter what color or place in society that they are. Mary taught me to sing *Hava Nagila*," and little did I know that I would marry a Jewish boy — the in-laws were very impressed. I appreciate all of you for filling in the picture of who she was. We're family and we have a place here and we thank you for opening that place for us."

Wendy followed Lori. "I'm the youngest. I also appreciate that you let us into your lives and Mary's. It is a family legacy that's important for us to know and for my nephews Zach and Ben to know this person. I admire her for forging a life as a pioneering Asian woman in the theater."

We were about to close the ceremony when Zach came forward, sat at the piano, and said, "This is for Mary." He performed a stunning modern jazz improvisation. When he finished he said, "This means so much to me. I had a lot of anger and resentment about this part of my family, that they just didn't give a shit about me. I've found that I don't have to hate. Even though Mary never wanted to meet me I now know that she was a good person. I can go on with that information."

May, seeming more fragile than she had been only the day before, stood by me at the piano. "I can't help but regret all that we missed of knowing Mary and what she missed of us." She began to sob, tears streaming over her delicate cheeks, her tiny body trembling, her words barely a whisper. "It's so important for us to be with people who knew Mary. And who, like Marnie, knew about the camps. I was also in Tule Lake."

With that she turned to me and buried her face in my shoulder.

I held her close, feeling the warmth of her body against mine, and absorbing the surprising information that she'd been in Tule Lake.

In closing I said, "My father told me that one of the saddest results of the incarceration of Japanese Americans was the disruption of the traditional family bond. Prior to camp, families had always shared meals as a unit in their homes, but in the camp mess halls, the families gradually split apart — the teenagers sat at different tables, forming peer bonds, separate from their parents. The women no longer cooked for their children and husbands, and the husbands lost their position as breadwinners, unable to put food on the table. Such a simple change had a devastating long-lasting impact on the families. I think maybe some of the rupture in Mary's family could have begun in Minidoka and Tule Lake camps. But at least today Mary is reunited with her family. Let's raise our glasses to that and together partake of the delicious food Michael has provided."

Instead of going straight home with fritz, I went to my office. I needed time alone to consider what had just transpired. As we were all hugging and saying goodbye, I had thought of a series of poems I'd written thirty years before, when I'd first tried to understand my relationship to Tule Lake. I wanted to give them to Lori and Wendy.

In the quiet of my studio, now emptied of Mary's possessions, I found the poems. Many were haiku, told in the various voices of young and old internees, Nisei and Issei alike. Only two were written from the point of view of Caucasians: the first was the rumination of a conscientious objector like my father, set during the early dark days of arrival, and the other was a long narrative in my voice about Mr. and Mrs. Takaetsue. I hadn't read the poem in years and I recited it aloud to myself.

Our America 1944

What a funny trio we made,
two old Issei, Mr. and Mrs. Takaetsue-san
and a three-year-old Caucasian girl,
bent into the wind,
as we walked hand in hand across the firebreak
over to the prisoner side.
Fierce black sand bit into us,
blown across the dry lake bed
where the tules no longer grew.

Even in the wind, Mrs. Takaetsue-san
stooped down to get a white shell
stuck in the black sand.
"Michiko," her husband said,
"It too cold for white child,
leave your shell for another day."

When he went to play Goh
with the other old men
in Block 10's community room,
she pulled the table to the potbelly stove
away from the cracks in the wall
where the wind and sand blew in.

She brought her shells
from the orange crate beside their bed.
Now we do lady work," she said.
"Now we lady build our mountain."

I sat across from her.
"You hand me shell," she said.
"I put them on."
Little shells of white,
Tiny caracoles, so brittle
They could snap in a three-year-old's hands.
But not in Mrs. Takaetsue-san's,
Not in the fingers tapered like candle flames.

We made towers,
Not the sentry towers at the gate,
Not towers with harsh search lights on top,
But pinnacles out of fairy tale books
built of homemade paste and caracoles.

"Here we stick them on," she said,
"and here." She bowed low
her nose close to the table,
her tongue tip between her lips.
Little white caracoles,
Climbing up and up,

To peaks and turrets.
"A palace we build,
a palace for the emperor."

I watched her.
I listened to her breathe.
"Up here," she pointed to a magic tower,
"Up here where the princess live,
away from all the wars."
Another shell, up on the top,
"Now we done. Now we have our palace.
No Tommy gun here."

When I finished, I understood. My dedication to Mary had less
to do with politics than I had thought. It was only political because
my caretakers were political prisoners as Mary had been. It accounted
for my shame in the company of Mary's family, my underlying need
to reconnect with people representing those whom I had yearned for
all these years.

Fritz has often cited a scene in my novel about Tule Lake where
the character based on my father goes to the barracks of a Nisei couple with whom he is very close. They have a three-year-old child, and
as he sits there talking with his friends, the mother, Mitsue, tenderly
bathes her daughter in a large tin washbasin. My father's character
is entranced, filled with rapturous love and longing. Fritz thinks the
child is a substitute for me, and also that my father's character is an
aspect of me, as though I'm looking back at an elegiac moment in
my life. I'd never felt he was correct in his interpretation until now.

PART III

Finding Mary

22

The Detective Work Begins

To the reader: What follows tells of a process that led me to reinterpret aspects of my own life, as well as Mary's, and unfolds the repercussions of racism and anti-Semitism in America. I hope the result will be a contribution to Mary Mon Toy's family as they come to see what a brave woman she was, and to future readers, in increasing an understanding of the profound and complex impact of the Incarceration on too many lives in America.

At the storage unit the next day, lori, wendy, may, Zach, and I dug into boxes, trunks, and crates until we unearthed Mary's birth certificate, confirming that she was born in Seattle, Washington to Mon Yusa Watanabe and Yoshizo Watanabe.

"If Mon was her mother's name, where did Toy come from?" I asked, still having trouble incorporating this new information.

"She had a friend named Toy, a dancer," May said. "Maybe she took the name from her."

I remembered seeing the name and flipped through a photo album until I came to a publicity shot of a dance team, "Toy and Wing," signed, "Dear Mary, With Love."

"Could it be her?" The woman was disarmingly beautiful.

"Dorothy Toy, that's the friend. She danced with Paul Wing. They were famous in the 1930s and forties," May said. "They called them the oriental Fred Astaire and Ginger Rogers."

"Do you know where the name Okada came from?"

"Okada?"

"Okada is the name on her Social Security and Medicare. Was it her husband's name?"

"I don't even know that she was married. I never met a husband."

"She said he was a Japanese national who was deported when war was declared. And there was another story of a Nisei husband she left behind in camp." Each time I opened my mouth the words sounded less plausible.

"Frank never mentioned any husband."

"What was Mary's mother like?" I asked, eager to change the subject. "Mary seemed to love her very much."

"She was a good person, but I didn't know her well. I felt uncomfortable with her. I sensed that she thought I should speak Japanese, and I didn't know the language at all. Frank and I went only a couple of times to visit Mon and Yoshizo at the estate, somewhere on Long Island Sound, where they worked after getting out of camp. They were live-ins. She was the maid and he was the gardener. But I remember she made us the most delicious hamburgers, with soy sauce mixed in."

Just hearing Mary's mother and father spoken of by name intrigued me. I had to know more.

Over the years, Mary's friends had said I should write a book about her, but Mary herself had never given any indication that she wanted that. If anything, it was she who would want to write the book, just as she had insisted on writing her own obituary.

She must not have wanted anyone to do an article about her or to write her obituary for fear of exposing what she'd seemingly hidden her whole adult life. Now I wanted the truth, or at least what lay behind the lie, or better said half-truths.

Maybe it was left to me to tell her story. But it raised a serious moral question about my right to expose the secret she had kept all those years. I had lived a lie about my Jewishness. It had necessitated complex subterfuges and psychological negotiations. The burden I carried was heavy and penetrated deep into my being, spreading through me like a virus, stunting my ability to grow into and own my true self, or worse, it kept me from knowing what my value in the world is. I've always had a two-pronged sense of self. I projected confidence in my ability to move through the world professionally, and even believed in my abilities to conquer any task, and to be known as a person who made things happen, but every success is accompanied by a self-denigrating internal voice that tells me I don't deserve to exist. This voice allies itself with my terror of being found out. I have sympathy for anyone who can't give up such a secret. But I also know the enormous relief of finally revealing oneself.

Mary was never able to totally let go of her cover. In deciding to write the truth about her, I determined that if her secret was illustrative of the power of shame, and the fear of exposure that lived within other people of Japanese descent as a result of their incarceration, it was important to understand if it had a lasting personal consequence for her.

I began my detective work worried that there wasn't enough information to fill in the gaps and blamed myself for not having interviewed Mary before the dementia had progressed too far. Discovering that she had dissembled about something as fundamental as her birthright, I had no trust in any of the stories she had told me. I'd only heard vague and conflicting versions of the husband or husbands. She was old when she died, and many of her friends and other valuable informants weren't available, either because of death or their own deteriorating memories. Mary Mon Toy wasn't a household name, so I feared there wouldn't be much material beyond her scrapbooks and albums. The chances were that I could come up with nothing substantive.

Who was Mary after all? Had she lied about everything? Lies accumulate, building on each other; I knew that only too well. The habit of lying is a guard against being found out, but in the underworld of the unconscious, the lies fester until the outside world becomes a minefield of projected danger.

To deny one's birthright carries a special burden. It strikes at the very center of who you are and the ontological terror doesn't dissipate over time, but grows, taking on proportions far beyond the reality of what would happen if you were found out. Mary had kept her silence. It might have accounted for her parents never seeing her perform. Maybe Mary was afraid they'd blow her cover. Or that they'd find out that she had denied her heritage.

As I discovered Mary's secret and related it to my own, it seemed absurd in the multicultural world I lived in to be frightened of revealing one's identity, though here we are again as I write, with fear rising across our country about being singled out and violently violated for one's race, religion, gender, and sexual orientation, as well as progressive attitudes, belief in science, and intellectualism.

Even as communities have bravely fought back, the veins of intolerance were tapped and exacerbated during Donald Trump's reign. As Fritz has always said, intolerance lies just beneath the surface in most countries, until sanctioned and unleashed by a leader.

It's similar to what Mary and I came up against, and hid from in post WWII America. Intolerance has a long, long history in America. It is an unseemly and dangerous part of us. In my case it was the virulent anti-Semitism I overheard among my classmates, and the personal shame and self-disgust that I felt when I learned that Jews had been annihilated.

I still remember as a ten-year-old coming across a book in the library of my parents' friends as an adult party was going on in their living room; the book was filled with photographs of the liberation of Nazi camps. In shock at what I was reading and witnessing, I closed the book and ran from the room, never telling my parents what I'd seen. In Mary's case reverberations from the wartime fear-mongering and hatred of anything Japanese remained well after the war ended.

Wᴇɴᴅʏ ᴡᴀᴛᴀɴᴀʙᴇ sᴇɴᴛ ᴍᴇ ʙɪᴏɢʀᴀᴘʜɪᴄᴀʟ ɪɴғᴏʀᴍᴀᴛɪᴏɴ ᴏɴ ʜᴇʀ grandparents, taken from Mary's father's immigration entry papers. Yoshizo Watanabe and Mon Yusa Watanabe were both born in Japan in Fukushima-ken — Yoshizo in 1884, and Mon Yusa in 1898.

Yoshizo immigrated to the United States, entering Seattle in October 1907. He returned to Japan in October 1913 to marry Mon Yusa on January 13, 1914. They returned to the United States together on February 2, 1914, ten years before the Oriental Exclusion Act.

Mary Teru Watanabe was born on June 3, 1916 and her brother Frank Chusei Watanabe was born on November 21, 1920. Unless Mary's birth certificate and Yoshizo's entry papers had been forged — and as much as I wished Mary's version of her birth were true — I could no longer deny that Mary and her brother were born to the same parents in mainland America and that those parents were both Japanese immigrants.

Mary with her parents and brother at her family home
pre-Incarceration, Seattle, circa mid to late 1930s.
From the left, Mary, Frank, Mon Yusa Watanabe, Yoshizo Watanabe

I WAS STILL PERPLEXED . . . WHERE DID THE NAME OKADA COME from? My theory about Toyokada had been refuted by May Watanabe's theory about Dorothy Toy. I knew Okada had to be a legal name because it was in Mary's Social Security files and on her pension checks from SAG (Screen Actors Guild) and AFTRA (American Federation of Television and Radio Artists).

This Okada must have been a man she married. But which one: the romantic Japanese national who had taught her to ski and play tennis and golf, the same man who had been forced to leave the country after Pearl Harbor, and who she said had died in Okinawa during the war; or was he the Nisei who had been a good catch when she married him, but who had turned to degeneracy in camp?

Shig and I at the
Summit at Snoqualmie, Washington

Going through her photographs, I was much taken with a tiny snapshot of Mary standing with a handsome young man, next to a car, in the mountains in winter. He is debonair in a white shirt, baggy trousers, and suspenders, the chic ski-style of the period. She wears similarly stylish loose-fitting ski pants. He has his arm around her and a foot propped on the car's running board. They are grinning with pleasure at the camera. It looked like love to me. On the reverse side of the picture she had written simply, "Shig and I." Perhaps this was Okada? But, again, which man, which identity.

THE DAY I SAT ON THE COLD FLOOR OF THE STORAGE UNIT, I CAME across a bundle of what were labeled in Mary's hand "Love Letters," dating from 1939 through 1940. Her young love was an erudite, flowery writer, working on all cylinders to impress. He addressed her as M.T. and later as M. Teru. He was studying at UC Berkeley, but wrote of their ski trip together in the Cascades. The letters were signed George, with no last name, though he also signed with his initials JGY. No Okada there, nor any Shig.

At one point he drew a picture of a candle at the end of the letter with: "P.P.S.: A candle to celebrate a first anniversary — A JACL dance, wasn't it?" This reference to the Japanese American Citizens League indicated that he was most likely Nisei, and not the tragically lost foreign lover.

In his final correspondence, dated "The Ides of April, nineteen forty" he proudly reported that he'd been elected to Phi Beta Kappa. "I suppose that I should feel very fine, especially in light of the Phi Beta Kappa key which has now been bestowed upon me. It was nice for me, but unfortunately someone within the last year killed a great deal of my ego. While I feel good on the left side of my heart, the other half is mocking me, debunking me, et al."

In the same letter he congratulated her on her engagement, and expressed his regret that by the time he'd be ready to settle down he'd "probably find that all the choice girls are gone."

A dead end in my search, but it was interesting to know that she was a love object of this bright, intellectual young man. Perhaps he was the one who taught her to ski, and perhaps by the time she told me the story she had conflated certain aspects. Maybe he died in the war, this lost love, and — with her imaginative skills — she turned him into a Japanese national and sent him to his death in Okinawa.

BUT EVEN MORE INTRIGUING WAS THE PICTURE OF A RISING MIDdle-class and rapidly-assimilating group of intellectual young Japanese Americans, with whom Mary associated in the late 1930s and early forties. The friends referred to in the letters skied, attended the best universities, and read the important books of their time. However Mary had to forgo college and go to work.

George wrote that it was ironic that, "you became a breadwinner rather than a coed. 'Tis a pity though that many times those who really could make use of [college] are unable to attend."

In later letters he admired her progress as an autodidact: "You seem to be keeping up with the literature of the times. I've read some of Gunther's *Inside Asia*, Lerner's *It is Later Than You Think*, Beard's *America in Mid-Passage*, Du Maurier's *Rebecca*, and Edman's *Philosopher's Holiday* . . . Edman quotes the great Spanish thinker Unamuno who very well expresses my predicament: 'The modern heart longs for what the modern mind no longer believes.'"

THESE YOUNG PEOPLE WERE LIKE MY PARENTS — COMING OF AGE at the same time — they shared intellectual pursuits, lived in and visited the same places — Berkeley and Seattle and the Cascades — and held similar political goals — radical, pacifist — George was a member of the ASUC (Associated Students of the University of California) Peace Committee fighting against compulsory ROTC (Reserve Officers' Training Corps), and made reference in other letters to Bayard Rustin . . . the African American pacifist and future civil rights leader and a hero to my father. George even attended a student conference of the Cooperative League, in Oregon.

Curious about what happened to this George, I called the Phi Beta Kappa office at Berkeley. A young woman answered and I told her the story of Mary and George. "I don't have a last name for him, but his initials were JGY. I don't expect there could have been that many Nisei elected to Phi Beta Kappa at that time," I explained.

"The records for 1940 are probably over at the Bancroft Library," she said. "You're in luck. I also work at the Bancroft. I can look for you since I now want to know about George myself."

"My aunt was elected to Phi Beta Kappa around that time, too," I said.

"Give me her name and I'll look for her."

Three hours later an e-mail arrived from her.

"I found him! His name was George Yasukochi. He was elected to Phi Beta Kappa in the spring of 1940, and so was your aunt."

My aunt Harriet had to have known George! If only she were still alive.

"You said you wanted to know if George was sent to a camp. He wasn't. I've attached his obituary for you to see what happened to him."

The obituary confirmed that he had not been incarcerated. It was his good fortune that he'd been active in the Berkeley Co-op when Roosevelt issued Executive Order 9066 — and that shortly before then the co-op had made arrangements for him to travel to New York City to study at the Rochdale Institute to be trained in co-op principles. He wasn't in the military zone when the order came down.

After the war he returned to the Bay Area and went to work at the Berkeley Co-op as their comptroller. He had devoted his life to consumer co-operatives. I could barely believe what I read. The Rochdale Institute was a familiar name in our household. My father had first learned co-op principles at the Berkeley Co-op in the late 1930s. My father had devoted his life to the co-op movement. My father and George Yasukochi, Mary's love, could easily have crossed paths over the years.

The obituary quoted his daughter, Valerie Yasukochi, who said that her father was an avid letter writer who preferred to put his thoughts on paper, sometimes feeling "more comfortable telling me things in writing than face-to-face." In another article Valerie said that he'd kept all his letters.

I set out in search of Valerie in the hope that George had saved Mary's letters to him. I located her in Berkeley and called, leaving a long, overly enthusiastic message on her answering machine, jabbering about Mary and the love letters and how the two of us had so many things in common in our backgrounds. My breath ran out as her message unit cut me off. I waited, feeling embarrassed by my manic flow of words. I was certain she'd never call back.

A few days later, I wrote her a much calmer e-mail reiterating my reason for calling, and added, "If you can find the time, could you possibly go through your father's letters to see if he saved any letters from a Mary Teru Watanabe?"

Immediately, my e-mail pinged. "I'm sorry," Valerie wrote. "I didn't know you'd called. I'm on the road. But I'll look through my father's files when I get home. I'm excited to hear from you. We'll have to get together one day."

I had my doubts that any of this would come to fruition, but I was happy that the possibility existed and that she didn't think I was a fool.

23

The Forced Removal —
Aliens and Non-Aliens Alike

I NOW KNEW THAT MARY'S BIRTH NAME HAD BEEN — WATANABE, AND that her first names were Mary and either Teruko or Teru, and that she had sometimes used Okada as a surname.

I wrote to the National Archives to ask if there were any files on her in Minidoka camp listing all the possible names as well as her date of birth.

The answer arrived quickly: Yes, they had a case file for Teruko Okada, born in 1916 to Yoshizo and Mon Watanabe. I could barely contain my exhilaration as I waited for the files to arrive.

I combed through Mary's photos, and one day I was removing the backing from a picture frame and a photograph fell out from behind other photos. By now I'd learned that Mary often had four or five photographs stacked up behind a framed picture, and usually the most interesting were the hidden ones — such as the cache of candid shots of Christine Jorgensen with people who appeared to be family members and theater associates, celebrating in a ship's stateroom at about the time Jorgensen returned from her sex change operation in Denmark. Mary was in attendance looking chic in a 1950s black-and-white-checked circle skirt, black sweater, and a long string of pearls.

This photo had nothing to with sex or glamour; it was a studio portrait of Mary as a teenager in a full-length white organza dress, a close version of my mother's white organza dress from Broadway High School graduation. Maybe Mary had told the truth about attending the same school as my mother.

I wrote to the Broadway High transcript office and they responded that they would look for both Mary Teruko Watanabe and Ruth Siegel.

The two transcripts arrived within days. Another mystery solved. My mother had graduated in 1933 and Mary in 1934, a year apart, even though they were exactly the same age.

In 1931 Mary had left for five months of travel to Japan to visit her relatives and had lost a year of school. She and my mother had walked the same halls in high school. Mary had taken chemistry; my grandmother could have been her teacher. Mary was in the Honor Society from 1931 to 1934, was president of the Broadway High A Capella Chorus in 1930, and was in the YWCA Business Girls Club from 1930 to 1934. Her hobbies were singing, piano playing, designing clothes, and collecting miniature shoes.

The transcripts gave home addresses for Mary and my mother. Mary had lived in the same house throughout all of her schooling; my mother had moved almost as often as we had when I was growing up. Charting my mother's various addresses on a map of Seattle, I found that for much of their school years, she and Mary had lived half a mile apart, or in New York City terms, ten short blocks, just as Mary and I had.

A PACKAGE FROM THE NATIONAL ARCHIVES ABOUT LISTINGS FROM the camp arrived a week later — and there was Shig. Shigesato Okada, twenty-nine years old, married to Mary Teru Watanabe on September 28, 1941, two months and nine days before the bombing of Pearl Harbor, not a propitious way to begin a marriage. He was a native-born Japanese American. They lived in Seattle and had a cabin in the Cascades ski resort of Snoqualmie. He and Mary were members of the Sno-owl Skiers from 1940 to 1942. Shig was the husband who was the skier.

I would later learn that he was a champion skier. He also played golf. The story of the handsome, romantic man who taught her to ski and play golf was starting to look like truth. He was a manager with C.T. Takahashi, a Seattle import-export firm. Mary had worked for another Seattle import-export firm, but she quit shortly before they married, which suggests that he made enough money to support the two of them.

They had both attended Wilson Business College in downtown Seattle from 1934 to 1935, where they most likely met. I immediately sent for the National Archive files of Shigesato Okada, Yoshizo Watanabe, Mon Watanabe, and Frank Watanabe.

PAGE AFTER PAGE OF DRY OFFICIAL DOCUMENTS EVENTUALLY YIELDED a narrative. Their story was rounded out by reading oral histories and documents written about that specific period in Seattle.

My first discovery was that at the time of evacuation, residents of Japanese descent were pinpointed primarily through the "race data field" of the 1940 census.

Confidentiality requirements that had governed the census since 1929 had been suspended under the War Powers Act of 1941.

Mary wasn't being inappropriately paranoid when the census taker tried to interview her at Vista. "Get rid of her," she had insisted. In 1941 the government had broken the covenant of privacy with her as a law-abiding American citizen, and it could happen again.

On April 24, 1942 the army slapped the first posters onto building walls and lampposts in Seattle's Japantown: "Instructions to All Persons of Japanese Ancestry, alien and non-alien. By using the term "non-alien," the announcements tried to circumvent any public relations issue that might result from sending American citizens to prison camps. "Non-alien" was the new opposite of "foreign." With this Orwellian turn of language, the War Relocation Authority stripped Nisei of citizenship nomenclature; they were only not-aliens, in the country of their birth.

Mary and Shig left Seattle on April 28, four days after the government's order to evacuate was announced. In those four days they had to dispose of all their earthly possessions except what they could carry by hand in two suitcases each and one sea-bag, like Yoshizo's duffel that Mary had saved. There were specific stipulations as to what property they could take: bedding and linens, but no mattress; toilet articles; extra clothing; sufficient knives, forks, spoons, plates, bowls, and cups; and essential personal effects

In those four days they had to arrange for the divestiture of all their properties — homes and businesses. They even had to find homes for their pets. I remembered when Mary was dying, in a moment of extreme agitation she had cried out, "I had to leave my dog on the street." I'd thought she meant Shannon, the beloved collie she'd had on West Eighty-eighth Street. I said, "No, Mary, remember you told me he was old and sick and you had to put him down." But she had been adamant: "I left him on the street. I prayed the garbage man would pick him up and take him home. I hope he was okay. I didn't want him to suffer." Maybe her dog was the sweet black Scottie standing in the snow in a 1941 photo in her family photo album.

In the intense rush to get ready, Mary and Shig closed down and locked up the ski cabin in Snoqualmie, and stored their belongings with — and put their faith in — a Caucasian caretaker.

They extracted all their personal items from their new apartment at 505 Eleventh Avenue, putting them in a padlocked room upstairs in the house owned by Mary's in-laws, Edward and Eva Ozawa, and entrusting the key to their Caucasian next-door neighbor, a Mrs. Force.

Mary helped her mother pack up the family home of twenty-plus years at 1011 East James Street, and moved some of their cartons to the Ozawa house. The remaining cartons went into the basements and attics of other Caucasian friends; the larger items — icebox, washing machine, piano, and furniture — went into the government-provided warehouse.

Years later I would come upon a circa late-1930s photograph of Mary, Yoshizo, Mon and Frank in the family home and there in the well-appointed living room was the upright piano.

Five of Yoshizo's medical books written in Japanese were confiscated as contraband, including one entitled *A Woman's Friend*, a gynecological self-help document.

Shig's three Kodak cameras were seized as contraband under the same order.

Mary and her brother Frank helped close down the dry-cleaning establishment that Yoshizo and Mon had built together over the previous ten years to supplement Yoshizo's income from his chiropractic practice. They would have sold off the fixtures for a pittance.

The government also warehoused cooking utensils and other smaller items if they were properly packed and crated, with the family's name and address written on the outside, as well as the family identity number assigned by the War Relocation Authority.

During the days leading to the evacuation one member of each family group had to find time to stand in line for hours to register and receive the identity number. This was the same number that children and adults wore on tags on their coats, as if they were on a school outing or on their way to a recreational camp, and that was attached to the family luggage on the day they were transported to Puyallup Assembly Center, and that was listed on all official documents during incarceration. Shig and Mary Okada's family number was 10902. Number 17326 was assigned to Mary's parents and Frank.

In the midst of the upheaval every prisoners had to report for a physical exam to ensure that no one carried any serious communicable diseases into camp.

As a child i witnessed and felt the psychological and physical stress — manifest in anger and at times misdirected rage at me — my mother evinced each time she packed up our meager furniture and personal belongings for the next move to the next crappy apartment when we came up short on money and couldn't afford the previous rent. Our moves were voluntary if you ignore our economic necessity. We didn't have the government breathing down our necks — except perhaps when we had to leave Burlington, Vermont during the McCarthy era. But we weren't packing to be transferred to a concentration camp.

Possessions were never important to our family except for my mother's Fiesta ware; we barely had any personal photos, no furniture other than the few second-hand pieces, no toys, and certainly no family heirlooms. The thought that people who valued their heritage and the artifacts of their culture and ancestors, and the very fine middle-class American possessions they had proudly accumulated, had to divest themselves of everything but what they could fit into two suitcases — two suitcases! — hit me hard.

I had known those facts, had even lectured on them on a book tour without experiencing the deep emotional dislocation they had to have felt, but now I learned it had happened to Mary, and it hurt.

I confided as much to Fritz. He first answered, "People can endure all sorts of hardships during war. We had to get out of our house with two hours' notice, and couldn't take any belongings except for clothing during Occupation so the American Army could move in." He stopped and thought a moment. "But we had lost the war, so it was our due. That was Mary's own government condemning her. It must have been devastating."

THERE WERE HEROES IN THE JAPANESE COMMUNITY IN THE MONTHS leading up to the evacuation orders. Dr. Mitsuo Paul Suzuki, a young Issei, who during that period when nobody knew his or her fate, calmly went about setting up a program to inoculate the community against typhoid fever, to ward off a possible public health crisis in the event that they were sent to camps. He organized vaccination sites on city streets on his own initiative, with the help of his wife and staff.

When Mary and Shig were racing to meet the deadline for boarding the first transports, Dr. Suzuki had already administered the three-part protocol, protecting them and hundreds of other evacuees.

Mary accomplished the gargantuan task of readying her family for the relocation with the additional stress of not knowing if she'd ever see her home or her personal items again, and that was compounded by uncertainty about what the government had in store for them. Rumors were rampant, including the possibility of Japanese American citizens being sent to Japan.

Mary's brother Frank was living at home while finishing his junior year at the University of Washington. When the curfew was put in place it was impossible for him to study at the library in the evenings or to socialize like an ordinary college student. Not only did it curtail his freedom, but it stigmatized him in the eyes of fellow white students.

Gordon Hirabayashi, a University of Washington senior at the time, has described in interviews how he would tear out of the library to get home as the curfew neared, until one day he stopped outside the library doors, and thought, "No, I'm going back to study with my friends." He returned to stay put with his Caucasian friends in the library stacks, enjoying the freedom of the American student that he was. They were frightened for him, but, "No one ever turned me in," Hirabayashi said decades later.

Frank, who was thoroughly assimilated, and eager to fit into Caucasian circles, was not a resister by nature or upbringing, observed the curfew. He was a sportsman, a team player, highly valued on varsity tennis and baseball teams. In a letter of support from the University of Washington, he was described as dependable and loyal: "He will play the game, in whatever situation he may be placed, effectively and with fine spirit."

The elder Watanabes had preached assimilation to Frank and Mary throughout their growing-up years. They'd insisted it was important to be and act American even though they themselves, as Issei, could not become citizens. Yoshizo and Mon were modern and determined in their desire that their children should meld into the Caucasian world, and in doing so further themselves.

All the letters of support written for the family by Caucasians spoke of how Mary and Frank mixed with ease in Caucasian circles at work, at school, and socially. Mary's father confided to a Caucasian neighbor in Seattle after the evacuation order, that he was ashamed of being Japanese and felt terrible to be ashamed of something he couldn't change. Families who had worked hard to assimilate, and regarded themselves as tried-and-true Americans, felt particularly betrayed by the government. Their shock and despair were similar to the disbelief and horror of thoroughly assimilated German Jews as the Nazi regime gained power and the racial laws were put into place, stripping away their rights as citizens.

No AMOUNT OF ASSIMILATION PROTECTED THEM WHEN THE ORDER came down to evacuate; there was no recourse for Mary. She had to join hundreds of others in downtown Seattle on that cold, rainy Tuesday morning waiting to board the first buses to Puyallup Assembly Center, a former fairground located thirty miles east of Seattle, cynically renamed Camp Harmony by the Wartime Civil Control Administration (WCCA), the civilian branch of the Army. Harmony was one of fifteen assembly centers that were hastily erected in a slap-dash manner to temporarily house the prisoners until the concentration camps were built. These assembly centers were not fit for human habitation.

The most infamous was in the Santa Anita racetrack, located thirteen miles from Los Angeles, where manure and straw still sullied the floors of stables that were used as living quarters for families.

After months in the assembly centers, the prisoners would be transported once again — to the ten camps established in harsh, inhospitable environments from the high deserts of California to the swamps of Arkansas. Most would live there for years.

Mary's parents and Frank were to follow later.

I see Mary, exhausted and sleep-deprived from packing until dawn, but slender and lovely, in hat and gloves, her hopes dashed of a new life with the handsome Shig. She wasn't one to cave in to depression, but she must have been chilled and shivering in the dank air, fearful for herself and Shig, and concerned for her parents' well-being and states of mind. It now fell to Frank to make certain that the last details were in place, and that Mon and Yoshizo were ready when their assigned group was transported to the assembly center.

Puyallup Assembly Center aka Camp Harmony, first days.

MARY AND SHIG WERE IN THE "LUCKY" FIRST CONTINGENT SENT TO the assembly center — lucky in that when they arrived they were issued two of the only three hundred available two-inch-thick mattresses stuffed with cotton. Later prisoners received empty mattress ticking, that they had to fill themselves with straw. Under low gray leaky skies, Mary and Shig slogged through mud to their new accommodations, an eighty-square-foot room in a crude barracks, built with no foundation, lifted with two-by-fours just inches above the soaked ground. Grooved floorboards kept some of the dampness from entering their living space, but the wood planking of the walls hadn't been cured and wide cracks had already developed, letting in rain.

The construction had been carried out with such sloppy haste that even the tarpaper on the roof hadn't been laid down properly so rainwater dripped from above, adding to their despair. They had one rough hewn door to the outside and one tiny window cut into the opposite wall. A single bare light bulb hung from the ceiling. There was no furniture except two metal single-bed frames and in the middle of the room a platform for a wood-burning stove that had to be assembled by Shig. Once it was working it didn't do much to warm the chilly space, because without dampers most of the heat was swept up and out the stovepipe.

Their private life was separated from the adjoining apartments by thin walls that didn't reach the ceiling, so that loud fights as well as sexual intimacies could be overheard up and down the line. It had to have been difficult for young, newly-married Mary to make love under such circumstances.

These "chicken hutches" were far worse, more primitive, than anything my father had described of the Tule Lake barracks.

IN 2001, A WEEK BEFORE 9/11, MARY OPENED UP TO A YOUNG African-American interviewer, Thomas de Frantz from "The Popular Balanchine Dossiers" doing research on the Broadway show "House of Flowers" in which Mary was performing:

> "We had to go to internment camp because my mother was Japanese, and I was half Japanese [and half Chinese]. So, they put us in a state fair ground, where they weren't ready for us. There were barracks and stalls and stables, and it was just awful, with guards all about and barbed wire and everything . . .. They didn't put the Germans away; they didn't put the Italians away, but because we were Japanese [they put us away]."

Waiting in line outside the Mess Hall in Puyallup Assembly Center

There was row-upon-row of identical inhospitable barracks built in the shadows of the stadium bleachers, each row with latrines and a mess hall at the far ends.

In the beginning there were only two small bath houses for every two hundred and fifty people, one for men and one for women. The walk to the communal latrine could be three city blocks long. When Mary went to the bathroom that first day, she found two adjacent splintery wooden planks with six holes cut in each, with no dividing partitions for privacy either between the planks or the holes. Using the toilet meant you sat back-to-back and side-by-side with others using the facility. Underneath the planks was a large zinc-lined pan to catch the refuse from all the toilets; the pan was supposed to be flushed with water every hour, but the schedule was unreliable.

Weeks later, the prisoners themselves put up partitions between pairs of seats, with a board behind each pair to provide minimal privacy. But there was no individual seating and no door to close, and nothing to ameliorate the horrible odor.

There were eight showers in each washroom and two sinks. People tried to time their showers to get a modicum of privacy, but those who were too modest simply gave up and remained dirty. When the last area of the assembly center was opened up, it could not accommodate the thousands of new people and the boilers broke down. Many people didn't have showers for weeks on end.

The mess hall for Section A where Mary and Shig lived was noisy and chaotic serving five hundred people at each meal. The lines were long to get in, and they had to wait outside for hours in the rain those first days and later, as summer came on, in the hot sun. In the beginning the mess crew served army field food, like tinned Viennese sausages; a shipment of spoiled sausages caused a camp wide outbreak of diarrhea, putting intense pressure on the already overtaxed sanitary system.

CIVIL RIGHTS WERE FURTHER STRIPPED WITH ROLL CALLS TWICE A day; Mary and Shig's room was checked at 9:00 a.m. and 9:30 p.m. to make sure they were present. Curfews mandated lights-out at 10:00 p.m. and forbade anyone to leave their rooms until 6:30 the next morning.

Exceptions were made for visits to the latrine in the middle of the night as searchlights from the watchtowers swept the area and followed all movement.

The Shinto religion was forbidden, as was any reading material in Japanese.

Camp police could enter any room at any time without a warrant.

Mary and Shig had arrived at Puyallup Assembly Center through a gate guarded by armed soldiers carrying bayoneted Tommy guns, passing between ten-foot fences with barbed wire on top. Mary had been married for exactly seven months; the honeymoon was over.

24

Personal Consequences
of the Incarceration

DISRUPTION OF THE FAMILY

TWO WEEKS AFTER SHIG AND MARY SETTLED IN ROOM A-2-87, Yoshizo and Mon arrived. Frank followed a month later. They were housed in section D, the last region to be occupied at the far end of the Puyallup fairgrounds. Mary needed a special pass to enter their area; sentries stood guard at the gate separating the sections and from there she had to be escorted by "chaperones"— other designated prisoners — into her family's quarters. It took planning and forethought to make the trip since waiting time had to be factored in. The gate was an impediment, one more curtailment of freedom, and one more disruption of the family unit.

MARY'S HEALTH

IN LOOKING BACK I SEE I MISSED CUES AS TO HOW MUCH MARY HAD physically suffered in camp.

She became ill early in her stay.

In late-May she had visited the clinic with pain in her lower right abdomen and complaints of severe constipation. An Issei physician prescribed a daily enema to be administered by Mary's mother. The next day it was suggested that ice packs be applied; the day after, codeine was prescribed because her pain had intensified. Within twenty-four hours Mary was rushed in an emergency vehicle to the Pierce

County Hospital outside the Assembly Center. She was in agony. They found that a large fecal mass, caused by severe constipation, was pressing against her right fallopian tube.

The pain lasted for a week and then gradually subsided as the remedies worked.

During the Pierce County Hospital visit, she was also told that she was pregnant.

IN THE FIRST WEEK OF AUGUST, MARY RAN A TEMPERATURE AND SUF-fered from significant tenderness, this time in her lower left abdomen. She went to the Assembly Center's clinic, where they discovered a "palpable mass the size of a three-month pregnancy." One doctor diagnosed a cystic mass as large as an orange, fixed and blending into the uterine lining. Another doctor thought it could be an ectopic pregnancy with the possibility of death.

On August 17 Yoshizo, Mon, and Frank were transferred to the high desert Minidoka camp in Hunt, Idaho. Mary and Shig followed three weeks later, after a thirty-hour grueling train ride.

Her pain had subsided just before they'd boarded the train.

THE ENVIRONMENT

THEY CLIMBED DOWN FROM THE TRAIN INTO BLAZING HOT SUN. THE temperature was a scorching high nineties, the air as dry as dust and a shock after the humid atmosphere of Seattle; it was an unforgiving climate for Mary's beautiful complexion. They were herded with the others onto old army buses and driven over gravel roads to the camp, where they were greeted at the gate by Mon, Yoshizo, and Frank.

Ever the optimist, Mary told an interviewer from the *Popular Balanchine Dossiers* in 2001, "There, they were ready for us. They had all the housing and the bathhouses, and the kitchen and everything, but they still had the guards, you know." In reality, according to historical documents, she and the other prisoners were met with more crude, unfinished barracks, intermittent running water, and no sewage system, compromised medical services, and pit latrines.

A five-mile barbed wire fence around the camp hadn't been completed, giving a semblance of freedom. They could have walked out into the seemingly infinite high desert, and if in a dream, just kept going, under a cloudless pale blue sky, though they'd be anything but anonymous in the white Idaho population, and most certainly would be captured and returned to the facility.

The imagined sense of freedom made it that much harder to bear the reality when the fence was eventually finished and the last of the watchtowers, eight in all, were in place. In that same interview she gave in 2001 she still maintained that she was half Chinese, similar to "the Eskimo children," or "papooses that they brought down from Alaska, because they were part Japanese. It was really unbelievable."

THE CAMP COVERED 68,000 ACRES, AND CONTAINED THE LARGEST city for hundreds of miles, with over 9,000 inhabitants, mostly from Seattle. At almost 4,000 feet above sea level, it was a harsh environment of sagebrush, petrified basaltic lava flows, and cinder cones. There were rattlesnakes and scorpions in abundance. By winter it would go down to thirty degrees below zero and the next summer it hit one hundred and fifteen, compounding the extreme discomfort of living in shack-like structures with no insulation, covered with black tar-paper.

During preparation for construction of camp buildings the earth had been scraped clean of vegetation, leaving open sandy ground between the barracks and along the firebreaks. It rained that November and the exposed surface turned to ankle-deep mud.

In summer when the mud dried, the camp was plagued with high winds and dust storms that bent the few spindly trees to the ground and turned the air an ominous yellow; the blowing, stabbing sand became so thick people couldn't see a foot ahead. Even with a bandana tied tightly over the face, fine dust penetrated the damp edges of eyes and entered firmly closed mouths so that evacuees ate grit for hours afterward. Dust breathed up into nasal passages caused severe nosebleeds.

Years later I couldn't help but wonder if Mary's nosebleeds, in the aftermath of the attack on the World Trade Center when we'd endured weeks of dense particulate-and-stench-polluted air, weren't a somatic recall of her days in Minidoka camp.

POLITICS

ADDED TO THE INHOSPITABLE PHYSICAL CONDITIONS WAS THE charged political climate in Idaho, led by Governor Clark Chase who had been militantly resistant to building the camp in his state.

Outspoken in his contempt for Japanese Americans, he proclaimed, "I don't trust any of them. They're all enemy aliens. Japs live like rats, breed like rats, and act like rats. Send them all back to Japan, then sink the island."

IN THE FIRST WEEK OF OCTOBER FEDERAL MARSHALS REMOVED SHIG from the new camp, and accompanied him back to Seattle to testify in a trial in which charges had been brought against his former employer, import-export businessman Charles Takahashi, owner of C.K. Takahashi, and another employee, Edward Ozawa — Shig's brother-in-law — for possible acts of treason.

Shig was accused of traveling to Mexico in 1941, allegedly to make a transfer of scrap iron to Japan through a third party, in violation of the Trading with Enemies Act.

Charles Takahashi and Ed Ozawa had already been arraigned by a federal grand jury under the same act. They had been sitting in the King County jail for eleven months, since shortly after Pearl Harbor, because they couldn't raise the bond of $25,000 per man. When Shig arrived in Seattle he was remanded to jail for ten days while he waited to testify. He later sardonically explained, "We'd all been evacuated from Seattle so the only alternative for me was naturally to stay in the jail."

He testified that he had traveled to Mexico on business for Taka-hashi, with one William T. Shenker whom the FBI described as a "disbarred Oregon Jewish attorney." Shig swore under oath that he had no knowledge of any sale to an enemy country. Though this incident would later have repercussions for him and Mary, for the time being he was free to rejoin Mary back in the concentration camp, transported under guard of the federal marshals.

Mary's health

On November 18 Mary visited the Minidoka hospital for a checkup. She had been menstruating regularly since the August visit, so even though her abdomen was enlarged and tender, it was evident that she wasn't pregnant. She thought she'd been eating too much, but the doctor discovered that her cyst had grown to the size of a grapefruit. The tumor was pushing against the right side of her abdomen, displacing the right ovary. That ovary contained a number of cystic growths.

The attending doctor was none other than Dr. Mitsuo Paul Suzuki, the young Issei who had undertaken to inoculate hundreds of Seattle residents against typhoid fever before they were forcibly removed from the city. She was finally in good hands. Nonetheless, an oophorectomy was performed to remove the left ovary, and dermoid cysts on the right ovary were excised. Mary remained in the camp hospital for a month until she had healed from the operation.

On a follow-up exam, more cysts were found in the right ovary. There was no mention in the records of another ovary removal, though her last exam stated that her "small right ovary" was palpable, which indicated that the situation had become a problem; she was started on Neelin, an estrogen-based hormone used as replacement therapy for post-menopausal symptoms.

A month later she was having a bad reaction to the drug; she had lesions on her face, and her skin was abnormally oily, and her fingernails were splitting. She was taken off the estrogen replacement.

Disruption of the Family

There was no respite for Mary and Shig. Their marriage wouldn't survive their imprisonment in Minidoka camp.

But why did they separate? Did government accusations against Shig play a part? The FBI described him as "an agitator, troublemaker, a member of a dangerous group." They said he was "dangerous because of his activities within the Puyallup Assembly Center and Minidoka Relocation Project." His name was included in a list of Minidoka residents "recommended for segregation from loyal Japanese."

Shig was cited by the FBI for being a member of the Cannery Union, "a suspected subversive organization, known to be controlled by Communists," when he'd worked as a laborer for the New England Fish Company in Seattle in the 1930s, painting him guilty with a wide anti-red brush. This would be a far cry from the Watanabe family's desire for their children to assimilate, which during wartime necessitated being upstanding loyal citizens, holding conservative political values.

Politics

From the beginning, in the assembly center and then in Minidoka, there were intense disagreements among the prisoners, with one faction wanting to co-operate with the administration, and another refusing to acquiesce to authority. Shig was in the latter group. The political divisiveness between factions in camp was immensely destructive to the population's sense of self and community, and the tensions exacerbated any discord already existing in private family lives.

Disruption of the Family

I've wondered if mon and yoshizo pressured Mary to separate from Shig out of fear that guilt by association with "troublemakers" might spread to their daughter, and jeopardize her future, their son's, and theirs, in the eyes of the government and within their community, forcing Mary to choose between loyalty to them and loyalty to her new husband.

Or was it Shig's drinking and gambling that became too much for her? "He was okay when we got married, but in camp all he did was drink and gamble," she had said to me. It's possible. A known gambler, Kiyoshi Roy Suyetani, was included by the FBI in Shig's "dangerous group."

I sensed from his files that Shig had become a very angry man — a completely understandable, and an appropriate response to the circumstances.

But Mary was a person who coped, who retained her optimism and humor to the end, using it to advantage even when as an old woman she lost control over her own life and memory. She would soon display a comparable mix of courtesy and firmness of purpose as she worked to get Shig and herself out of camp.

Or could Mary's inability to bear children have hastened the demise of their marriage? If that was the case, the Incarceration played its part. The stress of the upheaval and forced separation from her previous life and the lack of proper health care and sanitation in the early days of removal to Puyallup were undoubtedly factors leading to the tragic loss of her ability to bear a child.

"Maybe it wasn't so bad that I was sent to camp, otherwise I would be married and taking care of children," she had said many times.

But Mary loved children. She doted on the smallest neighbors living in her apartment building, taped their drawings to the outside of her door as though they were her grandchildren's art, gave them little presents, and listened intently to their stories. The children loved her in return.

Only in the last year of her life would she say she regretted never having a child. I had countered, "But you have me as your daughter." She gave me a look that said, "What temerity, what are you talking about?"

Because I had chosen not to have a child, I'd assumed we were the same. But now I imagined her saying, "I wish I'd had a baby and held her and brought her up." She once told me wistfully, "My baby would have been beautiful." Her longing had nothing to do with having an adult daughter to care for her in old age, nor did it have to do with making a choice. Choice had cruelly been taken from her. She must have mourned the dead fetus that had turned into the grapefruit-sized cyst that eventually left her unable to bear a child. But she had to put up a good front, to convince the world and herself that she didn't want to be a mother, another fabrication of self-preservation, a deception she perhaps grew to believe after years of repetition.

I HAD LET HER DOWN BY CONFUSING MY OWN ATTITUDES AND NEEDS with hers. I hadn't listened beneath the surface of her pronouncements for more complex feelings about motherhood. Maybe I hadn't wanted to allow any opening for examining my own ambivalence about having a child. It was easier to simply say that I didn't want to be a mother than to delve into why or why not.

Looking back now, given what I was to learn about her life, I believe she would have loved the opportunity to have that beautiful little girl. As for me, for a short period, I longed for a girl who I would call Mitzie, a mix of Marnie and Fritz, but I continued to fear that I would be a terrible mother.

I did a disservice to Mary, thinking we were the same.

Mary's health

Many years later when Mary and I visited the Actors Fund Residence in search of a suitable apartment for her, she angrily threw at me this observation: "You have to share a bathroom here!"

Then when she found a perfect unit in the Vista, and moved in there, she'd had terrible stomach trouble, including episodes of severe explosive diarrhea.

By the end of her life, she became obsessed with the bathroom, going back-and-forth all day long, eventually devolving into a compulsion to repeat a return to the toilet, only to flush, as though trying to expel and resolve her traumatic memory of camp and the horrific latrine situation that had led to her extreme constipation.

A Surprising Shared History

IN MY SEARCH FOR MARY I HAD COME UPON THE QUOTE FROM A MAN who vividly recounted, fifty years later, the experience as a young university student, of waiting for the transport to Puyallup Assembly Center. "The sight of hundreds of people assembled with assorted baggage lined up to board the buses at the embarkation point, with rifle-bearing soldiers standing around as guards, is still imprinted in my memory. I remember my acute sense of embitterment, humiliation, resentment, anger, depression, and concern as we rode the 30 miles to the Puyallup Fairground. The miserable facilities at this assembly center compounded these feelings."

At the end of his description I had been startled to read his name — Frank Miyamoto. He was the Nisei sociologist I'd first encountered in the Bancroft Library papers, who had written from Tule Lake, "There's one man in the administration that we can trust, it's Elberson"[my Father]. Finding Frank Miyamoto again in a new context brought me full circle. He must have gone from Puyallup to Tule Lake.

I combed the Internet for him; there were many references to his tenure at the University of Washington and his esteemed scholarly work, including a few items pertaining to my father in Tule Lake. I found an address for him in Seattle. My hopes rose. I clicked on the address praying for a phone number, and the notation came up — deceased. He had died the year before at the age of one hundred, the same age my father would have been had he lived. He and my father were young men together in the Tule Lake camp, two intellectuals just about to turn thirty, who had been graduate students at the University of Washington in overlapping years, who had actively shared and were shaped by the experience of the Incarceration.

Frank Miyamoto's Tule Lake journals had read like elegant and objective journalism. He hadn't fawned over my father. He'd respected his position on some issues, but had criticized him as well, saying he could be too intent on making the co-op work, at times pushing people too hard. I imagined him lingering after dinner in my parents' barracks — as I'd read other Nisei documenting such evenings in our barracks — seated with my father on the Sears and Roebuck sofa discussing and arguing over matters of the co-op, racism in America, and postulating about what the future held for those who had been torn away from their lives.

Miyamoto was a contemporary of Mary's who had gone to the same assembly center as she had, maybe even eaten in the mess hall with her and Shig, maybe they had been friends —a man who had suffered through the forced confinement as she had and gone forward into a successful career. No longer simply words on the page, he became for me a living, breathing participant in the life of my family during a critical period of their lives. I may even have looked up at him from my crib when he visited our barracks. How do I explain what I felt finding Frank Miyamoto again? I was discovering a place in America that I could call my own, a home town of prisoners with whom I shared not just a prison camp surrounded by barbed wire, but an emotional, intellectual, racial, and political history. I had been looking for Mary, and she was leading me back to myself and to my tiny family. I wished I could have been telling her as I went along what I found about the two of us, how connected we were, beyond what we could have imagined.

I OPENED MY COMPUTER IN MARCH OF 2013 TO AN E-MAIL FROM Valerie Yasukochi, the daughter of one of Mary's loves, George.

"My husband and I are coming to New York in July!"

Shortly before they were scheduled to arrive Valerie phoned to say she had been going through her father's correspondence files, and "I haven't found anything from Mary. He married my mother soon after he wrote the last letter. Maybe he destroyed them because of that. But I can bring you others from the early forties. There are some written from Tule Lake and Minidoka."

A day later an e-mail came from her. "What was your father's name again, and where was he in the '40s? before Tule Lake? In Wash state?"

I began an e-mail back to her: "His name was Donald Elberson. He received his undergraduate and his masters at the University of Washington. He went on to do Ph.D. work at Stanford in economics. He was somehow associated with the Berkeley Co-op . . . ."

Before I could finish, another ping sounded. It was Valerie again. "I found your father's name in a letter from a "Hank" who was at Tule Lake. Your father's name is Don Elberson!"

Minutes later another e-mail came through. "I think our parents knew each other! I came across a letter from a "Ted" dated 6/30/42, Tule Lake Colony . . . .. I found a sentence 'Bob Ota and Don Elberson are both here, and wish me to say hello to you when I write. Elberson is here in connection with the Co-op Movement.'"

It took me a moment to realize the full significance of the two sentences. Not only did Valerie's father know who my father was, but they had known each other before the camps. I had always assumed that my father's first connection with Japanese Americans was at Tule Lake. This one sentence told me that he had been involved with like-minded intellectuals and activists in the Nisei community before he went to Tule Lake. Frank Miyamoto writing that my father was the one person in the administration that could be trusted, could be read in a new way. Miyamoto perhaps knew my father from the University of Washington or at least had word of him before they'd met at Tule Lake. For me this was significant. Maybe my parents hadn't gone to Tule Lake camp on a simple wave of do-gooder's emotion, but rather they had taken the camp jobs, especially my father's co-op assignment, with acquaintance with the pre-camp lives of Japanese American activists and intellectuals, comrades-in-arms in some cases, peers who were enduring a grave setback.

I remembered Frank Miyamoto's acerbic comments about other liberal staff members, in particular one Quaker woman whom he considered a "bleeding heart." "Her pallid features stare out from behind a severe hair line and her earnest eyes have the glint of the reformer in them." Of a male staff member, he said, "I feel he wanted to sympathize and 'love' the evacuees too much." Miyamoto's sharp tongue was never applied to my father; on the contrary he argued directly and concretely, on an equal basis with him about the politics of the camp and the co-op.

Valerie wrote, "This connection is almost more than I can bear."

I felt the same. It was as though I had found kin. As my family had moved from place to place, the only children with whom I could feel completely comfortable were those whose parents were in the co-op movement. I didn't have to watch my words around them. I didn't have to hide that my father had been a pacifist during World War II because a number of their parents were Quakers. Valerie and I had the added connection of the Incarceration. She was instilled with the same philosophy of the co-operative movement, not a small influence in families such as ours, with parents who believed in the efficacy of people of all races and creeds joining together to achieve economic equality.

Valerie and I were the daughters of iconoclastic fathers who were committed to a political movement that had an enormous impact on people in the camps. My father had said this was a story not much spoken of on the outside during the war — for obvious reasons neither at the time — nor afterward. It was too progressive for the general American population to know, but Valerie and I knew it in our blood. In a sense we were sisters under the skin, and to me the most incredible aspect was that Mary had brought us together.

We made arrangements for Valerie to come to my office where I had all the material on Mary.

A heat wave had hit the city on the day of our meeting; temperatures were in the upper nineties and the humidity was over ninety percent.

Valerie arrived with her husband, a very nice Caucasian man in his sixties. By my calculations she should also have been in her early sixties, but she looked more like forty. Exceptionally pretty, with cropped hair, slender and fit, dressed in shorts and a singlet, she moved like a young person, her athletic body and expressive hands animating her speech. Hers was the verbal energy of an extremely smart person. She was emphatically her father's daughter.

She had brought copies of more letters from "Hank" and "Ted" as well as a publication by the Berkeley Historical Society entitled *A Conversation with George Yasukochi*, which included two photos of George dated 1940, the year of his last letters to Mary.

In one he was lounging on a bed in his dormitory room with a cheerleading megaphone to his lips, "singing a CAL song." The other was of him in his family home, posing before a gas fireplace in the parlor, a well-appointed room with fine floral wallpaper, heavy upholstered furniture, and an oriental rug, similar in terms of class status to the photo I'd seen of Mary's prewar family home.

He was dressed in formal attire for his graduation, complete with bow tie and double-breasted tuxedo jacket, looking very cute, with an engaging grin and a mischievous twinkle in his eyes behind his wire-rimmed glasses. No wonder Mary had saved his correspondence for seventy years. He would have made a charming, appropriate match, though he wasn't as sexually alluring as Shig, at least not in the photos. Mary had opted for the renegade Shig, but she had carried on a flirtatious, come-hither correspondence with George over the two years when she must have been closing in on her engagement. The seed of rebellion was in her long before she broke away from a conventional life.

The camp letters to George and *The Conversation with George Yasukochi* told a story of young men overcoming discrimination to reach high goals of achievement. George had commuted from home during his first two years at Berkeley because it was difficult to get a room as a non-Caucasian. But in his junior year he applied to Oxford House, a student co-op residence that operated on a non-discriminatory basis. This reminded me of my mother, who had to belong to a house for independents when she attended the University of Washington because the other housing — mostly run by the sororities — was restricted, which meant it did not allow Jews.

The Tule Lake letters came from "Hank" and "Ted" and others who were all George's fellow Oxford House Nisei graduates. Theirs was an intense comradeship among brilliant young men ready to step out into the world to test their abilities, but who, with the exception of George, now were caught in a no-man's land, imprisoned behind barbed wire in the Tule Lake camp with no sense of what the future would hold. They had finished their studies at the university so they weren't eligible to obtain leave-clearance to attend school as their younger siblings could. In the world beyond the gates there were no jobs available for Japanese Americans at their level of education.

Hank obtained a position in camp as a sanitary engineer, to operate and maintain the sewage disposal plant and pumping system for the Tule Lake community of 18,000. He made twelve dollars a month for his work. He got a lot of ribbing about odors, but he was grateful to get the useful experience and the opportunity to do work that he wouldn't be offered if he were on the "outside."

Discrimination on the West Coast had been so high before the war that most of the graduates could not look forward to much more than menial labor, even with their degrees from Berkeley — unless they moved east, as many would after they were released.

In one letter. Hank wrote, "Don Elberson, the Co-op specialist, is a right guy, but the head man, Smith . . . seems to want to force us into this Co-op system in the typical high-handed Caucasian manner, taking advantage of the color-line."

On December 22, 1942, as Hank looked for employment on the outside, he wrote, " . . . we were interviewed several weeks back regarding a job as industrial chemist in a gigantic Co-operative Association plant in Kansas City, MO., by Don Elberson, but that was all I heard." It recalled the letter from my father to the Consumer Cooperative Association in Kansas City in which he was furious at them for resisting hiring an Issei man on grounds that there would be racial reprisals from the local white community.

When she returned to California, Valerie sent me another packet that included her father George's retirement speech after sixty-years with the Berkeley Co-op, in which the voice of the young man who had written to Mary still lived: his wit, his circuitous paths for pursuing a passionate thought, as well as his seriousness of purpose and commitment to high-minded political positions. This time the writing was not directed at Mary nor did it make reference to her, but rather he spoke of his wife Bess, whom he married in 1942 after he "rescued Bess from the Tanforan internment camp horse stables... and thus she was doomed to a life as a Co-op widow." My mother would have nodded in recognition of what it was like to be married to a man ardently committed to making change in the world.

George went on, "As an American of Japanese ancestry, I can never forget that when the chips were down and war flared up in 1941 between the land of my parents and the land of my birth and beliefs, Co-op people were in the forefront among those that stood by our families in that traumatic situation."

To both Valerie's father and mine, the co-operative movement was close to a religion. It was not a perfect union of racial and economic justice, but at least it strove to meet those high ideals.

My father often said that the one and only good aspect of the internment was that it opened the Nisei to a wider world and eventually the world opened up to them. That comment had embarrassed me over the years, making me ashamed of his lapse into incorrect politics.

I never repeated his statement to people who had been incarcerated, nor to any friends who took strong leftist positions. But as I read these letters, I recalled the day Noboru Honda, who went on from Tule Lake to a highly successful career as an insurance broker in Chicago, had called me at my home when my father died. He said, "What I remember most about your dad was that he always said, 'Noby, think, analyze, and then think again.' I was unschooled when I got to camp because I had to quit after elementary school to provide for my brothers and sisters. I've used the advice for over fifty-five years. It has held me in good stead."

Years later the family of yoshimi shibata, another nisei with whom my father had worked closely in the Tule Lake co-op, contacted me because a personal film documentary was being made on his life. Shibata was disappearing deeper into dementia and couldn't articulate the experience of the co-op for a segment on Tule Lake. His wife and son said, "He loved your father and we thought perhaps you could come and be in the film and speak with him about his time there and his relationship to your father."

After the war Shibata had returned to Palo Alto from Chicago with two strong-arm men to forcibly reclaim the flower growing enterprise founded in 1906 by his father, and built over the years into a large retail and wholesale business.

It had been appropriated by Italian Americans when he'd been sent to camp. That had been a bitter pill for Yoshimi Shibata. It was similar to Mary's experience considering that Italy — like Japan — was a member of the Axis powers, yet Italian Americans were not interned as he was.

Once he had the farm back, he worked night and day, applying his intelligence and business smarts to turn the operation, Mt. Eden Floral Company, into the largest floral center on the west coast.

Shibata lived with his wife, Grace, in a beautiful, sprawling ranch-style home surrounded by over an acre of a manicured Japanese garden. His short-term memory was diminished and his recollections of his time in camp were indeed fading, but when he learned that I was my father's daughter he perked up, attaching himself to me with an intensity that could only be understood as transferred fondness; he held me physically close while we toured his gracious garden.

As we sat on an oversized moss-green sofa in their grand living room and the filming began, he came alive, forthcoming, and articulate for over an hour of intense interaction during the taping, recounting his leadership success in camp, but also painful episodes of that same period, and his fears when he had to summon the courage to take back what was rightfully his on his return to California.

He told how he had especially liked talking with my father. "We were good friends." He told of the politics of the co-op, his disagreements with the camp administrative polices, and issues of racism against Japanese Americans. He said my father was open to speaking his own mind and receptive to whatever he, Shibata, had to say.

Later at a luncheon in an upscale restaurant, he insisted on sitting by my side. He wouldn't let go of my hand, even as he dozed off from exhaustion. Whenever he woke during the lunch it was to repeat how my father and the co-op had saved him.

I was taken with how my father's interactions with this man had been transformed into feelings akin to love. My father was an exuberant and warm being, but he didn't speak of himself in personal terms. It was a different time, and people, especially those doing political work, rarely evinced any self-referential emotion, considered indulgent and immodest in the face of others' suffering.

IN MY FATHER'S CASE, THROUGHOUT MY CHILDHOOD I SAW HOW PEOPLE interpreted his political openness and respect for their opinions as love, even when they didn't put that name on it.

I mention this now because for me, in writing this book, the hardest part has been to feel I have the right to expose my opinions and loves and hates and ambivalence on the page, particularly in the shadow of Japanese American suffering. I've thought that my father and my mother wouldn't approve of any deviation from the purely political. But I've come to understand that my father found a way to feed his need for love by caring for others, as do I, apparently.

I also see that my father was not wrong in saying that the camp experience, though devastating for so many, did send young ambitious Nisei back out into the larger world with even greater determination to succeed. His ability and openness to acknowledge uncomfortable truths in pursuit of a deeper understanding of politics and history was admirable and necessary to advancing the arc of progress. This admission doesn't absolve our nation of the egregious act and shouldn't be construed as an apologia for any forced incarceration, past or future, based on race and ethnicity, but only as an acknowledgement that tragedies can sometimes breed surprising rewards, especially when people are as intent on moving forward as the Nisei were.

In Mary's case it was certainly true. When I continued to search for the details of her life after camp and saw how much was due to hard work and ambition and how much was luck, I had to concede that there was some validity to her statement that day on the park bench, "You know maybe it was good that I was sent to camp."

Even her choice to pass as Chinese American was fueled by her determination to go forward into the America that had betrayed her.

26

Permission to Leave the Camp
"It's a Shame the Girl's a Jap"

```
To: War Relocation Authority Board,
Washington, D. C.
Attention Mr. Dillon S. Myer, Director
Re:  Okada, Teru No. 10902
     Minidoka, WRA
     38-7-A
```

Dear Sir:

It is a shame that this girl is a Jap. She has a fine education, knows how to express herself in writing and has wit.

She never worked for me but I know of her ability as she was in and out of my building when she was working for the importing company. I have acted as her attorney in several small matters and found her to be a very fine girl. She associated mostly with the white girls in Seattle and from her general make up you would think her a Chinese girl rather than a Jap.

I believe her to be a loyal American, she being born here and raised in our schools. Of course this talk of sending American born Japs back to Japan and taking their American citizenship from them does not set very well

on their minds as it makes them lose faith in
the American Constitution.

This girl received a good training in
her home as her parents were clean in the
home and hard workers. She has a good education and if you could get a hold of some of
her correspondence, both in business and in
friendship you would soon find that she is a
very bright girl.

She would be a credit to any office as she
would attend to business and look out for the
interest of her employer.

Its [sic] a shame that she is a Jap.

Yours truly,

C.B.W. Raymond

IN FEBRUARY OF 1943, WHEN MARY APPLIED FOR SECURITY CLEAR-
ance to leave camp, her brother Frank had already been accepted and
was studying at Syracuse University.

In order to earn his leave clearance to attend Syracuse, Mary
— ever generous and responsible as the older sibling and the girl in
the family — had gone to great lengths in her letter to the National
Student Relocation Commission. She pledged the entire two hundred dollars in her and Shig's bank accounts toward Frank's tuition,
and offered to sell all her war bonds, which were worth one hundred
dollars. "Perhaps our total amount is insufficient to be of any aid,"
she wrote, "but our desire to help Frank is so strong that we have
arranged with friends to do likewise if necessary."

Once he was safely in the university, she plead Shig's and her
cases. They didn't let the authorities know they would be divorcing.

As with Frank's application, she had to obtain letters of support
from upstanding Caucasian citizens who had known her prior to
evacuation.

I found in the National Archives the above letter from attorney C. B. W. Raymond. He did speak the truth when he complimented her letter writing. In all her letters her use of language, syntax, clarity, allusion, and perfect grammar were far superior to any of those written by Caucasian friends on her behalf or by Washington, DC bureaucrats who would determine her future. Attorney Raymond was the first of twelve Caucasians in Seattle, Portland, and Pasadena on her list of references to petition. Fortunately the others told of years of friendship.

During the period when Mary was applying for leave clearance, the government had begun the notorious program of imposing mandatory camp wide loyalty oaths that would lead to intractable tensions throughout the community. Mary, Frank, Yoshizo, Mon, and Shig all signed "yes" to the two questions. I was surprised that Shig signed "yes" given his reputation with the authorities. His eagerness to get out of camp or pressure exerted on him by Mary might have convinced him it was best to do so. Or he was just a pragmatic man who decided that nothing could be gained by taking a principled stand. Or possibly he had never been a troublemaker and had been wrongly accused by an overzealous FBI and War Relocation Administration.

Mary and Shig had to have gainful employment waiting for them before they could be released, comparable to immigrants or refugees entering America. Mary wrote to a War Relocation supervisor in Toledo, Ohio inquiring about a listing for a public accountant for Shig and an opening for a stenographer for her. She told him they'd like to work in Toledo rather than Chicago because "we both feel that Chicago will be a duplicate of the pattern formerly laid on the West Coast, that is, congregation of Japanese Americans." This was unusual since many internees applied to go to Chicago precisely because there was a Japanese American community. She went on to explain that, "We shouldn't find it too difficult to intermingle with Caucasians having done so since childhood days."

She received a prompt reply informing her that Mr. Herman Weiner of the National Shoe Service Company of Toledo was offering Mary employment as a stenographer and for Shig, work as a stock clerk. They would each earn twenty-five dollars a week, though their payments were to be calculated differently. She would be paid for a forty-hour work week, while Shig would receive an hourly rate of fifty cents for forty hours, with enough overtime to make up the difference. In addition, during slack time in the shipping department, he could be trained as a glove cutter.

The letter ended with the caveat that though the citizens of Toledo had favorable attitudes toward Japanese Americans, housing could be a problem. In other words, Shig and Mary could come to work but they wouldn't be welcome to live in the Caucasian neighborhoods or any place else in Toledo. Mary responded that in the interim Shig had found work in Cleveland at the Federal Foundry Supply Company, where they would pay him $160.00 per month, plus overtime. I suspect that Shig, who held a management position in a company before his world fell apart, was insulted by the Toledo offer and had rejected it outright. Ever gracious, Mary thanked the supervisor for his help.

This is where Shig and Mary parted company. Though she traveled by train to Cleveland to see him in June, she didn't stay, but headed to New York City where she had found a position as a secretary and receptionist with the Community Service Society on East Twenty-third Street in Manhattan. She said goodbye to the handsome young man who had taught her to ski and play golf; gone was any fantasy of married life or any hope for a beautiful baby.

Shig's employment at the foundry supply company was abruptly terminated after only two weeks of employment. The reason given was that he was a security risk and therefore could not work in the defense industry. He was taken off the floor, finger-printed, and told to leave the plant immediately. A few days later, Shig moved to Chicago.

Eventually, Mary was able to attend the Juilliard School, but I did not find a recommendation letter from Eleanor Roosevelt in her records in the National Archives, and Juilliard destroys all applicants' admissions files after a few years. Eleanor Roosevelt may have used another channel, but a search of the Roosevelt archives turned up nothing, not even Mary's much touted visit by Mrs. Roosevelt to Minidoka camp.

Mary's story could have been an ego-saving construct of her coping mechanism or slippage in the less than meticulous record keeping of the War Relocation Authority.

Minidoka Concentration Camp with snow on the ground, Hunt, Idaho, 1942

Like other Issei, Yoshiko and Mon remained behind the barbed wire of Minidoka, even as their children left for work, school, and to fight the war in Europe — this was yet another way that families were torn apart by their incarceration.

Many were reluctant to leave camp, afraid to venture out into a world that was hostile to them, without the comfort and safety of their Japanese American community. They also didn't have the option of release from prison as it was supremely difficult to find work in America as aliens, or as Mary wrote in a letter to authorities, "Our parents brought us up to be good and loyal citizens though they were barred by law to become naturalized."

Mon and Yoshizo did not have a fluent command of written English and spoke with pronounced Japanese accents as was the case for any first-generation immigrant, but this was wartime and the Japanese were the enemy, so having such an accent was a real detriment that caused them embarrassment and an additional reason to be fearful.

LEAVING THEM BEHIND, ESPECIALLY LEAVING MON, MUST HAVE BEEN extremely painful for Mary. She had to put aside her enormous sorrow at age twenty-seven in order to venture out with no family to help her emotionally or financially, with only the $50 send-off stipend from the War Relocation Authority in her pocketbook. Her situation was comparable to a refugee who has been torn from life on another continent, to find a path alone into an unknown future. The quote that plays in my head as I think of her at this turning point, as she left camp, is of James Joyce's young artist going forth, "To forge in the smithy of my soul, the uncreated conscience of my race."

27

It's Not Over Yet

THERE ARE NO IMAGES OF MARY IN PUYALLUP OR MINIDOKA, OR OF Shig or the rest of her family. The reason is simple — during the time Shig and Mary were there, personal cameras were still forbidden inside the camp, though the ban was later lifted. Shig's Kodaks and another camera owned by Mon remained in a government warehouse.

Additionally, only official photographs were permitted, either those shot by the War Relocation Authority hires, such as Dorothea Lange, or by outside photographers of the government's choosing, including Ansel Adams, who each did studies of Manzanar camp, which were censored and idealized. As for Minidoka, the camp photos were taken by Francis L. Stewart and were for the most part skewed toward depicting a normalized and positive view of life in the camp. Photographs by Russell Lee follow the Issei men who went out of the camp into the fields to help with the war effort by harvesting beets. These more than any others depict the despondency and loneliness of their years of incarceration.

MARY'S FIRST POST-CAMP PHOTO, TAKEN IN THE EARLY WINTER OF 1943, was of a happy brother and sister standing in front of Juilliard School on Convent Avenue and 122nd Street in Manhattan. Frank wore his army uniform. You can almost read the balloon over their heads: We made it! He had graduated from Syracuse University and was attending the Army Language School in Minnesota. She had enrolled at Juilliard.

Mary in Riverside Park, NYC, May 1944, newly arrived in the City
Her expression hints of quiet joy and relief; she is finally free.

In a later snapshot Mary poses alone under a blossoming cherry tree in a park on northern Riverside Drive in Manhattan, wearing a stylish hat of the period and a two-piece suit, with a demure ruffled white collar peeking out. She's carrying white gloves and a handbag as she smiles sweetly into the camera. Her expression hints of quiet joy and relief; she is finally free.

But the truth be told — though they were out of the camps — the Incarceration continued to cast a long shadow, exercising a powerful grip on them.

When Mary arrived in New York in 1943, she moved to New Jersey to live with her Caucasian sponsors, another requirement for obtaining leave clearance. Think of it, having to get a sponsor in order to live in your country of birth.

Sixty years later she told an interviewer, "My sponsor was a Baptist minister. He and his wife lived in Ridgewood, New Jersey. Every morning I had to make their breakfast and catch the 8 a.m. bus to the city."

She worked an eight-hour day in midtown before traveling uptown for an evening music class, and afterward catching the bus back to New Jersey. She put in hours of practice time on weekends. "I was falling asleep because when I got home I had to help with the cooking, and then on the weekend I had to do the laundry. They had a wonderful maid in me. My instructor at Juilliard said, 'You can't keep this up . . .,' and she found me a room in International House, . . . a little, tiny room. You had to share the bathroom, too, you know, shower and everything."

Mary (seated against the center of the fireplace) in I-house
at a lecture by Dr. John R. Mott, winner of the Nobel Peace Prize in 1946.

I-House, as it's commonly called, was built in 1924 as a residence where men and women, mostly young, from around the world could live and learn together in a diverse community. The alumni include distinguished professionals who went on to great heights of success: Nigerian writer Chinua Achebe, Broadway star Patti LuPone, opera diva Leontyne Price, and future CEO of Citigroup, Vikram Pandit. Located in the Morningside Heights neighborhood of northern Manhattan, abutting Riverside Park and Grant's Tomb, its grand building sits adjacent to Sakura Park, a small, peaceful, two-acre green area with a dozen cherry trees donated in 1912 by the Committee of Japanese Residents of New York. The cherry trees that bloomed in frothy pink the next spring had to feel to Mary like a celebration of her freedom, though bittersweet, thinking of her parents back in the stark environment of the camp.

JUILLIARD SCHOOL OF MUSIC WAS AT THAT TIME DIVIDED INTO THE Institute of Musical Art and the Juilliard Graduate School. Mary enrolled in the Institute of Musical Art's Department of Special Classes, Voice Program and Extension Division on Claremont Avenue and 122nd Street, only steps from I-House and Sakura Park. The building, which still stands, is an elegant limestone structure adorned with stone carvings of violins, trombones, bagpipes, and musical notes high upon its facade. It was an extraordinary experience — both daunting and uplifting — for Mary to enter the building that fall of 1943, with light streaming into the grand foyer through large arched windows and a marble staircase with wrought-iron balustrades sweeping up to the second floor.

She matriculated in a special program for students who had to work for a living. Her voice teacher that first year was Muriel Tannehill Dansereau, a lyric soprano, who had found her the room in I-House.

In the winter semester of 1943 Mary took one hour of singing per week and two hours of Rudiments of Music and Elementary

Harmony. The second semester, spring of 1944, her schedule with Dansereau was the same.

"The school considered that I didn't have any money, so they let me have old music scores . . . there was a broken-down piano that I used for practice," Mary later told an interviewer.

Beyond her salary at the Community Service Society, and her part time work as a cashier in the cafeteria, where she ate her "meals for lunchtime and suppertime," the only extra money she had to fall back on was the fifty-dollar stipend which she hadn't yet spent.

AN UNSETTLING PICTURE EMERGED DURING THE YEARS SPANNING 1943 to 1945 that was as fraught with difficulty as the previous two.

Mary and Shig had formally separated, and their divorce was pending.

On a number of occasions in the early spring of 1944, she had to travel to Cleveland, and later to Chicago to deal with Shig's lawyer concerning their mutual property, and also with her parents' belongings that were mingled with Mary's in-laws' belongings and were in storage in Seattle.

THEN ON MARCH 18, 1944 ONE OF THE WAR RELOCATION AUTHORITY offices in Chicago ordered Shig to appear before a panel to determine if his temporary leave clearance should be rescinded, which would return him to Minidoka camp. He underwent intensive questioning about the scrap metal incident when he had traveled to Mexico for Charles Takahashi's company.

Ten tense days went by before he heard that he'd been cleared and awarded permanent leave clearance.

IN APRIL A MAJOR INCIDENT ERUPTED IN NEW YORK CITY. MAYOR Fiorello LaGuardia, a progressive Republican renowned for his strong positions supporting racial equality and immigrant rights, suddenly swerved and came out vociferously against the relocation of Japanese Americans to New York City from "west coast concentration camps." He went on an oratorical rampage filled with racially-tinged declarations against having Japanese Americans in New York, saying it was unfair "to turn these people loose," and accusing the federal government of "dumping" them on the city. He insisted they posed a danger to the city's military installations, war plants, and shipping facilities. He questioned their loyalty and said that they would impose a grave burden on the police force.

In reality, fewer than five hundred prisoners from the camps were slated for New York City, all of whom — like Mary and Shig — had been put through extensive tests of their loyalty by the War Relocation Authority.

Fierce letters flew back and forth between Mayor La Guardia and Interior Secretary Harold Ickes.

LaGuardia stated and restated his claims, and Secretary Ickes forcefully refuted them, and attacked La Guardia for "these opinions that seem ominously out of tune in a nation that is fighting for principles of democracy and freedom." Ickes accused LaGuardia of playing on the "discordant anthem of racial discrimination."

On April 28, 1944 the conflict broke onto the pages of the *New York Times*, which reprinted the entire text of LaGuardia's positions, and Ickes' statements supporting the Japanese Americans, "these homeless and blameless victims of a wartime military decision."

The whitewash being disseminated by the administration, obscured the fact that ultimately it had been Roosevelt's decision to send people of Japanese ancestry to the camps. The president, through his surrogate, was taking no responsibility for his role.

Mayor LaGuardia contended that if the government had determined that they were dangerous enough to be sent to concentration camps, then he had a right to reject their presence on his coast, and Ickes countered in a disingenuous letter dated April 22, 1944:

"They were moved into relocation centers under the juris-
diction of the War Relocation Authority not because they
were suspected of disloyalty, but because temporary homes
had to be provided while procedures for relocating them to
other communities were being developed," giving the federal
government time to determine their loyalty by "various intelligence agencies."

This Orwellian version would have come as a surprise to the one
hundred and twenty thousand people summarily uprooted and incarcerated for years behind barbed wire.

The conflict was a growing concern in the Japanese American
community in New York when on April 21 Mary was called in for
questioning before a War Relocation Authority panel in New York
City, for the purpose of reevaluating her own leave clearance, as they
had Shig's a month earlier.

The hearing officer in New York sent a letter to Leland Barrows,
director of the War Relocation Authority in Washington, DC on
April 24, 1944. She reported that, "Mrs. Okada stated she had no
idea why she was called for this hearing." In the letter they laid out
everything about her: her education, her various employments, particularly at the Japanese import-export house, her marriage, that she
was living in New York while her husband was residing in Chicago,
her trip as a teenager to Japan with her mother and brother to meet
her grandmother, that she had not attended Japanese cultural school,
but that she could read, write, and speak Japanese. It delineated her
parents' relationship to Japan, and her father's employment as a chiropractor and later a tailor. It stated that Yoshizo had never returned
to Japan. The letter reported that Frank had been at the University of
Syracuse, and that Mary's parents remained in camp. In the last two
paragraphs it quoted Mary as saying that Frank had never registered
with the Japanese Consul, nor had either of her parents applied for
repatriation, and that Mary had purchased United States War Bonds,

that she belonged to the YWCA and a private ski club, and that she refused to join the Japanese American Citizens League.

Mary's first theatrical career step could be marked by her performance that day. The hearing officer concluded her letter with this: "Throughout the interview Mrs. Okada was perfectly frank and did not seem at all nervous." As a result, she saw "no reason whatsoever for her 'Leave Clearance' being denied."

Emiko Tokunaga, choreographer, and biographer of Martha Graham's Japanese American lead dancer Yuriko, and long-time friend of Mary's, said that Mary was distressed for years after the hearing, afraid she would be sent either to Ellis Island, back to camp, or to the West Coast where she didn't feel welcome.

On June 3, Mary turned twenty-eight years old. A lot had changed for her in the preceding two years and in her mind the threat continued in the spring semester of 1944, with her parents still in camp and no foreseeable let-up in her precarious position in America.

Mary's divorce from Shig was finalized on November 20, 1944. Shig remarried a day later to a woman who had also been in Minidoka camp. He'd wasted no time finding a new wife, which, regardless of how Mary felt about him, had to have dealt another blow to her pride and self-esteem. Shig's legal ground for divorce from Mary was desertion. Under questioning, he stated that they had separated in Cleveland in May of 1943 when Mary left him to go to New York.

In his deposition, the lawyer asked what her vocation in New York City was, and Shig answered, "She is a stenographer."

Q: What else is she doing? A: She is studying music.

Q: Did she refuse to live with you? A: Yes, sir.

Shig's main witness to the charges of desertion was the lawyer Thomas Masuda, an activist friend from the days of the Puyallup Assembly Center and a member of the "troublemakers" group.

MARY FOCUSED A GOOD PART OF 1945 ON ARRANGING FOR HER PARENTS' move out of camp and the task fell to her because Frank was still in the Army Language School. The first step was to accompany Mon back to Seattle in order to reclaim their belongings from storage. Mary obtained leave from her job and from Juilliard, and rode the train across the country in late April, to arrive at the Union Pacific railroad depot in the town of Shoshone, Idaho with its Americana western-style main street of stark, flat-roofed, false-facade wooden frontier structures: general store, saloon, a few houses, and a hotel.

When she reached Minidoka, she would have passed through the gates to be processed again by armed guards, before walking down the dusty path through the blocks of dismal housing, breathing the old smells of mess hall food and inadequate sanitation, stopping to greet former acquaintances still languishing in camp. Small victory gardens had cropped up beside the barracks since she'd left, planted and maintained by the older generation.

During her ten-day stay she was assigned sleeping quarters in the same hospital where she'd had her ovaries removed. Mary tried to soothe her distraught father, and reassure him that she and her mother would return in less than two weeks from their trip. She hadn't seen either of them in over a year and a half. Yoshizo was depleted from his time in camp, appearing much older than his sixty years. Lovely Mon had also aged and was suffering from symptoms of menopause. Mon received a prescription for hormonal medication from the hospital before they left.

ON MAY 9 MON AND MARY WALKED OUT THE GATES AND WERE driven by a staff member to Twin Falls, where they boarded the train and began the journey north and west to Seattle, retracing the route they'd traveled to camp, this time with shades pulled up as the locomotive steamed through Idaho, paralleling the Snake River, gradually leaving behind the high prairie to meet rolling grass covered hills and flatlands. They crossed over to the small border town of Huntington, Oregon, went up through Baker City on the Oregon trail, and once out of the town of Le Grande the train began the long climb through the Blue Mountains, slowly taking the wide curves. It then followed the dramatic Columbia River Gorge, high cliffs rising on their right, the river on their left where the Washington state border was close enough to touch.

They would have changed trains in Portland before continuing the trip north through the Cascade Range. I envision the clouds opening as they neared Seattle with Mt. Rainier showing its flanks to

Mt. Rainier

welcome them into the mountains where Mary and Shig had skied and hiked through fragrant, cool lush pine forests.

I hope that Mary took Mon's hand as she had mine when we crossed the bay to Ellis Island that evening in 1998. The battle of emotions had to have been concentrated within each of them as they entered the city from which they'd been banished, a city of immigrant aspirations fulfilled for Mon and Yoshizo, and a place of relative acceptance for Frank, Shig, and Mary until the attack on Pearl Harbor shattered everything. I can only wish that Mary and Mon found solace in each other's company for this bittersweet—mostly bitter, I'm afraid — homecoming.

They had to hurry because Mon had only a temporary leave clearance, closely monitored by the authorities. She and Mary set themselves immediately to reclaiming the family property, only to meet with resistance.

At the last minute Shig sent a letter retracting permission for them to enter his sister-in-law's house. It took a lawyer's intervention to force him to back down, which he did, but not without a vindictive swipe at Mary. He stipulated in his terse three-line note that his "former wife" could take what was hers, "without breaking any personal property in the room."

When they were finally allowed entrance to the house they found an insecure padlock on the spare room door, one that could be easily removed by anyone. According to Mrs. Force, the Caucasian guardian of the property, the storeroom had been left in a turbulent condition by the sister-in-law at the time of the evacuation.

There were items missing from that room as well as from the government warehouse. Innumerable possessions entrusted to the caretaker of Mary and Shig's ski lodge had also disappeared; the bureaucratic quest to retrieve their belongings would go on for decades afterward and in most cases, came to an unsatisfactory end.

I once took Mary back to her old New York apartment building, thinking it would give her pleasure to see it again. But when Rose pushed her wheelchair up the path and stopped before the front door of 66 West Eighty-eighth Street, Mary wouldn't look at the building or at me. Her mouth was set.

I only realized my mistake a few sentences into my cheerful platitudes about what a wonderful place it had been to live. I signaled to Rose and we left quickly, but the damage had been done.

Mary wouldn't speak to me. She kept her head down and barely ate anything through our entire meal at her favorite restaurant, the place that served traditional Japanese country food. Returning to the restaurant was another misjudgment on my part. Mary's mind may have been scrambled, but her emotional sensitivity and acuity were not. Her home on West Eighty-eighth Street had been her salvation, her refuge, the place where she thought she'd live forever, never to be torn from as she had been from Seattle. Her apartment still existed in her mind as home, fully intact, a place she could return to, and I had forced her to see it was no longer hers, gone forever. Mary and her mother must have felt similar despair at being in Seattle again.

YOSHIZO ADDED MORE STRESS TO THE PROCESS OF LEAVING CAMP AS he was very fearful about finding work and a place to live in white society. He couldn't make a decision. He needed his son Frank to do it for him. His confidence had been shaken by the incarceration, and further eroded during his own attempts in the last few months to find work outside.

He had made inquiries about positions in health care and as a professor teaching chiropractic technique at a university, but they all came to nothing. He inquired about work in the garment industry in New York City — he was an accomplished tailor — but as a Japanese alien the American Federation of Labor refused him membership into the union. There was no way to get work without a union card.

Frank helped as much as he could from a distance, coming up with a few openings, but it was left to Mary to meet with prospective employers in New York, and send the information to Yoshizo and Mon in camp.

Frank couldn't get leave from the army to accompany his parents on their train trip two months later from Shoshone to Salt Lake City to Chicago where they were to change to the train for New York City.

Three times Yoshizo balked at the last minute and refused to leave camp. On each occasion Mary had to scrap the complicated carefully-laid plans, exchange train tickets, recoup money paid out, and cancel the job possibilities she had meticulously organized.

Mary persisted, making all the decisions for her parents. She secured positions for them as caretaker and housekeeper on an estate in Noroton, Connecticut on the Gold Coast of the Long Island Sound. The country home of D. K. Ludwig, where they were to reside, was described in contemporaneous newspaper accounts as modest only because Ludwig was an American shipping magnate with enough money to buy the entire neighboring town of Darien. He was an eccentric, obsessively private man, dubbed "the invisible billionaire" who would go on to garner the number one spot on the first Forbes "400 Richest Americans" list published in 1982. The job description

Frank in his Army uniform with Mary
in front of the Julliard School of Music

had said that he'd worked in Hawai'i, and was familiar with and sympathetic to Japanese culture.

Mary had again landed on her feet in a grand manner, using her ingenuity to cushion Mon and Yoshizo's traumatic return to the outside world. What other daughter could have found the richest man in America to employ her alien resident parents during wartime? Yoshizo and Mon settled into the Ludwig estate on July 9, 1945, one month before the bombing of Hiroshima and Nagasaki.

"The Slant Eyed Scandals"

Mary as the Chinese Chanteuse

IN THE SPRING OF 1946 MARY TURNED THIRTY. SHE DECIDED SHE needed to find work that would pay more than her salary at the Children's Aid Society. She was renting a room at 57 West Eighty-eighth Street, across from the building where she would eventually live for fifty years. The room was on the top floor of a low-income five-story walk-up building used for "SRO" or single room occupancy. She shared the small space in the run-down brownstone with another young woman. They didn't have enough money between them to purchase more than one bed and one convertible daybed and a few kitchen utensils. Mary had spent all of her extra savings on getting Frank and her parents out of camp.

But she was in New York City and she was ready and determined to find work singing on the stage; she was talented and she had the necessary get-up-and-go. Her teachers at Juilliard had told her that there would be no jobs for her in opera because she was Asian. Even *Madama Butterfly* wasn't ever cast with an Asian singer at the Metropolitan Opera.

They had steered her toward Musical Theater, though no one pointed out that on Broadway almost every Asian role was also played by whites. The producers thought nothing of having the white performers appear in Yellow Face, a racist protocol that would continue long after Black Face had become taboo.

A rare exception was Sono Osato, a singer and accomplished ballet dancer of mixed race — her father was Japanese and her mother Irish French-Canadian — who was one of the stars of Leonard Bernstein's *On the Town*.

Bernstein was intent on racially integrating his musical. Revolutionary for the times, he hired Negro dancers and singers for the ensemble, and Osato to play Ivy Smith, "Miss Turnstiles," the love object of Gabey, the white sailor-on-leave. The production remained on Broadway from December 1944 to February 1946 and even had performances during the three-day period when the atomic bombs were dropped on Japan. Osato's father had been interned as an enemy alien, but she was not sent to camp because she wasn't living in the West Coast military zone at the time. The production kept her racial identity unspecific, but people with race consciousness knew that she was Japanese American.

There was a documented outburst from Horace R. Clayton Jr., a Negro sociologist who happened to be in the audience days after hearing of the bombing of Hiroshima. "If I were half-Japanese I wouldn't be dancing with three American sailors at a time like this," Clayton said to his white wife. When his wife demurred and said that Osato was one hundred percent American, he snapped back, "She's a Jap, and I'm a nigger, and you're a white girl. Let none of us forget what we are."

Sono Osato was Mary's contemporary, born in Nebraska in 1919 — a Nisei who had broken through in a spectacular way and who, as a teenager had danced with the Ballet Russe.

When Mary searched the newspapers and trades for audition opportunities, Osato's success perhaps raised her expectations that she too could find an opening in a Broadway musical. One day she came upon an ad in the *Daily Mirror* for a new nightclub: "Wanted: Oriental showgirls, must be at least five feet six."

"Well, I was five six and able to move," she told an interviewer.

"It didn't state that I had to dance or anything. So, I went down and got the job . . . It was called The China Doll Club . . . .. It was quite the place, and it was an unusual place, because there weren't any Oriental night clubs before [in New York City]." And they were offering one hundred dollars a week.

A promotional postcard for the China Doll Club.

THE CHINA DOLL CLUB WAS THE BRAINCHILD OF IRISH AMERICAN restaurateur and impresario Tom Ball. He modeled it on Forbidden City in San Francisco, a going concern ever since it was opened in 1939 by Charlie Low, a Chinese impresario. The China Doll Club was advertised as a place where you could get the best Chinese food in the city along with an "all Chinese cabaret floor show."

The "Slant Eyed Scandals" at the China Doll Club was a production by Donn Arden, who would become famous as the Busby Berkley of Las Vegas, credited with having created the first showgirls. Nothing was spared on the costumes designed by Madame Berthe, a tiny Russian immigrant, a virtuoso at beading and fringes who would go on to create wardrobes for major theatrical productions.

Like other top nightclubs of the time, the production cost was in the vicinity of sixty thousand dollars. The showgirls, billed as "Lee Mortimer's China Dolls," wore Thai inspired headdresses, silk Chi-

A promotional postcard for the China Doll Club – Mary in lower left

nese tunics, as well as seductive, shortened versions of Carmen Miranda dresses with ruffles barely covering their behinds, and for the "Bubble Girls," gold lamé bikinis and ankle-length gold skirts that were removed in an erotic striptease, with oversized fans to strategically and tantalizingly obscure naked body parts.

This was a far cry from Bernstein's stylish musical, but it was a job and a start.

Lee Mortimer, a partner in the enterprise, wore two professional hats: nightclub purveyor and show business columnist. He and his fellow gossip columnists like the *Daily News'* Walter Winchell drummed up audiences.

The reviewers loved the show, and cited a number of acts including: "Ming and Ling, the Chinese Hillbillies"; Mara Kim, a ballet and creative dancer; the "Tai Sings," a ballroom dance couple; and Florence Hin Lowe, an acrobatic dancer who had been with the *Folies Bergere*.

Mary was given special notice among the "gorgeous and leggy, slant-eyed" showgirls.

The "Scandals" was described as occidental with an oriental spin, a mix of old-school Chinese acts, trendy rumbas, full-blooded American jokes, and current popular songs.

The producers had taken advantage of the burgeoning postwar interest in the Orient: soldiers were returning stateside, and many of them had served on the Pacific front and become infatuated with Asian women. The club played to the eroticizing of the exotic. It became an extremely popular locale, with audiences that included celebrities like Lucille Ball and Desi Arnaz.

THE CHINA DOLL CLUB OPERATED IN THE OLD LA CONGA CLUB, which had featured Latin music, and when Tito Puente and other Latin musicians performed in the club they held onto their gigs. Otherwise it was melting pot in microcosm . . . the waiters were Jewish, the cooks were Chinese, and all of the performers were of Asian descent. Father and son Ming and Ling were an ethnic and racial mix of Filipino and Caucasian, Mara Kim was Korean.

The majority of the performers in night club settings, adopted Chinese surnames to fit the bill, but in the case of those with Japanese surnames, sadly there was more at stake in the name changes.

The most famous case would become Jack Soo, born Goro Suzuki, who took a Chinese American identity after he was released from Topaz camp. He performed in nightclubs as Mary had done.

When he became a lead on Broadway in *Flower Drum Song*, he saw it as an opportunity to change back to his birth name, but the producers nixed the idea saying that the notable performer, Pat Suzuki, who was performing under her real name, was already in the cast, and they didn't want two Suzukis.

Jack went on to fame playing Sgt. Nick Yemana, an outspoken Japanese American character in the 1970s TV sitcom *Barney Miller*, but still acted under a Chinese surname until his death.

A group of China Doll Club showgirls, Mary top row center

In the past, Lee Mortimer, the big backer of the China Doll Club, had made snide hurtful comments about Japanese American performers. During the incarceration he glibly wrote, "The Japanese Dolls are vanishing, leaving the playful gentlemen who like to be seen around the exotic, slant-eyed lovelies to seek the company of the Chinese, Filipino, and Hawaiian charmers." But it was known in the Japanese community that he "had a thing for" Japanese women, and would later marry a Japanese American woman.

IN APRIL OF 1946 MARY DROPPED HER REAL NAME — TERUKO WATAnabe Okada — kept her American name, Mary, and took Mon's name, and created Mary Mon. In the newspaper notices she gradually became Mary Mon Toy, and a public relations story emerged describing how she was born in Hawaii to Chinese parents, while in other versions it was a Chinese father and a Korean mother, but nary a Japanese parent.

She must have felt terribly alone during this time even with Mon and Yoshizo nearby in Connecticut. She couldn't brag to them about any of her performance successes. They would be shocked to know that she was working in a club, parading scantily dressed before a boisterous white audience. She'd established her ethnic disguise, but it was necessary to remain alert at all times for any accidental slip-up.

A telegram from Lee Mortimer, inviting her to a party in his honor, was sent to her residence at 57 West Eighty-eighth Street — addressed to Miss Mary Mon, c/o Okada. Had she covered her ethnicity by saying she was staying in the apartment of someone named Okada? Did Mortimer know? It was arduous enough working her way into a field where Asians weren't welcome except as exotic token acts in the white entertainment world or curiosities at a Chinese club, without the need for this added balancing act.

Mary's choice to mask her ethnicity was based on real life concerns: she had to make a living; she wanted to continue performing; she wanted to be a star; the specter of the prison camp was still with her. The last camps had just been disbanded, but the impossible had happened before and she had almost been sent back. Perhaps the sailors and soldiers, who wolf-whistled and cheered and flirted with her between the acts had killed Japanese as recently as the previous year, and there were relatives in Japan, first cousins and aunts and uncles in Fukushima whom she hadn't heard from since well before the bombs fell on Hiroshima and Nagasaki.

MARY PERFORMED IN THREE SHOWS A NIGHT, THE LAST AT 2:30 A.M. An early publicity photo attests to her beauty, slender with a wasp waist and long shapely legs, though she hadn't quite mastered the pose; an awkward angle of her leg gives her away as a show business amateur. Welcoming in her demeanor, she was a tantalizing vessel for white male fantasy and safe enough a female presence to avoid being a threat to wives and girlfriends. She continued smiling sweetly, blowing kisses, and sitting during intermissions with men like her new boyfriend Robert MacDonald, a United States Air Force pilot.

She perfected her showgirl poses and privately developed her repertoire of American, French, and Italian songs, putting into practice all she'd learned at Juilliard, adding Yiddish and Irish tunes to round out the package until Lee Mortimer announced in his column on June 2, 1946, two short months after the club opened, "At the China Doll Club, one of my own little dolls — Mary Mon — stepped out of the chorus to tackle top femme singing spot, and stopped the show cold. She has a sensationally exciting voice of caressing quality, which none of us suspected."

29

Namesake
A Visit with Dorothy Toy

MARY'S SISTER-IN-LAW MAY WATANABE ASSUMED THAT MARY HAD BORROWED THE SURNAME of Toy from the tap dancer, Dorothy Toy.

I wanted to learn more about Dorothy whom I only knew from one photo; perhaps something about her would offer more insight into Mary at that time.

The Chinese American actor Lori Tan Chinn, who knew Mary and had performed with her in the last years of Mary's career, told me that Dorothy Toy was actually Japanese American, born Dorothy Takahashi in San Francisco, but grew up in Los Angeles.

Paul Wing, Toy's partner was Chinese American, and word had it that Dorothy Toy passed as Chinese American in order to escape being sent to a concentration camp.

As I inquired further, I heard rumors that a well-known Chinese American actress had informed on Dorothy Toy during the war, putting Dorothy in tremendous jeopardy. It was a federal violation of United States military orders not to report to camp if you lived in the western military zone when the executive order came down. You could be remanded to Federal prison if caught.

On the Internet, I came upon clips of Wing and Toy's movie performances, and an entry on Wing and Toy in a history of tap dancing in America edited by Rusty Frank, an independent contemporary tap dancer.

When I reached Rusty Frank by e-mail she wrote back that Dorothy was very much alive, and sent me her phone number in Oakland. "Just call her and say I gave you the number. She'll be fine with a cold call. She's amazing."

I couldn't believe my luck. I had reason to be in the Bay Area so I called and set up an appointment through Mark Wong, the man who took care of Ms. Toy. I followed up with a long letter of explanation to Dorothy, including that I had been born in the Tule Lake Camp.

Her house was slung low on a hill overlooking Oakland.

It was a warm hazy October day with a slight breeze that sent golden leaves floating and circling through the air as I waited outside until I was greeted at the front door by Mark, handsome and slender, in his early forties, his head stylishly shaved. He took the potted orchid I had brought. "Oh, she's going to love this."

And then there she was — diminutive, delicately beautiful, and astoundingly fit at ninety-three years old — dressed in black tights, a thick oversized royal blue sweater, and black Capezio ballet slippers. She hugged me tightly. "I'm so happy to see you," she cooed.

She led me downstairs to the dance studio where she still gave classes to young people.

Honeyed light streamed in through large windows and bounced off floor-to-ceiling practice mirrors. Photographs of her career with Paul Wing hung high on the walls above the mirrors.

"We started out in Los Angeles and then we went to Chicago and from there to New York." I asked her why they had gone to Chicago. "We were real hicks," she said, "We had to pull our act together. You can't go straight to New York if you're not sophisticated." Her conversation was effervescent, and it was quickly apparent that though her short-term memory was slipping — she asked me the same questions innumerable times — her long-term information corresponded remarkably well with what I'd already learned about her.

The China Doll Club on Fifty-first and Broadway was across the street from the back entrance of the Roxy Theater, a movie palace with live shows, where she and her partner, Paul Wing, had performed five times daily. "We'd finish our last show and race over to the China Doll Club in time to make the end of the dinner show there." After that they did two more China Doll shows, the eleven o'clock and the two-thirty a.m. "It was hard, but you can do anything when you're young."

She remembered Mary. "Mary Mon Toy! She was a beautiful girl. She had long legs and breasts. She was a showgirl. She was tall for an Oriental. You had to be tall to be a showgirl."

AFTER TWO HOURS OF SPIRITED EXCHANGE, LOOKING THROUGH photos of other performers at the club, and sharing tea and cookies that Mark set out for us, I broached the rumor that someone in the Asian performing community had jeopardized her security by notifying newspaper columnists that she was actually Japanese American. Her ebullience evaporated. Her face clouded with sadness, and she said quietly, "It was very difficult for me and my partner in those days." I offered up the name of the Chinese American actress, and she grew yet more serious. "Yes, she was a very cruel person. She hurt us terribly."

The trouble had first begun during the evacuation from the West Coast, when she and Paul Wing had been in San Diego doing a show with Chico Marx. "It came out in the newspaper about me — she'd told the columnists. We said to Chico we had to leave immediately. He kept saying, 'Don't go, I can talk to Immigration for you. I can tell the authorities to lay off.' We said, 'No, we don't want you to get into trouble. We have to leave.' It was hard, so hard, it was a good job, but we had to leave."

They went east, but even in New York City they weren't safe. They were especially frightened when the popular gossip columnist, Earl Wilson, made a pointed reference in his *New York Post* syndicated "Saloon Editor." "She planted the story with him. We went to Upstate New York and waited until things blew over. I don't know why a person would be so cruel to inform on us. Maybe she was jealous, but she hurt us terribly. It still hurts. You don't get over a thing like that."

Through it all her parents were in Topaz camp in Utah. I asked if she could write to them. "Oh, no," she said, "I couldn't have any contact with them. They could be punished or the authorities could come after me. But I wasn't worried. They were with my cousins. I knew my cousins would look out for them."

I could hear in her voice that she was still haunted by guilt for not being there to care for them as a dutiful Nisei daughter should.

When I asked if her mother had ever talked about her time in the camp, she said, "Oh, no, no, she never wanted to talk about that time. It was very terrible for her."

"Did you know that Mary Mon Toy was also Japanese American?" I asked. "Her family name was Watanabe."

Stunned by this information, she answered. "I didn't know that, I thought she was Chinese, but of course we didn't speak of those things back then."

A little later she asked me, "did you ever talk with Mary about the camps?"

"No, not really, very little actually," I said.

She shook her head. "You should have. She probably would have wanted to. What a pity."

"Are you comfortable speaking about what happened to you? I asked, "especially about not being able to communicate with your mother at the time?"

"Only with people who understand," she answered.

Suffering was still alive within Dorothy Toy after sixty-five years, and it underscored for me Mary's choice to pass as Chinese American, and why she continued unto death to say she'd been born in Hawai'i.

BACK IN MY HOTEL ROOM, I WAS FILLED WITH REMORSE THAT I hadn't talked more with Mary, wishing she had been able to speak in depth of her time in camp. There would have been so much for her to unburden.

I imagined Mary being a woman as warm as Dorothy, and what a comfort that would have been for me. Many times, after my visit with Dorothy, I would lie on the daybed in my office, with the tiny audio recorder on my chest, listening over and over to her soft voice, feeling it resonate through my body, speaking to me from afar. I told myself I was doing research, knowing full well it was more than that.

In August of 1946 "Mary Mon, Songstress," was interviewed for the *New York Post's* man-on-the-street column titled "What Do YOU Think?" A sophisticated photo of her accompanied the question for the day: "If you had your choice, where would you spend the rest of your life?" Mary's answer: "Right here in New York. In this city you can very easily lose your identity. People here are much more broadminded and tolerant, besides being cooperative and minding their own business when they should."

A clearer statement couldn't be made of her desire or was it simply necessity, to shed her Japanese ethnicity?

Rising Star

Oriental Songstress and "Miss Slant Eyes of 1948

MARY LEFT THE CHINA DOLL CLUB AFTER EIGHT MONTHS AND HER career began to take off.

She became the "Chinese Chanteuse," a sophisticate, her hair in a fashionable up-sweep, dressed in glittering floor-length gowns that clung to her svelte, curvaceous body.

Mary appeared in Montreal at the Gayety, a moderately classy club, in an all-white vaudeville variety show, along with puppeteers, ventriloquists, mimics, dog acts, aerial artists, and contortionists — tacky stuff, but it was a first move into white entertainment.

She soon advanced to being on the roster with performers like young comedian Joey Adams and Guy Kibbee, a successful Broadway and film actor, opening live stage shows at large movie palaces in New York, Washington, D.C. and Boston, and booked into the finest nightclubs.

Placard in front of a movie theater
Mary (upper left) is part of the
opening live entertainment

By THE SPRING OF 1948 MARY WAS THE TOP ACT AT BOSTON'S MUSIC BOX in the Copley Square Hotel, being a huge hit with Irish songs, opera arias, and Jewish folk songs.

Columnists extolled her beauty, her polished delivery, her rapport with the audience, her amazing ability to sing in at least five languages, and the fact that she was called back for many encores. They also cited her as the current "Miss Slant Eyes of 1948." No matter that she'd inoculated herself against anti-Japanese sentiment; she still had to endure ingrained prejudice against Asians, even couched in supposed compliments.

While appearing at the Music Box, she was invited to join a line-up of performers for the RKO Boston premier of the movie *Berlin Express*, featuring Robert Ryan and Merle Oberon. The star-studded stage show included Dorothy Lamour, Hildegarde, Eddie Foy Jr., Count Basie, Billy Eckstine — and Mary Mon Toy. In the pre-premier publicity, she was a show business "item," equal to these other big shots.

The *Boston Evening American* described the night as "once-in-a-lifetime thrill" for the four thousand Bostonians who attended the movie and variety show. Mary came out and stood solo in the spotlight. "Mary Mon Toy, Chinese song stylist from the Music Box, literally brought down the house with her magnificent voice and her gift for range which included haunting Irish airs and grand opera."

After the show Mary posed for photographs with a group of men, including Robert Ryan. She and Ryan sat close, their bodies touching, and the chemistry was palpable. Mary looked to be holding her own with the movie idol; it was the start of a long friendship.

Mary and Robert Ryan backstage at the RKO Boston theater premier of *Berlin Express*

By the end of 1948 Mary was performing in elegant clubs up and down the Eastern coast, but mostly in Philadelphia and New York City. She was working all the time, receiving glowing notices in the gossip columns.

Some of the places were less classy.

She became a regular in Harold Minksy's Follies at the Colonial Inn in Miami, Florida, described by a columnist as an "ultra-plush" venue — but the show was glorified burlesque, a cheapened version of the Paris *Folies Bergere.* It consisted of fourteen scenes, with showgirls, strippers, corny comedians spouting blue lines that drew raucous suggestive belly-laughs. The production was full of "nekkid women" who peeled down to bras and feathers. The big payoff was a dance act of a stripper with a couple of "muscle-boys who mauled the girl in an effective routine." Pretty raunchy, cheesy stuff, but Mary was the class act in the two big production numbers, dressed in her sleek, oriental-influenced dress, and backed up by a chorus of "babes." Not the best milieu, but her goal was to earn a living and stand out in a crowd; she kept her eyes on the prize no matter what venue she had to exploit to reach the heights. Her sights were set on eventually moving into legitimate theater with a preference for opera disproving her music instructor's advice that it was futile to try to enter that exclusive club as an Asian.

On February 6, 1949, she made a promising inroad toward that dream. She sang with the chorus ensemble of Kurt Weill's American Opera *Street Scene,* book by Elmer Rice and lyrics by Langston Hughes, in the concert hall of Manhattan's Ninety-second Street Young Men's and Young Women's Hebrew Association. It was an illustrious cast of Negro, white, and Asian singers. In the chorus with Mary was the great Robert McFerrin Sr., who would have to wait until 1955 for full recognition of his talent, when he became the first Black soloist at the Metropolitan Opera, beating Marion Anderson's debut by a few weeks. Kurt Weill sat in the audience at the Y that night. Going backstage to greet the cast, Weill wrote in Mary's libretto, "It was an evening to remember."

MARY PLAYED THE LEGENDARY PALACE THEATER IN THE SUMMER OF 1950 at the premier of *Peggy*, starring Diana Lynn, Charles Coburn, and Rock Hudson. She was in the white vaudeville lineup of eight acts that entertained the audience before the movie began. She teed off with the ballad "This Can't Be Love," and ended with a selection from the opera *Carmen*, a mix of the low and the high that was becoming her signature.

In the fall, after her Palace performance, she appeared as a regular at the Old Romanian on Allen Street on Manhattan's Lower East Side, a venerable Jewish restaurant and club that had recently been renovated and now seated five hundred patrons.

The elite opening night audience at the Old Romanian included Lou Walters of the Latin Quarter, who in a few years would play a major role in Mary's move into the really big time.

31

Ambition and Tough Negotiating

IN AUTUMN OF 1953, MARY WAS JUST WINDING DOWN AN AFFAIR
with the actor Kaie Deei, also known at Khigh Dheigh, though he
was born Kenneth Dickerson Jr. in Spring Lake, New Jersey. He was
hired solely for Asian roles despite being of Anglo-Egyptian-Suda-
nese ancestry. He was married and eight years older than Mary. They
made an interesting couple; he was passing as Asian, possibly so no
one would know of his North African heritage, while Mary was presenting as Chinese American.

He wrote to her from Boston where he was rehearsing for the
role of Mr. Sumata in the out-of-town tryouts of *Teahouse of the August Moon*, in preparation for the Broadway run. He was cast in the
same role in the television *Hallmark Hall of Fame* movie in 1962. He
went on to become a featured movie and television character actor
in Asian roles.

His was an odd case . . . he's often accused by Asian Americans
of performing in Yellow Face, but in fact because directors thought
he was Chinese, he was typecast in Asian roles, making him, as some
have said, an honorary Asian American actor with all the handicaps
of racial stereotyping.

I assume Mary knew he wasn't Asian, but in his letters there's
no sense that he confided in her or she in him. What is clear from
his letters is that he was pining for her from Boston. Mary had told
him she was going away and he was upset about the prospect of not
seeing her for a long time. He wrote how lonely he'd been and how

painfully he missed their "togetherness." Pouring his heart out, he descended into bathos: "The moments that each night should anticipate sleep with blissful calm become torturous years as my thoughts convulse and strain to reach and touch your dear heart and cheek, my love." You either adore receiving a letter like that or you want to run. For Mary, I suspect, it was a bit of both. In another letter he was ecstatic and relieved that they had finally spoken on the phone the day before, "Travel in safety and peace, "he wrote, "I love you with reverence and passion; with tenderness and violence."

Over-the-top purple prose became the standard content of letters from Mary's many lovers. Reading through her stacks of correspondence, I saw what a devil she was when it came to men, driving them wild with passion one moment only to turn around and take off, leaving them to their suffering.

It's unclear what Mary's travel plans Khigh Dheigh was alluding to in his letter. She was juggling two possible career choices. That same October she began work at Lou Walters's Desert Inn "Folies Bergere" in Las Vegas. While there she received a bid from Paris.

By then she had snagged top William Morris agent Dick Henry, who had begun negotiating a contract for the Nouvelle Eve Revue Cabaret Nightclub in Paris. In Dick Henry's letters he encouraged her to take the Nouvelle Eve deal. Mary was reluctant to settle for what was offered. Toughened up on the road performing in nightclubs, she'd become a shrewd pro, looking out for her own interests.

She worried about what sort of place the Nouvelle Eve Revue was. A London friend had written to her that it was some kind of strip joint; Dick Henry assured her that it was a very beautiful club, and that the starting salary at three hundred dollars a week was good for her career.

Even with no existing correspondence from Mary's side, her business acumen was apparent in the exchange of letters between Albert Tavel, a Paris representative, and Dick Henry. She herself had the contract translated, instead of relying on her agent's interpretation. She wanted several things changed. She didn't like that the management reserved the right to cancel the contract. Albert Tavel responded that they could cross out that clause. Mary questioned the intent of another clause that stated, "In order to create a cordial and animated atmosphere, the artists are at the disposition of the Management to play in the Room the roles which will be given them." Mr. Tavel countered, that it pertained only to the "frame of the show. I wish to tell you that there is no question of the artistes being asked to mix with the audience."

In reference to the clause that "the artist will wear Reard brassieres and panties furnished by the Management," Mary asked "the meaning of Reard brassieres and panties." She seemed satisfied with the explanation that they were simply the standard articles worn at Nouvelle Eve and "the management wants all the artistes to wear the same."

Mary wanted to know why they anticipated actions if they had to "ban the Spectacle." Mr. Tavel assured Mr. Henry that the show had never been banned, and he would cross out the clause. When she asked for clarification of the "Director's right to diffuse, publish, reproduce or sell," any photos, for the publicity of the house," Mr. Tavel answered succinctly, "There is no question and no obligation for MARY MON TOY as a singer, to do nudes." And lastly, when Dick Henry stated that, "MARY MON TOY will not pay more than 10% total commission on the salary, Mr. Tavel agreed to split "the 10% between our two offices." In his parting salvo, Mr. Tavel wrote, "I should like you to mention to Miss Mon Toy, that the management of the Nouvelle Eve is an extremely nice management, and that all artistes without exception have always been very happy there."

Her ambition was now equal to her bargaining ability. As she was negotiating for the job in Paris she was also angling for a far better situation — a run in Lou Walter's prestigious New York City Latin Quarter Club.

In the second week of November Dick Henry wrote that Mary had landed the Latin Quarter job, to start in January.

I visited nouvelle eve in 2010. it was a club still appreciated by connoisseurs of the old-style entertainment for its raw ebullient raunchiness as compared to the slickness of the bigger venues.

"We bring the girls in from the country, train them and then they're stolen away by the major establishments that pay more," the current owner, son of the man who ran it in Mary's era" told me. "The look of the place is unchanged from when your friend performed here. I try to keep it that way," he said with pride, detailing how he scoured flea markets for authentic replacement items.

The club had opened in 1898 presenting a topless revue, dubbed "*Gaîté Parisienne*" by the Paris smart set. During World War II the nightclub became a cinema and only in 1949 did it reopen as a variety show. The stage sets were designed by Erté, Lucien Berteaux, and Paul Bugnaux, the costumes by Balenciaga and Maggy Rouff with furs from Revillon.

The lobby's décor of Persian pink walls, magenta velvet settees, rose-colored bar, and faux Grecian figurines adorning gold-framed mirrors gave off the whiff of a bordello in 2010, but the intimate theater had orchestra and balcony seating for three hundred at cabaret tables sporting authentic Art Nouveau lamps that maintained a veneer of prior elegance. Midnight blue velvet curtains dotted with sparkling appliqués flanked the stage and the house's star-studded ceiling was painted in matching blue. The stage apron, jutting out beyond the proscenium arch, was constructed of large glass blocks lit from below with an exciting ever-changing rainbow of colors synchronized to the show's music.

But the magic disappeared behind the wings where the walls were painted high gloss oil-based-ochre like a New York tenement and a steel circular staircase led up to the dressing room, toilets and showers.

The dressing room was where the young women strapped on can-can boots, each weighing four pounds, in order to exert the most noise and impact when the performers stomped and kicked.

Climbing the stairs, I could almost hear the cruel boots on dancers' feet, clomping past me on their way down to perform. In the cramped dressing room before the long mirror with its shelf for makeup and toiletries, and the performers' chairs assembled in tight formation, I imagined the odors of perfume, sweat and greasepaint, as well as the intimate chatter of women as they gossiped and talked of their everyday lives. Had Mary been included in the conversations? Was her French good enough to form friendships? Or did she sit apart, aloof?

I RECALLED THEN THAT SHE HAD TOLD ME IN ONE OF HER MORE LUCID moments, that a large oil painting of a café's expansive, colorful awning, chairs, and tables that hung above her bed in the Vista residence, was the view from her room in Paris.

"Who painted it?" I had asked.

"I did," she said, in her most matter-of-fact voice. "I got tired of sitting by myself in my hotel room. An artist gave me a canvas and oils. I painted from my window."

It showed talent in the subtle use of color, the angled point of view, and how she'd taken command of the four-foot tall by three-foot wide canvas.

"Did you ever paint anything else?"

"No. I left after that. I went home."

32

"Les Mademoiselles de Paris"

The Latin Quarter

At the Desert Inn in Las Vegas, Mary had performed in a trio with Ruby "Curly Top" Richards and Lee Sharon as part of the "*Revue a la Folies Bergere*." The show was promoted as "an exciting, chic and entrancing Parisian Revue with stars of the Continental Stages . . . and the leading European Cafes and Theaters." The three women were featured as "*Les Mademoiselles des Paris*."

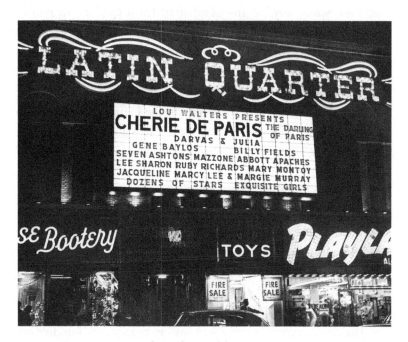

Latin Quarter Marquee

Lee Sharon was a blonde, blue-eyed Texas-born showgirl who had trained under Lili St. Cyr, the most famous contemporary stripper. She had recently returned from work in Japan at a club where she had caused something of a sensation as "Miss Happy-Limbs."

Richards, a former Cotton Club chorus girl, was just back from a two-year stint in the Paris *Folies Bergere*.

At thirty-eight-years-old Mary held her own with the much younger women, her body smooth, slender, and seductively proportioned in the revealing costumes.

Mary was billed as "*La Chinoise*," Ruby as "*La Creole*," and Lee as "*L'Americaine*." Ruby was born in St. Kitts, and grew up in Harlem, an American Black. Mary was born in the state of Washington, an Asian American, but only the blonde stripper could be presented as *L'Americaine*.

In January of 1954 "Les Mademoiselles de Paris" opened on "the great white way," at the Manhattan Latin Quarter, located in a wedge-shaped building at the north end of Times Square at the crossroads of Broadway and Seventh Avenue. The giant, scarlet landmark script of the Coca Cola sign splayed across the building's south wall calling attention to itself from all points in the neon-resplendent square. The locale was home not only to the Latin Quarter, but also to the downtown Cotton Club and the Palais Royal. It's been said that "that little block had more razzle and dazzle than any other spot" in the Big Apple.

The Latin Quarter was the defining height of nightclub prestige, known for the most gorgeous showgirls decked out in extraordinary costumes, a spectacular floor show with great headliners and fine food elegantly presented. Lou Walters prided himself on the cuisine.

Though the showgirls were scantily dressed, Walters didn't allow any nudity, except on the playbill, so you could take your wife and kids there for a night on the town.

The club's cavernous room had seating capacity for hundreds of people. Three times a night, as patrons finished their meals, settled in with more drinks, and busboys rushed to clear, the house lights went down and Buddy Marlowe's band burst into the theme song: "So this is Gay Paree, come along with me, we're stepping out to see the Latin Quarter," the cue for the *Les Mademoiselles de Paris* to strut into the spotlight dressed in feathers, sequined pasties, and wide-brimmed hats, their hands held high above their heads to better show off their scanty costumes — rumored to cost $40,000 apiece. They crossed the stage and moved onto the huge apron that thrust like a runway deep into the audience; guests at tables below the apron gazed up at the glamorous spectacle of the three gorgeous women.

Christine Jorgensen, the ex-GI recently returned from her sex change operation in Denmark, was a featured performer. She swept out in a long tulle gown with a mink stole, her blonde hair perfectly coiffed in a glamorous modified pageboy. The emcee introduced her to cheers, whistles, stomping, and no doubt a bit of snarky laughter. With perfect aplomb, ignoring any derision, she put the microphone to her lips and, in a deep voice, crooned a song.

RUBY'S STORY SYMBOLIZED THE significance of the racially mixed trio that Walters had brought together when most New York City clubs still had a non-mixing policy for audiences, and non-touching regulations across race lines for performers. Ruby was greeted that first night in New York with wild applause and shouts of the white fans from her uptown Cotton Club days. They'd come to welcome her home from Paris.

Five-foot-six-inch Ruby was a beauty, her sepia skin a few shades

To "Mary" All my love to you, and remember always it's the same??? Le Creole Ruby Richards

Les Mademoiselles de Paris, Latin Quarter, , 1954
l to r, Lee Sharon, Ruby Richards, Mary Mon Toy

darker than Mary's under the bright lights. In Paris she'd been treated like any other performer. According to Ebony magazine, even though she was the lone dark-skinned chorus girl, "she wasn't 'centered' to bring out the uniqueness of her skin." She could kiss a white man on stage without bringing down the censors and police. In her interviews in the white press Richards didn't compare the two nations' racial policies — she only made mention in the Negro press — but made sly comments about how she'd had to clean up her act a bit when she came back to make it acceptable to American audiences.

New York Age, the most important Afro-American newspaper wrote, "For glamour and pulchritude, Walters copped some long-stemmed hussies, in addition to our own Ruby 'Curly Top' Richards." The three, beyond being beautiful and titillating in their multiracial act, exuded pleasure and self-confidence in their on-and-off-stage photographs.

They weren't what the public characterizes as stereotypical show-girls. Mary spoke elegant English and was a proper lady in many ways, dressing demurely when not on stage, having perfect table manners, sending old-fashioned bread-and-butter thank-you notes to reviewers, columnists, and stagehands.

When not performing, Lee Sharon looked like a naive ingénue in photos with her long blonde ponytail and prim dresses.

As for Ruby, I've listened to an undated, shaky audio tape in which she converses with the cultural historian Delilah Jackson. She speaks in a cultured stage voice, much like Mary's, that is, until her perfect diction digresses in anger, and is abruptly interspersed with knowledgeable race-conscious name-calling of "motherfucker" this and that about theater people who weren't standing up for their rights, and with explicit references to a certain famous performer as "that Uncle Tom nigger."

To the one and only Emperesse
I wish for you the best out
of life always. I pray for
your health, happiness'
and friendship.
Love you lots
Lee

In the beginning both women liked Mary, judging by their inscriptions on the photos she kept in her albums. The most enigmatic and sisterly is Ruby's autograph: "To Mary, All my love to you and remember always It's the same????," which I construed as a reference to the song, "It's the Same the World Over," their big number together.

The question marks seemed a key to something other than what I presumed was a song about romantic love around the world. Was it a sardonic racial allusion to people who say that "we're all the same under the skin," or a sexual joke — one of Mary's favorites — about how white men think Asian women's vaginas are horizontal? Or was it just a high-school-yearbook throwaway when you can't think of what to write? But I couldn't imagine that these two women of color, who paraded barely dressed with the intent to excite, didn't share racial and raunchy jokes at the expense of the men in the all-white audience.

When I set out to find the lyrics for the song, the only one that kept popping up was titled "It's the Same the Whole World Over," a 1930s English music hall number about a poor girl who was taken advantage of by rich men who sleep with her and then move on leaving her with nothing. The repeated stanza is "It's the same the whole world over, It's the poor what gets the blame/It's the rich what gets the pleasure/Ain't it all a bloomin' shame?"

I continued the hunt, finding various versions with only slightly altered lyrics and always with the same meaning that the girls are ruined and left to fend for themselves.

REGARDLESS OF WHAT THEY WERE ACTUALLY PERFORMING OR WHAT the intent was of Ruby's autograph, discovering a possibility in the song of sexual exploitation opened up a place in me that I had closed long ago. I realized that my attachment to Mary wasn't only the bond of the camps, wasn't only my longing for Mr. and Mrs. Takaetsue, but rather I found something of myself in Mary's quest, and felt an affinity to Mary and Ruby in that nightclub setting with its nakedness and flirtation with the sordidness of being at the mercy of wealthy white men for whatever benefit their performances did or didn't bring, in other words, using whatever means to make a living and build a career.

A friend asked me, when I was considering writing about Mary, "Isn't that going to be a stretch for you? She's a showgirl. How can you relate to that, it's pretty low?"

Taken aback by her judgmental comment, I answered that I had a high regard for anyone who can get out on a stage night after night, and anyway that was not all Mary was, and the more I thought about it I realized it was not a stretch for me at all, on the contrary, what connected me to Mary beyond the camps was her having said to me that first day, straight out, "I'm a tits and ass showgirl." I loved her for it. The more deeply I probed her show business life, the more pleasure I felt when proudly repeating the moniker in describing to others who she was, who she had been. I enjoyed their startled expressions, that implied, *Is that an appropriate way to describe your Japanese American subject?*

Their reaction to the tawdry implication of "tits and ass" touched an essential part of me that has always identified with what I call being "street," and which causes me to feel out of place, to this very day, in the middle class and upper-class environments where I currently live my life. I can easily pass as privileged, which in many ways I've become but no one knows what I feel inside, how I hear a declassee tone in my voice, how I'm ashamed that I'm an autodidact, that I didn't go to the right schools, or grow up with comforts of any kind.

Ocean liner going-away party for Christine Jorgenson, at the left, and Mary on the right

CHRISTINE JORGENSEN AND MARY BECAME GOOD FRIENDS. THERE is photograph taken in an ocean liner stateroom, at a *bon voyage* party for Jorgensen, where a stylishly dressed Mary looks relaxed and happy, and a playful shot of them with Jorgensen laughing at a pair of inflated balloon-like balls the size of cantaloupes covering Mary's breasts. There are other pictures of a long nightclub table where Mary and Jorgenson are only two of three women present among a group of men, in which Christine is arm-wrestling a young man with Mary looking on, amused by the contest.

Mary was the only non-white person in the intimate group made up of Jorgensen's family and friends, including a small child, and a few male business associates. Mary and Christine kept up their friendship over time, with Christine sending postcards, sometimes about the men she'd met on her trips to Europe.

PROFOUND ISSUES — RACE, SEXUALITY, GENDER, AND, ETHNICITY — must have come together for Mary at the Latin Quarter. She was performing in the scantiest of costumes, exposing her nearly naked body to the world along with two women — one white, one Black — who had seemingly no shame at showing off their beautiful bodies and who excelled in risqué performances. She was sharing the stage with a Black woman who was outspoken about racial discrimination in America. Throw Christine Jorgensen into the mix, a man — an ex-GI, who had physically changed his sex organs to become the woman he'd always felt he was, who had been hidden in a male body, and who was now celebrating and showing off her new gender to the world.

It had to be liberating for Mary to be with women who dared to be themselves. They were outliers, women who didn't succumb to the restrictive mores of the 1950s. Mary may not have come out completely as herself, but for the time being she could bond with these women and be admired each night as an enticingly sexual beauty by scores of men, white men to be specific, and see her name, Mary Mon Toy, in lights on the Broadway marquee. I can't help but think that referring to herself as a "tits and ass" showgirl, even after all she later accomplished, had to do with this episode of sexual, gender, and racial freedom of expression.

The Showgirl and the Diplomat

MARY'S STEADY LOVER DURING HER RUN AT THE LATIN QUARTER WAS a member of the Permanent Mission of the Republic of the Philippines to the United Nations. Jose was married — his wife and child had remained in the Philippines — and he was madly, lustfully besotted with Mary.

Jose was small and delicate, unassuming in his demeanor — he called himself "an ordinary man" — who socialized with General and Mrs. Carlos Romulo. Romulo, the Philippines' first permanent representative to the UN later became the president of the United Nations General Assembly of the Security Council.

While Jose was professing his love to Mary, General Romulo was a candidate for the position.

It had to have been a heady yet decidedly complicated experience for Mary to attend diplomatic functions given the fact that a mere nine years before, in July of 1945, Romulo had served with General MacArthur in the fight to liberate the Philippines from Japanese control.

IN 1954 THE CRUELTY OF THE BATAAN DEATH MARCH OF APRIL 1942 was still a raw memory for Filipinos. 75,000 Filipino and American troops had been marched sixty-five miles to prison camps under arduous conditions, with thousands perishing along the way.

It must have been difficult for Mary to have entered their society as a person of Japanese descent, albeit as an American. She was placing herself close to the fire on this one. It's hard to imagine that she revealed her ethnicity to Jose, not doing so may have influenced how their affair played out in the end.

THE SHOWGIRL AND THE DIPLOMAT — A COMPELLING MATCH IN the early 1950s when nightlife in the big city was going strong. They had an equal bargain: Mary got a man with position and powerful friends; Jose had a glamorous showgirl who performed at the classiest nightclub in America, and introduced him to exotic, erotic, and quixotic people like Christine Jorgensen.

They began going out in January 1954, but he didn't put his feelings for her on paper until the spring. In that letter, clearly written after a sexual assignation, sent special delivery to her apartment on May 4, he wrote, "The bug bit me quite some time ago — last night, or rather this morning makes it official. In other words it's acute; I've got it bad — and I like it!"

In the next letter, on May 7, his over-the-top prose abounds ". . . each embrace in answer to mine, pulsating and breathless, cannot but be the culmination of that lifetime search for each other."

Rather precipitously, on May 13 he sent Mary an onionskin, carbon copy of a full-page, single-spaced typed missive he had written to his wife the day before, asking for a divorce. In that letter he wrote that their marriage had never worked, that his decision to separate should be no surprise to her since they'd been estranged for two years. He asked for her cooperation "because . . . there is another person concerned. Although she has not thought of marriage, my own feelings toward her preclude any doubts as to the final outcome."

WITHIN THE WEEK THE RELATIONSHIP WITH MARY SOURED. HE went to see her backstage at the Latin Quarter after the show and she told him she wanted to be alone, and sent him packing to his new bachelor residence at the Regent Hotel at 104th Street and Broadway, dressing him down in front of others. That was on Thursday.

On Friday Jose's wife called him long-distanced to say she wouldn't oppose his petition for a divorce, provided her interests were not harmed. Jose wrote to Mary to say, "I will still have to find out what her 'interests' are."

The next day a diplomatic pouch arrived from Manila, which brought him "to earth in a hurry, when I received information about how badly off I am financially and I remembered you saying you wouldn't be my wife until I could support you."

Jose's world was unraveling and to make matters worse, he couldn't keep any food down, not even water, and there were broad hints that he'd lost his virility.

At a breakfast with General and Mrs. Romulo, he was nervous and "jumpy." and Mrs. Romulo, her hand on his arm, asked him to tell her what was bothering him. He said he and Mary had had a "bad morning together," and he'd gone to the doctor who told him that there was nothing physically wrong with him, that it was emotional, and that he should stop fighting himself and stop drinking. Jose was ready to check into the hospital for a complete going over. He was a mess. Shades of grand opera.

His daily special delivery letters to Mary became self-denigrating in his expressions of endless love for her. But in his last letter he declined her demand that he drive her to Long Island for a party in honor of Jorgensen, accusing Mary of making him her "whipping boy," and in the next sentence counseling her to try to relax, that she worked too hard, even though he understood that "in your business things pile up."

He told her he loved her as much as when they first met, but then he began an analysis of her personality, contending that there were two of her, and he'd always love the "one who wants my worship and adoration. The one who gets all worked up, gets critical and at times, downright inconsiderate, takes a little more study, patience and very careful handling. My favorite tho, is the one whom I dream of as my wife to share my wonderful memories of the 'thunder and lightning' during which the 'earth swallowed me.' To the both of you, I love you. J."

WITH JOSE, AS WITH THE MANY OTHER LOVERS TO COME, IN THE end Mary asserted control and gained ultimate power by withholding her affections, provoking a blowup, and walking away.

Why were her relationships so short-lived? Perhaps if she didn't get what she wanted out of a bargain she had no more interest in it. Was it that Jose didn't have enough money anymore? Or she simply tired of men becoming too dependent on her.

Tragically, I think it was because if she let a lover get too close, especially in marriage, he'd learn how old she was, that she couldn't have children, and that she was Japanese American and had been incarcerated during the war.

In the stacks of love letters, she received over the years, there were indications that she was using men to advance her career, her social standing, and later on to gain monetarily from the affairs. This seemed the case with her flirtations and affairs with the three-time Prime Minister of Thailand, the Tony winning theater and movie actor Russ Brown (*Pajama Game* and *Damn Yankees*), Marlon Brando, and a Broadway stage manager, all of whom were married or otherwise unavailable, though in a position, to help. In order to survive she had had to use every means at her disposal — her talent, her beauty, her allure, her intellect, her seductiveness, her humor, and her wiles. She had been on her own all of her adult life, before, during, and after leaving the camp. There was no one to fall back on.

Learning more about this aspect of her life helped me to further understand her defensive stance in the world, her refusal to ask me or any of these men directly for emotional support. Only through sex, imperious demands, charming storytelling, or coy manipulation could she allow herself to engage emotionally.

There were moments — though fleeting — when Mary had allowed me in, when she genuinely said to me that she loved me and in doing so admitted she needed my love. Her relationship with Rose was more freeing of her emotional needs — she loved being mothered by Rose. She became a child again with Rose, and Rose in turn treated her like a stubborn toddler, cajoling and laughing without giving in to her demands and importuning.

I could hardly breathe as I recognized a similar dynamic in myself. I've never been able to ask for help from anyone — instead I present a face of competence, strength, and authority to the world, the kind of woman my father admired and my mother insisted that I be when she said, "I want you to grow up to be an independent woman"— never able to admit weakness, fearful and ashamed for people to know who I really was . . . that is everyone except Fritz.

With new insight I could hear Fritz complaining about my terrible sense of myself, my self-disgust, even my terror of being found out.

"I've never understood it in forty years of knowing you," he'd demand in frustration, "Why you are so ashamed of who you are? Why don't you let anyone in? Don't you see that people love you? *Um Gottes Willen*, they fall in love with you."

Cornered, I would answer, "They only love me because I fool them and charm them into submission. They only love me because I take care of *them*. They don't know who I am inside."

And he would answer, "Don't be so sure of that. You didn't fool me. I'd never fall in love with the person you describe as being so disgusting. It's an insult to me for you to think I would."

IN JOSE'S LAST LETTER TO MARY, HE TOLD HER THAT THE PEOPLE SHE worked with, in particular Ruby, could never steal her charm, beauty, graciousness, or talent. He pleaded with her not to try to get even with them for any slights, "fancied or real." She should try to be generous toward them, and understand that when they asked for advice, "they're admitting your superiority." He closed with, "Be kind. It becomes you. That is the Mary with whom I fell in love. She'll always be Queen, nay, 'Empress' in my heart. I love you. J."

With Jose she had allowed a different interaction than she would with the other men. She had shared her concerns about her work with him. She had let him dangerously close to her real feelings. Jose saw "the two of her."

"To the Empress," Ruby had written in autographs; perhaps a reference to her periodic haughty demeanor. Jose, to his credit, understood what was going on beneath the mask of superiority, Mary's paranoia — slights that were "fancied or real," Jose had said.

THAT PHRASE HAUNTED ME. I, TOO, WAS PARANOID, BUT I NEVER responded with haughtiness. On the contrary, I became more subservient. In that way we differed. *I have to be careful*, I thought, *not to confuse her psychology with mine*. Thinking back to my reaction to Fritz's mother, and how I lost a sense of myself when I felt dismissed and diminished, how on other occasions I could spin from lashing out at Fritz — the person I trusted most — to turn on myself, saying I wasn't worthy of living . . . that I was a gutter rat, a piece of shit, and falling into a fugue state, even gouging at my legs with my finger nails, drawing blood, until Fritz would have to grab hold of me to stop the self-punishment.

In order to truly understand the impact of the Incarceration on Mary, I had to see us as separate beings, and at the same time, try to get to the bottom of my own extreme deprecation of self. Was it just a manifestation of a white-middle-class woman's problem as people scornfully say, or something deeper, more complicated, and connected to an inability to deal with issues of racism and anti-Semitism and the impact of discrimination on both of us in our country?

It was my duty as a writer to find out.

I began to understand that only in self-knowledge, could I have a clear vision and true compassion and empathy for the plight of people jailed for their heritage. I still didn't quite get the dynamic, but

I had a glimmer of what I would face later, that Mary was different from me and that it would be a disservice to confuse and equate our responses to feeling harmed.

There is the possibility that Mary's perception of hurtful attacks by her fellow performers were real hostility, especially from Ruby, growing out of Ruby's envy for what was about to take place: Mary's big break, her chance to perform in a Broadway musical, in a role Ruby probably felt was her due on racial grounds, a role in the all-Negro *House of Flowers*.

34

The Changing Color of Broadway

"House of Flowers"

On a night in February 1954 Lou Walters came into the Latin Quarter dressing room with a seventeen-year-old Negro girl who was awkward and shy and, according to Mary, had no real style of her own. She said Walters told her, "Get this young girl ready, fix her up so she can go on."

The girl was the future star Diahann Carroll. She had won a radio talent contest on "Chance of a Lifetime," and her prize was to sing one evening during the intermission between the two shows at the Latin Quarter.

Her agent had rushed her from a cross-continental flight from California to a beauty parlor to get her hair cut. While she'd dozed in the chair, the stylist had cropped her hair so close that she looked like a young boy. Mary did her best. "I shaped her hair into a French pixie look, put eyelashes and makeup on her, stuffed little falsies into her bra, and shoved her out onto the stage."

Carroll was just off from shooting a small part in the movie *Carmen Jones*, the all-Black film rendition of the opera *Carmen*. "She had never sung before on a [stage], you know," Mary said. "She stood with her arms behind her back. She sang beautifully — "Why Was I Born?" [by Jerome Kern and Oscar Hammerstein, popularized by Billie Holliday]—and she received a wonderful hand."

After the show Mary had changed into street clothes and was swabbing her face with cold cream, removing traces of stage makeup, "We didn't know those bigwigs were sitting at the ringside table,"

Mary said later, "There were little pages like the Phillip Morris boy, dressed in that red uniform. They brought back a note saying they wanted to see Miss Carroll and they wanted to see Miss Mon Toy."

Mary and Carroll had received "a house card" from Broadway producer Saint Subber requesting the honor of their presence after the performance.

Mary in the Latin Quarter audience with gossip columnist Earl Wilson, 1954

This wasn't unusual for Mary. Even as an Asian, she'd been invited to sit down front in night clubs with radio and newspaper hotshots like gossip columnist Earl Wilson and celebrities like movie star Robert Ryan, and the World Heavyweight boxing champion Max Baer, but this was different — Saint Subber had produced the Broadway musical *Kiss Me Kate* only a year before.

Together, she and Diahann Carroll, appeared at the front table to find four men waiting: Saint Subber, young and sexy with a sultry pout; Peter Brook, the English director; Oliver Messel, a renowned

British set and costume designer; and the up-and-coming writer Truman Capote. Saint Subber treated Mary and Carroll with deference as he told them they were mounting a new Broadway musical called *Maison des Fleurs*, or *House of Flowers*, based on a novella by Capote, with music and lyrics by Harold Arlen, already famous for "Over the Rainbow," and choreography by the great George Balanchine.

He said, "…and we'd like you to come and audition at the Alvin Theater."

"So we went," Mary said.

House of Flowers production team, (top to bottom): Truman Capote (Author, lyricist), Harold Arlen (Composer), Jerry Arlen (musical conductor), Oliver Messel (designer), Peter Brook (director), Saint Subber (producer)

SET ON A HAITI-LIKE ISLAND IN THE WEST INDIES, *House of Flowers* would tell a story of two competing bordellos of local prostitutes, and an innocent love affair, played out against the backdrop of Mardi Gras.

House of Flowers, Mardi Gras scene, ensemble with Louis Jordan in flight
Mary is fourth from the left

"Madame Fleur" was the proprietor of one establishment, and "Madame Tango" is her competitor.

The plot revolved around Ottilie, Carroll's character, a neophyte whom Madame Fleur holds in abeyance for the future, when she would need a replacement for one of her aging girls. A rich white man from town, smitten with Ottilie's purity and loveliness, wants to hire her as his "live-in housekeeper." Difficulties arise when "Royal," a young Black fisherman from the hills outside of town, caught sight of Ottilie and fell in love with her as she did with him.

AT MARY'S AUDITION, GEORGE BALANCHINE ASKED HER, "CAN YOU dance?"

"Not really," she answered, "I'm a singer, not a dancer, but I know how to move."

He laughed. "That will do," he said. "We can teach you what you need."

BEFORE ARRIVING AT THE LATIN QUARTER, SAINT SUBBER AND THE others had been scouting Negro clubs around the city. They had already plucked Mary Louise from her singing gig at the Savannah Club in Greenwich Village. She became a member of the ensemble and Carroll's understudy.

Truman Capote and Harold Arlen poured the flattery on Margot Small, another future friend of Mary's, who was also performing at the Savannah Club. A light-skinned eighteen-year-old, just beginning a dance career, they told her she was a raving beauty. Wary, she refused to go to the theater. Capote and Arlen pursued her, even traveling uptown to her family's apartment in Harlem to plead with her, until she finally relented.

Glory Van Scott was dancing with the Talley Beatty Company when she heard about the tryouts. She was only recently out of finishing school in Chicago, a proper young lady from a family that prized the arts.

She arrived in New York City, with her hatbox, pearl earrings, pumps, and demure starched white collar. Glory had studied ballet, song, and acting with other gifted children, but in New York she was introduced to the pioneering dance technique of Katherine Dunham, with its Afro-centric underpinnings. It was her first theater audition ever and she had no idea what to expect; to her astonishment, there on the stage was the choreographer, George Balanchine, Mr. G. himself.

After the final round of tryouts, they called the names of the chosen few out of scores of performers for the "Tango Girls": "Leu Comacho definitely; Glory Van Scott, definitely; Margot Small, definitely;" and then "Mary Mon Toy, definitely."

The producers were seeking a certain type to play the prostitutes — beautiful girls who didn't look particularly American, who had a slightly foreign style. They wanted a range of skin tones, light skinned and dark and in between.

Mary was chosen because she helped replicate the racial mix of the islands. She was cast as "Mamselle Honolulu" in Madame Tango's house, a supporting principal with her name on the program, a major career step.

The *House of Flowers* cast was all Black except for two white actors — Ray Walston, who would soon become a film and theater star, and Dino DiLuca, an Italian actor, and one Asian, Mary Mon Toy. The first pool of talented performers was deep from top to bottom.

Pearl Bailey had just finished filming *Carmen Jones* when she took on the starring role of Madame Fleur.

Juanita Hall, who made her name in 1949 in *South Pacific* in the role of Bloody Mary, had the co-starring role of Madame Tango.

Diahann Carroll went on to win a Tony for best actress in *No Strings*, and a Golden Globe for her TV title role as *Julia*, and an Oscar nomination for the groundbreaking 1974 film *Claudine*.

House of Flowers production team (l to R): Jean Rosenthal (lighting designer, Oliver Messel (designer), Marlene Dietrich (friend of production), Vagn-Riis-Hansen (Sant Subber's manager and partner), Saint Subber (producer), man far right not identified.

Fredrick O'Neal, who was already a force in African American theater, television, and film, a radical unionist, and co-founder of Harlem's American Negro Theatre.

Josephine Premice would go on to be nominated for two Tony Awards.

Twenty-one-year-old Louis Johnson would become one of two Black lead dancers with the New York City Ballet.

Arthur Mitchell would found the Dance Theater of Harlem.

Walter Nicks, who served as Balanchine's dance master for the production, earned a scholarship to the American Ballet School.

Geoffrey Holder, who danced in the production, also earned a choreography credit which was almost unprecedented for a Negro choreographer on Broadway.

Carmen de Lavallade and Geoffrey Holder became part of the lore of the production when they fell in love during the run of the show and married the month after it closed.

Twenty-three-year-old Alvin Ailey founded Alvin Ailey Dance Theater in 1958.

Herbert Ross, who came on as the second choreographer/director, later directed the iconic film *Footloose*.

The production principals and performers were what today we would call a dream team, an illustrious group of people, glamorous and in demand.

Mary in the upper left window, Juanita Hall with telescope.

The musical was destined to be a seminal theatrical event, a transitional moment in the history of American theater, with its melding of Caribbean steel pans, authentic Vodou rituals, cutting-edge modern dance, and Broadway glitz. Audiences were to see a whole new school of Black dancers trained in classical ballet and avant-garde modern dance techniques performing in a Broadway musical, brilliant young performers and choreographers who would go on to change the artistic and racial landscape of theater and dance in America.

AND MARY WAS ABOUT TO BE A PART OF IT.

She showed up for the first rehearsal dressed to the hilt in a full-length mink. According to her, this is when Pearl Bailey said, "This here is a colored show, what we need with an oriental chick?" Mary snapped back, "I'm lending you atmosphere, and my own color, madam."

Mary later told an interviewer, "All the kids laughed, but Pearl Bailey never really liked me after that . . . she had me stuck on the balcony of one of the sets and the scrim hid my face and everybody said, 'What happened to the oriental girl?"

Mary also said that the other performers were mean to her in the beginning . . . they hid parts of her costume so she'd miss her cues. But she worked hard. "I paid my dues, and I gained the respect of the kids. I'm glad I didn't snitch on them. I didn't complain. I just kept on being oriental. You keep that stuff within you."

Costume fitting

Glory, on the other hand, said that she and Mary hit it off immediately, sharing a room when the production moved to Philadelphia for the out-of-town tryouts and their friendship continued through the rest of Mary's life. Glory called her "big sister"; she didn't know then that Mary was old enough to be her mother, "She was beautiful and certainly didn't look her age."

Mary Louise was intimidated by Mary, "She didn't like that I felt unsure of myself. I wasn't forceful like the others or ambitious enough. Mary was sophisticated. She'd even been to Europe."

Geoffrey Holder would tell me that Mary was gorgeous, and "We all loved her."

In a photo, Oliver Messel is adjusting the bodice of Mary's Mardi Gras dress. Her hair is loosely pinned up and her expression projects calm concentration, a new professional seriousness of purpose.

Friend and noted understudy Maureen Moore explained to me that being fitted for costumes is the best part of being in a production. It's the moment when your character gains a concrete reality. It's when you realize this is really going to happen, and for Mary it was a turning point in her career.

House of Flowers was classier than any of her preceding shows. She'd worn grand and intricate costumes at the China Doll Club, on the vaudeville circuit, and at the Latin Quarter, but none had the sophistication and pure good taste of Oliver Messel's award-winning designs. Mary recognized the quality of the design and execution — she had, as Mary Louise said, "been to Europe." When Pearl Bailey offered her own hand-me-downs to the girls, Mary declined, "I don't need them. I have real Diors of my own."

THOUGH THERE IS AN ORIGINAL CAST RECORDING OF THE EVOCATIVE songs, there is no film record of the musical other than a ten second snippet from dancer Geoffrey Holder's Banda performance. Still photographs capture Louis Johnson's incredible jumps and Walter Nicks high jinks, and to some degree the look of the stage and the energy of the production, but there is no documentation of the Balanchine, the Holder, or of the later Herbert Ross choreography, not even on paper.

The closest anyone has come to recreating it is for the Popular Balanchine Dossiers collection by Thomas de Frantz.

I spent my Christmas holiday in 2014, poring over de Frantz's documents and tapes collected in the Library of the Performing Arts at Lincoln Center. I watched and read interviews with the performers for hours on end. Mary's interview was only in transcription, but it captured her excitement, pride, and paranoia at being in the musical. In a video made in 2001, Margot Small and de Frantz try to recreate the dance steps of the Tango Girls.

House of Flowers' "Tango Belles," (l to r), Pearl Reynolds, Leu Camacho, Margot Small, Glory Van Scott and Mary Mon Toy,

He respectfully prods Margot Small into showing him the moves forty-six years after she appeared in *House of Flowers*. This gentle beanpole of a young man with shoulder length dreadlocks, and a contemporary sense of movement, tried to follow the zaftig older dancer as her muscle memory gradually reawakened. "No, no," she said to him, wiping sweat from her face and neck, repeating the sequence, "it was like this," slowly revealing the thread of influences from Katherine Dunham to Balanchine to Herbert Ross as she again became the young woman who had been pursued by Capote and Harold Arlen to play a Tango Girl. After a particularly sexual movement, she stopped and laughed, "I was so innocent back then. I had no idea what this was about." These were the steps that Mary danced as well, though she wasn't innocent about what they conveyed.

Five days into my time in the library, I read a passage by Glory Van Scott where she described standing in the wings watching the other dancers make their entrances, and how they'd smile at each other in recognition of their mutual joy.

Asked by Thomas de Frantz at the end of an interview if she had any last thoughts about performing in *House of Flowers*, Glory answered, "If I could give someone a gift, certainly an artist, I would give him the gift of having that as a first show. To be with the people I was with. To experience what I experienced as an artist with them." A statement of youthful esprit de corps and racial pride. How lucky Mary was to be a part of it, how rare such instances are in an artist's life.

But then I came upon the final version of the script, the one that was used once they returned to Broadway from tryouts in Philly.

In the first scene of the first act, Madame Fleur, played by Bailey, says of her competition, Madame Tango, "Now she's imported a Japanese lady. Some of what used to be our steadiest gentlemen, they are all so curious over this little old Jap."

It was a shock to read that line in 2014; what must it have been for Mary to see it in the script nine years after the end of the war? She had to have closed off a part of herself as night after night she endured the jingoistic and racist reference unable to complain without revealing her true identity.

Geoffrey Holder said when I interviewed him, "we loved Mary," which at first glance would seem a good thing, but in that word "we"

I now heard that she wasn't a part of the "we of us." Where they were embracing each other's talents in the historic production, Mary observed from a few steps outside their circle. She was still the old Jap, even among colleagues and close friends who seemingly overlooked the racism in that line, and weren't aware of the profound significance for her and her family in that one simple statement.

I wondered if the reference wasn't added after Mary showed up for the first rehearsal in her mink.

In Capote's original novella there is no Japanese prostitute. If Mary's story of Pearl Bailey challenging her right to be in the play is true, Bailey's animosity might have played some part in having the slur inserted. Another petty arrow in the act is slung directly by Bailey's character at Mary's real life and her rejection of Bailey's proffered gift of Dior dresses: "She's only recently off the banana boat from Paris."

By all accounts Bailey was involved in having Josephine Premice replaced when Premice — a huge talent — upstaged Bailey by receiving too large a hand with her very first song. Bailey also had the haunting song "Don't Like Goodbyes" taken away from Diahann Carroll and given to herself after Carroll stopped the show with it. It was in keeping with Bailey's competitive nature, that she would use her muscle to have those pointed lines added, to denigrate Mary's character.

It could explain Mary's grudge against Bailey fifty years later. By now in her career Mary projected power and self-assurance that could be intimidating, even to a burgeoning diva like Pearl Bailey. Mary was beautiful, could be arrogant, and had built a reputation for her Latin Quarter work, and for headlining in clubs up and down the East Coast. This was Pearl Bailey's first starring role in a Broadway show; for her a lot was riding on the hot new musical.

Maybe more important, Mary wasn't Black — but did Bailey know that she was Japanese American? Or was "Jap" chosen because the musical was set during World War II and "Jap" would be more potent than "Chink" or some other derogatory Asian reference? I asked Glory if Mary had ever spoken to her about the camps or that she had been incarcerated. Glory motioned with her hand, that Mary skimmed over it. "She didn't want to talk about it."

I said then that many people don't think the camps were so bad because they weren't the killing camps of Europe. Glory fixed me with her penetrating look and said, "There is more than one way to kill a soul."

During the run, a piece about Mary appeared in Irv Hirsch's "Night Shift" column in the *Trade Union Courier*, a show business trade newspaper covering theater, movies, radio, video, and the arts.

Show Girl Goes "East"
To Make a Success

It took over 5,000 miles to travel from her birthplace in Hawaii, and years of the rough road of show business, but pretty Mary Mon Toy finally made it as "Miss Honolulu" (she plays the role in the hit musical, "House of Flowers"). She almost didn't get there for one of her earlier inclinations led to her studying to be a teacher.

Born of Chinese and Korean parentage, she moved to California at the age of eight. With the theatrical urge planted early, she was selected, at the age of 16, along with several other high school mates, by Tom Ball to become one of the early well-known "China Dolls" at his N.Y. night club.

Later, she went back to take a degree in education at U.C.L.A. But acting called, and after several movie bits, she went into vaudeville, doing a singing and dancing act, which was followed by a mid-Western tour of night clubs. Back on Broadway, she was featured at the Latin Quarter, the show girl's Mecca, and in a solo at the Palace. More night clubs and modeling were followed by her present role.

She is also an ardent union member, Chorus Equity, AFTRA, and Variety Artists Guild being among her affiliations, and attends all meetings where possible, realizing their usefulness.

Despite the glamour of her profession, she's looking for the right man for marriage. Meanwhile her desire is to get ahead in musical comedy.

Her travels have taught her some discrimination still exists, particularly in the west, where she was once refused service privileges in a dress shop. But she takes such things in stride.

Mary has "gone east" instead of west to make a success.

It's breathtaking to see how she changed her ethnicity, birthplace, her education, and the particulars of the discrimination she'd met; they had all been altered, as had her age. She'd shaved off fourteen years. So convincing is this version that she must have begun to believe her own myth. She'd created a public history to hide the incarceration, but at what price to her authentic self? Though this was the first time she was outspoken about being discriminated against because of her race and it's the first record of her professing to be an "ardent" union member, which made me wonder if she'd picked up on talk of race and worker activism from the other cast members.

Wanting to know more about the musical and Mary's connection to it, and having the feeling that something significant had happened in the mounting of the production that had played an important role in the future careers of the performers, Mary included, I followed every lead to get an interview with Geoffrey Holder, who was outspoken about issues of race. Through a lucky circumstance, I was rewarded.

I interviewed Holder in his nursing home a few months before he died. He was a grand picture of a man even confined to a hospital bed. He wore a green, white, and red plaid shirt and had a long scarlet shawl dashingly wrapped around his neck. As we began his speech was somewhat garbled, and I had to lean close to understand him, but fifteen minutes into our conversation, his voice gained momentum and articulation when he suddenly veered off into an angry denunciation of "the director, that Englishman, a constipated man," who had "been rude" to the cast of dancers. Holder went on . . . Peter Brook had wanted them to perform the Cha-Cha, "his way, counting each step out. We said we didn't have to count, we knew how to do the Cha-Cha, we danced it every night after rehearsals at the Palladium. And then he called us 'you people.' We went to Pearl Bailey and Bailey went to Saint Subber, the producer, and said, it's either me or him. Subber folded and Herbert Ross, who worked as a choreographer on *Carmen Jones* with Pearl and Diahann, was brought in," resulting in Peter Brook being sidelined, and Balanchine let go, consolidating both jobs into one.

The producer, director, set and costume designer, lighting designer, writer, lyricist, orchestrator, stage manager, stage hands, and choreographers, save Holder, were all white while ninety-seven percent of the performers were Black. It was a plantation set-up and it could have perpetrated a plantation mentality on both sides, except that the young performers were too well-educated and trained in their artistic fields to feel subservient, and they had to have been cognizant of the rising winds of social change in America. Brown vs. the Board of Education had been adjudicated and desegregation unanimously supported by the Supreme Court in May of 1954.

Sit-ins at lunch counters were being planned at southern Black universities where some of the performers had studied, and a bus desegregation case was already in the courts having been filed in 1953 by an African American female Army private, Sara Keys, who was on furlough traveling on an interstate bus, when she was ordered in North Carolina to give up her seat to a white marine. By late 1954, the strategy was being planned for Rosa Parks' historic refusal to move from her seat on a city bus. This climate of new activism on civil rights had to have influenced the *House of Flowers* performers. When Brook referred to them as "you people," it became a historic moment in theater; a proud Black cast stood up to the white director and won.

Holder's anger was as raw after six decades, as if it had just happened. Next his fury spilled over onto me when I asked if he thought the mixed reception for the play had anything to do with the white reviewers not knowing how to deal with trained Black modern and ballet dancers.

"You're insulting me with that question," he shouted as he rose up in his bed, and with sudden ferocity launched a personal attack on me. "Why are you dressed like that? Why are you wearing stripes? They're so passé. And your hair." He swirled his hand over his head. "Why don't you comb it?"

Keep calm, I said to myself, you have to find a way through this. Don't shrink back. You need this interview. You worked too hard to get it.

"You should know that I changed my outfit five times before coming and left my bedroom in a chaos of rejected clothes," I said, opting for the truth as my defense.

"And why did you do that?" he asked in his deep baritone, with a hint of amused victory.

"You're a Tony winning director and famous costume designer, who even in bed in that perfect shirt and red scarf, are the height of style. I knew you'd judge me and sure enough you did."

He roared, throwing back his head, filling the room with his famous booming laugh.

A nurse entered with clean linens giving us each a moment to recoup. He imperiously told her to leave them on the bureau, that she'd have to wait to change his bed.

By the time she walked out we'd cooled off enough to go on with the interview. When I mentioned to him that I still heard white theater people blaming Pearl Bailey's diva ways for difficulties with the production, he only snapped back with mild irritation, "She was a strong woman, she had to be."

Notwithstanding our truce and parting hugs and kisses and his invitation to come back and visit him, I left his hospital room thinking how deep and unresolved the old racial wounds went, even for someone as supremely talented and accomplished a man as Holder, and how wide the gulf remained between us.

WHEN MARY HAD SPOKEN OVER THE YEARS ABOUT *HOUSE OF FLOWERS*, she mostly described herself as more experienced than the "kids in the cast"; she had taught them how to deal in the rough-and-tumble world of New York theaters. Then why was she so defensive? After my interview with Holder, I began to understand what was going on with her.

Though most of the "kids" had no show biz experience, hadn't gone through the hard knocks of vaudeville, many came out of a realm of high culture, of ballet and modern dance. Some of them already knew Balanchine, having danced with his company. Many were superbly trained in Afro-centric modern technique from studying under Katherine Dunham, Lester Horton, and Talley Beatty; they had a common goal and a shared language of avant-garde dance and Negro cultural history. A number of them had been to finishing school and college, or had gained a field of knowledge of Black musical heritage, like Mary Louise who had sung and toured with the great Cab Calloway. Their talent had been developed and noted by the powers that be, and some had the monetary support of their families.

It hadn't been that way for Mary. She was the one who had financially supported her family. She hadn't had extensive classical training, unless you counted her two years of night classes at Juilliard — even those were disrupted with leaving to get her parents out of camp. She'd been a showgirl and a lead singer on the vaudeville circuit, no mean accomplishment, but it wasn't classy and it wasn't high art. The closest she'd gotten was the ensemble in Kurt Weill's *Street Scene* for two performances.

The dedication and advanced training of these young people flew in the face of what was expected of Blacks at the time. White society and popular culture still depicted Negroes in movies and on the stage as undereducated, subservient, and capable only of singing the blues, tap dancing, and jitterbugging.

Mary knew better from her own interactions with Blacks in the nightclub acts and her stint with opera singers of the caliber of Robert McFerrin Sr. She could extrapolate from her experiences with racist distortions of Asians, but I suspect she carried some of her own racial prejudices back then as well as the compensatory need to feel superior to another subjugated race. But inferiority and stereotype weren't what Mary encountered in the rehearsals for *House of Flowers*. They were an incomparably smart and talented group with awareness of their own accomplishments, and disdain for those who weren't as talented as they. Even Herbert Ross felt he had to protect the young Alvin Ailey and Carmen de Lavallade when he brought them to New York from California. "They're a tough New York lot," he said.

HOUSE OF FLOWERS OPENED ON DECEMBER 30, 1954, TWO DAYS before the start of a new year, a racial harbinger of what was to come in America. The theater was packed, the front row filled with celebrities like Gloria Vanderbilt and her date for the night, Frank Sinatra. The ticket presales were huge; performances were sold out through March of the following year.

The book for the musical may not have been the best; even Geoffrey Holder called it a fairy tale with prostitutes. In adapting his original short story for the stage, Capote sentimentalized the drama, perhaps thinking he was making it more palatable for the general audience. What was lost in the show's book and the spoken dialogue, which often edged on hokey, was Capote's masterful use of language and his talent for the hard-bitten truths of lost souls. But the songs he collaborated on with Harold Arlen compensated for this failing. As Jennifer Dunning wrote, they were "achingly poetic," and considered by many now, as Arlen's masterwork. They evoke Caribbean floral scents and rhythms, island folklore, humor, romantic love, racial politics, sexual longing, anger, and lust. Songs like "A Sleeping Bee" and "Two Ladies in De Shade of a Banana Tree" crawl under your skin and into the brain so that for evermore their melodies continue to haunt.

Some reviewers appreciated the uniqueness of what was happening on the Alvin Theater stage. William Hawkins of the *New York World-Telegram* opened his review with "It's a gaudy, tropical, horticultural show, *House of Flowers* at the Alvin. New York has not had a first-rate Negro musical for too many years. It has never had one with such elegance and chic."

But Brooks Atkinson of the *New York Times* trashed the musical from the beginning to the end of his condescending review, culminating in his final paragraphs. "Every Negro show includes wonderful dancing. *House of Flowers* is no exception in that respect. Tall and short Negroes, adults and youngsters, torrid maidens in flashy costumes and bare-breasted bucks break out into a number of wild, grotesque, animalistic dances."

Reading this, I thought, *no wonder Geoffrey Holder had so personalized his attack on me.*

Atkinson also wrote "Mr. Capote, who found West Indian bordellos a pleasant place for drink and conversation . . . appears to have about as much feeling for their inhabitants as a eunuch in a harem." A snide slam at Capote's homosexuality, another cause for Holder's fury during our interview.

Inbred bias in keeping with mid-century American attitudes, must have affected and infected the critical response to *House of Flowers*. Unconsciously, they could have been looking for what Glory Van Scott called "good old 'Yassuh' theater." Some of those critics who wanted something new must have wanted a good-old-liberal preconceived new, and they weren't prepared for the radical new they got; it was too much for them to take in and contextualize.

What the reviewers were seeing was avant-garde art. Its influences, including bumps and grinds and muscular athletic moves, derived from Katherine Dunham's earlier work and adapted by Balanchine and Ross, would later be acclaimed in Bob Fosse's and Alvin Ailey's choreography. Like anything that breaks with the old, it's hard for people to gauge it in the beginning.

Mary Louise had no doubts about a reason for the mixed and, at times, hostile reviews, "The show was really up front with cross-race sexuality. *South Pacific* before that had been a good liberal play by comparison. This was about raw sexuality during the time the South was still segregated." She said it was about white sailors coming onto a Black island for sex, unlike *Porgy and Bess*, which was Black on Black. The sailors are never seen, but "the virile Black guys on the drums were there to get the sailors hot." Mary agreed. "We were kind of shocking. Bare chests and pasties and so on, I think in those days . . . well, it isn't like now."

What was most revolutionary and probably disturbing was how the sexual crossing of racial boundaries transgressed the mores of the time. Captain Jonas, played by white Ray Walston, and Black Pearl Bailey shared an on-stage, steamy sexual kiss. It's made clear that they've been lovers for a time. The kiss went unmentioned in all the reviews, which tells me that it was too hot to handle.

One can find a few other instances of cross racial kisses, such as the kiss between Ivy who was Asian and Gabey who was white in Bernstein's *On the Town*, but that was sweet rather than sexually charged. And it wasn't Black on white. This was 1954 when the Hays Code, which didn't allow any insinuation of an interracial sexual relationship, was still the censorious law in film and on television. As late as 1968, when Harry Belafonte appeared on a variety show on NBC, Petula Clark, a white singer, smiled at him and touched his arm, causing the show's sponsor, Plymouth Motors to panic and almost cut the segment until Clark, who owned and produced the special, said she'd kill the show unless it was aired intact. She won, but the mere fact of the controversy at that late date underscores how dangerous the *House of Flowers'* kiss was, fourteen years earlier. Nobody was bowing and scraping at the Alvin Theater. The stance on stage was one of self-assurance with in-your-face arrogance and some insolence thrown in. And something unusual even occurred within the more sentimentalized love between Ottile and Royal that set this musical apart from others of the period; Ottile chooses the young Black suitor over the older, moneyed white man.

This was no *South Pacific, Madama Butterfly* or *Teahouse of the August Moon* where the young innocent woman of color is left to pine for the white man when he abandons her to return to his white world. *House of Flowers* was revolutionary in its sexual daring and the critics, without explicitly saying why, warned potential theater goers: "Leave your sedate Aunt Minnie at home, or you'll have a lot of explaining to do . . . Adventures that would make even Sinbad the Sailor gasp."

*H*OUSE OF FLOWERS SURVIVED FOR A RESPECTABLE RUN: 165 performances — five months — and closed on May 21, 1955. The musical has lived for over half a century in the hearts and long memories of the players. Other performers, white and Black to this day include the songs in their repertoire and use them for auditions. Those who had the privilege of sitting in the audience never forgot it. *House of Flowers* remains a reference point among the cognizant, and one can rarely attend a theater or dance event with any of the original participants and not find reference to it in the *Playbill* and the same is true in biographies and histories of the principals.

The show advanced the future careers of many of the African American performers and cemented five decades of friendship for Mary with Glory and Mary Louise. I wondered if being in the production had shaped Mary's perceptions about race and had she been radicalized by what she was hearing from other cast members of the escalating civil rights movement; did it carry over to the next phase of her professional life, one that would deal directly with her own rights as an Asian American performer?

Racism in America was blatant in its cruelty in the 1950s, but as an artist of color you had to put the pressures of prejudice to one side — Glory, who experienced the shock of the brutal death of her cousin Emmett Till at the hands of Mississippi racists in August of 1955, said to me "I just keep going, you have to"—but when the exigencies of discrimination become too great to tolerate you needed the bravery and clout of the group to fight back.

That's what happened with the cast in *House of Flowers*. I learned a lesson listening to these actors, about the redemptive power of making art, the courage it takes for any artist to stay on the path, the importance of keeping a sense of self intact even when the world doesn't want what you produce, and the necessity of community when the powers that be want to shove you back off the curb into the street.

OVER THE YEARS, SADNESS ABOUT THE FAILURE OF MY NOVEL TO FIND a publisher had crept back into me, insecurity about my own abilities as a writer had risen to the surface again, and suspicion that no one would be interested in what I had to say. There were also moments in doing the research on Mary's life, much as I loved the adventure of discovery, when I felt her life was taking precedence over mine and that I was once again in her service. But I was learning from the determination of Mary and the cast of *House of Flowers*, that the arc of creative expression was as long as any other journey toward change in our country. Each failure couldn't be comprehended in the immediate time that it occurred, because something was percolating that was much larger than a single disappointment.

Mary, as with the cast, refused to be silenced; her courage would buttress me as I began to unravel my timidity in the face of resistance to my work. Where I beat myself up, she forged ahead, never feeling sorry for herself, thrilled with what the world tossed her way and proud of what progress she made for herself. Why was that? Where did her strength come from, and at what price?

35

The World of Suzie Wong

HOUSE OF FLOWERS DIDN'T HAVE CARRYING POWER FOR MARY'S career. She bounced around after the show closed, and rejoined the white vaudeville circuit, performing in her old haunts up and down the east coast from Miami to Montreal, all far from Broadway and the glamour she had tasted. Her act devolved into the tawdry in Miami. A columnist wrote, ". . . a neatly-stacked Oriental damsel, by the name of MARY MON TOY, is transformed from a shy cherry-blossom type to a lissome lass doing a geisha-girl version of an American strip tease . . .sort of a Japsy Gypsy Rose Lee."

There's a photo of Mary in a seedy club, seated on a bar stool looking prim and proper yet very uncomfortable as an unseemly white man leans his large belly into her, his leg touching her thigh, grinning suggestively for the camera.

How did she find herself in that situation, and why ever did she have to endure such indignity? I want to shove the man aside, and run with her from that sordid scene.

I remember similar incidents in my own life, and I recall my mother slapping me across my face and calling me a tramp when I came home falling down drunk at fifteen. I attended the same high school in Uniondale where she taught. She rarely went to the teacher's room, too upset to meet my teachers, who would confront her before her colleagues about my disruptive behavior in class and the bad crowd I hung out with. What would Mary's mother have done if she'd walked into that bar — a preposterous notion, I realize, but I sense that there's a key in this photograph to the difference between Mary and me. She protected her mother from such knowledge; I rebelled in defiance of my mother in order to hurt her.

After Miami, Mary did a number of screen tests for movies, the most important being for the part of Hana-ogi, Marlon Brando's love interest in *Sayonara*. That hope was dashed when it was awarded to Miiko Taka. "I was too tall for Brando, he was short, you know," was what Mary told me.

The more likely explanation was her age: she was forty-one years old to Brando's thirty-three, and Miiko Taka's thirty-two. Though Mary looked good on stage and in person, on the silver screen her age would show. And probably even more painful to Mary, Miiko Taka had no previous acting experience, was also from Seattle, and as a child had been incarcerated in the Gila Camp in Arizona, a fact Taka didn't hide. To add more disappointment, journalist Dorothy Kilgallen wrote in her syndicated "Voice of Broadway" column, "Mary Mon Toy, one of Brando's chief interests in the U. S. is trying to decode his latest dispatch from Japan where he's making *Sayo-nara*. He tells her he's taken up 'hot housekeeping' and she can't quite figure out what it means." What it meant was that he had moved on to a new Asian woman.

Mary's career picked up in the spring of 1958. She was hired for the popular Phil Silvers television show, *Sergeant Bilko*, along with other Asian American women performers from her China Doll Club days.

She found work doing television ads, both on camera and in voice-overs. Some of them came through a connection to her good friend Keye

Phil Silvers Show, Sgt Bilko with Mary Mon Toy and performers from earlier China Doll Club days

Luke, the Chinese American actor who had gained early prominence in film as Charlie Chan's "Number One Son."

After a while she earned regular TV work on her own through the Compton Ad Agency. She went to audition after audition for theater, TV, and film acting roles. When she came up empty, she settled for serving as hostess at restaurants or a greeter at mall openings. She modeled in department stores and did clothing shoots for newspapers and magazines in Montreal, combining them with singing gigs in the city's nightclubs. She performed in summer stock, regional theater, and supper clubs. Her files are filled with *Playbills* and press clipping for her performances in regional theater venues around the country, large and small. She never thought herself too fine to take minor work, seemingly not complaining that she was the only Asian playing the Asian roles with other cast members in Yellow Face. Though some regional papers did take note of the fact. She again was determined to meet her goal of being a working actor no matter how many avenues and detours she had to follow.

The resilience and stoicism she'd shown as an older woman served her well in maintaining her career for four decades. Much of her dogged perseverance and ingenuity had to do with the discipline instilled by her mother. She told me, "My mother said school came first. I had to finish my homework before I could go for singing lessons or play sports."

Mary's parents were not the only Issei who demanded academic excellence from their children. Mary's work ethic was as culturally determined as my own mother's high standards for herself that had stemmed from her Jewish background. Mary and she had more in common than their birth week, the high school they both went to, the proximity of their neighborhoods in Seattle, and the camp experience.

During the difficult periods Mary's generosity and sense of reciprocity with other performers grew, as did her emerging influence in the theater world. In 1957 Keye Luke had been trying to set up a project with Mary that never materialized, and he was as disappointed about it as Mary. By the end of the year, he was earning only minor roles, which he lamented in long letters to her. In late December Mary successfully interceded for him with Gene Kelly to get him a major placement as Wang chi-Yang in the up-coming *Flower Drum Song*.

Mary was a savvy networker, sending coconut candy to ad agency people as thanks for a job, orchids to actors when they made it to Broadway, gifts of appreciation to the backstage workers and the people in the box office, and thank-you notes to columnists, producers, reviewers, and fellow actors. She was a consummate professional out for herself, but a generous goal of her career building was to make it easier for Asian American actors who followed.

For a short time in the late 1950s there was a surge of theatrical and film opportunities for Asian American actors.

Mary's next big break came when she was cast in *The World of Suzie Wong*. Joshua Logan was the director of both that play and the movie *Sayonara* — so that while Mary's screen test for *Sayonara* had led to a disappointment, in the end it helped her to win a Broadway role. *Suzie Wong* opened on Broadway in October of 1958 and ran for 508 performances.

The show signaled a departure from the casting of Caucasians as Asians. Asian American actors filled most of the Hong Kong Chinese roles. One exception was awarding the starring spot to France Nuyen, a Eurasian French national, but at least she was of Asian heritage. Mary was cast as the bar girl, prostitute, Minnie Ho, "the girl who forgot to ask for pay because she liked her work so much." She was again on Broadway.

The New York reviews cited her skills in comedy. It was a major accomplishment and it substantially raised her visibility.

Later, as Mary toured with the national company of the show, Minnie Ho became a role identified with her. The only problem was, as Truman Capote wrote in his congratulatory opening-night telegram, "too bad it's another house."

Similar sympathy could be shown all the actresses in the play. They were on Broadway, but in stereotypical roles for Asian and Asian American women, roles with no real depth, stripped of meaningful material in order to entertain an American audience and make the interracial sex non-threatening. Paying for sex with a woman of another race wouldn't challenge the sanctity of marriage or the American anti-miscegenation laws that criminalized interracial marriage; in both the book and the play, sex with Asian prostitutes was lauded as a way to open the world of sensuality to white men.

On December 8, 1958, *FLOWER DRUM SONG* opened at the St. James Theater, across the street from the Broadhurst Theater where *The World of Suzie Wong* had been playing for a month. Though there have been many criticisms of *Flower Drum Song* in the Asian American community, it was a revolutionary moment in American theater because not only were most of the characters Chinese American, but with a few exceptions, they were played by Asian American actors. True it didn't deal in a complex, authentic cultural manner with issues of immigration and acculturation, but it was a Broadway musical, after all.

Flower Drum Song was about making it in America on American terms. There were no prostitutes in the play, maids or laundrymen or Dragon Ladies or Kung Fu villains, none of the stereotypes so ubiquitous in American theater and film. Instead there was a wealthy immigrant father, his assimilated university-student son, a picture bride right off the boat, and energetic, enterprising nightclub owners and performers in a thoroughly American-style nightclub in San Francisco's Chinatown.

Anyone watching the play or the movie had to come away awed by the overwhelmingly high level of talent in both. In the Asian American non-theatrical community *Flower Drum Song* became an affirmation of self that was passed down through many generations, first by attending the Broadway show, later the film when it came out, and eventually by viewing a prized DVD with children and grandchildren at home. In 2014 at the New-York Historical Society during an "Evening with Nancy Kwan," star of the film of *Flower Drum Song*, Asian American audience members of all ages took the microphone to say that they had watched the movie innumerable times and that it had meant so much to see people like themselves on the screen.

THE TWO YEARS ON BROADWAY WERE A HIGH POINT FOR MARY. Sent out by the producers to promote the show, she appeared on radio and television in top venues. She was being pursued by agents, one of whom was Tony Rivers, who would discover the comedian, Joan Rivers.

He wrote in October 1958, after having seen Mary in *The World of Suzie Wong*, " . . . you did such an outstanding job as MINNIE HO that I felt I had to write you these few lines . . . You no doubt have your own reasons for not coming to see me . . . However, I'm certain you will go a long way as a comedienne and I'm only sorry you were'nt [sic] my client in this case . . . Keep up the good work. I think you are a real talent."

Mary sang on Jack Paar's late night show. A person-about-town, her photograph was regularly headlined in the show business and gossip columns, including a pictorial spread of the softball competition between the casts of *Suzie Wong* and *The Flower Drum Song*, where Mary Mon Toy was the losing pitcher to Pat Suzuki of *Flower Drum*.

In 1960 she was a heralded member of the grand national road tour for *The World of Suzie Wong*, which travelled the entirety of the United States and up into Canada, with performances in twenty-five venues. Mary garnered press often with her photo at every stop, as well as honored billing in the Playbill programs and congratulatory telegrams and notes at various stops, including one for the play's opening at the legendary Riviera hotel in Las Vegas, saying, "Good luck! I love you madly, Duke Ellington."

Over time, it sometimes seemed like Mary knew and was known by everyone. In a 2014 remembrance in *The New Yorker*, of the famed Ruby Dee, who had recently died, Hilton Als, thinking back to his own young self as he had frequented his mentor Owen Dobson's apartment in the late 1970s, wrote, "I could barely look at Dee when I would see her at Owen's, in that penthouse on West Fifty-first Street, where his parties were legion. There, one saw one beauty after another: Josephine Premice, Derek Walcott, Mary Mon Toy — a whole colored world of mutual support."

Owen Dobson was a leading black director and poet, Josephine Premice, a transcendant actress, and Derek Walcott, a poet and future Nobel Prize winner in Literature, and of course, Mary Mon Toy, still known for her signature Broadway roles in *House of Flowers* and *The World of Suzie Wong*. Hilton Als goes on to write that for his young self, it was a "dream of Manhattan sophistication."

A Celebration of Suzie Wong

The World of Suzie Wong, the Broadway stage

The World of Suzie Wong, the Broadhurst Theater Playbill, France Nuyen

The World of Suzie Wong stage dress rehearsal, with Mary (third from left),
Joshua Logan, and William Shatner

William Shatner autographed photo, "To my Mary, who was never contrary,
always filled with joy."

Promoting *The World of Suzie Wong*, Jack Paar's *NBC Tonight Show*,
Jack Paar, Mary Mon Toy, and Steven Cheng

The World of Suzie Wong softball team. Central Park. Mary Mon Toy (third from
left behind the banner) was losing pitcher to Pat Suzuki of *The Flower Drum Song*,"

Mary Mon Toy at celebrity event to promote *The World of Suzie Wong*,
Front left to right: seated John Saxon and Anna May Wong, Mary standing

On the occasion of the announcement of the National Tour of *The World of Suzie
Wong*, Las Vegas venue, congratulatory telegram, Duke Ellington

"A big TV show is being readied for next year.
It will have 'Oriental' themes."
"Are they hiring Orientals?"

"No. It will be as phony as a $33 diamond."

The heyday for Asian American actors as a group was short-lived. In the late 1950s and 1960s even those who found themselves in starring roles in *The World of Suzie Wong* and *Flower Drum Song* both on Broadway and in films, soon discovered that they had no place to go after that.

Nancy Kwan said that upon reaching the pinnacle of her career, in film versions of both of those shows "there were no more comparable roles for me."

And in the case of France Nuyen, her substantial roles in *Suzie Wong* and *South Pacific* were never to be replicated.

She was also appalled by the racism in America, and just wanted to get back to France. Even though these two actresses were foreign-born and of mixed race — Caucasian and Asian, with features that weren't too Asian for the white American audiences — found no protection for them.

A syndicated article by Mary that appeared in a number of newspapers across the country in December of 1958 — toward the end of the run of *The World of Suzie Wong* on Broadway — captured her quintessential voice with something new . . . public, political outspokenness, expressed in her own behalf, about racial injustice. She said:

> "It's a devilish thing for Oriental talents that there is a multiplicity of Oriental shows on Broadway this season, . . . Ours and *Flower Drum* and the incoming *Rashomon*, but

when these are done we will all sit around quietly starving to death until 22 years hence when someone puts on a show 'requiring' Orientals. And then what will happen? What happens on TV?

Right now a big TV show is getting ready for after the first of the year. It will have Oriental themes. Are they hiring Orientals? No. It will be as phony as a $33 diamond.

Therefore, our only immediate job chance is the present circumstance of several Oriental shows. You remember the girl in *Teahouse of the August Moon*? (She played Miss Higa Jiga.) Great notices. What is she doing now . . . she is working as a clerk in a business office? No jobs for her rich talents."

Our economic concerns are not just ours. France Nuyen, our star, has them too, and is saving her money like mad. Young as she is, and with all the furor she has kindled, she feels when *Suzie* closes, "what happens to me?" She skyrocketed, you know, from a bakery counter to *South Pacific*, the movie.

Then this. Yul Brynner was a different problem. He is not truly Oriental, anyhow. He was male, his shaved head was useful to other stories, as the movies have proven. But an attractive girl of 19, however talented, who looks Oriental, has only a few chances. France is concerned about her future, and rightfully."

Please make a point of the problem of an Oriental talent in today's New York show business. It's very real. You see, you have an advantage. Occidentals can be made-up to look Oriental, but no makeup can make an Oriental look Occidental. It gives us a double hazard."

Reading Mary's article I realized how much anger she had been harboring. I'd convinced myself all those years that she had let the racial indignities slide off her, hadn't let prejudice get in her way. She'd always told me how happy she was with what she'd achieved in the theater world, how she had "done it her way," proclaiming, "What other oriental girl has made it to Broadway?"

I had thought she'd risen above any shame she'd felt about being incarcerated by the government, and that it was fear of being sent back that caused her to hide her ancestry from the world. But now I wondered, what if she did feel shame and what if shame was a cover for anger and what if her Pollyanna view was a cover for both shame and anger?

I had witnessed Mary's fury in her refusal to acknowledge Pearl Harbor Day. I had understood the anger underlying her silence after September 11, in her demand that I send away the census taker, in her closing down to lovers when they got too near, in her picking fights with them to protect her identity, her defensive stance toward Pearl Bailey in *House of Flowers*, her paranoia about the other performers at the Latin Quarter, and her rage at the man at the residence who told her to go back to China, but I'd somehow missed her anger at the injustice that touched her most directly, that which had held her back professionally, "Yellow Face" casting in America.

How could I have missed it? I was brought up in a family where race was openly addressed; I was privy to conversations in our home among my parents' Negro friends, which were punctuated with bitter laughter about being tired of white people asking their opinion on the "Negro issue." I remember a colleague of my mother's saying, "I'd like to turn the question on them and ask, 'How do you feel about white racism as a white person.'"

This same man involved me in a discussion of race over Thanksgiving dinner when I was home from my freshman year in college. Something I posited in our conversation impressed him enough to invite me to lead a class in a teacher training seminar he'd convened at the local university. I was a mere seventeen years old. He wanted me to give my insights on race to his all white class of future teachers.

Why did he ask me to teach it? Why didn't he confront and decode their limitations himself? He perhaps decided they'd hear it better from another white person. But more likely he didn't trust himself not to reveal his anger in this hard-won professional arena. He was a man for whom my mother had mounted a fight in Nassau County in order to integrate the school system by hiring him in 1954; the job at the university had evolved out of the excellence of his teaching techniques at the high school. He was elegant, refined, and tamped-down. All these years later I saw that I missed the anger he must have felt at the restrictions that were placed on him, but even more, the historical anger that he carried, of ancestors who came to America in chains, followed by centuries of suffering through slavery and Jim Crow, a simmering rage, greater than that of immigrants who come to the United States of their own volition and find discrimination, or the anger of Jews like my mother who had their admission to higher education limited by quotas in American universities, and were excluded from private clubs and housing.

The repressed anger of Issei and Nisei, who had been incarcerated for their race and ancestry, a searing erasure of the great American promise, came closer to that of Blacks. I'd admired the professor's decorum, and never suspected any inner conflict.

Both Mary and he were accomplished at camouflaging their true feelings before a white person, but I was astonished to see this blind spot in myself, I who had my own overabundance of anger, rage, and shame, and I, who prided myself on understanding the subtleties of cross-racial interactions, had missed it in Mary. It was like coming face to face with an old friend, myself in this instance, who is revealed to be an unattractively different person than you always thought she was.

The day I had this sudden insight I left my apartment in an agitated state and happened upon Jim Moody, my neighbor, a successful African American actor, known for his role in the movie *Fame*, based on his position as teacher of young people at the School for

Performing Arts, and with whom I'd often talked about Mary. I expressed my dismay at my failing and asked him how I could have missed her fury at being held back professionally because of her race given that I was brought up in the 1950s in a liberal household.

"Ah, the Liberal problem," he sighed, and I recognized immediately that he was saying we liberals don't want to cop to the boiling rage, instead we prefer the patient, non-violent, martyred soldiers in the fight for equality, the ones who rise above the fray. Then he said, about my writing the book, "Keep it complex. Race in America is a conundrum. There are a lot of layers."

But, as I walked away, I became defensive, thinking . . .

'I've marched in Black Lives Matter demonstrations, I understand the anguish and fury caused by the videos of Blacks being killed at point blank by the police, and to a lesser degree than Blacks and other groups of people of color did, I felt it myself. I support the outrage and the stances of Asian American performers in their fight against the continuing use of Yellow Face casting.'

I had many deep eye-opening discussions with my friend Lori Tan Chinn, the consummate and decades long, successful Broadway stage, film, and television actor, about the very high hurdles to maintaining a career when one is Asian American. And I had learned from a father who hadn't missed how racial anger could play out in unexpected ways.'

ONE SUMMER AFTER THE PEACE CORPS, I HAD A JOB RUNNING A DAY camp for children in the South Bronx. I was hired by the white director of the sponsoring community center. On my first day I met in his office with the board of directors of the camp, a group of middle-aged Black men who had been in prison, who had initiated the idea for the camp so that the children of their housing project would not end up in the same troubled circumstances that they had. They'd raised the money for the camp, recruited teens from the neighborhood as counselors, galvanized mothers and grandmothers to volunteer for field trips and help supervise daily activities, but the director had hired me, a twenty-three-year-old white woman to run the camp.

The meeting in the director's office, cramped with nine of us, was tense as he described how I would be in charge. At one point, he left the room and the seven board members began to argue among themselves. Their voices rose with shouts of accusation of cowardice and Uncle Tom-ism, when suddenly one husky man stood, pulled his arm back and with full force punched another man in the chest. Two others tried to physically call him off, but more punches were landed from both sides with a terrifying ferocity, until a board member yelled "fucking cool it," and then someone else called out, "the Man's coming," which served to stop the altercation, just before the director reentered the room.

The fight, the words hurled, had been about having allowed the director to take over the hiring, in other words without saying it directly, hiring me.

I was devastated and later I went to my father. "What happened in that room," I asked. Why had they come to blows? His answer was simple, "It was because they couldn't turn their anger against its source. They couldn't confront the white director, and couldn't go after you as his surrogate. Their sense of impotence and rage had to go somewhere. Tragically they let it out on each other."

It was the exact dynamic that occurred in the camps when the administration grew more oppressive during the loyalty oath debacle — when the oppression increases from above, the people who are hurt, hurt each other. Either that or they press the rage down and put on a happy face.

WHAT I HADN'T UNDERSTOOD ABOUT MARY WAS HOW DEEP HER rage went, tamped down by her unspoken frustration and sense of futility, nor how we had differed from each other in the genesis of our anger. Failing to see Mary as a separate person as I'd cared for her and followed up with research on her past, I'd missed the most obvious . . . what most differentiated us from each other . . . I had never experienced racism directly and she had. I had never had limitations put on my ambitions by outside forces, not even as a woman or a Jew.

I'd always gone for and gotten jobs that men could have had, "guy jobs" as I used to joke in the Peace Corps where we all, men and women, were treated with equally difficult jobs and gender-equivalent assignments; as a rock and folk concert producer when very few women were producers; as only the second female Program Director of a prominent metropolitan radio station. I didn't know what it felt like to go into an audition or job interview knowing that the first line of rejection would be your race, where talent and training wouldn't even be considered in the mix. I didn't know what it felt like to have your most distinguishing physiognomic feature, the shape of your eyes, render you suspect and foreign in a world of "round eyes." I didn't know what it felt like to be forcibly sent to a concentration camp, with little possibility of reprieve from the sentence of guilt by race and ethnicity.

I had focused instead on what Mary and I had in common, our knowledge of the camps, our Northwest heritage, the political milieu that informed our lives to a greater or lesser extent, that we were both artists, and the fact that we'd both passed as something other than who we were born as. I'd thought her battles with her lovers were akin to my own with Fritz. I'd equated our shame and our necessity to present a false identity to the world, basing it on my own reasons for masking my Jewishness. I missed what purposes her need to take on another identity served for her and how her needs differed substantively from mine. I missed that what distinguished Mary's anger from mine was the direction of the rage: hers was aimed outward at a world that held her back and at a political policy that had mistreated her and her people.

I began to see that my rage drew on infantile terrors of being torn from the loving people who had cared for me in the camp, followed by years of instability and disruption, always on the move from one place to another where I didn't fit and where I had to adjust to each new challenge without the support and stability of a warm, nurturing family life.

Even my discovery of the impact of the McCarthy witch hunts, though disruptive and deeply hurtful to my family, wasn't exactly comparable.

It was after that episode that I increasingly hid who I was but even that was more due to the physical and psychological repercussions within the privacy of my home life, the way we as a family unit turned against each other, I, in my rebellion, my mother in her anger at my father and his inability to fight back, and my father in his impotent rage at the circumstances.

Mary had put her anger to work in the service of forging her career and making the best of any situation. Hers was a conscious adult act to show the world she couldn't be kept down.

I, beginning from earliest childhood, built a world of my own making in order to be safe, creating a self that I believed I could control. In the process, I turned against my real self, focusing my rage inward, ever more punishing for not ever being good enough, fearing that if I weren't perfect, I'd be found out and destroyed and the earth would disappear around me and beneath my feet, as it did on a number of occasions.

Any shame that Mary felt about being sent to camp, was superseded by her anger at the injustice. In fact, maybe I was wrong about her; perhaps she felt no shame at all, but rather felt justified in being angry because she believed in herself and her right to succeed as much as white actors did. While for me, shame was an overriding response to my fear of being found out for who I really was, an unworthy child, unworthy of parental love or anyone's love. It took learning about me, facing my own pain and blind spots to be able to truly see, with a new clarity, the nature of the pressure on Mary. She led me to myself so that I could eventually find her.

I have difficulty admitting to how wrong I got it, how little I understood about myself and how it resulted in not truly knowing Mary. And even more perhaps, is the shame I feel about revealing my troubles to the reader in the face of others who encounter concrete oppression on a daily basis. Oppression that can kill the soul, as Glory would say, and even the body.

But there are a lot of layers in this race conundrum, as my neighbor Jim reminded me. It's that "liberal thing," the curse of turning away from one's own struggles in order to have sympathy for the other, while doing so results in a counterproductive, bifurcated sympathy given more easily when the "other" is cheerful, forgiving and non-violent, and righteous, but not self-righteous, no never self-righteous. To misunderstand the implicit anger that stems from real terrors of bodily harm from those in power and real exclusions from the fruits of society, real deaths, and real enslavement and real imprisonment is to miss that though anger often turns inward, it doesn't always have to, doesn't always have to be transmuted into shame and guilt and used against oneself, but can be put to work in a most productive manner by saying to the world and to oneself, I can succeed, I can be productive, I can love myself, I can fully embrace my love for another, despite whatever you bastards throw at me.

If I'd had this insight earlier maybe I could have loved my mother more. She was like Mary, she used her anger at the real discrimination she met as a Jew in America to spearhead a stellar performance at the university leading to a productive career, and in the process, she found a husband and had a child. Where things fell apart for her was that she, like me, her daughter, didn't grow up in a warm family and wasn't fortified emotionally. And tragically for the two of us, I didn't want to be like her. I found her aggressiveness unappealing and my father's modesty and wanting to work behind the scenes much more attractive and a model I continue to follow to this day. To my detriment, I fear.

Mary came from a loving family, and a strong ethnic upbringing, a mother who created a safe passage for her into young adulthood even in a racist society. She was already an adult when the good life she had anticipated was ripped from her.

And when she was released from camp, even though she was relieved to be out, she reentered an America that vilified her race and ethnicity, and placed limitations on her aspirations as an artist. She had to have been exceedingly angry and even vengeful about what she had lost in camp — her husband, her capacity to have children, and valuable time and the critical years to build a career. But her attitude served her well, up to a point.

I WENT BACK TO A SCRIPT I HAD COME ACROSS IN MARY'S BELONGINGS. She was performing at the El Morocco in Montreal during the lean years following *House of Flowers*. She was introduced as a "singing star" by the emcee, "fresh from Broadway where she was featured in the musical hit, *House of Flowers*." She entered to "Two Ladies in de Shade of de Banana Tree" and began with specifically autobiographical lyrics.

The gentleman is a dope . . . and not my cup of tea
A singing star's not what I am—it's what I want to be!
Give me a song to sing, and a place to sing it
And I'll give it everything I've got
I don't care if it's opera (*trill*)
Or something really lowdown and hot!

She went on . . .

But ladies and gentlemen, it almost never works out
that way . . . let me explain."

The Desert Inn in Vegas said they'd give me a chance
I told them how I'd studied singing here and in France
They took one look at me and I was hired — to dance!
That's why I want to sing!

Lou Walters of the Latin Quarter gave me a call
He said he had an opera scene . . . a fancy-dress ball
I wound up wearing opera hose — but that's about all
That's why I want to sing!

When "*House of Flowers*" called me — what a chance
At last an opportunity to show off my voice!
But how did I end up? The madam's number one . . . choice!
That's why I want to sing . . .
Next was her own rendition of "The Lady is a Tramp."
This Marlon Brando can't move me an inch . . .
James Dean might make it, but just in a pinch . . .
But Humphrey Bogart — why he'd be a cinch!
That's why the lady is a tramp.

Used to be proper, and believe me, it's true
And I would like to be that way now, too
But fellows ask me . . . so what can I do?
That's why the lady is a tramp . . .
There used to be some girls around here
Who were so dear . . .
Not me —
I'm free!
You think you've had it?
Well — meet the new champ!
That's why the lady is . . .
I said the lady is . . .
That's why the lady is . . . a tramp.

On an earlier reading the sexually explicit lyrics had felt poignant in light of her disappointment and frustration at being restrained as a singer, and principally an opera singer. She had incorporated opera from her Juilliard days into many of her vaudeville and early night-club acts, but in these lyrics, she told the story of what happened to her when she finally began to make some headway into the big time. She became less free to do as she pleased; others determined who she should be and how she should present herself. She was hired to be alluring and titillating at the Latin Quarter, dressed in pasties and other revealing costumes — "opera hose" are sexy, thigh-high sheer stockings held up by garters, reminiscent of a prostitute's seductive garb — and she was barely given the opportunity to sing, except for schlock songs composed by a minor talent. In *House of Flowers* she danced and sang with others from a marvelous libretto, but she had no solo, and she played a prostitute.

On second reading, Mary's intent in the lyrics and performance seemed anything but poignant; rather she was taking charge, assert-ing her right to be on stage, flaunting her sexuality and her anger and challenging the convention of a sexually compliant Asian wom-an. The lyrics were more Mae West than Sinatra in their bawdiness. Mary had moxie, an old-fashioned term, whereas underlying the re-written lyrics of these songs, and dressed in *faux* self-denigration was a daring, modern, and self-exposing assertion of a sexual life and an aggressive revelation of professional aspirations.

Her anger had become more explicit. I was convinced that the race consciousness, outrage, and outspokenness she witnessed during her close associations with Blacks in *House of Flowers* freed her to use her resentment productively. Again, Hilton Als words played in my head. He'd seen Mary as part of a "whole colored world of mutual support." Josephine Premice had shortly appeared in *House of Flowers*.

EVEN SO, MARY WAS STILL PASSING AS CHINESE AMERICAN. I recognized myself in her diversionary tactic. During my university years, which began in 1959, the time contemporaneous with Mary's phony-as-a-$33 diamond-interview, I continued to pass as gentile even as I took public stands at my university against Jim Crow in the South.

When I was rushed by the sororities, I refused to join on the grounds that they discriminated against Blacks and Jews, never letting on that I was Jewish. The sorority girls would corner me in my dormitory, furious that I wouldn't join. They couldn't understand my resistance. To them I was a popular all-American blonde coed, albeit peroxide blonde, with a Christian last name, not knowing that I rejected the sororities to honor my mother who had been denied membership in any sorority at the University of Washington.

As a white person, creating a disguise was easy, but what a much more powerful anti-discrimination statement I would have made if I'd simply told them who I was. How furious they would have been having to back off once they knew I was Jewish, having to rescind the invitation because the national sorority wouldn't have allowed them to take me —a convenient cover for their own anti-Semitism. I was too frightened to declare myself, too alone with my secret.

In my research into my parents' tenure in Tule Lake I had come upon a transcript of the James Sakoda interview with my father, conducted in my mother's presence. They had been talking about the racism of some staff when Sakoda digressed, writing that one of the staff, " . . . had made an anti-Jewish remark in the company of evacuees," which he thought unseemly. He wrote that my father "was going to speak with the camp director about it." Though my mother remained silent during this give-and-take, I saw that she did have my father to come to her defense, or at least she could confide in him about whatever insults she experienced.

Mary didn't have recourse to such support. Having no one to share your distress about overheard slights about Japanese Americans and vicious racial, ethnic, or anti-Semitic comments is a lonely place to be. In my case, I couldn't tell my mother I was passing because I would have had to admit that I was denying the part of me that came from her. I had no place to join in with Jews for comfort, identity, and solidarity.

Shortly before my mother died, I asked her if her family had had Seders. She answered with unusual tender warmth, "Oh, yes, we went to Grandma Annie's. It was a big family group." She had so effectively eradicated that part of her heritage when she married my father that I didn't even know what a Seder was until, in my thirties and living in New York City I was invited to join a friend's ritual dinner. That evening, and every year since when I've attended a Seder, I choke up during the reading of the Haggadah, picturing my mother at my great-grandmother Annie's house — knowing I'm there at the table for both of us.

WHERE DID MARY GO FOR SOLACE AS AN ADULT? I WONDERED IF SHE had longed to openly express her Japanese side. She had her mother and father, who eventually lived in an apartment in Queens. She could visit them and eat her mother's homemade Japanese food, talk about family and friends in Japan and America, enjoy the memories of her Japanese upbringing.

But she couldn't tell her parents the whole truth, couldn't include them in her success, proudly showing them the innumerable press clippings, which could also reveal her deception. What probably sustained her were memories of the years before the war living in an ethnically Japanese home, visiting her relatives in Japan as a teenager, and the nurturance of a loving mother who closely watched over her upbringing and imparted the value of her heritage. I'm sure she carried Mon's love within her, which accounted for her courage in the larger white world. But the unexpressed anger had to have become a handicap.

It's said we become the lies we tell about ourselves. I increasingly saw the truth of that as I began to search Mary's life as well as my own past. As I tried to remember what I thought and felt throughout my childhood when I worked to fit in to middle-American culture, it took great effort to recall my inner life. My shame and terror of inadvertently revealing my true self became attached like a virus to every aspect of me, including the confluence of sexual and artistic identity.

A version of self-denial had also to be operating in Mary as she continued to omit a whole portion of her identity. She may have had difficulty owning what she had accomplished. Perhaps she constantly retold the set-piece stories of her successes as a defense against that empty place in her, to convince herself that she'd really achieved what she said she had. Would she have been more successful if she'd let go of her fabrications and told the real history of her heroic rise from the camps to Broadway? She would have had a community of Japanese Americans to lean on for emotional support, and telling her story might have released her talent from the exhausting pressure of hiding. It could have been a powerful narrative for the press, but in reality, the press wouldn't have covered such a story because no one was interested in knowing.

White America remained almost willfully ignorant about the camps until the 1990s, and/or if they had heard they were startlingly uniformed about the details of the internment or argued that it had been necessary to incarcerate Japanese Americans because we were at war with Japan and their loyalty was questionable. Even in 1999 when I'd toured with my novel about Tule Lake, I received angry call-ins during radio shows saying it was right to "jail the Japs" for our protection.

The more discerning Caucasian population began to seriously examine the Incarceration only after a few popular novels were written by white authors, notably David Guterson's 1999 *Snow Falling on Cedars*, which told an acceptably sentimental view of the Incarceration. It didn't matter that brilliant, powerful novels and memoirs by Nisei authors had been published by university and independent presses well before that time: Miné Okudo's 1946 graphic memoir *Citizen 13660*; Monica Sone's 1953 memoir *Nisei Daughter*; Jeanne

Wakatsuki Huston and James Huston's 1973 memoir *Farewell to Manzanar*, John Okada's hard-hitting, modernist 1957 novel *No-No Boy*, and Yoshiko Uchida's 1982 memoir, *Desert Exile: The Uprooting of a Japanese American Family*.

SHORTLY AFTER I WROTE THIS CHAPTER, I RECEIVED A BIOGRAPHER'S dream gift.

A woman tracked me down on the Internet, and called to say that she had been going through her deceased father's personal items, and had come across letters from Mary Mon Toy to him. She wondered if I would like to take a look, with the understanding that I could quote from them, but could never divulge who her father was. She thought that her father had had an affair with Mary in the late 1940s which resulted in his separation from the family. He eventually went back to his wife. The letters indicated that he and Mary had resumed their relationship in 1958.

I have many letters from Mary's lovers to her, but none from Mary to her lovers. I said "yes."

All I will reveal about this man is that he is white and at the time he met Mary and later when he wrote these letters, he was a small-town New England banker. His daughter thinks that he first met Mary when she was the lead act at the Music Box in the Copley Square Hotel in Boston, but we haven't been able to confirm that.

The letters arrived. I recognized Mary's handwriting and her distinctive voice, flirtatious, smart, show-offy about recent accomplishments and potential gigs. He was sending her money and expensive items. She was finagling for what she wanted. It was clear that he was a nice man, kind, and concerned about her. And as his daughter said to me when she sent the letters, "you know, I liked Mary as I read them." This from the daughter who had suffered from the initial breakup of her family. I read them with that in mind, and I, too, saw that there was nothing pernicious in her interactions, he clearly adored her, and she was genuinely caring of him in return. And then

I came upon this in what appears to be her last letter to him. The date is "Saturday night, at home." It is during the Christmas holiday season.

> "My dear [blank], At the risk of repeating myself, may I put on paper how warm and cordial your thoughts and mine intertwined (sic) All in all you are indeed a nice person and deserve the good fortune you enjoy . . . a lovely, good wife and mother of three lovely offspring. You have much to look forward to in their growing lives and the happiness (word undecipherable) together and shared. . . .
> In retrospect, I suddenly see a much forelorner picture of my future. Particularly, on holidays and such. But instead of letting it get me down I guess I'll remain the 'eternally happy kid,' appreciative of little sips of nectar life's cup offers."

She goes on to regale him with "happy kid," glamorous stories of her life in the city after which she thanks him for his presents along with suggestions on where he could buy other gifts for her, all itemized. She closes with advice on how to protect himself and his family by secreting and destroying her photographs and letters.

> "It's not a good policy to have them lying around. Y'know, in case of accidents or such and your private papers are gone over by the executor of estate. Don't mean to be morbid — darling — just 'cool,' Kiss, m"

When I next spoke with his daughter, I said how moved I was by Mary's candid expression of vulnerability. His daughter agreed.

MARY'S FATHER, Yoshizo, DIED AN AMERICAN CITIZEN IN 1968. NATURALIZATION had finally been opened to him in 1952 when the prohibition against Japanese immigrants becoming American citizens was deemed unconstitutional. He died a Buddhist, even though his camp records state that he was a Baptist, a possible diversionary attempt by him to prove his loyalty to Christian America.

Okoden envelopes, the traditional Buddhist funeral gift, were sent by friends to the family with five-and ten-dollar bills enclosed.

Mon, Mary's mother, became a naturalized American citizen in 1955. She died of breast cancer in 1972, six months after her final trip to Japan with Mary to visit relatives and have a last look at her country of birth. They arrived in Tokyo and ended their stay two weeks later in Hiroshima.

When Mon died, Mary received Okoden from Japan and from the cities in America where Japanese Americans had settled postwar and post-camp: Denver, Lansing, Salt Lake City, and New York. The letters in English were sent to Mary's apartment on West Eighty-eighth Street, addressed to Mary Teruko Okada, Teru Watanabe, Mary Watanabe, or Mrs. Mary Okada, and a scattering to Mary Mon Toy from Caucasian friends. I imagine her writing out all the possible combinations for the postman.

There were other letters in Japanese that were mailed to a Mr. Shigesato Nishioka on West Twenty-fourth Street, for translation and reply in Japanese. Each envelope bore, in Mary's hand, the amount of the contribution and the date of her thank-you note. Ever the dutiful Japanese daughter, she fulfilled her responsibilities to her parents to the end.

Mon was cremated and Mary had her remains sent to Japan to be buried in the Tokyo cemetery where Frank and Mary were later interred.

When Mary died and I told her niece, Lori, that she, like their father Frank, wanted to be buried in Japan with their mother, Lori was bewildered by their choice. "They were so American, so assimilated. My father's wish came out of nowhere for me," she said. "Why would they want to do that?"

At the time I had no answer for her, but as I thought about it I saw a similarity between Mary and Frank and post-Holocaust Jews who energetically assimilated directly after the war: many of those Jews got nose jobs, married across religions, celebrated Christmas, let Jewish traditions and rituals fall by the wayside. But then as they gradually absorbed the horrors of the Holocaust, they began to take on a stronger Jewish identity than before the war. For Mary and Frank, the event that heightened their loyalty to their parents' ethnicity and their own heritage must be the Incarceration.

Mon's death was an enormous loss for Mary; she often spoke of her sadness. She loved her mother's beauty and kindness, and judging by the photographs Mon was lovely in a soft gentle way. But Mary's sadness must have been about more than the death of a mother. Mon was Mary's tie to her young life before the camps. After Minidoka, and after Mon, Yoshizo, and Frank's deaths, her hold on life in a Japanese American family and community, and as a Nisei, was never the same. The connection had been broken. She had the geisha doll that Mon made, the family photographs, a needlepoint tapestry that she often proudly told me Mon had hand-stitched, but she no longer had Mon and her ways. Her longing was to reconnect one day. When I sent off her remains to Japan, I hadn't fully understood the meaning of her need.

Mary's ashes arrived in Tokyo in January; the Kato family waited until spring to inter her, when the cherry blossoms would be in bloom, they wrote me. That April, by e-mail, I received photos of the Buddhist burial, complete with Buddhist priest, rituals Mary must have realized I would never have known to fulfill for her here in America.

I asked Mary's friend Emiko Tokunaga if and where, once her family was gone, she thought Mary found a connection to her ethnic heritage. Emiko said that Mary had loved her own mother, Utako. Utako Tokunaga was a fine seamstress who would periodically visit New York City from Salt Lake City, to design costumes for Emiko and her

sister Yasuko's dance company, Tokunaga Dance Ko. Mary met Utako during one of her stays and after that, whenever they got together
Mary and Utako always spoke Japanese interspersed with English.

"Perhaps Mother brought back her remembrances of being Japanese, of her Japanese heritage," Emiko said. When Utako taught
Emiko to make the rice-cakes, *ohagi*, from scratch, Utako insisted
that they give some to Mary and even took a taxi up to Mary's apartment to deliver them. "The Japanese gift-giving tradition was deeply
ingrained in Mother, and she wanted to share something that Mary
missed," Emiko said. When Utako was recuperating from a series of
surgeries, half a dozen white roses would arrive at the family home
in Utah every month for half a year, a gift from Mary. "Mother was
touched by the roses, and she could not believe that Mary remembered her so lovingly."

IN 1974, MARY HAD A SMALL PART IN THE OFF-BROADWAY PLAY *Santa
Anita '42*, which was set in the notorious Santa Anita racetrack assembly center in California, a place comparable to the Puyallup assembly center. Surprised to find Mary listed in the playbill and in the
many New York City major reviews, I contacted the director, Steven
Robman, to ask if he remembered her and if she had told him that
she was Japanese American and that she and her family had been
incarcerated.

He remembered her fondly and said that she had told him she
was half Chinese American and half Japanese American, but that
no, she hadn't shared her wartime stories, "which is weird when you
consider the subject matter of the play. Actors are usually very willing to talk about personal experiences that bear on the text being
rehearsed, so it would be quite telling if Mary chose not to reveal her
background during that time."

Slipped into her copy of the script I discovered a letter to Mary
from Bill Hosokawa, author of the seminal cultural history *Nisei: The
Quiet Americans*. He had addressed her as Dear Teru and apologized

to her for not having responded to the playwright, Alan Knee, who, on Mary's initiative, had sent him a copy of the *Santa Anita '42* script for comments. She had clearly written to Hosokawa as Teru Watanabe Okada.

Soon after this I was reading Louis Fiset's book about the Puyallup Assembly Center, and in the chapter on dissension in the camp I discovered that Hosokawa — whom I'd always been aware of as a conservative force in the Japanese American community — was identified by the administration of Puyallup Assembly Center as one of the group of "troublemakers" that included Mary's husband Shig. Hosokawa had resisted repressive acts of the administration. As punishment, in August of 1942 Hosokawa, his wife, and infant son were banished from Puyallup with four hours' notice and sent to the just-opened Heart Mountain Camp in Wyoming.

Bill Hosokawa knew Shig and Mary and the history she had left behind. In writing to him she was treading dangerously close to her real story and to the secrets she had kept for decades.

Maybe Hosokawa didn't want to return to the upsetting episode either. When he finally wrote to the playwright, it was to critique the script tactfully, saying he would have liked clearer explanations of the Japanese internment story and much less "allusion and symbolism." Mary had found a way to prod the playwright into giving a more authentic version of the camp experience without exposing to the cast, many of whom were Nisei, the director, and the playwright, that she had been incarcerated.

Resistance and Activism

ON MAY 25, 1968 MARY WALKED THE PICKET LINE IN FRONT OF THE
City Center Theater in Manhattan wearing a pillbox hat similar to the
chic model Jackie Kennedy popularized, a pastel suit with a black velvet collar, and a simple white blouse beneath the jacket. She wore stylishly oversized sunglasses
and sported a pixie haircut.

Hanging from her neck
was a placard stating, "If
Caucasians are given Ori-
ental roles, why doesn't it
work both ways?" Signs
brandished by other dem-
onstrators read: "Mr. Rodgers: Save on Yellow Greasepaint, Texas Dirt and Black
Wigs — hire Orientals"
and "Do the Anti-Racial
Discrimination Laws Stop
at the Box Office?"

They were protest-
ing the almost total lack
of Asian Americans in
City Center's revival of *The
King and I.*

King and I demonstration against
Yellow Face casting organized
by Oriental Actors of America.
"If Caucasians are given Oriental roles, why
doesn't it work both ways."

"Mr." Rodgers was Richard Rodgers, composer of *The King and I*, and of *Flower Drum Song*. One would think that, of all people, he had an abundance of Asian American performers to draw from, but of the nine featured Asian roles, eight were being played by non-Asians; even the understudies were non-Asian.

What was not commonly known at the time was that there were potentially ten featured Asian roles. The model for Anna in the *King and I*, Anna Leonowens, was not the romanticized white Brit of the musical. She was mixed-race Anglo Indian on her mother's side. Leonowens had passed as upper-class British for her entire life, claiming she was born in Wales — and not in Bombay as was the case — and leaving out the fact of her mother's race. She had never, in fact, been to England at the time she went to Siam to tutor the children of the king. It's hard to miss the irony of the parallel between Asian Americans' compromised professional careers and that of the model for the archetypal liberal story of cross-racial romance.

The demonstrators' demands weren't addressed. The play went on in Yellow Face, with only Yuriko, the great Martha Graham soloist, in the major role of Eliza, performing a dance of flight from oppression based on Uncle Tom's Cabin. Yuriko had been incarcerated in Gila camp. She was the wife of Charles Kikuchi whose book on his experiences in camp had led me to my family's files at Bancroft Library. The world was getting smaller: the connections to the Incarceration were piling up. And a radicalized Mary, unbeknownst to me when she was alive, had taken to the streets to denounce the ongoing injustice.

On november, 23, 1984 "mary mon toy: Actress First" was headlined in a wide-ranging, personal interview in *Back Stage*, an American entertainment industry trade publication as part of their series, "Striding Toward Affirmative Action: Taking Your Own Reins." A longtime member of AFTRA — the American Federation of Television and Radio Artists, and SAG, the Screen Actors Guild, Mary told how, "While I've never gotten jobs through

Gerry Goodstein

Rene Sanchez, Ana Margarita Martinez-Casado and Ofelia Gonzalez in Repertorio Español's production of Gloria Gonzalez's "Cafe Con Leche."

E. Claude Richards, actor and playwright

Mary Mon Toy, actress

"Ritual of a Body in Moon" La Mama/TWITAS (Third World Theatre Arts Festival), Ismael Ivo, dancer/choreographer; Dudu Tucci, composer/percussionist.

Striding Toward Affirmative Action:

Taking Your Own Reins

creative community, of your diversity, of your strength and of your spirit." The

contemporary lifestyle of non-traditional Jewish life: either overtly or

a new musical that will be announced later in the year.

Vargas Llosa, Jose Donoso and Manuel Puig. The plays will be translated into English with possible future production at INTAR. This move gives strength to the growing impact Latin American literature has been making in the last decade.

INTAR's yearly series of play

Back Stage, Mary's views on discrimination and affirmative action in the theater.
See Appendix 2 for the full interview

AFTRA or SAG seminars or open-door lotteries, our unions actively assist members to do so . . . I've gone to EPI interviews [open call auditions] and sat and waited at Equity only to be told "If we decide to use a minority . . ." This particular one was for IBM. You'd think they'd want an Asian actor what with technology what it is today." Later in the piece, she counsels, "If you feel you're right for the part . . . stand firm . . . [you're a union] member and should be given the same courtesy as non-minority members."

Also in the interview, she describes how she found roles on her own through friends and connections. Of those, most poignantly she says, "A few of the non-traditional roles I've played were Anna in *Ladies Night in a Turkish Bath*, and Mammy Pleasant in *The Cat and the Canary.* . . . The most enjoyable non-traditional role I played was Charlotta, in Chekov's *The Cherry Orchard* . . . With each performance I realized how contemporary is Chekov. I hated to see the limited performances end. Someday I hope I'll get a chance to play more Chekov roles." Sadly, she never did.

Mary on the front line of AFTRA
(American Federation of Television and Radio Artists)
demonstration against Apartheid.

In march of 1986 aftra joined with the associated actors and Artistes of America to demonstrate in front of the Permanent Mission of South Africa to the United Nations, to commemorate the twenty-sixth anniversary of the Sharpeville massacre in South Africa, when police opened fire on peaceful protesters, killing eighty-nine and wounding over three hundred.

It was a rally that Glory Van Scott had encouraged Mary to join. Frederick O'Neal, who had performed in *House of Flowers*, was the keynote speaker. In the AFTRA coverage of the demonstration Mary was again front-and-center of the gathering, holding the lead AF-TRA banner with other actors. Smiling for the camera, she looked comfortable and even happy in her role as a demonstrator against injustice.

It was strange to find her in the photographs, but they explained one reason for her choice of me as a friend and caretaker . . . a shared politics. She had recognized my activism. She'd said she trusted me because her brother had read my novel set in the Tule Lake camp, and told her I understood what they'd been through. She also had read a manuscript of my book to help me with certain Japanese usage. A principal character in the book, the radical activist in the co-op, could have been based on Shig and or George who was a member of the Berkeley Co-op.

In going through her belongings earlier I had found that she collected my press coverage, including articles about my family's history in the Tule Lake camp which she'd marked up in red. She knew where I stood. Why hadn't she told me directly why she'd chosen me? We could have talked politics. I could have asked her about the connection between her incarceration and her activism. We lost out on so much because of our reticence with each other. I now wanted to know if she was politicized before she met Shig or if he'd introduced her to racial and economic politics. He was a union man, a member of the Cannery Union which was one of the most radical on the west coast. Was that part of why she was attracted to him?

George Yasukochi was a progressive thinker and a pacifist; was that why she carried on the correspondence with him? I would ask her if, when she marched, she wished that she could have told her compatriots that she understood what it meant to live under apartheid because she had been imprisoned by the state for her race and ethnicity?

What a sadness that neither of us could open up and confide in the other, she for her reasons and I for mine. We'd hidden out true selves for too long to speak candidly of our deepest political feelings about such a profound experience. We'd developed covers that told the world we were not to be completely taken seriously. Though even skirting the issues we'd found each other and fulfilled some part of our need to be known for what we knew and who we were.

I ASK MYSELF, WHAT DID MY MOTHER AND MARY HAVE IN COMMON? Both were outliers for their times. Mary was Japanese American at a tragic time for Americans of Japanese descent. She pursued a desire to be a performer, which was unusual for Japanese American women. She was a divorcee when divorce was uncommon. She never remarried. She took many lovers. She never had children. My mother was Jewish when Jews were discriminated against in this country and were being exterminated overseas. She was brilliant and highly educated and didn't want to be confined in the role of mother and wife.

Mary earned her own way and was parsimonious as she husbanded her savings. My mother was the primary breadwinner in our family. She was a woman who considered her work a vocation. In the late 1940s it was the rare teacher who was married, and rarer still to have small children. My mother had strong convictions about women's rights long before the second wave of feminism. Like my mother, Mary was intrepid as she strove to meet her goals. It was what made then both appealing and difficult to tolerate at times.

It's interesting that I chose to take care of their emotional needs and, in the end of their lives, their physical necessities. I was there for them, when they needed me most. With my mother as she lay dying, I put aside my anger, or as it says in the bible, I put aside childish things, and it held me in good stead, because the anger never returned.

I wasn't completely done with her and me, and when I met Mary a month after her death, I was ripe for being lured into another mother-daughter challenge, one complicated by race, ethnicity, history, and politics. I had said to Fritz when Mary died on Pearl Harbor Day that she knew how to create a perfect dramatic finish, but I, from the very beginning of our friendship, must have intuited the symbolic and circular nature of our story. We are our choices in life. I chose to take care of Mary, no matter how reluctantly I let myself be drawn in and how much I fought the responsibility, and she chose me to be the one she entrusted with her later life and death.

The more I searched Mary's past, the more I recognized my own shame. It's not easy to let go of. But I understand how I've adapted differently than Mary did.

I found one man who taught me how to love. I didn't parade my body upon the stage as she did. Instead, I toned down my public image hoping people would overlook me and not see beneath the surface to my desire for unconditional love. I camouflaged my need to be taken care of, and my shame at having such a need by obsessively taking care of others.

Whenever I was overtaken with the compulsion to help someone, it was usually because I was feeling bereft. I wanted love, so I gave it. I wanted succor, so I soothed another.

I know what the reader is thinking: How could she have missed the obvious clues of this in her interaction with Mary? But the answer is in our humanness and the power of our unconscious. What better person to use as the canvas of my need for family, than a Japanese American woman who had been incarcerated in a camp like the one where I was born, and a place where I had been nurtured by a married couple of her same race and ethnicity, the people from whom I'd learned to reach out beyond the confines of my own family for love.

A friend once said to me, "you didn't have a childhood." At the time I thought, what a foolish thing to say; I had a childhood, more interesting than most. Someone else said, your childhood was stolen from you. She explained her comment by saying it was stolen because my parent's needs and political work had come before my own.

IN MARY'S CASE HER YOUNG ADULTHOOD WAS STOLEN FROM HER JUST as it was beginning to take flight. She valiantly fought to make up for lost time by turning herself into an artist. Mary gave me courage to write this book. As I researched and worked on it each day, often thinking I wouldn't be able to finish, that even if I did no one would want it as they hadn't wanted my last novel, I said to myself, she kept at it, so can I.

There weren't and still aren't many women performers who work steadily for four decades. Until very recently there were still woefully few serious and major roles for Asian American actors, and some still filled by Caucasians playing in Yellow Face. So how do I evaluate a career like Mary's? How do I place it in the history of the performing arts?

In the 1970s and 1980s — in her sixties and seventies — she continued to find jobs. Her ten-year stint from 1975 to 1984 in a recurring role as Mrs. Lem on the soap opera *Ryan's Hope*, where she played the owner of a Chinese restaurant, was important and unusual in that she didn't speak in broken English as was too often required of Asian American actors. She was not made into a joke: Mrs. Lem dressed elegantly and was gracious and charming with the patrons of the restaurant. Mary was playing one version of her actual self, the proper side she presented on formal occasions.

She had other comparable television roles in pilots such as *Nurse*, where she is a nurse with a non-Asian name — Marge Bailey — who happened to look Asian. In *One of Our Own* she played Dr. Grace Chang, again with no foreign accent.

Nurse, Mary in a pilot for a television series

In 1977, she appeared in the PBS special *Jade Snow Wong*, the story of writer and ceramist Jade Snow Wong. Mary plays Jade Snow's mother. It is an understated, nuanced, and subtle performance in which her character evolves from an immigrant factory worker who speaks no English, into an elegant sophisticated woman. Mary effortlessly held the screen each time she appeared.

In the movie *All That Jazz* she had a cameo as a hospital nutritionist, played with no accent, attending to the out-of-control choreographer Bob Fosse. Was it possible that she had insisted on playing these roles not as caricatures but as serious women?

Kojak television series, "Chinatown Murders." Mary (at left) on-set in Chinatown with Telly Savalas and Johnny Kai.

Mary was almost sixty when she landed a part on the TV show *Kojak*, starring Telly Savalas as a New York City cop. It was a job that Lori Tan Chinn said all the female Asian American actors went after, but Mary got it. It was a serious dramatic role.

I may be partial, but I think her performance was by far the best of the cast — as did Cecil Smith the great *Los Angeles Times* reviewer in an otherwise dismissive review of the two-part episode — though she barely spoke and when she did it was in Chinese, or at least a phonetic transcription of the language.

Her script was filled with her transliterations and stenographic notes to herself. Her friend Emiko told me that Mary did intensive research for every role she performed.

Even in her silence on screen she conveyed the conflict of this elderly Chinese immigrant grandmother who must turn over her granddaughter and grandson to the police. There was no pidgin language silliness, no stereotyping.

In one scene Telly Savalas speaks through a translator to the old woman Mary is playing, saying, "It's not just language and culture that stands between us and I'm deeply sorry for that." The viewer realizes he means racism, because earlier there have been a number of pointed references to racial discord. The moment of understanding between them is very moving. I couldn't help thinking as I watched their silent communication that Mary was hearing that line as a direct apology for racist attitudes in America or even for her imprisonment or at the least, she was using the

Mary with Telly Savalas

emotional, historical reference as grist for her beautiful performance.

Her makeup for the part was quite horrible, akin to Cicely Tyson's mask-like aging in *Autobiography of Miss Jane Pittman*. You can barely recognize Mary, almost a metaphor for the fact that she masked herself throughout her career. Perhaps being hidden allowed her to do her best work.

The show was rebroadcast around the world, many times over; one can still find it on the Internet. Her brother Frank wrote to Mary from Hawai'i to say how sad it was that "mom and dad weren't alive to see you. They would have been so proud." This would have been the show they could have seen, and it would have ameliorated Mary's greatest regret . . . "that my parents never saw me perform."

One person wrote on a blog after reading her obituary in the *New York Times*, that hers was the unheralded story of performers who went out each day and trod the boards. "You think about the thousands of performers who have come through New York in its long history as an entertainment capital; of the .01% who actually make it big; the large number who pass through without making their mark. Then you have the Mary Mon Toys, who work solidly their entire careers without breaking through."

I once asked Glory Van Scott if she thought Mary had had a successful career, and if she believed that if Mary hadn't had the impediments of race and age she would have been very successful.

Glory answered that Mary was definitely successful, but that given her talent, her work ethic, her charm, and her determination, "she would have been way up there" if she hadn't had those handicaps.

I then asked if staying alive in the business was harder for Mary than for Black performers. She immediately answered, "Much harder for Mary because she was always out there on her own. We had each other to lean on."

I've learned from Mary and her friends what it takes to be an artist. It means you find your own path and follow it even when you don't break through into fame. You do it because you have something to offer and because you have a need to ply your art. Geoffrey Holder spoke of that courage when he said of Pearl Bailey, "She's a strong woman, she had to be."

John Butler, a white choreographer who worked with Black dancers, including choreographing *Portrait of Billie* for Carmen De Lavallade, said to her and her dance partner Dudley Williams, in rehearsal, that they had the "courage to take the risks, that's what an artist is all about."

Did Mary have that kind of creative courage? I'm not sure, but she did have the strength to get out there and grab what she wanted as a performer which is another form of valor. I learned from her that you can't listen to the outside world, you have to do what you have to do and be grateful for what you accomplish.

Writing this book took me to surprising places. It opened me to a world within me that I hadn't been ready to embrace in the past, to acceptance of that locus where my creativity, personal identity, and politics converge.

38

Reparations/Redress

IN 1990 MARY RECEIVED A LETTER FROM THEN PRESIDENT GEORGE H. W. Bush apologizing for the internment of Japanese Americans and awarding her a check of $20,000 for the losses she had endured when she was incarcerated. She joked that it was too bad it had to come from Bush, but she was happy to receive it.

I happened to know the man who was an activist participant in spearheading the fight for reparations or, as it was called, Redress. His name was William Hohri and he was as iconoclastic in his way as Mary was in hers. She would have liked him and I think he would have gotten a kick out of her. For all I know they may have met.

As a teenager he had been incarcerated in Manzanar camp with his parents. As an adult he worked for civil rights and peace causes, which led him to his role as an advocate for the rights of other Japanese Americans who had been incarcerated. In 1983 he became the main plaintiff in a class action lawsuit — Hohri v. The United States — which demanded redress of $220,000 for each American citizen who had been sent to camp. That would have amounted to a federal payout of twenty-seven billion dollars. The government mounted a vigorous defense as the case found its way to the Supreme Court.

Hohri *et al* eventually lost on a technicality in 1987, but the fear that he and the other activists would continue their fight — as indeed they did — pushed Congress to pass a bill apologizing to Japanese Americans and allotting the $20,000 to each person who had been sent to the camps. Ronald Reagan signed the bill in 1988 and the first checks were mailed out in 1990 to only those who were alive as of the bill's passage on August 10, 1988. If someone had died between that date and when the check was issued beginning two years later, their heirs received the Redress payment.

William Hohri had often complained to me in a jocular tone, . . .though with a bite . . .that JAs, as he called his fellow Nisei, were too modest, too self-effacing to fight for their rights. Many had resisted his efforts with the lawsuit and when the money became available, they thought they should donate their redress money to a good cause. He would argue with them, trying to convince them otherwise.

One day a manila envelope arrived in my mailbox. In it was a five-by-seven black-and-white photo of William with a devilish grin, standing by a Japanese sports car. When I looked closely, I saw that the vanity plate spelled out "REDRESS." His note to me said, "I spent it on myself and am showing the country that I did."

I wish I could hear Mary letting loose with one of her deep resonant laughs at seeing the picture.

EPILOGUE

Shortly before the 2016 election, I went to Rosh Hashanah services at the Jacob Javits Center on the far west side of Manhattan overlooking the Hudson River. I was seated among thousands of people in a huge atrium with a ceiling and west and east walls constructed of squares of glass. It was the same space where Hillary planned to hold her post-election celebration, chosen for its glass ceiling.

The rabbi was the leader of this "gay synagogue," which observes the High Holidays at the Javits Center so that its huge congregation and others can worship together.

She opened her remarks with a welcome of inclusion saying all are at home here — "believers and non-believers; gay and straight and transgender; Jews and Muslims and Buddhist and Christians and witches; and everyone no matter how we identified ourselves." Among a multitude of categories, she included people who were Jewish but never knew their religion and with a sigh I relaxed. I had a place here.

The music was a mix of chants and prayers, folk songs, classical, and Broadway show tunes. There was a wonderful chorus and an extraordinary sound system . . . how could it not be considering that many in the audience were in show business.

We joined together to sing and pray in freedom and the safety of numbers. The sermon that evening centered on a new book by a German entitled *Hitler* in which the author's description of the Chancellor's rise in power was parallel, to an ominous degree, to the rise of Trump.

I didn't fast the next week on Yom Kippur, nor did I attend the morning or afternoon services, and I arrived late at the closing ceremony.

When I again walked into the giant hall, I was swept up in the thousands of voices swelling with glory and defiance.

As the sun dipped in the west over the Hudson, we were enveloped in a rosy glow, followed by dusky gloaming, and finally slowly it was nearly dark. We turned as one to witness the brilliant moon rise in the eastern windows to shine its white beam down upon us.

I had been standing throughout the changing light, trying to join my voice with the others even though I didn't know the Hebrew, and suddenly I couldn't breathe and I collapsed into my chair. I had seen an image of myself as a small blonde girl leaping and running through the fields behind our farmhouse in Shelburne and thought, "you innocent child, you had no idea that you were Jewish."

The next thing I saw was my mother sitting at the breakfast table, just as I had come down stairs each morning. She was staring, without affect, into space. It was then that I believed she was putting poison in my orange juice.

I calculated the year. It was 1946.

The worst of the stories were emerging out of Germany, of the camps, of the millions who had perished; and my mother was isolated in a farmhouse without her family, with no friends as yet that she could trust, with my father who again was always out and about, and she had no way to practice her religion without breaking their pact to not observe their respective religions.

In the enveloping darkness, I wept for her and wished she were there with me, where we could be Jews together, sharing our rich heritage. I could say how sorry I was that I hadn't understood what she had lost, what she had sacrificed for love. I would say how sorry I was that I had hidden my identity all those years.

What I wish now for others, like Mary, who find their lives torn asunder by politics, racism, ethnocentrism, incarceration, gender discrimination, poverty, and violence — all the darker forces of history — is that they can find their way to physical safety, and to a place within themselves where there is no need for shame or hiding.

Nidoto Nai Yoni, Let It Not Happen Again.

ACKNOWLEDGMENTS

SOME BOOKS TAKE A LIFETIME TO WRITE AND THIS IS ONE, FOR better or worse. In the process over the years many generous people taught, read, edited, critiqued, published my work, and kept me going with their confidence and good will, when my own will gave out. Many of them have no idea know how much they helped; this is my attempt to thank them.

My gratitude and sentimental education began long before I thought to write this book. First on the list are my parents Don and Ruth Elberson who led the way when they chose to bring me into the world in the tar-paper covered hospital in Tule Lake Camp, which informed my view of America for the rest of my life.å

Many years intervened between publishing a novel loosely based on my parents' experiences in Tule Lake Camp and writing about my friendship with Mary Mon Toy, during which I met a handful of her friends who would eventually become the village that supported her. They were Michael Estwanik, Stan Schneir, Dianne Carrion, Dr. Glory Van Scott, Mary Louise and Bill Britten, Maureen Moore, Cely Onrubia and Rose Baptiste. Without their bountiful generosity and dedication to Mary, I could never have completed the task of caring for her in the last years of her life.

When Mary died and I began to do research for this book, others came into my world to help. Lori Tan Chinn, the successful actor and comedian, was instrumental in developing my consciousness of the profound forces arrayed to hinder progress in building a theatrical career as an Asian American. Emiko Tokunaga and her sister, Yasuko Tokunaga, of the Tokunaga Dance Ko, focused my understanding on the particular problems Mary Mon Toy faced upon leaving camp to re-enter America. Emi was one of the few people Mary confided in about her reasons for passing as Chinese American. Early on I made the acquaintance of Brian Niiya, a young, brilliant historian of the Japanese American Incarceration. Working together on a short biography of Mary for Densho.org, (meaning "to pass on to the next generation,") he honored her contributions, and never made judgments of her life choices, including that she had masked her ethnicity. Additionally, he discovered sources of articles on her life pre-incarceration. When I suggested creating a virtual archive of Mary's life and work, he introduced me to the Densho archivists, Caitlin Oiye Coon and Micah Merryman, who took the incipient idea, and with the utmost professional effort, support, and sophisticated technological systems, set about to carefully preserve Mary Mon Toy's theatrical and family history. Their enthusiasm never abated from start to finish. They also introduced me to the curator at the Wing Luke Museum in Seattle where Mary's physical archive will reside.

Which brings me to the Watanabe family who allowed me to enter and share their family story, not an easy thing to do. They were essential to my understanding of Mary, particularly as they corrected false information and provided their own lovely memories of Auntie Mary, the glamorous and daring actress who broke barriers to Asian American inclusion in the performing arts. Mary's nieces, Wendy Watanabe, and Lori Watanabe Saginaw, have followed in their aunt's footsteps in their own fights for social justice. Knowing them and their mother, May Ohmura Watanabe, has immeasurably enriched my life.

I am indebted to the readers of various versions of my manuscript who committed hours, days and even weeks of their time and expertise to help me bring my intentions to the fore. They are in the order of their reading: Lorraine Bodger, Peter Steiner, Jane Cook, Victoria Olsen, Carla Peterson, Jill Norgren, Jane Kinney-Denning, Sheila Kohler, William Andrews, Pat Auspos, Brian Niiya, and Sydney Ladensohn Stern.

Through the years of research, writing, and COVID lockdown, long-time friends and colleagues kept me hopeful and sane with

walks, runs, Zooms, encouragement, reliable advice, pertinent articles, constructive observations, and concentrated listening: Bonnie
Bellow, Brett Harvey, Carol Ascher, Laurie Lisle, Mimi Hart, Sherry
Perlstein, Karin Bacon, Sheila Kohler, Deirdre Bonifaz, Julia Fisch-
er, Charles Ruas, Jane Ciabattari, Janet Brof, Kate Wenner, Cesar
Chelala, Silvia Chelala, Eva Rado, Nina Gershon, Roxanne Edwards,
and Trudy Kramer. Natalie Anita Brady arrived unexpectedly in my
life, bringing with her the joy of family connection. Ruth Danon
guided me toward my own agency.

For additional creative and personal sustenance, there have been
the Duxbury Colony women: Kathi Aguero, Lee Briccetti, Sally
Brady, Erica Funkhouser, Lydia Kann Nettler, Judith Benet Richard-
son, and Susan Taft Quinn.

A decade ago, I was fortunate to be invited to join the WOM-
EN WRITING WOMEN'S LIVES Seminar Group, composed
of an extraordinary group of biographers and memoirists, whose
melding of passion for ideas and high scholarship I have tried to
emulate: Dorothy O. Helly, Kate Culkin, Blanche Wiesen Cook,
Alix Kates Shulman, Julie Van Haaften, Ava Chinn, Barbara Fisher,
Carla Peterson, Jill Norgren, Dianne Jacobs, Sydney Ladensohn
Stern, Kathy Chamberlain, Pat Auspos, and Victoria Olsen to
name but a few.

There are others who helped in a multitude of ways to get this
book on track and to keep it moving toward publication.

Yue Ma, at MOCA, Museum of the Chinese in America, was
the first person to introduce me to the importance of the China Doll
Club for Asian American performers.

Arthur Dong, film producer/director/archivist, and Rusty Frank,
tap dancer/writer/editor, shared essential information, names, con-
tacts, and helped identify photos of Asian American performers.

Thomas De Frantz, of the Popular Balanchine Dossiers, conducted an invaluable interview with Mary, and later offered his insights to
me on the historic significance of *House of Flowers*.

The Shibata Family, from whom I learned of my father's goodness as well as their own courage and determination to overcome the trauma of the camps.

Valerie Yasukochi, a sister in arms, who shared her father's story of the Berkeley Co-op and his letters from university friends incarcerated in Tule Lake Camp.

James Moody, actor and neighbor, who uttered the words, "Ah, the liberal dilemma," initiating a turning point in my understanding of the limitations of sympathy and empathy in matters of race.

Gary Lee Kraut literally opened the doors during the off-season for my visit to the Nouvelle Eve Club in Paris.

Russell Tremayne contributed his knowledge of both the white and the Japanese American with on-going stories of Minidoka camp, during one entire day while we drove through the Idaho countryside, visiting points of embarkation for the prisoners, and walked the dusty paths where Mary and her family had been incarcerated.

Setsuko Sato Winchester toughened my perspective on the Incarceration, through her outspoken political stands and the artistic integrity of her Yellow Bowl Project.

Terry Shtob generously consulted on how to assemble and protect archival material for mailing Mary Mon Toy's personal collection to Densho.org.

Stan Schneir spent countless hours helping me to choose, repair, and organize dozens of photographs.

The people at Pro Image photography lab who did emergency reclamation of old photos, with special thanks to Naia Burton and Elizabeth Choi.

Cordelia Kennedy von Conta, my childhood friend in Vermont—in whose farmhouse I felt safe during hours of play—helped confirm much of what I had only imagined of the "Red Scare" period on our lives.

Every writer needs a person who conveys confidence in one's abilities. For me, that has been John Coyne, who supported, championed, and promoted my work, from the beginning in 1994, on the manifold website, *Peace Corps Readers and Writers*, and since 2004 called *Peace Corps Worldwide*, which promulgates the accomplishments of current and former Peace Corps volunteers in their continuing service to their communities and country, as well as the stories they brought home from their overseas assignments. John, a prolific writer himself, has worked over the years to create an American literary canon of published works by Returned Peace Corps authors.

From the beginning John has worked in partnership with Marian Haley Beil, the Editor in Chief of the publishing arm of Peace Corps Worldwide, and the imprint Peace Corps Writers.

Marian has brought hundreds of novels, memoirs, and other non-fiction books to life and to the attention of the wider world. I am honored that she agreed to personally work on my book. With creativity and dedication to detail, she designed, edited, and shepherded my manuscript into being. This memoir/biography would not have found itself between covers without her. I bow in admiration and gratitude.

As a former Peace Corps Volunteer and a person born in the infamous Tule Lake Camp, my life has come full circle with this book.

And finally, I thank my good fortune for Fritz Mueller, who has supported me throughout the effort, with his deep, reliable knowledge, good judgment, and great capacity for love.

Terminology and Usage

During the many years I worked on this book, the political, racial, ethnic terms of usage changed. I have done my best to go back and edit the book so that it rises to the newly considered determinations, with certain exceptions.

I have not altered any of the language in the supporting historically contemporaneous endnote sources. I have also not altered usage in verbatim dialogue, such as when Mary Mon Toy and Dorothy Toy refer to themselves as "Oriental," even long after it is not accepted usage in the community. The few times "slant-eyes" is used, it is always in a historical context, with quotations marks and a clear sense that I see it as objectionable.

For the sections pertaining to the Incarceration, when in my own voice, I have attempted to adhere to the considered determinations set out in the following Densho.org statement:"

> In the 1940s, government officials and military leaders used euphemisms to describe their punitive and unjust actions against people of Japanese ancestry in the United States. The deceptiveness of that language can now be judged according to evidence from many sources, most notably the government's own congressionally-ordered investigation, documented in Personal Justice Denied (1982-83), the report of the U.S. Commission on Wartime Relocation and Internment of Civilians (CWRIC).
>
> Today, these decades-old euphemisms persist in textbooks, news sources, and other platforms—meaning that most Americans learn about this history through a distorted lens that diminishes the harsh realities of Japanese American WWII incarceration.

For more detailed determinations on the words Forced Removal vs Evacuation, Incarceration vs Interment, Japanese American vs Japanese, Concentration Camps vs "Relocation Centers," and Issei, Nisei, Sansei, Yonsei as well as an explanation for the concept of Words Matter, the reader can turn to the site: Terminology - Densho: Japanese American Incarceration and Japanese Internment.

Regarding racial terms outside of the Japanese American material, I have for the most part adhered to the term Black, as opposed to African American. There are a few times that I have used the word Negro in an historically contemporaneous context. When Mary Mon Toy uses the word "Eskimo," I have not changed it.

On a few occasions I have used the derogatory word for a Black person and the derogatory word for a Japanese American; each time the word occurred in actual historical dialogue.

SELECTED BIBLIOGRAPHY

Abe, Frank (Author), Nimura, Tamiko (Author), Ishikawa, Ross (Illustrator), *Hearby Refuse: Resistance to Wartime Incarceration*, Chin Music Press, Inc., 2021

Arendt, Hannah, *The Jew as Pariah: Jewish Identity and Politics in the Modern Age*, Grove Press, Inc., New York, 1978

Armor, John and Wright. Peter, Adams, Ansel, photography, Hersey, John, commentary, *Manzanar*, Times Books, Random House, New York and Toronto, 1988

Austin, Allan W. *From Concentration Camp to Campus: Japanese American Students and World War II*, Urbana: University of Illinois Press, 2004.

Awner, Max, Interviewer, *A Conversation with George Yasukochi: Controller of Consumers Cooperative of Berkeley, 1956-1982*, Berkeley Oral History Project of the Berkeley Historical Society, Berkeley, CA, 1995

Bosworth, Allan R., *America's Concentration Camps*, W. W. Norton & Company, Inc., New York, 1967

Capote, Truman, *Breakfast at Tiffany's*, (Novella and Short Stories), *House of Flowers*, 103, Random House, 1958, reissued Penguin Classics, Penguin Books LTD, London, England, 2000

Dunning, Jennifer, *Geoffrey Holder: A Life in Theater, Dance and Art*, Harry N. Abrams, New York, 2001

Fiset, Louis, *Camp Harmony: Seattle's Japanese Americans and the Puyallup Assembly Center*, University of Illinois Press, Urbana and Chicago, 2009

Frank, Rusty E., *Editor, Tap! The Greatest Tap Dance Stars and their Stories 1900-1955*, Da Capo Press, New York, 1954

Gesensway, Deborah and Roseman, Mindy, *Beyond Words: Images from America's Concentration Camps*, Cornell University Press, Ithaca and London, 1988

Gordon, Linda and Gary Y. Okihiro, *Impounded: Dorothea Lange and the Censored Images of Japanese American Internment in World War II*. W. W. Norton, New York, 2006

Harth, Erica, *Last Witnesses: Reflections on the Wartime Internment of Japanese Americans*, Palgrave Ltd., St. Martin's Press, New York, NY and Houndmills, Basingstoke, Hampshire, England, 2001

Helwig, Frederike (Photographer), Waak, Anne (Editor), *Kriegskinder: Portraits of a Forgotten Generation*, Hatje Cantz, Berlin and Stuttgart, Germany, 2018

Higa, Karin M., *The View from Within: Japanese American Art from the Internment Camps 1942-1945*, Japanese American National Museum, UCLA Wight Art Gallery, and the UCLA Asian American Studies Center at the Wight Art Gallery, Los Angeles, 1992, distributed by University of Washington Press, Seattle

Hohri, William Minoru, *Repairing America: An Account of the Movement for Japanese-American Redress*, Washington State University Press, Pullman, Washington, 1988

Hosokawa, Bill, *Nisei: The Quiet Americans*, William Morrow and Company, Inc., New York, 1969

Houston, Jeanne Wakatsuki, and James D. Houston, *Farewell to Manzanar*, Boston: Houghton Mifflin, 1973.

Huang, Yunte, *Charlie Chan: The Untold Story of the Honorable Detective and his Rendezvous with American History*, W. W. Norton & Company, New York, London, 2010

Inada, Lawson Fusao, Editor, *only what we carry: The Japanese Internment Experience*, Heyday Books, Berkeley, California, California Historical Society, San Francisco, California, 2000

Jacoby, Harold Stanley, *Tule Lake: From Relocation to Segregation*, Comstock Bonanza Press, Grass Valley, California, 1996

James, Thomas, *Exile Within: The Schooling of Japanese Americans 1942-1945*, Massachusetts, London England, Harvard University Press, 1987

Johns, Barbara, *Signs of Home: The Paintings and Wartime Diary of Kamekichi Tokita*, The University of Washington Press, Seattle, 2011

Kikuchi, Charles, *The Kikuchi Diary: Chronicle from an American Concentration Camp*, Edited by John Modell, University of Illinois Press, Urbana and Chicago, 1993

Kim, Kristine, *Henry Sugimoto: Painting an American Experience*, Japanese American National Museum, Los Angeles, California and Heyday Books, Berkeley, California, 2000

Kim Lee, Esther, *A History of Asian American Theater*, New York: Cambridge University Press, 2006

Kitagawa, Daisuke, *Issei and Nisei: The Internment Years*, A Continuum Book, The Seabury Press, New York, NY, 1974

Kochiyama, Yuri, *Fisherman's Daughter, An Oral History Vol. 1*, Community Documentation Workshop at St. Mark's Church-in-the-Bowery, New York City, 1981

Long, Richard A., *The Black Tradition in American Dance*, New York: Rizzoli International Publications, 1989

Matsudo Gruenewald, Mary, *Looking Like the Enemy: My Story of Imprisonment in Japanese-American Internment Camps*, New Sage Press, Troutdale, Oregon, 2005

Mirikitani, Janice, Editor, *AIIIEEEEE, A Japanese American Anthology*, The Japanese American Anthology Committee, San Francisco, California, 1980

Mirikitani, Janice, *We the Dangerous: New and Selected Poems*, Celestial Arts, Berkeley, California, 1995

Miyamoto, S. Frank, *Social Solidarity Among the Japanese in Seattle*, With a New Introduction by the Author, University of Washington Press, Published in cooperation with the Asian American Studies Program, Seattle and London, originally published in 1939, reissued in 1984

Muller, Eric L. (Editor), Manbo, Bill (Photographer), *Colors of Confinement: Rare Kodachrome Photographs of Japanese American Incarceration in World War II*, University of North Carolina Press, Chapel Hill, 2012

Nakano, Jiro and Nakano, Kay (Editors and Translators), Hoshida, George (Illustrator), *Poets behind Barbed Wire*, Bamboo Ridge Press, Honolulu, Hawaii, 1983

Niiya, Brian, Editor, *Japanese American History: An A-to-Z Reference from 1868 to the Present*, The Japanese American National Museum, Los Angeles, Facts on File, Inc. 11 Penn Plaza, New York, NY, 1993.

Okada, John, *No-No Boy*, Combined Asian American Resources Project, Inc., San Francisco, 1976

Okubo, Miné, *Citizen 13660*, University of Washington Press, Seattle and London, 1946-1994

Rebec, Estelle and Rogin, Martin, *War Relocation Authority Tule Lake Relocation/Segregation Center, 1942-1946*, The National Archives, Washington, 1955

Sears, John F. *Jews in Refuge Must Be Given: Eleanor Roosevelt, the Jewish Plight, and the Founding of Israel*, Purdue University Press, West Lafayette, Indiana, 2021.

Shibata, Yoshimi, *Across Two Worlds: Memoirs of a Nisei Flower Grower*, Mt. Eden Floral Company, www.mteden.com, Mountain View, CA 2006

Sone, Monica, *Nisei Daughter*, University of Washington Press, Seattle, Washington and London, England, Copyright 1953, published by Little, Brown and Company, later edition with S. Frank Miyamoto introduction, 1979

Takami, David A., *Divided Destiny: A History of Japanese Americans in Seattle*, University of Washington Press, Seattle and London, Wing Luke Asian Museum, Seattle, 1998

Takei, Barbara and Tachibana, Judy, *Tule Lake Revisited: A Brief History and Guide to the Tule Lake Concentration Camp Site*, Second Edition, The Tule Lake Committee, 2012.

Takei, George, *To the Stars: The Autobiography of George Takei, Star Trek's Mr. Sulu*, Pocket Books, Simon & Schuster Inc. New York, NY, 1994

Takezawa, Yasuko I., *Breaking the Silence: Redress and Japanese American Ethnicity*, Cornell University Press, Ithaca and London, 1995

Tamura, Teresa, *MINIDOKA: An American Concentration Camp*, Caxton Press, Caldwell, Idaho, 2013

Thomas, Dorothy Swaine and Nishimoto, Richard S., *The Spoilage: Japanese American Evacuation and Resettlement*, Berkeley: University of California Press, 1946)

Tokunaga, Emiko, *Yuriko, An American Japanese Dancer: To Wash in the Rain and Polish with the Wind*, Tokunaga Dance Ko., 2008

Tremayne, Russell M., Editor, Shallat, Todd, Co-editor, *Surviving Minidoka: The Legacy of WWII Japanese American Incarceration*, Boise State University College of Social Sciences and Public Affairs in partnership with College of Southern Idaho, 2013

Tule Lake Committee, *Kinenhi: Reflections on Tule Lake*, Library of Congress Catalog Number 79-93361, 1980

Turner, Stanton B., *The Years of Harvest: A History of the Tule Lake Basin*, 49th Avenue Press, Eugene, Oregon, 1988

Uchida, Yoshiko, *Desert Exile: The Uprooting of a Japanese American Family*, University of Washington Press, Seattle and London, 1982

Weglyn, Michi, *Years of Infamy: The Untold Story of America's Concentration Camps*, William Morrow and Company, Inc., New York, NY, 1976

Winston, Rick, *Red Scare in the Green Mountains*, Rootstock Publishing, 2018

Yamada, Mitsuye, *Camp Notes and Other Poems*, Shameless Hussy Press, Berkeley, California, 1976

Yamamoto, Traise, *Masking Selves, Making Objects: Japanese American Women, Identity, and the Body*, University of California Press, Berkeley/Los Angeles/London, 1999

Audio, Video & Film Bibliography

And Then They Came for Us, DVD of film, Abby Ginzberg (producer/Director) and Ken Schneider (Co-producer/Editor), Ginzberg Productions, Berkeley, California, 2017

Flower Drum Song, Rogers and Hammerstein musical, DVD of film, A Ross Hunter Production, A special edition, Universal Pictures Company, 1961

Forbidden City U. S. A, Collector's Edition, Stories from Chinese America, Collection Vol. 2 Deep Focus Productions, Inc. The Arthur Dong Collection, California, 2010

House of Flowers, CD of songs from the original Broadway Production, CBS Special Products, New York City, recorded in 1955

Long Story Short: A Film by Christine Choy and Jodi Long Produced by Film News Now and Wahini Dakini Productions, 2008

Moving Memories, Early home movies taken by Japanese American prisoners in the 1920s and 1930s, Karen L. Ishizuka, (Producer), Robert A. Nakamura (Creator/Editor), Japanese American National Museum, Los Angeles, (Date Missing)

Rabbit in the Moon, documentary/memoir about the lingering effects of the Incarceration, Emiko Omori (Producer/Director/Cinematographer/Editor), New Day Films, Hohokus, New Jersey, 1999

Resistance at Tule Lake, Konrad Aderer (Director), Third World Newsreel, 2018

Something Strong Within, A film by Robert A. Nakamura, (Director/Editor) and Karen L. Ishizuka (Producer/Writer), created for the exhibition, "America's Concentration Camps: Remembering the Japanese American Experience, Japanese American National Museum, Los Angeles, (date missing)

The World of Suzie Wong, DVD of film, Richard Quine (Director), Ray Stark (Producer) Warner Brothers Archive Collection 2013, from 1960 Paramount British Pictures Ltd, 1960, Burbank, California

To Be Takei: A Star's Trek for Life, Liberty, and Love, DVD of film, Jennifer Kroot & Tina Kroot (Producers), Jennifer Kroot (Writer/Director), Bill Weber (Editor/co-director), Rainbow Shooting Stars pictures LLC, California, 2014

You Don't Know Jack: The Jack Soo Story, A film by Jeff Adachi (written, directed, and produced by Jeff Adachi. DVD, AAMM Productions, 2011

INTERVIEWS

Bill Britten and Mary Louise Britten   Spring 2011

Lori Tan Chinn   Spring 2010

Author interview with parents, Don Elberson (DE) and Ruth Siegel Elberson (RSE), notes on paper,   1970s

Geoffrey Holder   May 6, 2014

Yoshimi Shibata video   June 25, 2005

Dorothy Toy aka Shigeko Takahashi   October, 10, 2010

Dr. Glory Van Scott   April, 27, 2011

Notes on My End Notes

The Showgirl and the Writer is a three-pronged narrative, each of the segments requiring separate and interconnected research.

One strand is my Caucasian family's relationship to the Incarceration of Japanese Americans during World War II. It covers their experience working in the Tule Lake High Security Camp and the aftermath on our lives individually and as a family unit, including my marriage.

The second focus is my friendship with Mary Mon Toy, the Japanese American "Showgirl" of the title and how our attachment raised questions of why such a friendship was initiated and persisted.

And third, are the psychological, political, moral questions raised while following the trajectory of Mary Mon Toy's post camp life and career as an Asian American performer.

Part I: My Story

For material on my parents' work and life in the Tule Lake Camp I have used War Relocation Authority (WRA) Papers, National Archives and Records Service, (NARA), and the day-to-day Journals of Nisei correspondents in camp, recruited by the Berkeley/ Bancroft University of California anthropologist, Dorothy Swaine Thomas, for the Japanese American Evacuation and Resettlement Records (JERS). I have corroborated information through interviews I conducted with my parents in the late 1970s at their home in Puerto Rico, as well as through other historical timelines and commentary.

Most of my story and that of my husband, are derived from memory. My husband lived through WWII in Germany. Since memory is an elusive and often unreliable source, I've backed up his recollections with British records of the bombing of his hometown city of Augsburg and statements by his contemporaries who also were *Kriegskinder*, or war-children. In my case, through family stories and documents, governmental, artistic, and witness narratives, I've tried to understand what the lasting psychological effect of historical and political events has been on my life.

Part II: Mary and Me

I began writing the section about my friendship with Mary Mon Toy shortly after she died, when my memory of her was still vivid, though again, hindsight can be unfaithful. I've corroborated and/ or rejected my day-to-day impressions and learned more through interviews with her friends and colleagues .

Part III: Finding Mary

Mary Mon Toy's version of her personal story posed its own problems. After her death, I learned how unreliable her statements had been about certain aspects of her life. I began to seek factual truth by pouring over her vast collection of personal and career memorabilia, gathered during her career as an Asian American performer in postwar America. I have since made a gift of her entire collection to Densho.org, the preeminent website documenting the Incarceration during WWII so that future scholars have an opportunity to reach their own conclusions. The collection resides as a virtual archive of Mary Mon Toy's performance history in the Mary Mon Toy Theatrical Collection (ddr-densho-367) and a separate archive on her family life in the Mary Mon Toy Family Collection (ddr-densho-488). The material has been scanned and moved to the Wing Luke Museum where it will reside as the physical Archive for Mary Mon Toy.

To further test the reality of her life, I reached beyond her self-generated collection for information on the time of her incarceration and that of her immediate family. The War Relocation (WRA) Authority National Archives Papers, National Archives and Records Service, (NARA) were essential. The Roosevelt era is our government's most documented period in American history, and the individual case study files on those imprisoned yield intimate and detailed private material. The tragic incarceration of people of Japanese descent is a boon to researchers, though at times personally invasive.

I cross-referenced the material I found on Mary Mon Toy and her family with books and oral histories that contained detailed information on all the camps: dates of entry, construction, sanitary conditions, housing, food, general environment, etc. I am indebted to Louis Fiset for his book, *Camp Harmony: Seattle's Japanese Americans and the Puyallup Assembly Center*, which was an incalculably valuable resource.

The Encyclopedia at Densho.org, under the guidance of the historian Brian Niiya also provided vast general and particularized information on the camps and the history and life of those who were imprisoned there.

I had many sources to follow for the precipitous rise of Mary Mon Toy's career post Incarceration, but none was more informative and useful in understanding the coming together of her artistic ambitions and political growth than the Popular Balanchine Dossiers, 1927-2004 (bulk 1927-1962)The Balanchine Foundation, House of Flowers, Compiled by Tommy DeFrantz (1954), Library of the Performing Arts, New York Public Library.

THE END NOTES

FORWARD • PREFACE • HOW IT BEGAN

Page xxiv   "Later, when there was no evidence of disloyalty among the population," The dangerous economics of racial resentment during World War II, Gwynn Guilford, Quartz, February 13, 2018 https://qz.com/1201502/japanese-internment-camps-during-world-war-ii-are-a-lesson-in-the-scary-economics-of-racial-resentment

Page xxiv   For further reading on the subject: Americans Betrayed, Morton M. Grodzins. Chicago: The University of Chicago Press, 1949, For a review of Americans Betrayed: https://chicagounbound.uchicago.edu/cgi/viewcontent.cgi?article=2643&context=uclrev

PART I – MY STORY
CHAPTER 1 • THE FIRST CAUCASIAN BABY

Page 5   "My birth was announced in a staff newsletter: " Edwin Bates, Tule Lake Staff Newsletter, War Relocation Authority Papers, National Archives and Records Service (NARA), Washington, D.C., Field Basic Documentation, August 7, 1942, 2

Page 8   "Lines of tarpaper-covered barracks were still being thrown up." DESCRIPTION OF TULE LAKE JAPANESE COLONY James Sakoda, Journal, (JERS) the Bancroft Library, Tule Lake, R20-81, June 22, 1942, 1-5

Page 8   OAC (On-line Archive of California) https://oac.cdlib.org/ark:/13030/k66m36j8/?brand=oac4

Page 8   "Lines of tarpaper-covered barracks were still being thrown up." See also Barbara Takei's description of Tule Lake: https://encyclopedia.densho.org/Tule%20Lake as well as her book, *Tule Lake Revisited: A Brief History and Guide to the Tule Lake Concentration Camp Site*, Second Edition, Takei, Barbara and Tachibana, Judy, The Tule Lake Committee, 2012

Pages 9-10   "There were no desks or chairs, not even a clock in the room." Interview by Author (MM) with Don Elberson (DE) and Ruth Siegel Elberson (RSE), Puerto Rico circa late 1970s, 25

Page 10   "People were pretty damn shaken coming off the trains," Interview by Author (MM) with Don Elberson (DE) and Ruth Siegel Elberson (RSE), Puerto Rico circa late 1970s, 25

Page 13   " . . . do it for me, do it for Fumi." Frank Shotaro Miyamoto, Community Council Minutes, R21:06, August 11, 1942

Page 13   " . . . Baby plays with rattle, daddy plays with co-op" James Sakoda, Journal, (JERS) 67/14c, the Bancroft Library, Part II Section 5-Tule Lake, R20-81, December 25, 1942, 836

Page 15   "It was many years later" The story of my great grandparents' homesteading in Devil's Lake, North Dakota can be found in the Sons of Jacob Cemetery site. Louis Kahan Family History, Sons of Jacob Cemetery (sojnorthdakota.org)

Page 15   My grandmother, Sarah Edna Siegel's description of Homesteading in Devil's Lake, North Dakota can be found in an audio interview with her; University of Washington archives, https://digitalcollections.lib.washington.edu/digital/collection/ohc/id/1771/

Page 15   " . . . she must have had her feelings about his not fighting."
The strongest indication I can find of my Grandmother's Zionist posi-
tion on the plight of Jews in *Refuge Must Be Given: Eleanor Roosevelt, the
Jewish Plight, and the Founding of Israel,* John F. Sears, Purdue University
Press, West Lafayette, Indiana, 2021, 170-171. The correspondence be-
tween my grandmother and Eleanor Roosevelt can be found in: Sarah
Siegel to ER, August 21, 1946; ER to Siegel, September 5, 1946; Folder:
Sia-Sil; Correspondence 1945-1952; Eleanor Roosevelt Papers (hereaf-
ter) ERP); FDR Library (hereafter: FDRL).

Page 17   "His case, Ozawa v. United States, made it to the United States Supreme Court . . .." Ozawa vs United States, OCTOBER
TERM: 1922. Statement of the Case. 260 U. S. TAKAO OZAWA v.
UNITED STATES. CERTIFICATE FROM THE CIRCUIT COURT
OF IAPPEALS FOR THE NINTH CIRCUIT. No. 1. Argued October
3, 4, 1922.-Decided November 13, 1922 https://tile.loc.gov/storageser-
vices/service/ll/usrep/usrep260/usrep260178/usrep260178.pdf

Page 17   "His case, Ozawa v. United States, made it to the United
States Supreme Court..." For further reading: The following is an in-
depth analysis and description of Ozawa's conceptualizing of his position on whiteness. California Law Review VOL. 97 JUNE 2009 No.
3 Copyright © 2009 by California Law Review, Inc. *Yellow by Law,*
Devon W. Carbado, 1-60 https://www.dismantlingracism.org/up-
loads/4/3/5/7/43579015/yellow_by_law.pdf

Page 18   "The situation in Tule Lake and the other nine camps worsened after January of 1943." For an overview: Densho.org, Catalyst, The
"Loyalty Page Questionnaire" of 1943 Opened a Wound That Has Yet
to Heal. https://densho.org/catalyst/the-loyalty-questionnaire-of-1943-
opened-a-wound-that-has-yet-to-heal/

Pages 18-19   For a primary source discussion of the Loyalty Oath registration from the staff views, including my father's, Don Elberson, see: May 12, 1943 B. BILLIGMEIER Registration # Reports, 1-38 https://digitalassets.lib.berkeley.edu/jarda/ucb/text/reduced/cubanc6714_b257r20_0007_2.pdf

Page 19   "My father said the word from Washington D. C was that it was to be the "black camp." Interview by Author (MM) with Don Elberson (DE) and Ruth Siegel Elberson (RSE), Puerto Rico circa late 1970s.

Page 19   "As political philosopher Hannah Arendt said" in *Thinking Without a Banister, Essays in Understanding, 1953-1975*, Edited by Jerome Kohn, Schocken Books, March 6, 2018, 132-133.

Page 19   Also, in keeping with what Hannah Arendt said: Relating loss of citizenship to the Japanese American Incarceration, A punishment more primitive than torture: Anne McMillan, International Bar Association, https://www.ibanet.org/article/0973ca3c-1549-4489-b0f4-0dc418085c28

Page 20   "My mother said, the evacuees had a right to demonstrate . . .." Interview with Mrs. Ruth Elberson. Investigating Un-American Propaganda Activities in the United States Hearing before a Special Committee on Un-American Activities, House of Representatives, 78th Congress, First Session, Volume 16, November 29-December 1943, 10142-10143

Page 21   " . . . yellow monkeys" to their faces, or worse. " Robert Billigmeier, The Caucasian Staff at Tule Lake, (JERS), 67/14c, the Bancroft Library, R20:01, n.d., 8-9

Page 21   "Your wail was heartbreaking, unearthly." Interview by Author Marnie Mueller (MM) of Ruth Siegel Elberson (RSE), Puerto Rico circa late 1970s.

Page 22   "I was adamantly against . . .." Interview by Author (MM) with Don Elberson (DE) and Ruth Siegel Elberson (RSE), Puerto Rico circa late 1970s.

Page 22   "Some people expect the gratitude of a serf . . .." Robert Billigmeier, The Caucasian Staff at Tule Lake, (JERS) 67/14c, the Bancroft Library, R20:01, n.d., 12

Page 22   "They called me a 'Jap Lover'" Interview by Author (MM) with Don Elberson (DE) and Ruth Siegel Elberson (RSE), Puerto Rico circa late 1970s.

Page 23   "I don't think it was helpful . . .." Interview by Author (MM) with Don Elberson (DE) and Ruth Siegel Elberson (RSE), Puerto Rico circa late 1970s, 25

CHAPTER 2 • AMIDST THE DARK FORCES OF AMERICA

Page 25   "In late 1943 Tule Lake my father began to travel back and forth from camp to the Washington DC War Relocation Authority headquarters and from there to a long stint in Manzanar camp followed by accompanying a group of Nisei leaders on the train to Chicago for a major Co-op meeting." Manzanar Free Press, Elberson to Assist Evacuees in Co-operative Method Relocation, December 4, 1943, 1

Page 25   "you'd cling to every man..." Interview by Author (MM) with Don Elberson (DE) and Ruth Seigel Elberson (RSE), Puerto Rico circa late 1970s. In the author's possession.

Page 33   "People who had worked for the 1948 Henry Wallace campaign for President were especially targeted by Loeb." The Rutland Herald, THE RED SCARE, A history" lesson for Vermont, PAUL HELLER, Aug 11, 2018 Updated Oct 30, 2018, https://www.rutlandherald.com/the-red-scare/article_03824920-9254-5e0b-b569-57a7871a5ff4.html

Page 33   "People who had worked for the 1948 Henry Wallace campaign for President were especially targeted by Loeb. A direct source,
Winston, Rick, *Red Scare in the Green Mountains*, Rootstock Publishing,
2018

Page 33   "People who had worked for the 1948 Henry Wallace campaign." Rick Winston, Classical Film Lectures and Programs, The Mc-
Carthy Era and the Burlington Press, http://rickwinston.org/the-mccar-
thy-era-and-the-burlington-press/

Page 33   "People who had worked for the 1948 Henry Wallace campaign." Rick Winston, Classical Film Lectures and Programs, The Mc-
Carthy Era and the Burlington Press, http://rickwinston.org/the-mccar-
thy-era-and-the-burlington-press/

Page 35   "My mother was Jewish" Woodsmoke Productions and Vermont Historical Society, "The Case of Alex B. Novikoff," *The Green
Mountain Chronicles* radio broadcast and background information, original broadcast 1988-89. https://vermonthistory.org/case-of-alex-b-no-
vikoff-1953

Page 35   "William Loeb had also gone way out of his way to disprove
"rumors," that he himself was Jewish," New England Historical Society,
Eleven Things You Didn't Know about William Loeb, 7. https://newen-
glandhistoricalsociety.com/11-things-didnt-know-william-loeb/

Page 38   ". . .for the United Housing Foundation," COOPERA-
TORNEWS, New York, The co-op and condo resource, *From Amalgam-
ated to Central Park, West, The History of Cooperative Housing*, Debra A
Estok, April 2008 https://cooperatornews.com/article/from-amalgamat-
ed-to-central-park-west

Page 38   "They finally hired him a year on in." United Housing Foundation Files Collection Number: 6129, Kheel Center for Labor-Man-
agement Documentation and Archives, Cornell University Library
Guide to the United Housing Foundation Files (cornell.edu)

Page 44   "He reminded me that while my mother and I had driven to Chicago." https://densho.org/catalyst/10-things-you-might-not-know-about-jerome/

Page 51   " . . . where I found *Years of Infamy: The Untold Story of America's Concentration Camps,*" Weglyn, Michi, *Years of Infamy: The Untold Story of America's Concentration Camps,* William Morrow and Company, Inc., New York, NY, 1976

Page 51   "...where I found *Years of Infamy: The Untold Story of America's Concentration Camps,*" For more on Michi Weglyn, https://encyclopedia.densho.org/Michi_Nishiura_Weglyn/

Page 52   "One day in 1991 I was reading Thomas James's Exile *Within: The Schooling of Japanese Americans 1942-1945* (1987)." A Nisei Block Manager had written to him. Knowing my father, I extrapolated that the man trusted him enough to speak his mind. "School has started. What a school! Yes, I can appreciate the efforts made by the WRA, but---I oftentimes wonder. Do you know the real existing conditions? How, I wonder, how are we going to make real Americans out of these innocent young children. Teaching them the principles of Democracy, "I pledge allegiance to the flag. One nation, indivisible, with liberty and justice for all" while — they are penned up. Barbed wire fences, guard towers all around playing their search lights on us at night, guards with tommy guns, pistols, despair — God! Oh, what is this? We who were born here, reared here, educated here, we are bewildered . . . my children ask me: "Daddy, why can't we go home? Why do we have to stay here? ..." What can I tell them---tell them because we are Americans but of Japanese ancestry. No, heavens, no! Then what are we to tell them? There replies would be: I didn't learn anything like that in school, where one type of Americans should be put into a camp." Weekly activities report to Don Elberson from Block Manager 51, Tule Lake Relocation Center, September 19, 1942, BAN (The Bancroft Library) 6714 R2.08.

Another statement directly appealing to my father a few days later, confirmed what I thought. From the Archive of Robert Billigmeier, 18 https://cdn.calisphere.org/data/13030/mp/k68s4pmp/files/k68s4p-mp-FID1.pdf , As reported by Robert Billigmeier:

> "Following is interesting evidence of that confidence, (it) appeared in a Nisei block manager's report dated September 21, 1942 as concluding remarks."
> . . .. "Attention MR. ELBERSON. Whether or not it is a fact, information has reached us to the effect that you may be transferred to another Project which we understand would be in the nature of a promotion. as for the promotion, we don't question that it is in order for we feel that you have justly earned such and if such is so, congratulations are in order. However, I am voicing the sentiment of our Ward as well as the sentiment of the entire Project. Your work, your understanding of us and our problems, your character and your personality commands our respect and admiration, our sentiment is so wholehearted that we do not want to lose a man of your caliber. We are very anxious to have you remain here and to serve us if it is humanly possible. We may be greedy in voicing to our sentiment, but we are sincere in our statement and we hope that your promotion can be had remaining right here in this Project. Men of your caliber are few and far between and we are human and selfish enough to want to keep you here." Signed, Hh

Page 53   "It's rather inconceivable to me that the employment of one Japanese . . .." Don Elberson letter to Merlin Miller, WRA Papers, National Archives, NARA, Subject Classified General File, February 10, 1943, 2.

Page 54   " . . . Japanese Evacuation and Relocation Study, a project initiated in 1942 by Berkeley sociologist Dorothy Swaine Thomas." For an
overview: Densho.org, the Japanese American Evacuation and Resettlement Study, https://encyclopedia.densho.org/Japanese_American_Evac-
uation_and_Resettlement_Study/

For the documents. https://bancroft.berkeley.edu/collections/jais/ The
Japanese America Evacuation and Resettlement Study (JERS), A digital
archive in Bancroft Library, University of California, Berkeley, California.

Page 54   "And they were there, daily journals written by two Nisei intellectuals . . .." For an interesting retrospective view of the young Nisei
who were active participants in the day-to-day compilation of the Japanese American Evacuation and Resettlement Records including their
interface with Caucasian liberals on staff, and their brilliant originali-
ty as social scientists, I recommend Arthur A. Hansen's 1988 interview
with Professor James M. Sakoda for the Japanese American Project of
the Oral History Program at California State University, Fullerton. The
attached is the second interview of two, which took place on August 10,
1988, at the home of Professor James A. Sakoda and his wife, Hattie,
at 411 County Road in Barrington, Rhode Island. Japanese American
World War II Oral History Project: Part III: Analysts, 386-446

http://texts.cdlib.org/view?docId=ft0p30026h;NAAN=13030&doc.
view=content&chunk.id=d0e36541&toc.depth=1&brand=cali-
sphere&anchor.id=0%20:%20See%20also%20for%20informa-
tion%20on%20Arthur%20A.%20Hansen,%20https://encyclopedia.
densho.org/authors/Arthur%20A.%20Hansen/

Page 54   "Sakoda was a pioneering figure in computer programming…" Overlooked No More: James Sakoda, Whose Wartime Internment Inspired a Social Science Tool, *The New York Times*, By Elizabeth
Landau and Ben Klemens, May 8, 2023, May 15, 2023, Section B, 7
Overlooked No More: James Sakoda, Whose Wartime Internment Inspired a Social Science Tool - *The New York Times* (nytimes.com)

Page 54   "Miyamoto returned after the Incarceration to the University of Washington." Densho.org, Encyclopedia, S. Frank Miyamoto,
https://encyclopedia.densho.org/S._Frank_Miyamoto/

Page 55   "Fumi as a "gritty young gal who sure knows how to dress."
James Sakoda, Journal, JERS 67/14c.,Bancroft Library, Part II: Section
5-Tule Lake, R20:81, January 20, 1943, 918

Page 55   "I learned from Frank Miyamoto that my father preferred
to work behind the scenes." The Cooperative Movement in Tule Lake,
(JERS), 67/14c, The Bancroft Library, Part II, Section 5-Tule Lake,
R20:86, 6

Page 55   "Don has no experience with racial minority groups,' James
M. Sakoda, Journal, Japanese American Evacuation and Resettlement
Records, (JERS), R20:81,The Bancroft Library, Part II : Section 5-Tule
Lake, January 28, 1943, 964

PART II – MARY AND ME
CHAPTER 4 • WHAT SHE TOLD ME

Page 64   Formerly the Actors Fund, currently, https://entertainment-
community.org/ and The Screen Actors Guild, https://www.sagaftra.org/

CHAPTER 5 • BLUE EYES, BRANDO, SAMMY DAVIS JR., AND A HUSBAND

Page 73   "Kimiye Tsunemitsu at nineteen, had just left camp and was traveling alone on a train to New York City." Later to perform as Trudy Long," https://densho.org/catalyst/mary-mon-toy-nisei-entertainers-be-came-chinese-wwii/

Trudy Long, as herself, appearing in, *Long Story Short: A Film by Christine Choy and Jodi Long*, Produced by Film News Now and Wahini Dakini Productions, 2008, https://www.amazon.com/Long-Story-Short-Larry/dp/B00407VQPM

CHAPTER 6 • TOGETHER ON ELLIS ISLAND

Page 75   "A written invitation arrived from Mary." World War II Incarceration of Japanese Americans Featured in Ellis Island Exhibit, Japanese American National Museum, Press release, March 25, 1998. https://www.janm.org/press/release/world-war-ii-incarceration-japanese-americans-featured-ellis-island-exhibit

Page 75   "Leading up to the event." "What Is a Concentration Camp? Ellis Island Exhibit Prompts a Debate," Somini Sengupta, *The New York Times*, March 8, 1998, 35. https://www.nytimes.com/1998/03/08/nyregion/what-is-a-concentration-camp-ellis-island-exhibit-prompts-a-debate.html

Page 75-76 Senator Daniel Inouye, who was on the board of the." Densho.org, Encyclopedia Senator Daniel Inouye. https://encyclopedia.densho.org/Daniel_Inouye/#:~:text=Hawai'i%20Senator%20Daniel%20K,the%20442nd%20Regimental%20Combat%20Team%20

Page 80 (1) "She understudied for the part of Mei Li," *These Filipino Theater Actors Were the Stars of Their Time*, Spot. PH, Alex Castro, July 4, 2017, Cely Carrillo is Cely Onrubia in the article. Her daughter, Cynthia Onrubia is also in the article. https://www.spot.ph/arts-culture/arts-culture-peoplepar-ties/70561/6-early-filipino-broadway-stars-a1801-20170704-lfrm

Also, on Cely Carrillo Onrubia: Oral history interview with Cely Carrillo Onrubia, 1986 Columbia University Libraries, Time-Based Media https://dlc.library.columbia.edu/time_based_media/10.7916/d8-sjnm-0d10

Page 80 "Cely's daughter Cynthia Onrubia is a famous dancer and choreographer." Internet Broadway Data Base, IBDB for Cynthia Onrubia. https://www.ibdb.com/broadway-cast-staff/cynthia-carrillo-onru-bia-81370

Page 80-81 "It was a lesson that would be repeated over my years with Mary." Regarding Cely Carrillo Onrubia, Mary's loyal friend, it was a lesson I did not learn early enough. In all the time I knew Cely, when she helped Mary in her last years, and after Mary's death, when I would be invited to Cely's home for a dinner of her delicious Filipino food, she never let on to how extensive her own career was. It was a surprise for me to find Brian Camp's Blog, in which he highlighted Cely's major role in *The Hour of the Tiger*, an episode of *The Virginian*, a popular NBC western series that ran in a 90-minute time slot from 1962 to 1971. *Brian Camp's Film and Anime Blog, Asians in TV Westerns*, "The Virginian: The Hour of the Tiger," December 17, 2019. https://briandanacamp.wordpress.com/2019/12/17/asians-in-tv-westerns-the-virginian-hour-of-the-tiger/

CHAPTER 7 · REACTING TO 9/11

Page 85 "It was in February of 1944." A contemporaneous document from the British nighttime bombing of Augsburg, Germany on February 25, 1944. William Uyen pilot in the Bombing of Augsburg. https://www.jankersten.nl/WilliamUyen/19440225.html

Page 85   "It was in February of 1944." Another contemporaneous handwritten document recording in pencil the number of bombs dropped on Augsburg on 25.2.1944 https://ibccdigitalarchive.lincoln.ac.uk/omeka/files/original/408/7878/SChattertonJ159568v10731.2.jpg

Page 86   "As they came of age in the 1950s and 1960s." Helwig, Frederike (Photographer), Waak, Anne (Editor), *Kriegskinder: Portraits of a Forgotten Generation*, Hatje Cantz, Berlin and Stuttgart, Germany, 2018

Page 86 "As they came of age in the 1950s and 1960s." WNYC-FM radio podcast, The New Yorker Radio Hour, "Germany's Traumatized Kriegskinder Speak Out," Eric Molinsky and Owen Agnew, October 14, 2016. https://www.wnycstudios.org/podcasts/tnyradiohour/segments/germanys-traumatized-kriegskinder-speak-out

Page 87   "I trod carefully with Mary." "*Of Spies and G-Men: How the U.S. Government Turned Japanese Americans into Enemies of the State*," Catalyst, Densho.org, By Nina Wallace, Densho Communications Coordinator, September 29, 2017. https://densho.org/catalyst/of-spies-and-gmen/

Page 88   "When I gently said to Mary." For one view of the effect of the Incarceration on the response to 9/11: *How memories of Japanese American imprisonment during WWII guided the US response to 9/11 The terrorist attacks on Sep. 11, 2001, could have divided the nation, but lessons from World War II, when Japanese Americans were placed in internment camps, helped the government avoid repeating past mistakes.* Susan H. Kamei, USCDornsife, University of Southern California, September 3, 2021, https://dornsife.usc.edu/news/stories/3543/japanese-american-imprisonment-us-response-to-9-11/

Page 88   "When I gently said to Mary." For an analytic comparison of the consequences of 12/7/1942 (Pearl Harbor Attack) and 9/11: Eric L. Muller, 12/7 AND 9/11: *War, Liberties, and the Lessons of History*, West Virginia University, The research repository@WVU, Volume 104/Issue 3, Article 7 https://researchrepository.wvu.edu/cgi/viewcontent.cgi?article=1472&context=wvlr

CHAPTER 9 · GLIMMERS OF LOVE

Page 101   "A man in the building, Michael Estwanik," *StageBuzz.com*, October 20, 2011 Interview with Michael Putman Estwanik of The American Songbook Project, Byrne Harrison, http://www.stagebuzz.com/2011/10/interview-with-michael-putman-estwanik.html

Page 103   "I'm here to document the great event," https://www.stanschnier.com/untitled, Stan (aka "Stan Lee") also played Bass with the Incredible String Band in the 1970s

Page 103   "She'd recently told me that Mary Louise (Jones Britten)" Verified in audio interview with Mary Louise and Bill Britten and Marnie Mueller, April 2011, In the author's possession.

Page 103   "Bill was the original Bozo the Clown…" Bill Britten / Wonderama / TVparty!/ Classic TV http://www.tvparty.com/50-bill-britten2.html

Page 104   "She's an understudy to all the greats, " *Moore To Love*, Filichia sings the praises of Maureen Moore, the worthy understudy for *Gypsy's*, Bernadette Peters, New York City , October 1, 2003, https://www.theatermania.com/new-york-city-theater/news/moore-to-love_3944.html/

Page 199   "Mary had once said, "in those days, Chinese and Japanese didn't get along. Objections came from both sides of the family." ." Thomas DeFrantz, The George Balanchine Foundation, Popular Balanchine: Oral History, New York Public Library for the Performing Arts at Lincoln Center, *House of Flowers* interview with Mary Mon Toy, September 7, 2001, 2

Page 201   "I held her close, feeling the warmth of her body." For more on May Ohmura Watanabe I recommend a 19 part video interview with her on https://ddr.densho.org/narrators/902/, ddr-densho-1000-454-1 — May Ohmura Watanabe Segment 1 | Densho Digital Repository, Recorded, December 18, 2018

Page 201   "My father told me that one of the saddest results of the incarceration." For reading on the psychological and sociological impact, both bad and good, of the Incarceration on individuals and families, a good place to begin is: Densho. org, Encyclopedia, Psychological effects of camp, Donna K. Nagata, author of The Legacy of Injustice: Exploring the Cross Generational Injustice of the Japanese American internment, New York : Plenum Press, 1993 https://encyclopedia.densho.org/Psychological_effects_of_camp/

PART III – FINDING MARY
CHAPTER 22 • THE DETECTIVE WORK BEGINS

Page 211   "Yoshizo Watanabe and Mon Yusa Watanabe were both born in Japan," The full information I received from Wendy Watanabe will be available in: Densho.org, Mary Mon Toy Family Collection (ddr-densho-488) and the Wing Luke Museum, Seattle.

Page 212   "The day I sat on the cold floor of the storage unit, I had come across a bundle of what were labeled in Mary's hand "Love Letters," dating from 1939 through 1940." Copies of "love Letters" from George Yasukochi, 1939-1940: Densho.org, Mary Mon Toy Family Collection (ddr-densho-488) and the Wing Luke Museum, Seattle.

Page 213   "This reference to the Japanese American Citizens League," For information on the Japanese American Citizens League, https://en-cyclopedia.densho.org/Japanese_American_Citizens_League/

Page 215   "I've attached his obituary." SF GATE, George Yasukochi – Berkeley Coops Official, Erin Hallessy, November 24, 2004. https://www.sfgate.com/bayarea/article/George-Yasukochi-Berkeley-Co-ops-official-2669669.php

Page 215   "The Rochdale Institute was a familiar name in our household. My father had first learned co-op principles at the Berkeley Co-op. International Cooperative Alliance, uniting, representing, and serving co-operatives worldwide," The Present Application of the Rochdale Principles of Co-operation (1937), https://web.archive.org/web/20091029163330/http://www.ica.coop/coop/principles-revisions.html#1937

CHAPTER 23 • EVACUATION

Page 218 "The two transcripts arrived within days." Watanabe, Teru, M. Date of Graduation June 14, 1934, Broadway High School, Seattle Public Schools, MS 21-171, Student Records, PO BOX 34165, Seattle, Washington; Siegel, Ruth, Date of Graduation, June 15, 1933, Broadway High School, Seattle Public Schools, MS 21-171, Student Records, PO BOX 34165, Seattle, Washington.

Page 218   "Shigesato Okada, twenty-nine years old, married to Mary Teru
Watanabe on September 28, 1941," Marriage certificate, State of Washington, 755, Series A, 70497 Mary Teru Watanabe Shigesato Okada.

Page 218   "I would later learn that he was a champion skier." TERU
WATANABE RELATES ENGAGEMENT Mr. and Mrs. Yoshizo Watanabe. of Seattle, announced the engagement of their only daughter. Miss
Mary Teru, to Shigesato Okada, son of Mrs. Kotaro Watanabe of Loma,
Montana, and Mr. Shigotada Okada. of this city, last night. The troth
was revealed at the bride-elect's residence. Miss Watanabe is a prominent member of the Aeolian Society. She is a graduate of Broadway high
school and Wilson's Business College. Mr. Okada, graduate also of Wilson's Business College and (Franklin high school, is a well- known skier,
being first president of the Rokka Ski club. Last year he won the slalom
and downhill championship of the Northwest in a competition against
the Vancouver Fuji club. Taihoku Nippō1940.11.29 — Hoji Shinbun
Digital Collection (hoover.org), Japanese Diaspora Initiative, Stanford
University, From Taihoku Nippō, 1940.11.29, 8

Page 219   "My first discovery was that at the time of evacuation," Louis
Fiset, *Camp Harmony: Seattle's Japanese Americans and the Puyallup Assembly Center*, 55-57

Page 219   "Mary and Shig left Seattle on April 28," (WRA) Administration, (NARA) Teru Okada, Puyallup Assembly Center, Entry Date
4-28-42, Case File, DOB 6/3/1916, 18W3, BOX 4840, 8/24/1; Shigesato Okada, Puyallup Assembly Center, Entry Date 4-28-42, DOB;
5/1/1914 BOX 4838,8/24/1

Page 221   "Mary and her brother Frank helped close down the dry-cleaning establishment." (WRA) (NARA), Evacuee Case File, Yoshizo Watanabe, DOB: 3/21/1884m /BOX 6678, 10/8/1, War Relocation Application for Leave Clearance, Employment, Proprietor of Dexter Cleaners,
Seattle, 1935-1942.

Page 222   "Dr. Mitsuo Paul Suzuki, a young Issei," Fiset, Louis. *Camp Harmony: Seattle's Japanese Americans and the Puyallup Assembly Center*, Chapter 4 PUYALLUP ASSEMBLY CENTER 70 -71.

Page 223   "Gordon Hirabayashi, a University of Washington senior at the time,"45 YEARS LATER, AN APOLOGY FROM THE U.S. GOVERNMENT, Perspectives, Nancy Joseph, College of Arts and Sciences, University of Washington, March 13, 2000 https://artsci.washington. edu/news/2000-02/45-years-later-apology-us-government, For more detail see: Fiset, Louis. Camp Harmony: Seattle's Japanese Americans and the Puyallup Assembly Center, Chapter 5, EXILE, 81-83

Page 223   "In a letter of support from the University of Washington, he was described as dependable and loyal:" (WRA) (NARA) Individual Record for Frank Chusei Watanabe, Case File, DOB 11/22/1920, BOX 6631, 10/6/6: Letters in support of Leave Clearance for Frank Chusei Watanabe, University of Washington, Department of General Studies, from H.B. Densmore, Chairman, General Studies, lead letter, n.d.

Page 224   "All the letters of support written for the family by Caucasians..." For example: Letter from Mrs. Robert C. Ridgway to Mr. Dillon S. Meyer, Director, War Relocation Authority, Barr Building, Washington, D. C, "The fact that the two Watanabe children are among the most thoroughly Americanized group of second-generation Japanese in Seattle can undoubtedly be traced to the fact that their parents have constantly encouraged them to become integrated into the American community, and have made much progress in this direction themselves." June 7, 1943, (WRA) (NARA), Evacuee Case File, Yoshizo Watanabe, DOB: 3/21/1884m /BOX 6678, 10/8/1

Page 224   "Mary's father confided to a Caucasian neighbor" Letter of support for Leave Clearance for Yoshizo Watanabe from Miss Muriel Jones, Seattle, to Mr. Dillon S. Meyer, Director, War Relocation Authority, Barr Building, Washington, D. C, May 24, 1943, (WRA), (NARA), Evacuee Case File, Yoshizo Watanabe, DOB: 3/21/1884m /BOX 6678, 10/8/1

Page 224   "Harmony was one of fifteen assembly centers," https://encyclopedia.densho.org/Puyallup_(detention_facility)/, Fiset, Louis. *Camp Harmony: Seattle's Japanese Americans and the Puyallup Assembly Center*, Chapter 4 PUYALLUP ASSEMBLY CENTER, 61-66

Page 225   "Mary and Shig were in the "lucky" *Camp Harmony: Seattle's Japanese Americans and the Puyallup Assembly Center*, Louis Fiset, Chapter 5, EXILE, 84

Page 225   ". . . an eighty square-foot room in a crude barracks, built with no foundation," University Libraries, University of Washington, Special Collections, Camp Harmony Exhibit, Housing, Japanese Evacuation Report #11. Written by Joseph Conard of the Seattle Office of the American Friends Service Committee dated May 11, 1942. Joseph Conard, Collector, Box 4. Hoover Institution Archive

Page 226   "We had to go to internment camp because my mother was Japanese," In 2001, a week before 9/11, Mary opened up to a young African American interviewer, Thomas de Frantz from The Popular Balanchine Dossiers doing research on *House of Flowers*: Thomas DeFrantz, The George Balanchine Foundation, Popular Balanchine: Oral History, New York Public Library for the Performing Arts at Lincoln Center, *House of Flowers* interview with Mary Mon Toy, September 7, 2001, 2

Page 227   "When Mary went to the bathroom that first day, " University Libraries, University of Washington, Special Collections, Camp Harmony Exhibit, Housing https://www.lib.washington.edu/specialcollections/collections/exhibits/harmony/exhibit/housing

Page 228   "The mess hall for Section A," University Libraries, University of Washington, Special Collections, Camp Harmony Exhibit, Food, Nakashima, Ted, "Concentration Camps: U.S. Style." *New Republic*, Volume 106, June 15, 1942, pg. 822, Food — UW Libraries (washington.edu) https://www.lib.washington.edu/specialcollections/collections/exhibits/harmony/exhibit/Food

Page 228   "The mess hall for Section A," Fiset, Louis. *Camp Harmony: Seattle's Japanese Americans and the Puyallup Assembly Center.* Chapter 6 SETTLING IN, 100-101, https://www.lib.washington.edu/specialcollections/collections/exhibits/harmony/exhibit/settlingin

Page 228   "Civil rights were further stripped with roll calls twice a day;" University Libraries, University of Washington, Special Collections, Camp Harmony Exhibit, civil liberties, "Roll Call Started." Camp Harmony Newsletter, June 12, 1942, https://www.lib.washington.edu/specialcollections/collections/exhibits/harmony/exhibit/civil

CHAPTER 24 •PERSONAL CONSEQUENCES OF THE INCARCERATION

Page 229   "Mary needed a special pass to enter their area;", DISRUPTION OF THE FAMILY, Information from Fiset, Louis, *Camp Harmony: Seattle's Japanese Americans and the Puyallup Assembly Center,* University of Illinois Press, Urbana and Chicago, 2009, Chapter 6, SETTLING IN, 103, For an added condensed overview of Puyallup detention center, see Louis Fiset's article in the Densho encyclopedia, https://encyclopedia.densho.org/Puyallup_%28detention_facility%29/

Page 229   "An Issei physician prescribed a daily enema to be administered by Mary's mother." MARY'S HEALTH, Hospital Record of Treatment, 5/18/42 and 5/19/42, Enema given by mother (Mon Watanabe), War Relocation Authority (WRA) National Archives & Records Administration, (NARA)Individual Record Case File, Okada, Teru, DOB; 6/3/1916, 18/W3, BOX 4840, 8/24/1

Page 230   "In the first week of August," MARY'S HEALTH, 8/4/42, (WRA) (NARA)Individual Record Okada, Teru, DOB; 6/3/1916, 18/ W3, BOX 4840, 8/24/1

Page 230   "after a thirty-hour grueling train ride…" "The thirty-hour ordeal…"MARY'S HEALTH, Information from Fiset, *Louis, Camp Harmony: Seattle's Japanese Americans and the Puyallup Assembly Center*, 2009, Chapter 9, Leaving Camp Harmony, 158-163

Page 230   "There, they were ready for us." THE ENVIRONMENT, Interview with Mary Mon Toy, The George Balanchine Popular Balanchine Foundation: Oral History, Thomas DeFrantz, New York Public Library for the Performing Arts at Lincoln Center, September 7, 2001, 2

Page 231   "In reality, according to historical documents," THE ENVIRONMENT, Fiset, Louis, *Camp Harmony: Seattle's Japanese Americans and the Puyallup Assembly Center*, Chapter 9, Leaving Camp Harmony, 161-163

Page 231   "The five-mile barbed wire fence around the camp" THE ENVIRONMENT, Minidoka | Densho Encyclopedia, Brian Niiya, See sections: "Unfinished," "Blocks-Barracks," and "Unrest." See also, a heritage history by Hanako Wakatsuki in Densho encyclopedia, https:// encyclopedia.densho.org/media/encyc-legacy/Minidoka.html

Page 232   "In the first week of October federal marshals removed Shig." POLITICS, Fiset, Louis, Camp Harmony: Seattle's Japanese Americans and the Puyallup Assembly Center, Chapter 2, War Comes to Japantown, 29

Page 233   (1) "He later sardonically explained," POLITICS, Interview in 1944 after Shigesato Okada had left Minidoka Camp having received leave clearance, and was now applying for work in Chicago.: Indefinite Leave hearing of Shigesato Okada, 65 West Maple Street, Chicago, Illinois, at the request of Harry L. Stafford, Project Director, Minidoka Relocation Center, Hunt Idaho. Hearing conducted by Edward M. Joyce, Relocation Officer, on March 18, 1944, (WRA) (NARA) Individual Record Case File Okada, Shigesato DOB; 5/1/1914 BOX 4838, 8/24/ 1, 2

Page 233   "He testified that he had traveled to Mexico on business." POLITICS, Confidential report 9/28/42 (WRA), (NARA) Individual Record case file: Okada, Shigesato DOB; 5/1/1914 BOX 4838, 8/24/ 1, 2

Page 233   "The attending doctor was none other than Dr. Mitsuo Paul Suzuki," MARY'S HEALTH, for more on Dr. Suzuki, here is Testimony of Nobuko Yanagimachi Suzuki , wife of Dr. Mitsuo Paul Suzuki, about his work in both Puyallup Assembly center and later the Minidoka camp. https://downloads.densho.org/ddr-densho-67/ddr-densho-67-219-mezzanine-210e46e4e1.pdf

CHAPTER 25 • A SURPRISING SHARED HISTORY

Page 239   "In my search for Mary I had come upon the quote," Louis Fiset, *Camp Harmony: Seattle's Japanese Americans*, 96, also from Frank Shotaro Miyamoto "Reminiscences of JERS," (JERS), 144

Page 241   "Minutes later another e-mail came through," Letters from "Ted" from "Tule Lake Colony" to George Yasukochi, June 30, 1942, In the author's files, courtesy of Valerie Yasukochi

Page 242   "Her pallid features . . .. Frank Shotaro Miyamoto, Diary, (JERS), Bancroft Library, R20:18, February 17, 1943, 1

Page 242   "I feel he wanted to sympathize and 'love' the evacuees too much." Frank Shotaro Miyamoto, Diary, (JERS), Bancroft Library, R20:18, October 27, 1942, 2

Page 243   "She had brought copies of more letters," *A Conversation with George Yasukochi: Controller of Consumers Cooperative: Controller of Consumers Cooperative of Berkeley, 1956-1982,* Transcribed by Berkeley Oral History Project of the Berkeley Historical Society, Copyright 1995, Berkeley Historical Society, 71 pages, Photos of a young George Yasukochi, 5

Page 244   "Don Elberson, the Co-op specialist, is a right guy," "Letters from "Hank" in Tule Lake to George Yasukochi, "Tulelake (sic) Summer Resort," Newell California, August 22, 1942.

Page 245   ", "...we were interviewed several weeks back regarding a job, "Tulelake (sic) Summer Resort," Newell California, December 22, 1942

Page 246   "After the war Shibata had returned to Palo Alto, Shibata, Yoshimi, *Across Two Worlds: Memoirs of a Nisei Flower Grower,* Mt. Eden Floral Company, Mountain View, CA 2006

"Page 247   "As we sat on an oversized moss-green sofa in their grand living room," June 25, 2005, video documenting the interview with Yoshimi Shibata. In the author's files, courtesy of the Shibata family.

Page 247   "recounting his leadership success in camp," a video in which Grace Eto Shibata talks about her husband going to see a psychiatrist. Grace and Shimi spoke with me about how that helped him to process episodes in his life prior to the incarceration, as well as the psychological impact of being imprisoned in Tule Lake, https://www.youtube.com/watch?v=KrlUkXQ0Rt8

Page 248   "I also see that my father was not wrong," Bill Hosokawa discusses the more positive aspects of the WWII incarceration (en-den-shovh-hbill-01-0023-1) | Primary Sources | Densho Encyclopedia

Page 248   "I also see that my father was not wrong," For more on the professional opportunities post-camp for Nisei, I again recommend Arthur A. Hansen's 1988 interview with Professor James M. Sakoda for the Japanese American Project of the Oral History Program at California State University, Fullerton, Japanese American World War II Oral History Project: Part III: Analysts, http://texts.cdlib.org/view?docId=ft0p30026h;NAAN=13030&doc.view=content&chunk.id=d0e36541&toc.depth=1&brand=calisphere&anchor.id=0

See also for information on Arthur A. Hansen, https://encyclopedia.densho.org/authors/Arthur%20A.%20Hansen/

CHAPTER 26 • PERMISSION TO LEAVE THE CAMP

Page 249   "It is a shame that this girl is a Jap." (WRA), (NARA)Individual Record Case file for Okada, Teru, DOB; 6/3/1916, 18/W3, BOX 4840, 8/24/1 War Relocation Board, Washington, DC, from C. B. W. Raymond, Attention Mr. Dillon S. Meyer, Director, Re: Okada, Teru No. 10902 Minidoka, WRA, 38-7-A., No Date.

Page 250   "In February 1943, when Mary applied for security clearance, "https://encyclopedia.densho.org/National_Japanese_American_Student_Relocation_Council/ , Alan W. Austin and James, Thomas. Exile Within: The Schooling of Japanese Americans, 1942-1945, Chapter 4, Educating "Projectiles of Democracy,"116-130

Page 250   "Perhaps our total amount is insufficient to be of any aid," Handwritten letter from Mary Teruko Okada to Mr. Joseph Conard, Executive Secretary, West Coast Area, National Student Relocation Committee, September 14, 1942, sent from Hunt Branch 38-7-A, WRA, Twin Falls, Idaho, or in other words, Minidoka Camp. She included a copy of a letter from her bank, which stated that she has $151.96 in her savings account which she wants to go toward her brother's tuition. She also stated that she and her husband have $100 in War Bonds which she wants also to go to Frank. She wrote, "As his sister, I'm pretty fond of

Frank...Our parents brought us both up to be good and loyal citizens though they were barred by law to become naturalized." She thanked Mr. Conrad for "the thoroughness of your committee." She signed off by saying, "I hardly think you will be disappointed by any American student of Japanese ancestry whom you relocate to various colleges: (WRA), (NARA)Individual Record Case File Case file for Okada, Teru, DOB; 6/3/1916, 18/W3, BOX 4840, 8/24/1

Page 250   "Once he was safely in the university, she plead Shig's and her case." (WRA) (NARA)Individual Record Case File Case file, Okada, Teru, DOB; 6/3/1916, 18/W3, BOX 4840, 8/24/1 War Relocation Application for Leave Clearance, Approval for Teru Okada, Teru Okada, June 18, 1943 Case file for Okada, Teru, DOB; 6/3/1916, 18/W3, BOX 4840, 8/24/1, War Relocation Application for Leave Clearance, Approved for Shigesato Okada, April 5, 1943, Shigesato DOB; 5/1/1914 BOX 4838, 8/24/ 1

Page 251   "Attorney Raymond was the first of five Caucasians." Application for Leave Clearance, 6/1943, (WRA), (NARA)Individual Record Case File for Okada, Teru, DOB; 6/3/1916, 18/W3, BOX 4840, 8/24/1

Page 251 "Mary and Shig had to have gainful employment," Multiple letters back and forth with William J. Fluke, Relocation Officer of WRA, 615 Ohio Building, Toledo, Ohio. Included in the initial letter (May 11, 1943) was a list of twelve additional personal references. She closed saying, "My husband and I are able to furnish more references if you so wish." May 11, 1943 through May 23, 1943, four (4) letters. In her final letter, Mary politely declined the Toledo, Ohio offers of employment, (WRA) (NARA)Individual Record case file for Okada, Teru, DOB; 6/3/1916, 18/W3, BOX 4840, 8/24/1

Page 252 "Shig's employment at the foundry," Memo from the Office of the Provost Marshal General, Personal Security Division, Japanese American Branch, Subject: Okada, Shigesato, To Firm: Federal Foundry Supply Company, Cleveland, Ohio, which included extensive confidential material about his "subversive" activities before and during camp, concluding with Recommendation: It is recommended that SHIGESATO OKADA not be employed by the Federal Supply Company or any other plant or firm important to the United States Government. 9/2/43, (WRA) (NARA)Individual Record Okada, Shigesato DOB; 5/1/1914 BOX 4838, 8/24/ 1

Page 252 "He was taken off the floor, finger-printed, and told to leave the plant immediately." Report on removal of Shigesato Okada from Employment at the Foundry Supply Company, War Department Continuous Security District Office, Cleveland, Ohio, September 17, 1943, to Office of the Provost Marshal General Army Services Forces, Washington, DC., (WRA) (NARA)Individual Record Case File Okada, Shigesato DOB; 5/1/1914 BOX 4838, 8/24/ 1

Page 253 "Many were reluctant to leave camp," For an interesting analysis of some reasons Issei were unwilling to leave Minidoka Camp in the end, I again recommend Arthur A. Hansen's 1988 interview with Professor James M. Sakoda for the Japanese American Project of the Oral History Program at California State University, Fullerton, Japanese American World War II Oral History Project: Part III: Analysts, 405-408

http://texts.cdlib.org/view?docId=ft0p30026h;NAAN=13030&doc.view=content&chunk.id=d0e36541&toc.depth=1&brand=calisphere&anchor.id=0

Page 255   "As for Minidoka, the camp photos were taken by Francis L. Stewart," https://encyclopedia.densho.org/Francis_L._Stewart/

Page 255   "Lee's Incarceration work is less known than that of Dorothea Lange and Ansel Adams," https://encyclopedia.densho.org/Russell_Lee/ and more on Russell Lee's photos of beet farmers. http://www.ochcom.org/pdf/Lee-overview.pdf,

Page 257   (1)"My sponsor was a Baptist minister." Balanchine Popular dossiers Interview with Mary Mon Toy by Thomas De Frantz, September 7, 2001, 2, Sponsorship in Ridgewood, New Jersey confirmed in, War Relocation Authority (WRA) National Archives & Records Administration, (NARA)Individual Record Teru Okada, DOB; 6/3/1916, 18W3, BOX 4840, 8/24/1

Page 257   "She worked an eight-hour day in midtown," Caption: Photo of Mrs. Mary Okada at her typewriter in NYC. " Resettlement Program Affords Opportunity for Nisei Women to Apply Specialized Talents. " Pacific Citizen, Dec. 25, 1943, 18.

Page 257   (2) "My instructor at Juilliard said, 'You can't keep this up…'" Balanchine Popular dossiers Interview with Mary Mon Toy by Thomas De Frantz, September 7, 2001, 2

Page 258   "I-House, as it is commonly called," International House website: https://www.ihouse-nyc.org/alumni/noteablealumni/

Page 258   "Juilliard School of Music was at that time divided into the Institute of Musical Art and the Juilliard Graduate School." Juilliard School of Music/Institute of Musical Art catalog 1943/44, selected pages, courtesy of The Juilliard School Archivist, 60 Lincoln Center Plaza, New York, NY 10023

Page 258   "The building, which still stands, is an elegant limestone structure," The Juilliard School of Music, Shreve, Lamb and Harmon Architects, The Architectural Record, 1932, 385-393 and the Architectural History for the Manhattan School of Music, the original home of the Institute of Musical Art, www.msm.edu/About-MSM/Campus/Architectual-History, courtesy of The Juilliard School Archivist, 60 Lincoln Center Plaza, New York, NY 10023, 1 and 2

Page 258   "In the winter semester of 1943," Transcripts for Mary Teru Okada, The Department of Special Courses, Entered September 27, 1943, courtesy of The Juilliard School Archivist, 60 Lincoln Center Plaza, New York, NY 10023

Page 259   "The school considered that I didn't have any money," Balanchine Popular dossiers Interview with Mary Mon Toy by Thomas De Frantz, September 7, 2001, 2

Page 259   "Ten tense days went by," This from Edward W. Joyce, relocation officer, War Relocation Authority, Chicago, Illinois, "We could ascertain nothing…to indicate that the subject was as alleged, 'an agitator, trouble maker, and classified as dangerous . . .", (WRA) (NARA)Individual Record Shigesato Okada BOX 4838, DOB; 5/1/1914, 8/24/1, Indefinite Leave Hearing of Shigesato Okada, March 18, 1944, 4

Page 260   "Fierce letters flew back and forth between Mayor La Guardia and Interior Secretary Harold Ickes," .https://guides.laguardia.edu/internment/archives, go to Archival Documents ld.php (laguardia.edu) which contains the actual correspondence between Fiorello LaGuardia and Harold Ickes as a pdf, 4/11/44 through 4/24/44, four letters. But they are almost indecipherable. This researcher had to hold them up to the light and trace the words.

Page 260   "On April 28, 1944 the conflict broke onto the pages of the New York Times," ICKES HITS MAYOR ON LOYAL JAPANESE: CALLS STAND DISCORDANT Mayor's Record in Behalf of Race Equality and Justice Is Contrasted with New Views, New York Times, April 28, 1944, 8

Page 260   "Mayor LaGuardia contended…" The Secretary of the Interior, Washington, From Harold Ickes, Secretary of the Interior to "My Dear Fiorello," to be found in, the third letter in the series. ld.php (laguardia. edu), see also: LaGuardia and Wagner Archives: Mayor La Guardia, Japanese Internment and World War II: 70 Years Later (laguardiawagnerarchives.blogspot.com)

Page 261   "The conflict was a growing concern in the Japanese American community in New York:" See: https://digitalassets.lib.berkeley.edu/jarda/ucb/text/cubanc6714_b326w02_0065.pdf

Page 261   "The conflict was a growing concern in the Japanese American community in New York:" For more on the conflict between Mayor La Guardia and Japanese Americans see: Fiorello H. La Guardia and the Making of Modern New York, Thomas Kessner, McGraw-Hill, 1/1/1989, 536-538

Page 261   ". . . on April 21 Mary was called in for questioning before a War Relocation Authority panel," On April 1, 1944, a confidential report was sent from Leland Barrows, Acting Director of the War Relocation Authority to Harold S. Fistere, Relocation Supervisor in New York City, saying, "We have recently received a statement from the Japanese-American Joint Board that it cannot recommend the granting of indefinite leave to the subject: Teru Okada, 500 Riverside Drive (International House) New York City." Attached was a statement, "briefly summarizing the adverse factors which may have led the Joint Board to make an unfavorable recommendation in the subject's case." It was the confidential report describing Shig's trip to Mexico and that he was a "dangerous agitator in Camp." (WRA) (NARA)Individual Record Files for Teru Okada, DOB; 6/3/1916, 18W3, BOX 4840, 8/24/1

Page 261   "The hearing officer in New York sent a letter to Leland Barrows," Letter to Leland Barrows, Subject Teru Okada, from Mary H. S. Hayes, Relocation Officer in Charge, New York Office, April 24, 1944, (WRA), (NARA),Individual Record Case File for Teru Okada, DOB; 6/3/1916, 18W3, BOX 4840, 8/24/1,

Page 262   "Shig remarried a day later.." Date of Shig's remarriage found in Shig's second wife's obituary. Peggy Okada Obituary (2010) - Seattle, WA - The Seattle Times (legacy.com), July 11, 2010

Page 262   'Under questioning, he stated that they had separated in Clevelan,." From Deposition, Dorothy Brown, Clerk of the Circuit Court of Cook County, Illinois, Divorce File copies, 44S-13620, Shigesato Okada, Mary Teru Okada, Archives Req #13-2514, November 1944

Page 262   "Mary focused a good part of 1945 on arranging for her parents' move out of camp." letter from E. Price Steiding, Relocation Office in Charge, New York District Office to Mr. Harry Stafford, Project Director, Minidoka Relocation Center, Hunt, Idaho, arrangements for Mary Watanabe to accompany her mother to Seattle to identify the family's property, March 28, 1945. (WRA), (NARA), Teru Okada, DOB; 6/3/1916, 18W3, BOX 4840, 8/24/1

Page 263   "On May 9 Mon and Mary walked out the gates . . .", Mon and Mary visit Seattle, Short-Term Pass, Date of authorized departure, April 28, 1945, Expiration Date May 12, 1945, extended to May 26, 1945. (WRA) (NARA)Individual Record case file for Mon Watanabe, DOB; 2/25/1898, 18W3, BOX 6657, 10/74

Page 265   "It took a lawyer's intervention to force him to back down,"
Letter to Mrs. Edna G. Perraton, Legal Aid Bureau, Chicago, Illinois,
May 22, 1945, from Claude C. Walker, Sr. Property Advisor, 309 Walk-
er Building, Seattle, Washington, (WRA) (NARA)Individual Record
Teru Okada, DOB; 6/3/1916, 18W3, BOX 4840, 8/24/1

"Page 265   He stipulated in his terse three-line note," April 23, 1945 letter from Shigesato Okada, "Dear Teru," (WRA) (NARA)Individual Record case file, Teru Okada, DOB; 6/3/1916, 18W3, BOX 4840, 8/24/1,

Page 265   "According to Mrs. Force, the Caucasian guardian of the
property," A two-page formal Affidavit, dated May 1947, from "We the
Undersigned" at 4010 48th Avenue, Seattle, Washington, attesting to
the "turbulent condition" of the rooms. (WRA) (NARA)Individual Record case file, Teru Okada, DOB; 6/3/1916, 18W3, BOX 4840, 8/24/1

Page 266   Yoshizo added more stress to the process of leaving camp,"
Extensive correspondence about his attempt to find work and his fear
of leaving camp without his son, Frank Chusei Watanabe (NARA)In-
dividual Record case files for: Teru Okada, DOB; 6/3/1916, 18W3,
BOX 4840, 8/24/1; Mon Watanabe, DOB; 2/25/1898, 18W3, BOX
6657; Frank Chusei Watanabe, DOB; 11/22/1920, BOX 6631, 10/6/6;
Yoshizo Watanabe, DOB; 3/21/1884, BOX 6678, 10/8/1

Page 267   "Mary persisted, making the decision for her parents," Many
instructions for transport of Watanabe belongs to D. K. Ludwig home
in June of 1945, (WRA) (NARA)Individual Record for Mon Watanabe,
DOB; 2/25/1898, 18W3, BOX 6657, 10/74 also in War Relocation Authority (WRA) National Archives & Records Administration, (NARA)
Individual Record files, Teru Okada, DOB; 6/3/1916, 18W3, BOX
4840, 8/24/1

Page 267   "He [D.K. Ludwig] was an eccentric, obsessively private man, dubbed "the invisible billionaire" who would go on to garner the number one spot on the first Forbes "400 Richest Americans," list published in 1982." https://www.nytimes.com/1992/08/29/us/daniel-ludwig-billionaire-businessman-dies-at-95.html?src=pm, August 29, 1992, Section 1, Page 26 https://en.wikipedia.org/wiki/Daniel_K._Ludwig

CHAPTER 28 • "THE SLANT-EYED SCANDALS"

Page 270   "They didn't have enough money between them," Letter from Mon and Yoshizo Watanabe, explaining why there were remaining for the time being in the Hostel on 168 Clinton Street, Brooklyn, NY while they waited for their sponsor/work assignment, because Mary's living situation is minimal. Letter to a Mrs. Caward (WRA) (NARA)Individual Record Teru Okada, DOB; 6/3/1916, 18W3, BOX 4840, 8/24/1, June 12, 1945, 2

Page 270   "A rare exception was Sono Osato . . .,"National Endowment for the Humanities, Feature, *The Original Miss Turnstiles*: Sono Osato Starred on Broadway, Provocative casting On the Town. Carol J. Oja HUMANITIES, January/February 2015, Volume 36, Number 1,https://www.neh.gov/humanities/2015/januaryfebruary/feature/the-original-miss-turnstiles

Page 271   "She's a Jap, and I'm a nigger, and you're a white girl." Oxford University Press's Academic Insights for the Thinking Word, OUPBlog, On the Town, flashpoint for Social Distress, Carol J. Oja, September 23, 2014. Sono Osato, Also see, *Long Old Road* (Trident Press, 1965) Horace R. Cayton Jr

Page 271   "One day she came upon an ad in the Daily Mirror . . .." The Popular Balanchine Dossiers (PBD), Compiled by Tommy DeFrantz (1954), Interview with Mary Mon Toy September 7, 2001, 1

Page 272   "The China Doll Club was the brainchild of Irish American restaurateur…" It Could Only Happen on Broadway, Frank Quinn, *Sunday Mirror Magazine*, May 12, 1946

Page 272   The China Doll Club was the brainchild of Irish American restaurateur…." Chop Suey Circuit & China Doll Nightclub – Museum of Chinese in America (mocanyc.org)

Page 272   "The China Doll Club was advertised as a place where you could get the best Chinese food . . .." Café Life in New York, The China Doll has Something Different in Entertainment and Fine Native Cuisine, Virginia Forbes, *The New York Sun*, Thursday, May 2, 1946

Page 272   "The "Slant Eyed Scandals" at the China Doll Club was produced by Donn Arden . . .," Nightlife, China Dolls Show New and Bigtime, Lee Mortimer, *Sunday Mirror*, April 7, 1946, 28

Page 273   "Lee Mortimer, a partner in the enterprise, wore two professional hats:" China Doll Imports Gals from Coast, Lee Mortimer, *New York Post*, Wednesday, April 3, 1946.

Page 273   "The reviewers loved the show, and cited a number of acts including," New York Nite Life, Lou Grossman, *The Orchestra World*, May 1946

Page 273   "The "Scandals" was described as occidental with an oriental spin…", "Tips on Tables, Surging Crowds Dampen Joyful China Doll Debut," Robert Dana, *New York World-Telegram*, Tuesday, April 9, 1946

Page 273 "The "Scandals" was described as occidental with an oriental spin…"Also, Nick Kenny Speaking: *Daily Mirror*, Tuesday, April 9, 1946

Page 274   " . . . but in the case of those with Japanese surnames, https://densho.org/catalyst/mary-mon-toy-nisei-entertainers-became-chinese-wwii/

Page 274   "The most famous case would become Jack Soo," You Don't
Know Jack: The Jack Soo Story ww.jacksoo.com, *You Don't Know Jack:
The Jack Soo Story*, A film by Jeff Adachi ,written, directed, and produced
by Jeff Adachi. DVD, AAMM Productions, 2011

Pages 275   "The Japanese Dolls are vanishing, leaving the playful gentlemen." "Broadway Breaks Even on Oriental Beauty" Lee Mortimer, *The
American Weekly*, July 12, 1942.

Page 275   "In April 1946 Mary dropped her real name—Teruko Watanabe Okada—" See China Doll Postcard image on page 258, with her
new name.

Page 275   "A telegram from Lee Mortimer..." March 8, 1946, "Dear
Mary, I'm to be Guest of Honor at Leon and Eddie's this Sunday evening
at midnight. Many of the kids are coming, hope you can come and join
the party. Regards, Lee Mortimer." Densho.org, Mary Mon Toy Theatrical Collection (ddr-densho-367) and the Mary Mon Toy Archive in the
Wing Luke Museum, Seattle

Page 276   "Lee Mortimer announced in his column on June 2, 1946,"
Lee Mortimer column, "Nightlife," *Daily Mirror*, June 2, 1946

Page 276   " . . . until Lee Mortimer announced in his column on June 2,
1946, two short months after the club opened, " "Mary's coming out as
a solo singer also mentioned in On and Off Broadway, Irving Slossberg,
East Side News, Saturday, July 27, 1946

Page 276   " . . . until Lee Mortimer announced in his column on June
2, 1946," Mary makes more news. "Oriental...Mary Mon fills the spotlight as songstress at China Doll." *The Journal American* with head shot
photo of Mary Mon, August 24, 1946

Page 276   " . . . Mary Mon—stepped out of the chorus to tackle top femme singing spot," More mention of Mary as a singer, "At China Doll, new, typically brass-banded Broadway cellar, it is worth it to suffer your neighbor's elbow in your Yaha Dow (rum and lime in a fresh coconut) to listen to Mary Mon, a Chinese girl with a voice like . . .,well with a voice!" *Glamour Magazine*, Manhattan Mood, James and Peta Fuller, November 1946

CHAPTER 29 • NAMESAKE: A VISIT WITH DOROTHY TOY

Page 277   "It was a federal violation of United States military orders. . . .." United States Courts educational material on the Fred Korematsu landmark case regarding non-compliance with the federal authority requiring him to be remanded from the military zone to the Concentration Camp. Facts and Case Summary — Korematsu v. U.S., https://www.uscourts.gov/educational-resources/educational-activities/facts-and-case-summary-korematsu-v-us

Page 277   "It was a federal violation of United States military orders . . .." The Enduring Legacy of Fred Korematsu, Densho.org, Catalyst, Natasha Varner, https://densho.org/catalyst/fred-korematsu/

Page 277   "On the Internet, I came upon clips of Wing and Toy's movie performances . . .." Frank, Rusty E., Editor, "The Chinese Fred Astaire and Ginger Rogers," *Tap! The Greatest Tap Dance Stars and their Stories 1900-1955*, Da Capo Press, New York, 1954, Thomas Chinn, 102-110

Page 278-280 "Her house was slung low on a hill overlooking Oakland." The entire chapter's verbatim dialogue is taken from an audio interview with Dorothy Toy on Oct. 21, 2010 at her home in Oakland, California, conducted by the author. In the author's possession; copies are to be made available at Densho.org, Mary Mon Toy Theatrical Collection (ddr-densho-367), and the Wing Luke Museum, Seattle.

Page 281   "If you had your choice, where would you spend the rest of your life?" *New York Post*, Man on the Street, "What do YOU Think?" Monday, August 12, 1946

CHAPTER 30 • RISING STAR: ORIENTAL SONGSTRESS AND "MISS SLANT EYES OF 1948"

Page 283 2   "She appeared in Montreal at the Gayety," *Montreal Daily Star*, Vaudeville at Gayety: Attractive Variety Show Proves Popular, Monday March 10, 1947, and Montreal Herald, Good Acts at Gayety, March 12, 1947, 15

Page 283 1   "She became the "Chinese Chanteuse." "Mary Mon Toy, Chinese Emceetress (sic) at the Casino Royal, wears a bustled and silver embroidered white satin gown with the chic of a Parisienne…" *Washington Post*, Ringside Table, date and columnist unknown, Mary Mon Toy scrapbook, Mary Mon Toy Theatrical Collection (ddr-densho-367), and the Wing Luke Museum, Seattle

Page 283 3   "She soon advanced to being on the roster with performers…" " Tips on Tables" column, "Show Business Need New Names; Here are Some Candidates," Harold Fine, The *Washington Daily News*, Feb. 17, 1948, 33.

Page 284   "They also cited her as the current "Miss Slant Eyes of 1948." *The Spotlight* column, Youngstown, Ohio, October 21, 1948

Page 284   "The Boston Evening American described the night as "once-in-a-lifetime thrill," "Berlin Express' Premier Hailed Hub's Best Show," *Boston Evening American*, May 6, 1948.

Page 284   "it was the start of a long friendship." What I had first thought was a romantic attachment, I later came to see was a friendship. Two letters to Mary from Robert Ryan from the time he was suffering from a cancer that would prove fatal, in which he thanks her for checks she has sent him to tide him over when he couldn't work, but says he can't accept them and that he has "taken a film instead," Lolly-Madonna XXX, shot in Tennessee. July 20, 1972, Letter mailed from Tennessee, and December 12, 1972, return address 88 Central Park West, NYC, Densho.org, Mary Mon Toy Theatrical Collection (ddr-densho-367), and the Wing Luke Museum of the Asian Pacific American Experience.

Page 285   "She became a regular in Harold Minksy's Follies," *Miami Daily* News, Round Town, with Herb Rau, Follies Bergere, American Style, Thursday, December 22, 1949, 10-B

Page 285   "She sang with the chorus ensemble of Kurt Weill's American Opera Street Scene," Program for Street Scene February 6, 1949, also a Program for A Birthday Memorial Tribute to Kurt Weill, March 2, 1952 Theresa L. Kaufmann Auditorium, Young Men's and Young Women's Hebrew Association, 92nd Street Y, Mary Mon Toy Theatrical Collection (ddr-densho-367), and the Wing Luke Museum, Seattle

Page 285   "In the chorus with Mary was the great Robert McFerrin Sr," *ROBERT McFerrin Sr.: Was First Black Man to Sing with the Met*, By Adam Bernstein, Washington Post Staff Writer, Wednesday, November 29, 2006, Robert McFerrin Sr.; Was First Black Man to Sing With the Met (washingtonpost.com)

Page 286   "Weill wrote in Mary's libretto," The libretto signed by Kurt Weill to Mary February 6, 1949 in Mary Mon Toy is in the Mary Mon Toy archive in Wing Luke Museum, Seattle.

Page 286   "Mary played the legendary Palace Theater," "Pat Rooney Fills Up Palace Again," week of July 20, 1950, clip from unidentified New York City newspaper, in Mary Mon Toy's scrapbook, Mary Mon Toy Theatrical Collection (ddr-densho-367), and the Wing Luke Museum

Page 286   "In the fall, after her Palace performance," Lee Mortimer column, "Nightlife," *Daily Mirror*, week of Oct. 15, 1950, "Famous B'way Niteclub Isn't There at All."

Page 286   "... for sight and sound appeal, charming Mary Mon Toy,"
New Year's Eve 1950 at the Old Romanian, Gotham Guide, Gean Orlin,
"When the Stars Come Out" Tear sheet in Mary Mon Toy Theatrical
Collection (ddr-densho-367), and the Wing Luke Museum.

CHAPTER 31 • ONE AMBITION AND TOUGH NEGOTIATING

Page 287   "His was an odd case:" Library of Congress Blogs, National
Audio-Visual Conservation Center, ISSN 2692-1898, Remembering
TV's "Khan! "August 17, 2022, Cary O'Dell, Khigh Dheigh https://
blogs.loc.gov/now-see-hear/2022/08/remembering-tvs-khan/

Page 287   "What is clear from his letters . . .." Mary Mon Toy Theatrical Collection (ddr-densho-367) and the Mary Mon Toy Archive in the
Wing Luke Museum

Page 288   "The moments that each night should anticipate..." A postcard
of The Buddha Amitabha and attendants, A D. 593, Museum of Fine
Arts, Boston, Mary Mon Toy Theatrical Collection (ddr-densho-367)
and the Mary Mon Toy Archive in the Wing Luke Museum

Page 288   "I love you with reverence and passion; with tenderness and
violence." Mary Mon Toy Theatrical Collection (ddr-densho-367) and
the Mary Mon Toy Archive in the Wing Luke Museum

Page 288   "In Dick Henry's letters he encouraged her to take the Nouvelle Eve deal." Two letters from Dick Henry to Mary Mon Toy regarding performing at Nouvelle Eve, November 2, 1953 and November 9,
1953, Mary Mon Toy Theatrical Collection (ddr-densho-367) and the
Mary Mon Toy Archive in the Wing Luke Museum

Page 288   "Even with no existing correspondence from Mary's side," Exchanges between Albert Tavel and Dick Henry regarding Mary Mon Toy's contract for performing at the Nouvelle Eve nightclub, Paris, France, circa 1953/54, no exact date, Mary Mon Toy Theatrical Collection, (ddr-densho-367) and the Mary Mon Toy Archive in the Wing Luke Museum

Page 290   "I visited Nouvelle Eve in 2010." The son of the original owner was Adrien Pierini, an affable young man who proudly gave me the program for the 2010 version of La Nouvelle Eve, which gives a pictorial sense of the nightclub past and present, Mary Mon Toy Theatrical Collection (ddr-densho-367) and the Mary Mon Toy Archive in the Wing Luke Museum.

CHAPTER 32 • LES MADEMOISELLES DE PARIS:
THE LATIN QUARTER

Page 293   "At the Desert Inn in Las Vegas," Las Vegas TALK OF THE TOWN, *Las Vegas Sun*, Sean Flannelly, October 15, 1953.

Page 293   "At the Desert Inn in Las Vegas," "This is the break-in for the extravaganza which check in for the New York Latin Quarter, latter part of November." Folies Bergères, Desert Inn Las Vegas, *Variety*, Unit Review, October 30, 1953

Page 293   "At the Desert Inn in Las Vegas," Ads and programs for The Painted Desert Room, Mary Mon Toy Theatrical Collection (ddr-densho-367) and the Mary Mon Toy Archive in the Wing Luke Museum

Page 294   "It's been said that "that little block had more razzle and dazzle," "Site of the Latin Quarter Giving Way to a Tower,' David W. Dunlap, *New York Times*, February 13, 1989, Section B, Page 2

Page 294   "The Latin Quarter was the defining height of nightclub prestige," Lou Walters, Nightclub Impresario and Founder of Latin Quarter, Dies, Louis Calta, The New York Times, August 16, 1977, 36

Page 294   "The Latin Quarter was the defining height of nightclub prestige" Ads, menus, press coverage of the three Mademoiselle's, stage photos, candid photos, promotional material, and programs for The Latin
Quarter in Mary's time, Mary Mon Toy Theatrical Collection (ddr-den-
sho-367) and the Mary Mon Toy Archive in the Wing Luke Museum

Page 294   "She had recently returned from work in Japan..." http://www.
glamourgirlsofthesilverscreen.com/show/161/Lee+Sharon/index.html

Page 295   "According to Ebony magazine," "New Stars of Folie Berge-
re: Two American Negroes take big roles in Parisian Show (Babe Wal-
lace and Ruby "Curly Top" Richards)," *Ebony*, 1954, 71, Copyright ©
Johnson Publishing Company, Inc. and *French Disregard for Race Amazes
American Artists,* Ebony, 1954, 72-76, Copyright © Johnson Publishing
Company, Inc.

Page 295   "In her interviews in the white press." Ruby Richards is Valentine Pinup - *Jet Magazine*, February 18, 1954, Ruby Richards is Val-
entine Pinup - *Jet Magazine*, February ... | Flickr

Page 295   For additional information on Ruby Richards and other overlooked — by American historians — Black women performers in Paris:
Storytelling Portraits, A new exhibition of artist Man Ray's works exam-
ines the lesser-known subjects of his photography in Paris, Karen New-
ton, "Style Weekly, Arts, Events, Books," Richmond, Virginia, August
31, 2021. https://www.styleweekly.com/richmond/storytelling-por-
traits/Content?oid=17824959

Page 296   "*New York Age*, the most important Afro-American newspaper
wrote,." *The New York Age* (New York, New York) · 23 Jan 1954, Sat, 9

Page 296   "As for Ruby, I've listened to an undated, shaky audio tape."
*Jackson, Delilah, Delilah Jackson Papers>*Audiovisual Materials, Series 8,
Audiovisual materials 1930s-1980s, Boxes AV 1-21, LP 1, and CLP5,
Box V7, Ruby Richards Interview, Digital/digitized copy available in
the Reading Room: id b8k7m, Emory University, Stuart A. Rose Manuscript, Archives, and Rare Book Library, Atlanta, GA 30322, 404-727-
6887, rose.library@emory.edu

Page 297   "It's the Same the Whole World Over," a 1930s English music
hall number," https://monologues.co.uk/musichall/Songs-S/She-Was-
Poor-But-Honest

Page 298   "Christine Jorgensen and Mary became good friends." Mary
and Christine kept up their friendship over time, with Christine sending
postcards sometimes about the men she met on her trips to Europe. A
sample postcard from Christine Jorgenson to Mary, "Hi there, Held over
in Stockholm. Such terrific business and such a good time. All those
blonde swedes. Off to Paris and Rome soon. Love, Chris," August 30,
1954, Mary Mon Toy Theatrical Collection (ddr-densho-367) and the
Mary Mon Toy Archive in the Wing Luke Museum.

CHAPTER 33 • THE SHOWGIRL AND THE DIPLOMAT

Page 301   "in July of 1945, Romulo had served with General MacArthur." History, Art, & Archives, United States House of Representatives,
Romulo, Carlos Peña, 1899-1985, https://history.house.gov/People/De-
tail/20605,   https://www.nationalww2museum.org/war/articles/macar-
thur-philippine-islands-liberated-1945

Page 301   "...the Bataan Death March in April of 1942 was still a raw
memory for Filipinos," U.S. Army site, Asian Americans and Pacific
Islanders in the U.S. Army, AAPI History – Key Events, 1942 – 1943,
The Bataan Death March. https://www.army.mil/asianpacificamericans/
bataandeathmarch.html, For a first-hand description, *I Saw the Fall of
the Philippines,* Carlos P. Romulo, Doubleday, January 1, 1942

Page 301   "...the Bataan Death March in April of 1942..." U.S. Army site, Asian Americans and Pacific Islanders in the U.S. Army, AAPI History – Key Events, 1942 – 1943, The Bataan Death March. https://www.army.mil/asianpacificamericans/bataandeathmarch.html, Also, for a first-hand description, *I Saw the Fall of the Philippines*, Carlos P. Romulo, Doubleday, January 1, 1942

Page 302   "The showgirl and the diplomat—a compelling match in the early 1950s..." "Jose Villanueva, head of the Philippine UN Group, is sending flowers to Mary Mon Toy, the Latin ¼'s Oriental pip." It Happened Last Night, Earl Wilson, *New York Post*, May 5, 1954,

Page 302   "The showgirl and the diplomat—a compelling match in the early 1950s…" "...a fascinating foursome about town consists of Rory Calhoun, his dancing wife, Lita Baron, and Jose Villanueva, of the Philippine Delegation to the UN, squiring Mary Mon Toy. She's the Chinese Toy Doll who recently closed at the Latin Quarter and who holds a degree of sociology from U.C.L.A., *New York Tribune*, Early Bird, Coast to Coast, Hy Gardner, June 10, 1954

Page 302   "The bug bit me quite some time ago—" Special Delivery letter from Philippine Mission to the United Nations, Jose V, to Mary Mon Toy, Tuesday, May 4, 1954, written at 9:15 AM, Mary Mon Toy Theatrical Collection (ddr-densho-367) and the Mary Mon Toy Archive in the Wing Luke Museum

Page 302   "In the next letter, on May 7," Hand delivered from the Philippine Delegation to the United Nations, New York, "Adored," May 7, Mary Mon Toy Theatrical Collection (ddr-densho-367) and the Mary Mon Toy Archive in the Wing Luke Museum

Page 302   "Rather precipitously, on May 13 he sent Mary an onionskin,"
Special Delivery letter from Philippine Mission to the United Nations,
Jose V, to Mary Mon Toy, Jose V to Mary Mon Toy, May 13, 1954, 8
PM. Mary Mon Toy Theatrical Collection (ddr-densho-367) and the
Mary Mon Toy Archive in the Wing Luke Museum

Page 303   "At a breakfast with General and Mrs. Romulo," Another let-
ter on Thursday, May 7 at 4 PM, Jose wrote about the breakfast. Mary
Mon Toy Theatrical Collection (ddr-densho-367) and the Mary Mon
Toy Archive in the Wing Luke Museum

Page 303   "He went to see her backstage at the Latin Quarter after the
show," May 22, 1954, 1 O'clock in the morning. Mary Mon Toy Theatrical Collection (ddr-densho-367) and the Mary Mon Toy Archive in
the Wing Luke Museum

Page 303   "On Friday Jose's wife called him long-distanced," Letter,
May 22, 1954, 1 O'clock in the morning. Mary Mon Toy Theatrical
Collection (ddr-densho-367) and the Mary Mon Toy Archive in the
Wing Luke Museum, Seattle

Page 303   "But in his last letter he declined her demand." Date unknown. Mary Mon Toy Theatrical Collection (ddr-densho-367) and
the Mary Mon Toy Archive in the Wing Luke Museum

Page 304   "In the stacks of love letters," Letters from Russ Brown, George
Eckert, and others. Mary Mon Toy Theatrical Collection (ddr-den-
sho-367) and the Mary Mon Toy Archive in the Wing Luke Museum

Page 305   "In Jose's last letter to Mary," Date unknown. Mary Mon Toy
Theatrical Collection (ddr-densho-367) and the Mary Mon Toy Archive
in the Wing Luke Museum.

Page 309   *House of Flowers* "The girl was the future star Diahann Carroll." A different perspective on that night at the Latin Quarter. https://
interviews.televisionacademy.com/shows/chance-lifetime

Page 313   "We can teach you what you need." Glory Van Scott confirmed that Mary was hired as a singer and that she only had to be able to
move well in the ensembles. Author interview with Dr. Glory Van Scott,
4/27/2011, Mary Mon Toy Theatrical Collection (ddr-densho-367) and
the Wing Luke Museum.

Page 313   "They had already plucked Mary Louise from her singing gig
at the Savannah Club." Author interview with Mary Louise and Bill
Britten, Spring 2011, Mary Mon Toy Theatrical Collection (ddr-den-
sho-367) and the Wing Luke Museum.

Page 313   "After the final round of tryouts, they called the names of the
chosen few out of scores of performers for the Tango Girls:" Thomas De-
Frantz, The George Balanchine Foundation, Popular Balanchine: Oral
History, New York Public Library for the Performing Arts at Lincoln
Center, *House of Flowers* interview with Glory Van Scott, September 27,
2001, 2

Page 313   "The producers were seeking a certain type to play the prosti-
tutes," Thomas DeFrantz, The George Balanchine Foundation, Popular
Balanchine: Oral History, *House of Flowers* interview with Glory Van
Scott, September 27, 2001, 6

Page 318   "In a video made in 2001 Margot Small and DeFrantz" New
York Public Library Digital Collections, House of Flowers dance session,
Margot Small Barnes with Thomas DeFrantz, The George Balanchine
Foundation, Popular Balanchine: Oral History, 2001 https://digital-
collections.nypl.org/search/index?utf8=%E2%9C%93&keywords=-
house++of+flowers+dance+session+Margot+small+barnes

Page 319   "But Madame Tango, she's on board all right. And now she's imported a Japanese lady." *House of Flowers* \ script, Act I-1-13, Madame Fleur, Thomas DeFrantz, The George Balanchine Foundation, Popular Balanchine: Oral History, *House of Flowers*

Page 319   "Five days into my time in the library, I read a passage by Glory Van Scott," Thomas DeFrantz, The George Balanchine Foundation, Popular Balanchine: Oral History, *House of Flowers* interview with Glory Van Scott, September 27, 2001, 12

Page 319   "If I could give someone a gift, certainly an artist," Thomas DeFrantz, The George Balanchine Foundation, Popular Balanchine: Oral History, *House of Flowers* interview with Glory Van Scott, September 27, 2001, 21

Page 320   "In Capote's original novella there is no Japanese prostitute." Truman Capote, "Breakfast at Tiffany's," *House of Flowers*, pp 103-121, Penguin Books Ltd, 80 Strand, London WC2E ORL, England

Page 320   "She's only recently off the banana boat from Paris. *House of Flowers* script, Act I Scene 5, Madame Fleur, Thomas DeFrantz, The George Balanchine Foundation, Popular Balanchine: Oral History, *House of Flowers*

Page 320   "Bailey also had the haunting song "Don't Like Goodbyes" taken away from Diahann" Capote on Pearl Bailey and hiring her "which is one thing we shouldn't have done. Pearl began kicking up almost right away as we went into rehearsal. She overpowered poor little Diahann Carroll who'd not done anything on stage, taking away most of her songs." Lewis Funke, "Capote's Flower People," *The New York Times*, 9/17/1967 pp. 183, 188, 189, Times Machine: September 17, 1967 - NYTimes.com

Page 322   "I interviewed Holder in his nursing home..." Audio recording
of Geoffrey Holder with author, in the author's possession, May 6, 2014,
Holder died October 6, 2014 https://www.nytimes.com/2014/10/07/
arts/geoffrey-holder-dancer-choreographer-and-man-of-flair-dies-at-84.
html

Page 323   "Sara Keys, who was on furlough traveling on an interstate
bus," *The quietly defiant, unlikely fighter: Pfc. Sarah Keys and the fight for
justice and humanity*, United States Army military article, T. Anthony
Bell February 25, 2014

Page 323   " the strategy was being planned for Rosa Parks..." The Martin
Luther King, Jr, Research and Education Institute, Stanford University,
Encyclopedia, Parks, Rosa, biography February 4, 1913 to October 24,
2005

Page 326   "The theater was packed," "On opening night, there was
Gloria Vanderbilt Di Cicco Stokowski sitting with Frank Sinatra, first
row on the aisle...Oh, the place was full of celebrities and that curious
category of people who are not celebrities but whom celebrities know,
and who pretend not to be impressed by celebrities...There was an overabundance of the Gay Boys in their '54-55 uniform, which is the black
suit with the narrow pants; too, too Edwardian. " John O'Hara, "Appointment with O'Hara," Collier's, March 4, 1955, pp 6-7

Page 326   "The ticket presales were huge;" There was a good amount of
pre-publicity, including an above the fold photo on the first page of the
New York Times, Section Two, Drama, with Juanita Hall, Pearl Reynolds, Mary Mon Toy, and Leu Comacho, Sunday, December 26, 1954.
And "Truman (Capote) Goes Toulouse (Lautrec)" with photo of the
Tango Girls, Mary Mon Toy in the foreground. Cue Magazine, December 18, 1954, 15 Tear sheet in the Mary Mon Toy Theatrical Collection
(ddr-densho-367) and the Wing Luke Museum.

Page 327   "As Jennifer Dunning wrote, they were "achingly poetic,"" Dunning, Jennifer, *Geoffrey Holder: A Life in Theater, Dance and Art*, Harry N. Abrams, New York, 2001

Page 327   "William Hawkins of the *New York World-Telegram* opened his review," *House of Flowers* really Blossoms Out, William Hawkins, *New York World-Telegram and Sun*, Friday December 31, 1954, 16

Page 327   "But Brooks Atkinson of the New York Times trashed the musical," Theater: Truman Capote's Musical, Brooks Atkinson, *The New York Times*, Friday, December 31, 1954

Page 327   "Inbred bias in keeping with mid-century American attitudes…" "The show's distinctive nature—black and devilishly erotic—led to failure." *Coming up Roses*: The Broadway Musical in the 1950s, Ethan Mordden, Oxford University Press, November 26, 2000, 92-93

Page 327   "Unconsciously, they could have been looking for what Glory Van Scott called "good old 'Yassuh' theater." Author interview with Dr. Glory Van Scott, 4/27/2011, Mary Mon Toy Theatrical

Page 328 "Mary Louise had no doubts about a reason for the mixed and at times hostile reviews." Author interview with Mary Louise and Bill Britten, Bill Britten and Mary Louise Britten Spring 2011, Mary Mon Toy Theatrical Collection (ddr-densho-367) and the Wing Luke Museum.

Page 328 "We were kind of shocking…" Thomas DeFrantz, The George Balanchine Foundation, Popular Balanchine: Oral History, House of Flowers interview with Mary Mon Toy, September 7, 2001, 13

Page 328 "Ray Walston, and Black Pearl Bailey shared an on-stage, steamy sexual kiss. "*House of Flowers* script, Act I-4-40, Madame Fleur (Pearl Bailey) and Captain Jonas (Ray Walston) kiss. Thomas DeFrantz, The George Balanchine Foundation, Popular Balanchine: Oral History, New York Public Library for the Performing Arts at Lincoln Center, House of Flowers

Page 328 "This was 1954 when the Hays Code," Appendix 2, The Motion Picture Production Code of 1930, Particular Applications of the
Code and the Reasons Therefore (Addenda to 1930 Code), Appendix
1, 362-363, II Sex, Number 6. MISCEGINATION (sex between the
white and black races) is forbidden. https://www.umsl.edu/~gradyf/
theory/1930code.pdf, and Pre-Code Hollywood: Sex, Immorality,
and Insurrection in American Cinema, 1930–1934, Columbia University Press, Thomas Doherty, 1999, http://cup.columbia.edu/book/
pre-code-hollywood/9780231110952

Page 328 "As late as 1968, when Harry Belafonte appeared on a variety
show on NBC." Spokane Daily Chronicle, "A Tempest in TV Tube is
Sparked by Touch," March 5, 1968, p. 54

Page 329 "Leave your sedate Aunt Millie at home, or you'll have a lot of
explaining to do." Robert Coleman, Daily Mirror, 1/January, 1955,

Page 330 "I just keep going, you have to," Author interview with Dr. Glory
Van Scott, 4/27/2011, Mary Mon Toy Theatrical Collection (ddr-densho-367) and the Wing Luke Museum.

CHAPTER 35 • THE WORLD OF SUZIE WONG

Page 333 "A columnist wrote, "… a neatly-stacked Oriental damsel, by
the name of MARY MON TOY." The Saxony, Partial newspaper credit,
but no columnist attribution in damaged tear sheet, in Mary Mon Toy's
papers, *Miami Sunday News*, February 1957, Mary Mon Toy Theatrical
Collection (ddr-densho-367), and Mary Mon Toy archive at the Wing
Luke Museum

Page 334 "To add more disappointment, Dorothy Kilgallen wrote…"
The Voice of Broadway, Dorothy Kilgallen, "*Has Bug Bitten*," The Celebrities: Mary Mon Toy, *New York Journal American*, February 28, 1957

Page 334   "Mary's career picked up in the spring of 1958," For photos, reviews, playbills, scripts see the Densho.org, Mary Mon Toy Theatrical Collection (ddr-densho-367) and the Mary Mon Toy Archive in the Wing Luke Museum

Page 336   "In late December Mary successfully interceded for him with Gene Kelly" Keye Luke wrote a long letter to say that he had been under the weather from two car accidents and that he had had trouble finding work but things had turned for the better as a result of hearing from the agency handling *Flower Drum Song*, to thank her for her help, "Then about a week ago, your efforts in my behalf took effect…I want to thank you again Maria, for all your help. I deeply appreciate it even though of late I have been much harassed by the (indecipherable) that has made my pen very derelict." The Mary Mon Toy Theatrical Collection (ddr-densho-367), and Mary Mon Toy archive at the Wing Luke Museum

Page 336   "Mary's next big break came when she was cast in *The World of Suzie Wong*." Pasted into one of Mary's scrapbooks is a tear sheet from a magazine; it's a photograph of an audition, with 8 actors holding scripts, lined up on the stage. Mary is in the center reading. Joshua Logan is on the right in the orchestra with hands on his hips, observing the audition. Mary has written in the margin, "Final Reading — I got the Part." Mary Mon Toy Theatrical Collection (ddr-densho-367) and the Mary Mon Toy Archive in the Wing Luke Museum

Page 336   "*Suzie Wong* opened on Broadway in October of 1958 and ran for 508 performances." Three days before the opening in NYC, this review appeared in *Variety*, "Legit Tryout," *The World of Suzie Wong*, world Premiere at the Shubert, Boston. "Outstanding is Mary Mon Toy as Minie (sic) Hoe (sic), the one who always forgets to ask for the money Miss Mon Toy, a dazzling looker, nabs a whole bevy of laughs in her characterization of brassy Oriental floozy." Friday, September 12, 1958

Page 336   "The only problem was, as Truman Capote wrote in this congratulatory opening-night telegram, "too bad it's another house." Mary Mon Toy Theatrical Collection (ddr-densho-367) and the Mary Mon Toy Archive in the Wing Luke Museum

Page 338   "*Suzie Wong* opened on Broadway in October of 1958 and ran for 508 performances." "He wrote in October 1958, after having seen Mary in *The World of Suzie Wong*," Letter from Tony Rivers, the agent who discovered Joan Rivers," To Miss Mary Mon Toy, Tony Rivers Associates, Inc. October 15, 1958, the day after opening night of The World of Suzie Wong, Mary Mon Toy Theatrical Collection (ddr-densho-367), the physical Mary Mon Toy archive at the Wing Luke Museum

Page 338   *Author's note*: This was the one and only indication I came across in my research that there were rumors Mary was Nisei. Even so, the journalist, Larry S. Tajiri, had her birthplace wrong as well repeating the falsehood that Mary had attended UCLA. "The World of Suzie Wong" is entering the final months of its year-long run. Among the performers of Japanese ancestry who played in "Suzie Wong" since the beginning of its run last November are Takayo Doran, who left the cast when husband was transferred to the west coast, Jeri Miyazaki, Clifford Arashi, John Mamo, Ichisuki Ishikawa and several others. A girl who bills herself as Mary Mon Toy in the " Suzie Wong" cast is reportedly a Honolulu Nisei who attended UCLA and Juilliard. She made her Broadway debut in "House of Flowers" as Mamselle Honolulu, and has sung in Parisian bistros as well as in Broadway's Latin Quarter and in Las Vegas and Miami." Pacific Citizen, Vagaries, Reporting From New York, Larry S. Tajiri, September 4, 1959, 3 https://pacificcitizen.org/wp-content/uploads/archives-menu/Vol.049_%2310_Sep_04_1959.pdf

For additional information on the correspondent Larry S. Tajiri see: https://encyclopedia.densho.org/Larry_Tajiri/

Page 338   "In 1960 she was a heralded member of the grand national road tour for The World of Suzie Wong, which travelled the entirety of the United States and up into Canada, for one year, with performances in twenty-five venues." See *Playbills* and reviews in the Mary Mon Toy Theatrical Collection (ddr-densho-367) and Mary Mon Toy Archive in the Wing Luke Museum.

CHAPTER 36 •
"A BIG TV SHOW IS BEING READIED FOR NEXT YEAR. IT WILL HAVE ORIENTAL THEMES." "ARE THEY HIRING ORIENTALS?" "NO. IT WILL BE AS PHONY AS A $33 DIAMOND.

Page 345   "She [France Nuyen] was also appalled by the racism in America, and just wanted to get back to France." France Nuyen, in an interview with *New World* columnist, Sidney Field after she had gained considerable success in film and theater, spoke of before and after her fame in America. As Fields wrote, "when she [Nuyen] was in Hollywood making her two movies, she lived alone for a year and a half in a tiny room in a motel run by Mexicans…she couldn't visit San Diego, because she was Chinese and presumably a threat to the naval base there." "This is a racist country," she said. "I am more discriminated than in France. If you are Chinese or Japanese you cannot live in Beverly Hills or Malibu. And Negro men are picked up if they cross Beverly Hills after one a.m. You think that is right? I do not. I have not the courage to go where I would be kicked out. But it hurts me for my friends." But her world is different now. "Yes. I can eat what I want when I want it. And I can go anywhere without being kicked out because I am yellow." Is fame the passport to acceptance in America? New World, Sidney Field's column "Only Human." Circa October 21, 1958. Mary Mon Toy's scrapbook, Densho.org, Mary Mon Toy Theatrical Collection (ddr-densho-367) and the Mary Mon Toy Archive in the Wing Luke Museum

Page 345   "It's a devilish thing for Oriental talents that there is a multiplicity of Oriental shows on Broadway this season," *Cumberland Evening Times*, Maryland, syndicated, Friday December 19, 1958, 10

Page 354-355   "She was performing at the El Morocco in Montreal during the lean years following *House of Flowers*" El Morocco was one of the most prestigious and popular in the 1940s and 1950s. It was located at 1445, rue Lambert-Closse, Montreal, Canada, Mary Mon Toy complete "Routine Sheet…El Morocco," 1955, 1-5, Mary Mon Toy Theatrical Collection (ddr-densho-367) and the Mary Mon Toy Archive in the Wing Luke Museum

Page 357   "They had been talking about the racism of some staff when Sakoda digressed, writing that one of the staff, "…had made an anti-Jewish remark in the company of evacuees," which he thought unseemly." James M. Sakado, Journal, (JES), 67/14c, The Bancroft Library, Part II: Section 5-Tule Lake, R20:81, January 28, 1943, 964

Page 359   "It didn't matter that brilliant, powerful novels and memoirs by Nisei authors had been published," See Bibliography for more titles.

Page 362   "When Mon died, Mary received Okoden from Japan and from the cities in America where Japanese Americans had settled postwar and post-camp: Denver, Lansing, Salt Lake City, and New York." Okoden envelopes are in Mary Mon Toy Family Collection (ddr-densho-488), and the Mary Mon Toy Archive in the Wing Luke Museum

Page 364   "Perhaps Mother brought back her remembrances of being Japanese." "She met my mother during her stay in New York City (when she came to design costumes for our dance company, Tokunaga Dance Ko) and they always spoke some Japanese interspersed with English. Perhaps Mother brought back her remembrances of being Japanese. Regarding the "ohagi" I mentioned that Mother helped me learn how to make these rice cakes from scratch, and wanted to share the finish product with Mary. Since we did not have access to deliver the dessert (Mother was not able to travel), so we hired a cab to deliver the ohagi to Mary's apartment. The Japanese gift giving tradition was deeply ingrained in Mother, and she wanted to share something that Mary missed. Whenever Mary met me (and infrequently with Mother) it brought out her Japanese heritage." Emiko Tokunaga email to Marnie Mueller 6/19/15, Mary Mon Toy Theatrical Collection (ddr-densho-367) and the Mary Mon Toy Archive in the Wing Luke Museum.

Page 364   "When Utako was recuperating from a series of surgeries, half a dozen white roses would arrive at the family home in Utah every month for half a year, a gift from Mary." Email from Emiko Tokunaga to Marnie Mueller, May 22, 2013, Mary Mon Toy Theatrical Collection (ddr-densho-367) and the Mary Mon Toy Archive in the Wing Luke Museum

Page 364   "In 1974, Mary had a small part in the off-Broadway play *Santa Anita '42*," 17 reviews of *Santa Anita '42*, Mary Mon Toy Theatrical Collection (ddr-densho-367) and the Mary Mon Toy Archive in the Wing Luke Museum

Page 364   "He remembered her fondly and said that she had told him she was half Chinese American" Email from Steven Robman to Marnie Mueller, 7/31/14, Mary Mon Toy Theatrical Collection (ddr-densho-367) and the Mary Mon Toy Archive in the Wing Luke Museum

Page 364   "He had addressed her as *Dear Teru*." Letter from Bill Hosokawa to Teru, January 11, 1974, Mary Mon Toy Theatrical Collection (ddr-densho-367) and the Mary Mon Toy Archive in the Wing Luke Museum

Page 365   As punishment, in August of 1942 Hosokawa," *Camp Harmony, Seattle's Japanese Americans and the Puyallup Assembly Center*, Louis Fiset, Chapter 8, Dissension, 149

Page 365   "When he finally wrote to the playwright," Letter from Bill

Hosokawa to Alan Knee, April 2, 1974, Mary Mon Toy Theatrical Collection (ddr-densho-367) and the Mary Mon Toy Archive in the Wing Luke Museum

CHAPTER 37 · RESISTANCE AND ACTIVISM

Page 367   "On May 25, 1968 Mary walked the picket line in front of the City Center Theater," Flyers, a press release, and more photos in Mary Mon Toy Theatrical Collection (ddr-densho-367) and the Wing Luke Museum.

Page 368   "Anna Leonowens, the model for Anna in the King and I," .Bombay Anna: The Real Story and Remarkable Adventures of the King and I Governess, University of California Press, Susan Morgan, July 2008

Page 368   "On November 23, 1984 Mary Mon Toy: Actress First was headlined in a wide-ranging, personal interview in *Back Stage*, an American entertainment industry trade publication." It was part of their series, "Striding Toward Affirmative Action: Taking Your Own Reins," Mary Mon Toy: Actress First, November 23, 1984, 1

"*Back Stage* asked Mary Mon Toy to share her experiences as a Chinese/American performer with us." Here is her entire answer:

> "I'm a member of AEA, AFTRA, AGVA, and SAG. While I have never gotten jobs through AFTRA and SAG seminars and open-door lotteries, our unions actively assist members to do so via meetings and contacts with casting directors and agents. Once I got a call from AEA asking me to recommend a male indigenous Chinese for the NBC "David Letterman Show." Normally you would think the network would contact AFTRA not AEA, but it's my guess that someone at NBC knew someone at AEA personally. I was happy to recommend

an elderly actor who had an accent and experience as a restaurateur. He got the job and is collecting tv residuals from the show.

I've gone to EPI interviews and sat and waited at Equity only to be told, "If we decide to use a minority…" This particular one was for IBM. You'd think they'd want an Asian actor what with technology world-wide being as it is today.

Polarization starts young. I was walking my half-shepherd half-collie dog when a Hispanic kid asked, "What kind of dog is that?" I told him and he brought up, "How come you don't have a Chinese dog?" By the same token, an interviewer asked me why I didn't join Asian theater companies. I told him while I'm a contributor to them for the fine work they're producing, I strongly feel we minorities should be considered for roles other than traditional. If Blacks and Caucasians are considered and hired for Asian roles, which they have been, we should be given the same consideration. In other words, it should work both ways.

A few of the non-traditional roles I've played were Anna, the masseuse, in *Ladies Night in a Turkish Bath* and Mommy Pleasant in *The Cat and the Canary*. Both roles were obtained because I was doing summer stock and had been hired for Bloody Mary in *South* Pacific and Lady Thiang in *The King and I*. The most enjoyable non-traditional role I played was Charlotta in Chekov's *The Cherry Orchard*, at the New Media Repertory (Tier I). I met a friend and well-respected actor on the bus. He mentioned that his wife (fine actress) was directing the aforementioned play. Soon after, she called me and asked if she could come over with the script. I read the part of Charlotta and agreed to do it. I met the company, some of whom had done the play a few months before. The rest of us newcomers had to catch up on the Russian pronunciation. The cast was integrated with Blacks, Greek, European, Jewish and even a Dutch-Indonesian. It's uncanny how costumes and hair-dos can turn your character and attitude toward the playwright's target. None of us tried to make-up as Russians. I enhanced my high cheekbones with rouge and used lots of eye shadow to make my eyes even more Mongolian, who inhabit Siberia. With each performance I realized how contemporary is Chekov. I hated to see the limited performances end. Someday I hope I'll get the chance to play more Chekov roles.

My advice, if I may, to fellow minority performers is to go to all union calls. There's always a chance a casting director might veer from the usual road and decide to take a gamble. Don't be easily dismissed by anyone at these calls. If you feel you're right for the part and there's reluctance on their part, stand firm. You're an Equity, AFTRA, AGVA, SAG, AGMA member and should be given the same courtesy as non-minority members.

I sadly regret very few minority members are seen in ELT productions which would be an excellent showcase. So many have gone on from there but no minorities. If you do get an audition and are not right for the part, notify a fellow actor who might be right. There are so few jobs for us that we must help each other.

Slowly we're being hired: viz., the Chinese man-servant chauffeur in *Falcon Crest* and the war bride in the just-off-the-air *AfterMASH*, the hospital receptionist in "E.R," and the police chief in *Hawaiian Heat*. On soaps there's a restaurant owner in *Ryan's Hope* every now and then. And possibly others.

If you love acting, not just that you're in show biz, hone your craft — keep learning, trying-out, maintaining good health for without it you're out — and most of all don't give up!!

Page 370   "In March of 1986 AFTRA joined with the Associated Actors and Artistes of America to demonstrate…" *AFTRA Magazine* published by the National Office of the American Federation of Television and Radio Artists, AFL-CIO, NY Rallies Against Apartheid, Winter 1986., Volume 19 Number 1, 3

Page 374   "In the 1970s and 1980s, in her sixties and seventies, she (Mary Mon Toy) continued to find jobs." https://www.imdb.com/name/nm0870273/, full credits

Page 374   "In 1977, she appeared in the PBS special Jade Snow Wong,." Jade Snow Wong, Public Broadcasting System (PBS) on https://vimeo.com/126857095

Page 374   "In the movie *All That Jazz* she (Mary Mon Toy) had a cameo as a hospital nutritionist," https://www.imdb.com/title/tt00000000000078754/fullcredits

Page 375   "Mary was almost sixty when she landed a part on the TV show *Kojak*, starring Telly Savalas as a New York City cop." *Columbine*, the in-house publication for CBS employees about the filming *KOJAK*, *The Chinatown Murders*, December 1974, Front page, plus full pages 4 and 5, with photos. *Kojak: The Chinatown Murders Part 2* . Originally broadcast on Sept. 15, 1974. [Mary Mon Toy plays Grandma Mai Ling in this 1974 episode of the TV detective series.]

Page 375   "I may be partial but I think her performance was by far the best of the cast — as did Cecil Smith," "there were some interesting performances, notably...Mary Mon Toy's papery, old Chinese grand-mother..." *Kojak* a Casualty in Ratings Wars, Cecil Smith, *Los Angeles Times*, Thursday, September 19, 1974—Part IV, 19

Page 376   "One person wrote on a blog after reading her obituary in the *New York Times*." Bowery Boys: New York City History, In the *Times:* There's Something About Mary, February 2, 2010. https://www.bowery-boyshistory.com/2010/02/in-times-theres-something-about-mary.html

Page 377   "I once asked Glory Van Scott if she thought Mary had had a successful career..." Author interview with Dr. Glory Van Scott, 4/27/2011, Mary Mon Toy Theatrical Collection (ddr-densho-367) and the Wing Luke Museum. Chapter Thirty Eight

CHAPTER 38 • REPARATIONS/REDRESS

Page 379 "As an adult he worked for civil rights and peace causes," Densho. org: Encyclopedia, William Hohri, https://encyclopedia.densho.org/ William_Hohri/

Page 379 "In 1983 he became the main plaintiff in a class action lawsuit— Hohri v. The United States—" William Hori dies at 83: Sought Money for Internees, Douglas Martin, New York Times, November. 24, 2010, Section A, 25 https://www.nytimes.com/2010/11/24/us/24hohri.html

Page 379   "Ronald Reagan signed the bill in 1988." Densho.org: Ency-clopedia, Redress Movement https://encyclopedia.densho.org/Redress_ movement/

Photo Credits

California Ethnic & Multicultural Archives (CEMA), UC Santa Barbara Library, Billigmeier Archives, by permission of Billigmeier Family: p. 3

Zinn Arthur: pp. xxi, 311, 312, 314, 315, 316, 318,

Reames Studio, Glenville, Illinois: p. xxii

Stan Schnier: pp. 106, 107, 197, 198

Lucille Coberly: p. 47

Don Elberson: p. 17

Cely Onrubia: p. 63

Tay Takano: p. 89

Wing Luke Museum, photo by Tay Takano, copyright 2020, courtesy of Wing Luke Museum, Seattle, WA: p. 205

James Kollar Studio, Radio City Music Hall: p. 191

Courtesy of Museum of History & Industry, MOHAI, Seattle: pp. 224, 227

Densho Digital Repository: pp. 9, 253

Courtesy of MOCA, Museum of Chinese in America, New York City: pp. 258, 260

Moss Photo, New York: pp. 295, 296, 297

Photo by Friedman-Abeles ©The New York Public Library for the Performing Arts: pp. 339, 340, 341

Photo by Gaby of Montreal: p. 341

From Mary Mon Toy personal files. To date no attribution found: pp. xx, xxiii, 343 (2), 137, 205, 212, 256, 257, 267, 255, 283, 284, 310, 334, 369, 370, 374, 375, 376

Cy Ollivierre: p. 367

Photographer Richard Nieves: p. 342

Kem Lee Studio, San Francisco: p. 188

Shigesato Okada: p. 264

Screen shot from China News Services: p. 342

Verna Photographers, Brooklyn, NY: p.29

Made in United States
North Haven, CT
03 September 2023

41092123R00271